P9-CFY-891

JAMES O'TOOLE has been a Time/Life correspondent, a McKinsey & Company management consultant, and chairman of the influential HEW task force on "Work in America." O'Toole currently holds the University Associates' Chair of Management at the University of Southern California's business school, where he is also editor of the nation's leading university-based business magazine *New Management*.

Vanguard Manage- ment

Redesigning the Corporate Future

Vanguard Management

Redesigning the Corporate Future

JAMES O'TOOLE

B
BERKLEY BOOKS, NEW YORK

This Berkley book contains the complete text of the original hardcover edition.

VANGUARD MANAGEMENT

A Berkley Book/published by arrangement with
Doubleday & Company, Inc.

PRINTING HISTORY
Doubleday edition/August 1985
Berkley trade paperback edition/October 1987

ISBN: 0-425-10349-8

A BERKLEY BOOK® TM 757,375
Berkley Books are published by The Berkley Publishing Group,
200 Madison Avenue, New York, NY 10016.
The name "BERKLEY" and the "B" logo
are trademarks belonging to Berkley Publishing Corporation.

PRINTED IN CANADA

10 9 8 7 6 5 4 3 2 1

To Erin O'Toole and Kerry O'Toole

ACKNOWLEDGMENTS

I am indebted to the managers and workers of the eight Vanguard corporations—Atlantic Richfield, Control Data, Dayton-Hudson, Deere, Honeywell, Levi Strauss, Motorola, and Weyerhaeuser—for their gracious cooperation during all stages of the preparation of this book. They gave generously and patiently of their time in countless interviews and in response to my pestering queries and numerous requests for ever more information. Thanks seem somehow insufficient when the debt is for the very existence of a project that has occupied my last three years. All I can hope is that these good people will be repaid in the most appropriate and meaningful fashion: by the growing acceptance of their New Management philosophy.

I also wish to thank three other practitioners of the New Management—Max DePree of Herman Miller, Jan Erteszek of the Olga Company, and Joline Godfrey of Polaroid—for offering me living demonstrations that there is an alternative model of managerial eminence to the one traditionally taught in business schools. And, within the unique business school where I am fortunate to teach, I am proud to have colleagues who are actively recreating the field of management studies: my thanks to three of these, Warren Bennis, Edward Lawler, and Larry Greiner for their patient tutoring and thoughtful critiques of an earlier draft of this book. Acknowledgment is also due to nearly sixty graduate students at the University of Southern California's business school who, over the last three years, allowed me the privilege of refining the thesis of this book in lively classroom exchanges with them.

Writing a book is a lonely endeavor that requires more self-confidence to see through to completion than most mortals find within themselves. I was fortunate to have friends and advisers to turn to when my reserves of confidence were low. Jack Steele, Bill Leigh, Mortimer Adler, Jacques Barzun, Judith Garwood, and Marilyn O'Toole each provided a boost of encouragement at exactly the time I needed it most. Another source of confidence and clearheaded advice was my editor, Adrian Zackheim, who was supportive of this project from the beginning when all he had to go on was faith in my inchoate vision. I am also indebted to the three people who turned my sloppy manuscript into type— Kim Wallace, Sheila Thomas, and René Gay—not only for the professional quality of their work, but because they, too, provided regular and frequent encouragement. They said they liked reading what they were typing, and that was terribly important to me.

CONTENTS

PART THREE
How Vanguard Leaders Change, Lead, and Sustain Their Organizations

Preface to the Paperback Edition

WHY GOOD COMPANIES GET INTO TROUBLE

In 1984, I concluded some four years of research about a group of companies that I was convinced were among the best managed in the U.S. I called them the "vanguard" because I believed that they could serve as future models for all large, publicly held corporations. These were companies that were both highly profitable *and* socially responsible. In fact, they did well by doing good. But, before the ink was dry on the hardback edition of this book, my exemplary list of corporations had begun to read more like a litany of has-beens than the roll-call from the business hall of fame I had intended. Several critics leapt on a number of my less-fortunate corporate examples (Atlantic Richfield, Levi Strauss and Control Data) and offered these as "proof" that the principles espoused in the book were misguided. Setting aside the point that one cannot logically disprove a proposition simply by discrediting the examples used to illustrate it, I nevertheless must admit that the curmudgeons of the business world have raised an interesting point: Specifically, that none of the authors of the many recent books on management has been able to produce a list of good companies that is enduring (*In Search of Excellence*'s list had a half-life of about six months).

Failures of Hot-Tub Management

This fact has led me to undertake some considerable headscratching about why it is that so many good companies these days suddenly find themselves up to their collective crotches in crocodiles—and the crocodiles win. The most cynical explanation is that the employee-centered, "humanistic" philosophies practiced by many so-called excellent companies ultimately backfire and lead to financial ruin.

There is, alas, a *prima facie* case to be made against the once-fabled "right brain" style of management that favors intuition, informality, hugging, white wine busts and the like. Recall that during the era when the personal computer and semi-conductor businesses were booming, such high-tech idols as Atari, Apple, D.E.C., H.P., Osborne, and Intel appeared to all the world to be captained by managerial geniuses. In hindsight, we now see that their hot-tubs-and-sabbaticals approach was more a consequence than a cause of their being on the ascent side of a product cycle during which demand for computers temporarily exceeded supply. In this regard, it is instructive to travel the length of the Silicon Valley today. With only a few remarkable exceptions, the fabled "progressive" managers of yesterday have turned into get-tough, left-brain clones of the old-fashioned tyrants who manage in the Monongohela Valley. *Sic transit humanitas!*

Still, this doesn't mean that humanistic management *caused* the current high-tech decline, any more than it was responsible for the boom period in Silicon Valley's recent past. The truth is that all companies go through periods of boom and bust. Given a highly dynamic competitive environment, how could it be otherwise? What company hasn't had a bad quarter (or a bad year) in recent times? Even those who have topped *Fortune*'s annual list of "most prestigious" corporations have stumbled of late—witness IBM's PCjr, HP's struggles with personal computers, and Dow-Jones's embarrassing "Heard on the Street" column fiasco. The lesson here is that there are no perfect companies (as there are no men or women without faults). Moreover, simplistic theories about the cause of managerial failure—like simplistic theories about the source of managerial excellence—won't wash on careful analysis.

Since all companies get into trouble from time to time, perfection is thus not a valid criterion for excellence. A truer test of a company's greatness is how its managers behave during bad times. In this regard, consider a Midwestern high-tech company that has weathered the vicissitudes of the computer market with far greater stability than have its glitzy Silicon Valley rivals. That company is *New Management* magazine's 1985 Vanguard Award winner, Motorola. Motorola is not a denizen of lotus land; it is headquartered in the suburbs of that quintessential smokestack town, Chicago. And Motorola is not led by the kind of charismatic, splashy, larger-than-life, obsessive characters who spend twelve-hour-days "walking around" their Silicon Valley plants telling every employee how to do his or her job. In contrast, Motorola's leaders are thoughtful, careful, analytical types who are dedicated to institutionalizing the structures, systems, and habits that empower all employees to do their own jobs without constant coercion and direction.

Recall that in Silicon Valley's good old days, managers attempted to manipulate their employees with public manifestations of love—celebrations in which productive workers received praise (and hugs) for their efforts. In contrast, all Motorola's 60,000 domestic employees are part of self-managing work teams, and all are eligible for an up to 41% monthly bonus based on their team's performance. While Motorola's managers believe that there is never any excuse for failing to give productive employees recognition for their efforts, they also recognize that the real currencies of organizational life are money and power—two things that the egotistical stars of many high-tech companies appear to have trouble sharing.

In the heyday of Silicon Valley there was tons of talk about "culture" and oodles of effort dedicated to contriving symbolic actions and fabricated myths to communicate corporate affection for employees (one would have believed that high-tech workers were entitled to a hot-tub break whenever they became stressed-out from more than two hours of straight work). But those same companies undercut whatever value they derived from their symbols and rhetoric when they engaged in massive layoffs at the onset of each of the recent semi-conductor recessions. In distinction, Motorola plans ahead and is often—but not always—able to utilize reduced work weeks in lieu of morale-destroying layoffs. Most important, when recessions hit Motorola they respond in a fashion alien to the inhabitants of Silicon Valley: They do *nothing* fundamentally different than in good times. Of course, they respond by making appropriate strategic, tactical and product changes; but the company's fundamental principles—including employee participation in decision making, sharing of productivity gains, "open and complete argument on controversial issues," honesty, integrity, and the goal of "zero product defects"—are never compromised. Contrast this to the crisis management that occurred at such high-tech companies as Atari and Osborne when they first got into trouble.

Management As a Moral Undertaking

What Motorola's managers understand—and what allows them to cope with the effects of recessions better than their Aquarian competitors—is that management is basically a *moral undertaking*. Am I saying that viewing business as a moral undertaking will guarantee success, or that failure to do so will cause a good company to go bad? Sorry, life isn't that simple. I'm merely asserting that no company has ever gotten into financial hot water by taking the high road. No company has ever produced red ink *because* it behaved ethically, *because* it invested for the long term, *because* it treated employees with respect, or *because* it put something back into host communities. Of course, companies that do none of those things succeed, too. Yet, the low road is fraught with risk. For it is often the case that corporations that play fast and loose end by alienating customers, vendors, employees, and stockholders—witness E. F. Hutton, General Dynamics, A. H. Robbins and J. P. Stevens.

Indeed, all I am claiming is that managers have a *choice*. As there are no rules that free managers from the terrible responsibility of choosing what products to market and what strategies to pursue, managers must also choose whether to treat employees well or to treat them poorly, and whether to produce safe, high-quality goods or shoddy ones. There is no guarantee what the financial consequences of such choices will be. Corporations that mistreat employees and peddle inferior products may either succeed or fail; the same can be predicted for those that show respect for employees and customers. Nonetheless, that this choice *even exists* comes as news to most managers, for they have been led to believe that success is only possible by taking the low road, by pursuing the quick buck. Heretofore, they have believed that doing good was inimical to doing well.

But there is now evidence that managers are free to make a choice that few had thought open to them: They can choose to conduct their work lives with the same high principles with which they conduct their private lives. The companies I have studied—including Motorola, Dayton Hudson, Deere, Herman Miller and W. T. Gore— dispel the myth that the only way to succeed in business is at the expense of employees, customers and society. Important, the high road these companies pursue is *not* one of altruism, it is *not* pious or trendy "social responsibility," and it is *not* do-goodism. Much as an individual can lead a moral life without being a social worker or a Mother Teresa, a corporation can behave morally by leading a principled existence—what Aristotle called a "good life" in the individual context.

Four Principles of Excellence

From an organizational perspective, leading a good life entails *balancing the legitimate claims of all the corporation's constituencies*—suppliers, dealers, employees, host communities, as well as shareowners and managers. For example, Deere has a policy they call "mutual advantage" that they extend to all their various constituencies. When this principle is applied to dealer relations, it means that the company won't dump unsalable inventory on their tractor dealers in order to make corporate books look good in the short run (as is the practice, for instance, in the auto industry). A few years back, Levi Strauss executives behaved similarly when they cancelled all white-collar and executive raises immediately after gaining a significant wage give-back from their unionized employees. Contrast this to the attitude displayed at GM a few months later when executives voted themselves sizable bonuses hard on the heels of winning significant concessions from the UAW. Important, when Deere and Levi practice such "moral symmetry" they are *not* engaged in altruism; they simply see that treating employees, unions, and dealers with respect is in the best interest of investors in the long term. The real question is why auto executives continually choose to shoot themselves in the foot by acting expediently.

Dedication to high purpose is another moral precept that guides great companies. Again, this is a principle that GM violated in the 1970s when they proudly echoed Alfred Sloan's famous line that "We are in the business of making money, not cars." That worked fine until GM ran into competition from Toyota and Nissan executives who said, in sharp contrast, that *they* were in the business of making high-quality cars in order to bring jobs to their resource-poor island nation. Now, which company is most likely to attract, maintain and motivate the most dedicated and productive employees—one that offers them a noble vision, or one that shows contempt for the quality of its own product? In Johnson & Johnson's famous Credo, in Deere's Green Bulletin, and in the other "constitutions" of great companies, the stated purpose of business is to provide society with the high quality goods and services it needs in order to generate the profits necessary to maintain employment and to improve the nation's standard of living. Profits are an obvious necessity in this view —the more profit the better, in fact. But profits are seen as means, *not* as ends . . . an important moral distinction that not only builds employee commitment but addresses head-on the criticisms of anti-business legislators who seek excuses for increased corporate taxa-tion and regulation.

Continuous learning is another principle that is religiously ad-hered to in great companies. Again, using GM in the 1970s as an example of a good company that got into trouble, we see what hap-pens when a corporation becomes complacent and arrogantly be-lieves that it has "solved" the problem of management. For decades, GM's managers repeated over and over the once-successful policies developed by Alfred Sloan in the 1920s until they finally hit upon an environment in which these concepts were no longer valid. High-priced gas, changed consumer preferences, Japanese competition, new worker values, and government regulation brought home to GM in the late 1970s the lesson that nothing fails like success. In the best companies, in distinction, everyone is constantly challenging past premises and *un*learning the things that once led to success but promise failure in the future. On a visit to Motorola, I was surprised when a young manager buttonholed CEO Robert Galvin: "I heard what you had to say at this morning's meeting, Bob, and I'm going to prove you wrong; I'm going to shoot you down!" I thought the kid's career was kaput, but there was Galvin, beaming proudly as he ex-plained to me, "That's how we became the nation's leading producer of semiconductors." Indeed, it's through such listening to *all* of their constituencies that great companies stay flexible, and are thus able to meet ever-changing competitive challenges.

The final principle I'll mention is *high aim.* Contrast GM's satisfac-tion in the 1970s with being the world's *biggest* auto manufacturer, to the quite opposite aspirations of Lee Iacocca that Chrysler should become "the *best* at everything we do." It is a sad commentary on the state of American business that an executive can become a na-tional hero merely by dedicating himself to what ought to have been a given. If the old goal at Chrysler (and at GM, at U.S. Steel, and so forth) wasn't to be the best, good Lord, what *were* they aiming for? Fortunately, a few corporations have had high aim for decades. Day-ton Hudson—America's fastest growing retailer, the retail industry leader in customer service, the leader of all American businesses in terms of community service (and, *New Management*'s 1984 Vanguard winner)—has as its goal "To be premier in every aspect of our busi-ness." Significantly, when I recently visited DH's headquarters, I found healthy dissatisfaction with the fact that they were not yet number one in tapping their human resources. If one wishes to avoid failures, better a dissatisfied management than a complacent one.

Falling from Grace

If eminent companies succeed through commitment to such moral principles, why is it that some such companies nonetheless go bad? Having observed the precipitous recent decline of three of the corporations I had studied and in this book cited for their "excellence," I think I've begun to understand the process by which they did themselves in. First hand, I observed the tragedy of ARCO (the amazing shrinking oil company). For nearly a decade, ARCO had been a paradigm of the values just described, yet they self-destructed with meteoric determination. When the price of oil plummeted, ARCO's immediate reaction was to abandon the very characteristics that had led to their distinction. Formerly, ARCO had been statesmenlike leaders of their industry, masters at flexible, long-term planning, gloriously entrepreneurial, and always careful to assess the impact of their activities on host communities. But, almost overnight, the company reverted to the "tough-minded" practices of their least-imaginative competitors (and, in so doing, they not only added to the depth of their fall, but may have destroyed corporate morale to the extent that a full recovery is problematic). How could this have occurred? In corporation after corporation the same pattern found at ARCO repeats itself. When times get rough, the guys in the black hats gain credibility because they offer this clear, unambiguous response to any crisis: "Cut out all the gooey malarky, and get tough!" In the absence of confident leadership, such calls for expedient behavior carry the day because they promise immediate results. ARCO had been made particularly vulnerable to such expedience because the architect of their old culture, Thorton Bradshaw, had recently left the company (and was off saving RCA when the price of oil collapsed). Fortunately, after taking two steps backwards, ARCO now has a new CEO dedicated to restoring the levels of performance and moral leadership enjoyed under the tutelage of Bradshaw.

Control Data Corporation's fall has been even more precipitous . . . and tragic. Perhaps no other corporation had had a better fix on what business must do to avoid further governmental interference in the economy. But CDC then violated the very principles on which their philosophy rested. They arrogantly ignored the needs of their stakeholders, treating customers in a cavalier fashion, and dealing with partners in their community-based joint ventures with contempt. They also became a non-learning organization, too slow to tailor their fine educational software for use in personal computers, and failing to develop a competitive next generation of peripherals for that same home market. Significantly, they did not fail (as some on Wall Street claim) *because* of their efforts "to find profitable ways of meeting society's unmet needs." Instead, they failed *in spite* of this enterprising orientation.

Levi Strauss presents the most instructive case of why the good go bad—and of the heavy toll that must inevitably be paid as a consequence of succumbing to short-term amorality. In a headlong rush to achieve the insatiable levels of growth demanded by stock speculators, Levi aborted their historical principles—mistreating the very dealers who had participated in their earlier success, cutting corners here and there to look good *now*, and ultimately laying off long-term employees for the first time in their history. Having failed to meet the desires of Wall Street, while in the process losing the traits that had once made the company special, the heirs of Levi Strauss then realized they had made the wrong choice. Significantly, they have now chosen to take the company private (at great expense) in order to return to the time-consuming path of building lasting business relationships, and allowing entrepreneurial ideas time to develop— activities that the investing community was too impatient to endure.

Drawing the Right Conclusions

In each of these three cases cynics have drawn the wrong conclusion: They have claimed that ARCO, CDC, and Levi slipped *because* they were intent on doing well by doing good. In fact, these companies got into trouble when, faced with difficult external challenges, they betrayed their principles instead of staying the course. This is not to say that these three companies ended up with any choice other than to lay off employees; rather, prior, expedient decisions led them to the sad point where they had no other choice. Moreover, the examples of Motorola and Herman Miller illustrate that the final chapters of the stories of good companies needn't be ones of moral transgression and economic failure.

The cynics are right of course; the low road is easier and, no doubt, can lead to success. But my point is this: If managers come to see that they can succeed by taking *either* the high or the low road, won't many of them choose to pursue the higher course, even if it is more difficult? If some of these managers should then fail (as many must in a capitalist economy), won't they at least have the comfort of having known they gave the effort the *best* of everything that was in them?

And that's the point to keep in mind as you read this book . . .

Vanguard Management

Redesigning the Corporate Future

PROLOGUE:

EXECUTIVE SUITE

> There is nothing new under the sun.
> —ECCLESIASTES 1:9

The year is 1954. Eisenhower is President. The Supreme Court outlaws school segregation. McCarthy has been silenced. Hemingway wins the Nobel Prize for Literature. There is a severe post-Korean War economic recession. Yogi Berra is the Most Valuable Player in the American League.

While 1954 may not be a banner year economically or athletically, it is a vintage year cinematically. In Hollywood, the black and white era is running to the end of the reel, but it is going out with vitality—with unforgettable pictures like *On the Waterfront, The Country Girl,* and the now almost forgotten *Executive Suite.* To be hailed in years to come mainly by insomniac "Late Show" TV watchers and trivia freaks, *Executive Suite* is nonetheless a classic of the behind-closed-doors courtroom and boardroom genre.

Suite's dense plot is based on a novel by Cameron Hawley. The story concerns the maneuverings and machinations of ten characters (all played by big Hollywood stars) who are attempting to choose the successor to one Avery Bullard, president of the Tredway furniture-manufacturing company. We never meet Bullard. Indeed, the film opens with his sudden death, and we see only the back of his head as he is sprawled out on a New York sidewalk. His death triggers some shady inside dealing by board member Louis Calhern. (We'll call the characters by the names of the actors who played the parts—after all, this is the star system at its zenith.) Calhern sells his stock short in anticipation of a sell-off when the news of Bullard's untimely death hits The Street. But Calhern's shenanigans are (improbably) uncovered by Fredric March, the

Tredway VP for finance. March abets the transaction in exchange for Calhern's pledge to support March in his egotistic bid to succeed Bullard. March plays his part with delicious mendacity and deceitfulness. He is to the black hat born and never during the ninety-minute drama does he doff it. Consistently, he oozes and connives. He blackmails marketing VP Paul Douglas, a lovable schlemiel who is having an extramarital affair with his secretary, Shelley Winters. And March variously badgers or lies to the other board members in his ambitious grab for the brass ring. The other members of the board (it is predominantly an "inside board") include the heir apparent, Walter Pidgeon, a suave and urbane senior VP who nonetheless decides to step down and not pursue the top rung (he apparently lacks what will one day be called the "fire in the belly" needed for the top job); VP for manufacturing, Dean Jagger (a monosyllabic engineer, good-hearted but unsophisticated in the ways of corporate politics); and William Holden, VP for R&D, who is working on a "miracle substance" that promises to revolutionize the furniture industry, if only he can maintain top management support for one more round of expensive experiments.

Holden is the protagonist; the white hat is his to wave in March's face. Holden is young, handsome, and fit (there is no hint of the baggy-eyed dipso of later years). He is married to America's sweetheart, June Allyson. Alas, June does not want Bill to be president of Tredway, fearing that the single-minded fellow will spend even less time with their already (in her view) neglected progeny. So when Walter Pidgeon comes to the Holden home to recruit Bill for the savior role, lovely June prevaricates. Bill, she says, is "out of town" until after the board meeting.

To complicate matters further, there is Barbara Stanwyck, heiress to the Tredway fortune and lover of the deceased Avery Bullard. She is distraught at the news of his death as only Barbara Stanwyck can be distraught. In a moment of Academy Award-level hysteria, it appears to all the world that she is about to join her dear Avery in eternal peace by leaping from the twenty-third-floor window of the Tower (as the executive suite is dramatically named). Only in Hollywood are furniture-manufacturing firms found in high-rise buildings (to be charitable, it would be terribly difficult to create a convincing executive suite in one of those nondescript one-story North Carolina furniture plants). But Miss Stanwyck has a change of heart. She postpones her leap, at least until after the board meeting (curiosity, apparently, winning out over bereavement). And June Allyson, torn by guilt, 'fesses up to hubby Bill Holden. In the nick of time, she chauffeurs him to the boardroom where the meeting is in progress. March, all sleazy and sweaty lest cinemagoers forget he is the bad guy, is giving his campaign speech as we pick up the dialogue:

MARCH: When the average stockholder buys Tredway stock he makes an *investment.* The only reason he *makes* it is to get a *return.* That is why I believe a corporation today must be governed to be what its owners *want* it to be—have *paid* for it to be—a *financial institution* yielding the highest and safest *return on investment!*

(March eyeballs all the board members sitting intently around the table.)

Do you know why more and more corporations today are drawing their leaders from the ranks of comptrollers and investment bankers? Because the problems that come to the president's office today are *predominantly financial!*

At this point PIDGEON cuts in: I get it—manufacturing and selling don't *count* anymore . . .

(Pidgeon appears to have scored points with Dean Jagger, manufacturing VP, and Paul Douglas, marketing VP).

But MARCH is clever: Of course they count, Walter. But they're not ends in themselves, only the means to the end . . . It's a matter of management levels. I just said it: At the presidential level, the emphasis, *must* be *financial* . . . Take our own case . . .

(he looks at Jagger)

Dean and his staff have done a wonderful job of reducing costs on our finishing operation . . .

(he glances at Holden)

And we all appreciate the creative effort Bill's poured into our experimental program at the Pike Street plant . . .

(he addresses them all)

But the truth is—such efforts add comparatively little to our net earnings—even when they *succeed.* Last year they contributed *less than a quarter* of what we gained from one new tax-accounting procedure I got the government to approve . . .

(he looks around to make his point)

. . . So you see, that single piece of work, *all purely financial in nature* . . .

PIDGEON cuts him off again: *We see* all right! While Jagger and Holden are turning out product, you figure-jugglers and chart men are busy flyspecking it with decimal points! Well, we've had enough of it! Some of us are sick to our stomachs from it!

MARCH: (his face grows crimson; his voice shakes with emotion) And *I've* had enough of *that* attitude! I know how I've been regarded around here by most of you! Efficiency has become a dirty word! Budget control has a bad odor! Well, *that's my job—* my *responsibility!* And if I have to step on toes and hurt feelings in the process, that can't be helped!

(he looks at Pidgeon)

But *nobody* is going to say I ever had anything but the best interests of this company at heart while I was doing it! Take a look at the record of the last three years! Fight *that* record! *My* record!

HOLDEN almost whispers: *Your* record, March?

(March turns to him hotly)

MARCH: It couldn't have been done without me!

(Stanwyck looks up sharply; March hesitates, sensing he may have gone too far)

Understand—I don't mean to belittle Mr. Bullard . . . We all recognize his magnificent contributions to this company during its period of growth—

HOLDEN: In other words, Avery Bullard was the right kind of man to save this company from disaster . . .

(Holden is getting to his feet now, sensing this is the moment to move in)

. . . to build it up, and set it on its way . . . But now we need a *different* kind of management . . . one that will dedicate itself to paying the maximum dividend to the stockholders . . . Is that it?

MARCH: I don't know that I'd express it in exactly those terms . . . But . . . yes . . . that's substantially what I do mean.

HOLDEN: (he looks down at his hands; his tone is suspiciously casual) March, let me ask you something . . . The president of a company like Tredway would have to be a man of outstanding qualities, wouldn't he?

MARCH: Naturally . . .

HOLDEN: . . . A man prepared to make a good many personal sacrifices . . . willing to devote himself to the company, mind and heart, body and soul . . .

MARCH: If he were the right man, there'd be no worry on that score . . .

(Holden looks up with a sudden snap of his voice)

HOLDEN: Why? (all eyes go to him) *Why would he do it? What would his incentive be?*

MARCH: Outside of salary? There's such a thing as success, isn't there! . . . a sense of accomplishment?

HOLDEN: Exactly! And let's assume, March, that you're the man . . . running Tredway Corporation *your* way. Would *you* be satisfied to measure your life's work by how much you'd raised the dividend? Would you regard your life as a success just because you'd managed to get the dividend up to three dollars —or four—or five or six or seven? Would that be enough? Is that what you want for your obituary—the dividend record of Tredway Corporation?

MARCH: Are you suggesting that earnings aren't important?

HOLDEN: I'm suggesting no such thing and you know it!

(he turns to the others; and during the next speeches the camera pans to the faces around the table and to lovely June listening at the door)

March is right when he says we have an obligation to our stockholders—but it's a bigger obligation than raising the dividend! We have an obligation to keep this company *alive*—not just this year, or the next, or the year after that! Stop growing and you die! *There's* your waste, March! *There's* your inefficiency! Turn your back on experimentation and planning for tomorrow because they don't contribute to dividends *today*— and you won't *have* a tomorrow! Because there won't be any *company!*

MARCH: Avery Bullard didn't seem to think my policies were exactly destroying this company!

HOLDEN: No—he didn't. And he was wrong! The way a lot of people are wrong these days—grabbing for the quick and easy

—the *sure thing!* That's just lack of faith in the future! It's something that's in the air today—the groping of a lot of men who know they've lost their faith, but aren't sure what it is, or how they happened to lose it! Avery Bullard was one of them . . . He'd been so busy building a great production machine he finally lost sight of why he was building it—or why he was the man he was—if he ever really knew . . .

(in the sudden silence, Stanwyck's voice is heard . . . quiet but intense)

STANWYCK: Do *you* know, Mr. Holden?

HOLDEN: Yes . . . I think I do . . . Avery Bullard was driven by pride—pride in himself—the urge to do things no other man on earth could do . . . He was the man at the top of the Tower . . . needing no one . . . wanting no one . . . only himself. That's what it took to satisfy his pride . . .

(Stanwyck's eyes are misty)

That was his strength . . . and that was his *weakness,* too . . .

JAGGER: Why *shouldn't* a man have pride . . . if he's earned it?

HOLDEN: All right! But it shouldn't set him apart from those he's working with! The force behind a great company has to be more than the pride of *one* man! It has to be the pride of men working together—the pride of thousands! You can't make men work for money alone! You starve their souls when you try it . . .

(he turns to March)

. . . and you can starve a company to death the same way!

(and now to the others)

Avery Bullard must have known that once . . . but he'd become a little lost these last few years. The company'd been saved. There were no more battles to win. He had to find something *else* now to feed his pride—bigger sales—more profits—something!

(he strides to a small table in the corner)

That's when we started doing things like *this!*

(he picks up the table; the papers on it scatter to the floor)

The K-F Line!

(he moves toward Douglas with the table)

Paul . . . are your boys *proud* when they go out and sell this stuff—when they know the finish is going to crack and veneer split off and the legs come loose . . . ?

(Douglas begins to smile)

MARCH: Now wait a minute! That's price merchandise! It serves a definite purpose in the profit structure of this company! We're not cheating anyone—!

HOLDEN: *Ourselves!*

MARCH: . . . At that price the customer knows exactly what he's going to get!

(Holden yanks mightily on the table legs and rips one off, shouting)

HOLDEN: *This!*

(he raises the table above his head and smashes it against the floor)

This is what Tredway has come to mean!

(he points to the wreckage)

What do you suppose the people think of us when they buy it? How do you suppose the men in the factories feel when they *make* it? What must they think of a management that's willing to stoop to selling this kind of junk in order to add a dime a year to the dividend? Do you know there're men at Pike Street who've refused to *work* on the K-F Line . . .

(Jagger nods)

. . . who've taken a seven-dollar-a-week cut to get transferred to something else . . . ?

(March tries to save the situation)

MARCH: After all, that's only *part* of our business. Eventually we can cut down on the line . . .

HOLDEN: We'll *drop* that line! We'll never again ask a man to do anything that will poison his pride in himself or his work! We'll *have* a line of low-priced furniture—a new and different line— as different from anything we're making today as a modern automobile is different from a covered wagon!

(he looks at Douglas)

That's what you want, Paul, isn't it? What you've *always* wanted—merchandise that'll sell because it has *beauty* and *function* and *value*—not because the buyers like your scotch or think you're a good egg . . . !

(Douglas grins. Holden turns to Jagger)

The kind of stuff you'll be able to feel in your *guts*, Dean, when you know it's coming off *your* production line . . . !

(he looks at March)

A product *you'll* be able to budget to the nearest hundredth of a cent, March, because it'll be scientifically and efficiently designed . . . !

(he turns to Stanwyck)

Something you'll be *proud* to have your name on, Miss Stanwyck . . . !

(and now he includes them all)

We're going to give the people what they *need*—at prices they can afford to pay! And as fresh needs come up we'll satisfy *them too* . . . with something *new* and even *more* exciting! When we achieve *that*, we'll *really* start to grow! We're not going to die—*we're going to live!* And it's going to take every bit of business sense and creative energy in this company, from the mills and factories right up to the top of the Tower! We're going to do it *together—every one of us—right here at Tredway!*

(there is a moment of electric silence, then suddenly Pidgeon slaps the table)

PIDGEON: I'm with you, Bill!

(March's eyes dart about. Douglas is getting to his feet in the face of March's threatening glance.)

DOUGLAS: I take great pleasure in nominating Mr. William Holden for the presidency of Tredway Corporation!

Holden is elected, and they all live happily ever after. *Finis.*

Retrospective

Old Bill knew how to manage, that's for sure. He cared about product quality. He believed in planning for, and investing in, the long term. He saw the need for risk taking, technological innovation, and increased productivity; moreover, he realized that these were achievable only through teamwork. He was a leader who could express to his team the simple truth that most business inevitably boils down to two basic activities—making and selling things. But most important, he saw that success in management was *not* predicated on technique. Instead, his underlying assumption was that the art of management is to continually meet the corporation's changing responsibilities to all of those who have a stake in it—employees, customers, local communities, suppliers, dealers, as well as shareholders. For corporations to succeed in the long run, Holden believed that they must respond to the competing claims of their various constituencies with balance, with "moral symmetry." To Holden, there was no secret to success, no magic formula or theory that would lead to corporate eminence. There was only the hard and constant work of responding ethically to *all* manner of change—social, political, technological, competitive, and economic. Author Cameron Hawley thus created for Holden a timeless, commonsense philosophy, one that any manager in any era could do worse than to embrace.

Unhappily, life does not imitate art. Over the two decades that followed the release of *Executive Suite*, it was the philosophical carbon copies of Fredric March who were to win the boardroom debates and rise to the control of America's executive suites. In hindsight, we now see that the get-rich-quick approach prevailed in corporation after corporation. The financial viewpoint—in which management's sole responsibility is to stockholders—rose to ascendancy. "Clean hands" management—in which corporate leaders devoted themselves to the acquisition game and to tax manipulation at the expense of production and marketing—became the rule. The *ends* of meeting the needs of society, consumers, and employees were confused with the *means* of attaining short-term profits.

Unlike March, however, America's corporate leaders were not congenitally immoral, greedy, and callous. Instead, they were simply misguided and misled. And it is easy to see why they chose to follow the path they did. The philosophy they embraced was based on the tested practices of the nation's greatest pre-Korean War corporate successes (in such heavy industries as metals, autos, and chemicals). Understandably, then, corporate leaders were susceptible to the countless theories, techniques, formulae, methods, and rules advanced by consultants, business professors, and authors that were based on the get-rich-quick practices of the nation's largest firms. (Not coincidentally, in the middle of this era a Broadway smash hit was entitled *How to Succeed in*

Business Without Really Trying.) Because financial schemes had worked in the past—and because they appeared to be working at the time—they were embraced as laws, encoded, permaplaqued, and hung in executive suites from Altoona to Yuma. Thus, not only experience but the bestselling management books of the era were reinforcing the philosophy of the nation's Fredric Marches. They honestly believed they were excellent managers.

In fact, the March approach got American corporations through the fifties in fine fettle. And, in the sixties, it worked so well that the American corporation became the envy of the world. (France's Servan-Schreiber published *The American Challenge,* warning Europeans to either copy U.S. managerial practices or risk having such superbly managed American corporations as U.S. Steel, Chrysler, Ford, ITT, and Sperry Univac take over their economies!) This was a heady time. Managers knew how to churn out steady increases in quarterly profits, so they asked, "Why rock the boat?" Not a bad question when you are *Numero Uno.* But, first OPEC, then the Japanese, then new technologies and, finally, a lasting recession showed them why.

The 1970s were a disaster for American business. The corporate philosophies that had succeeded during the relatively undynamic fifties and sixties (a time in which American industry enjoyed an artificial advantage over its still war-ravaged competitors) were inappropriate in the new, highly competitive world markets of the seventies. By 1980, the American economy was on the mat, and it was clear to all who bothered to think about it that the extant philosophy of the nation's industrial managers was incapable of getting the country up on its feet and back into the fight.

Of course, this philosophy had been as patently wrong in the early 1950s as it was thirty years later, but the Bill Holdens of industry who had advocated a more fruitful course were ignored. They were unheeded not only because things seemed fine at the time (the disposition of the American character is not to fix the apparently unbroken), but because of the managerial abhorrence of ambiguity that was equally opposed to the changes they advocated. When the flesh-and blood Bill Holdens rose in corporate boardrooms and offered their complicated messages, they got clobbered by people who responded with a packaged set of rules that "guaranteed" corporate excellence. To American managers (who were as attracted by decisiveness as they were repelled by ambiguity) the Holden message seemed soft, muddleheaded, confused. Thus, only on celluloid were the Holdens heeded. In real life, when they held out their visions of corporate eminence, eyes glazed over, vice presidents nodded off, and the Fredric Marches rubbed their hands with the smug satisfaction of a prosecutor watching the defense attorney dig his client's grave.

PART ONE

INTRODUCTION:
HOW THE NEW MANAGEMENT
IS DIFFERENT FROM
TRADITIONAL MANAGEMENT

1.

THE ELUSIVE ELEMENTS
OF CORPORATE EMINENCE

Happy families are all alike;
every unhappy family is unhappy in its own way.
—LEO TOLSTOY

. . . Here we go again. American executives are once more
hopelessly enamored with oversimple solutions to the complex
tasks of management. Of course, some progress has been made
since the release of *Executive Suite*. Thanks to the economic
devastations of the late 1970s, many American managers—but by
no means all—now recognize that devotion to Fredric March's
financial flyspecking leads only to the swamps of stagnation. But
progress on a long journey does not signify arrival at one's ultimate destination. The clearest evidence of managerial failure to
understand the true cause of America's industrial decline is the
current fascination with finding *the* set of corporate characteristics that guarantee success. In effect, American managers have
still missed the point of *Executive Suite*. They have seen the
movie, understood the plot, absorbed the details (to the point of
figuring out whodunit), but they have nonetheless failed to grasp
the underlying moral of the story: Management is not a *problem*
to be solved by applying a set of solutions; rather, it is a *process* of
continuous response to the ever-changing environment and the
never-satisfied needs of the many and diverse constituencies that
a corporation serves. As T. S. Eliot might have written, American
managers had the experience, but they missed the meaning.

Today, the dominant managerial idea is that "There are many
roads to failure, but only one path to success." The purpose of this
book is to put the lie to that Tolstoyan notion. In these pages I
offer evidence that managerial eminence comes only from per-

sistent dedication to the kinds of high principles articulated by the William Holden character in *Executive Suite*. My first task is to demonstrate that there is no easier way, no theory X, Y, or Z, no secrets from the Orient, no one-minute quickie, no set of common rules that will permit a corporation to achieve lasting eminence. I must show that nothing can substitute for the hard work entailed in truly great management. Once having dispelled the myth of the easier way, my next task will be to show that the high road is not only passable in good times and bad, but that it leads to eminence.

I call this high road the New Management philosophy, although, in fact, it is not new at all. It wasn't even invented by William Holden! It has a lineage that extends back at least to the Age of the Enlightenment. In more modern times, it has been advocated by such writers as Mary Parker Follett, Chester Bernard, and Peter Drucker. It is "new" only in that it has been recently implemented by some eight of the largest American corporations. I've named these "the Vanguard" because I believe they will serve as models for large American corporations in the future. Indeed, I believe that the survival of competitive corporate capitalism *depends* on the willingness of American managers to adopt the New Management philosophy of the Vanguard. And, if they do, I suspect that the entire society would benefit greatly in the process.

This is a book about reform, not about revolution. The principles of the New Management require no centralized, national industrial policy on the one hand nor, on the other, a return to a frontier economy in which the buyer must beware and the least fortunate citizens must have double-strength bootstraps. Such extreme approaches to remaking the economy are ignorant of the process by which change occurs in this incredibly complex, pluralistic society. The American system—except in times of dire emergency—is immune to radical change. Countless checks and balances insure that change builds *incrementally* on the existing structure. Whether this is good or bad is irrelevant: It is what *is*, and one must start from there. Of course, change does occur, but it almost always does so within the context of prevailing values, traditional practices, and the existing allocation of power.

The evidence presented in this book offers some hope that, by building on the best aspects of the current system of corporate capitalism, the seemingly contradictory national goals of political liberty, economic efficiency, social equality, and a high quality of life are *mutually achievable*. What is most remarkable about the process of reform I advocate is that large, private corporations are presented as engines of social justice. Moreover, I argue that these corporations can probably become so without further government regulation of their internal workings, and without further governmental interference in the workings of the broader economy.

My approach also rejects the notion that the American public will ever again accept a Fredric March, "public be damned, I work for my shareowners" approach, or the currently vogue notion that a strong consumer orientation is a sufficient measure of corporate performance. Hence, I reject the impractical and undesirable proposals of both the left and right and focus, instead, on the difficult task of *reeducating the managers of the nation's leading corporations*. If American managers were formerly taught a philosophy that got their corporations into economic and social hot water, they can just as well now be taught a different philosophy that will lead to the high standard of living and high quality of life that all Americans seek. And they *are* educable; the behavior of the managers in the eight Vanguard corporations described in these pages makes that point.

In the chapters that follow, I illustrate how the Vanguard corporations are different from the Old Guard, how they changed their philosophy from traditional practices to the New Management, and what the consequences of that change have been for shareholders, employees, customers, and society. In making my case, I do not use as examples of the Old Guard the obvious basket cases of capitalism. Instead, I examine the very *best* of traditionally managed firms—such obviously successful and respected firms as IBM, General Motors, Du Pont, and Kodak. My reason for questioning the practices of firms that most people consider excellent is that there is little to be learned by knocking down strawmen. Everyone recognizes that the practices of Penn Central, Continental Illinois, and Kaiser Steel have been outmoded and self-defeating; hence, my argument for change must be made against those traditionally managed corporations for whom the strongest case for excellence can be made. Admittedly, this strategy is risky. To a great many managers, questioning the virtue of an IBM is tantamount to desecration of the flag! But since the future of the entire system is at stake, it is incumbent upon me to make the strongest case and to draw the clearest possible distinctions between the New Management and the Old. Without such clarity it will be far too easy for managers to look at the behavior of Vanguard and say, "but we're already doing that." My point is that most corporations are *not* practicing the New Management.

But I am getting ahead of my story. The first question I must address is Tolstoy's: Is there really only one road to success? At first blush, the notion of a single road to business eminence is enticing. But are all happy companies really the same? Can one discover the same characteristics at Apple Computers that one finds at Sony, or Royal Dutch Shell? Is Digital Equipment managed like Intel? Was bankrupt Chrysler returned to health by adopting the practices that made Hewlett-Packard successful?

Comparing Apples to Avocados

Without denying the possibility of finding basic similarities among great companies, it would nonetheless seem to be the case that each corporation is unique, and its uniqueness is determined by three factors: The society of which it is a part, the economics of the industry of which it is a part, and the company's own peculiar history.

Taking the first of these, significant *national cultural differences* have been conveniently ignored in several recent studies in which authors have been caught up in Nipponmania. In desperate search for the American equivalent of Sony, Japanese-style companies have been advanced as models of excellence to which all U.S. companies should aspire. But have the Japanese really created universally applicable practices? Would most Americans desire to work in companies that require Japanese-like conformity and regimentation? No matter how great a company might be, can it serve as a model of excellence for most Americans if they would have to abandon their individuality or significantly alter their personal values in order to succeed in their careers? Based on the persistence of traits of independence in the American national character, I think not.

The second significant distinction concerns the enormous *differences found between industries*. For example, the fast-growing, high-technology companies of Silicon Valley are often held up as models that all American managers should emulate. But what passes as good management in the computer industry may not work in, say, the steel industry. What is easy to do in Silicon Valley may be devilishly hard to achieve in the Monongahela Valley. Why? Because one industry may have an educated, white-collar work force in which the values of owners and workers are compatible, whereas another industry may have a poorly educated, blue-collar work force in which the interests of managers and workers are mutually antagonistic. One industry may face tough international competition, another may have a virtual monopoly on the good or service it offers. One may be in a fast-growing business, another industry may be in decline. Such differences have significant consequences for managers. For example, growth permits all kinds of expenditures—on employee training, on new plant and equipment—that tend to make the performance of a company look good. It is often said that growth masks mismanagement, and the absence of growth uncovers a multitude of past sins.

Hence, to tell declining steel companies to emulate the managerial practices of the booming Silicon Valley may be to suggest to prickly pears to try harder to become avocados. If the steel industry had the resources that the personal computer industry has had recently (as the result of phenomenal demand for computers), the practices of steel managers might come a little closer to excellence.

The third layer of necessary distinctions concerns important *historical differences* between companies. Acme and Zenith are both in the widget business, both are successful, both use the same technologies, and both compete in the same markets. But can the same managerial practices be prescribed for both? Probably not, if they differ in terms of their histories (one may be family-run, the other directed by professional managers), in terms of their locations (one may be located in a small town where peer pressure on employees to perform is great, while the other is in a large city where employees are strangers to each other after working hours), and in terms of their work force demographics (one may have a relatively young work force with high technical sophistication, the other may have older workers who suffer from computer phobia).

There are, thus, at least three levels of significant differences found in corporations: national character, industry economics, and company history. If one ignores the first, one may be led to advocate inappropriate Japanese practices for American companies. If one ignores the second, one may be led to advocate high-tech practices for low-tech industries. If one ignores the third, one may be led to advocate small-town-America practices that are likely to fail in big-city corporations.

While such distinctions obviously complicate the picture, they don't preclude the possibility of common characteristics that transcend national, industrial, and firm boundaries. One way to test the Tolstoyan hypothesis would be to identify a group of firms that most people agree are well managed, then see if they all have any traits in common. The trick is to come up with a list of firms that generates some consensus. While it is not easy to arrive at such a consensus, our test is not stymied for want of lists of great corporations.

Ranking the Great Corporations

In fact, listing the "ten best-managed companies in America" has become an executive parlor game. Since there are no rules, everybody can play; since there is no objective way to score, everybody is a winner. Who can resist odds like that? Not I. For what it is worth here, in alphabetical order, is my list of America's best-managed companies: Peter Burwash International, Chapparal Steel, Fel-Pro, W. L. Gore, Herman Miller, Kollmorgen, Lincoln Electric, Lord Corporation, and Olga. (I lose confidence after naming only nine—who says there is no pressure in this silly game?) Unlike my unnamed tenth nominee, I can confidently defend these companies on the grounds that they do everything well. They stick to the basics (they make high-quality products and provide excellent customer service). They provide job security for their workers (who are also major stockholders in most of these companies). They are each led by farsighted, risk-taking CEOs ("Bill Holdens" who clearly articulate a high moral and social purpose for their firms—and practice what they preach). And they make oodles of money (year after year, they outperform their competitors on all common financial yardsticks). Unfortunately, nobody is going to buy this list.

Why not? Because when E. F. Hutton talks, it is not the names of these excellent firms that he whispers in his client's ears. The names of these companies seldom find their way into the pages of the *Wall Street Journal.* These companies are relatively unknown because they are small- to medium-sized firms with only 300 to 3,000 employees. None is large enough to qualify for the *Fortune* 500, and only one makes the list of the nation's top 1,000 industrial firms. The stock of several of these companies is privately held; others are traded only over the counter.

While they are *terrae incognitae* to Wall Street analysts, these companies are nonetheless well known to many professors of management and to many corporate consultants. Over the last fifteen years, these small companies (and a few others like them) have been advanced by experts as models of business excellence. In response, the leaders of the nation's giant corporations have soundly rejected these models, arguing: "You are comparing apples to oranges. What they do may be fine for small companies, but it would never work in a big company like ours with a billion dollars in sales." At one level, I'm inclined to agree with these corporate leaders. There must be some reason why these small companies fail to grow large. Perhaps they become overly focused on improving what they do and miss opportunities for innovation and expansion?

Hence, if we are to discover the roots of eminence, it will clearly do no good to use small company examples—for no matter how good those companies might be, big company executives will reject them as models. But what big companies should one choose as models of excellence? It would seem that any list will appear arbitrary, for one's list depends on how one defines success. If one's measure is return on sales, then the Tupperware division of Dart & Kraft (with something like a 30 percent annual return over the last decade) will surely make, if not top, one's list. If one's criterion is customer service, the Frito-Lay division of PepsiCo must be included. If it is growth one is after, then Apple Computers is a must. If one is taken by corporate entrepreneurship, 3M is clearly a winner. Employee-oriented behavior? One cannot leave off Hewlett-Packard. Market share? It's hard to beat IBM. Exports? Boeing is near the top, if it isn't the nation's leading earner of foreign exchange. Philanthropy? Among the nation's one thousand largest firms only Cummins Engine and Dayton-Hudson donate 5 percent of their taxable income. Or what about some other common measures of excellence: Success in research and development? Productivity? Innovation? Return on stockholders' equity? Sales per employee? Clearly, one's list of great companies will be determined by whatever characteristics of performance one finds important. Thus, the exercise of deriving the characteristics of eminence from a list of great companies immediately becomes circular!

Where Would You Want to Work?

Curiously, I have found that the best way to deal with a subjective issue is to ask a subjective question. In particular, I have found that it is possible to gain a high degree of consensus among *informed* people about the ranking of the best-managed corporations by asking the following absurdly simple question: "If you could choose to work in any *large* American corporation, which one would it be?" The question seems to capture a basketful of complexities—it allows people to subconsciously factor in many amorphous and unparallel considerations and measures, yet still evokes remarkably clear and consistent replies. Over the last three years, I've interviewed over two hundred people—all individuals with considerable knowledge about *Fortune* 500 corporations—and almost always they cite one of the following eight companies when I ask them where they would want to work: Atlantic Richfield, Control Data, Dayton-Hudson, Deere, Honeywell, Levi Strauss, Motorola, and Weyerhaeuser. One or more of these corporations tend to make the lists of the well-informed business journalists, professors of management, consultants, corporate executives, and corporate critics I've interviewed. Several other companies that are mentioned—though less frequently and, I believe, with less conviction—include Johnson & Johnson, Digital Equipment, Dana, TRW, Hewlett-Packard, and, before they encountered serious financial difficulties, Cummins Engine, Polaroid, and Xerox. But no other corporation has been cited more than once. It is this set of corporations I have designated as the Vanguard and who are the focus of this book.

Uneasy about this list? Think about it. If you were to choose to work for a large American corporation, which one would it be? What would you look for in a potential employer? What characteristics would attract you? What corporate structure, systems, processes, policies, programs, and procedures would be consistent with your needs and values? Would you look for a company that paid well and had a generous employee benefit package? That was profitable and growing? That offered interesting and challenging tasks? That had working conditions flexible enough to meet your individual and family obligations? That fostered a sense of community and fellowship among employees? That treated all employees with respect? That offered equal opportunity to every worker without regard to sex, age, race, or religion? Certainly, these are concerns that Americans frequently raise with employers when they go job hunting.

In addition, many job applicants will inquire about a company's reputation before they apply for (or accept) a job. They may ask friends, ex-employees, and other informed outsiders about a company's economic and social performance. Does the company make and sell safe, high-quality products? Is it responsive to consumer needs and complaints? Does it charge a fair price for its product or service? Does it have high ethical standards? Does it tell the truth to its consumers, dealers, suppliers, shareholders, and employees? Does it obey the law? Does it pay its bills in a timely fashion? Does it produce a fair economic return for its shareholders? Does it bring out innovative products? Does it develop long-term business relationships by providing the goods and services consumers and society need and want? Does it put something back into the communities of which it is part?

These are some of the questions that may have gone through your mind as you considered the characteristics of a company where you could work without moral, social, economic, or career reservations. Indeed, if you are like most Americans, you would probably want to have positive answers to most (if not all) such questions before you were satisfied that a company was truly great. The research I've conducted indicates that most Americans evaluate the performance of corporations "holistically." That is, they apply a complex yardstick that incorporates all manner of personal, social, political, technological, and economic measures. In fact, while most of the people I have interviewed have been willing to make additions to almost any suggested list of measures of corporate performance, few are willing to settle for any *single* criterion. The more they discuss the issue, the more they want to make the inquiry ever more complex. For example, most of those I have interviewed have said that it is *necessary* for a corporation to be profitable before they would consider working for it, but few suggested that profitability is a *sufficient* reason to work for a company. In short, Americans tend to reject simple, narrow measures of corporate performance. Instead, they prefer to look at the fuller picture.

On the face of it, the question of where one would want to work might seem a too indirect way of identifying great companies. But, on closer consideration, it makes sense that a question that allows each individual's mind to do the complex data processing involved in value choice would work better than a simpler question that forced people to make unreal choices (or to accept measures they personally found inappropriate). The consensus I found is, thus, both remarkable and understandable. But it is *useful* only if we can then go on to identify the characteristics that these companies have in common.

Characteristics the Vanguard Share with All Fine Companies

In search of these characteristics, I started gathering printed data about the eight Vanguard corporations (and the runners-up). Then, to see what it was like to actually work in these companies, I assigned some sixty graduate students in three of my classes at the University of Southern California to interview middle managers in each firm. These candidates for the Master of Business Administration degree not only unearthed a great deal of information about the companies, they also kept me honest in my thinking with their pertinent questions and healthy skepticism. The students were looking for jobs in good companies and weren't about to brook any professorial woolly-mindedness. I also made it a point to visit each of the eight Vanguard companies personally, interviewing at least six or seven top executives (more in most cases), including the Chief Executive Officer (with one exception). And, whenever possible, I spoke with first-level employees in the offices, stores, and factories of these companies to gain the perspective of those who actually do the work involved in making a good or providing a service.

The process was as frustrating as it was educational. On the surface, these companies had little in common: They were in different industries in different parts of the country; some were capital intensive, others depended on labor; some were high tech, others not; some were old companies, others relatively new. But, digging a little deeper, it was possible to find a few general characteristics that most of the Vanguard (and many of the runners-up) had in common. As opposed to traditionally run companies, I discovered that these firms tended to have the following characteristics:

• *The Vanguard Are People-Oriented.* At Hewlett-Packard, workers participate in the decisions that immediately affect their own jobs, and they share directly in the profits that come from increases in their own productivity, as well as sharing in stock ownership.

At Honeywell, lifetime training is part of every worker's job. Millions are spent annually to upgrade the skills of the work force. And not just their technical skills—Honeywell is retraining all of its supervisors and middle managers, teaching them that they should play the role of consultants to workers, not policemen. The company is showing supervisors that it is better for the company when managers are seen as authorities, not authoritarians, better when they exercise their expertise than their power.

• *The Leaders of the Vanguard Are Visible.* The era of the executive washroom, executive elevator, executive suite, and executive lunchroom is over in Vanguard companies. The clean-hands society—in which the boss does financial magic but doesn't know production from marketing—has ended in these firms. Recognizing that in too many companies top management has been overpaid and underworked, in the Vanguard, top managers spend time in the trenches. There is real communication upward and downward. At Motorola there is a series of committees starting at the shop floor with direct links to top management. Robert Galvin, Motorola's CEO, discusses corporate policy with young managers in a cafeteria that is open to all employees.

• *The Vanguard Plan for Employment Stability.* Hewlett-Packard has a "social contract" with workers that they won't be laid off. During downswings in the economy, they work part-time and at reduced pay. Control Data has set up "rings of defense" to provide employment security. The first ring is long-range investments that provide for steady employment by allowing the company to introduce new, advanced products during economic downturns. The other rings include the use of part-timers, the use of contractors, job sharing, and reduced work weeks. By planning in this way, Control Data believes they can avoid morale-destroying layoffs. (As we shall see, the Vanguard's plans for full employment occasionally go awry.)

• *The Vanguard Have a Consumer Orientation.* At Deere, Levi, and Motorola, a secret to success is simply making the best product possible. At Dayton-Hudson the customer is always right: There is a no-questions-ever-asked return policy. At none of the Vanguard companies is the quick buck ever pursued. The goal, instead, is to establish long-term business relationships by providing what the customer needs. In traditional companies, managers often have both eyes on the stock market. Vanguard managers, in contrast, keep one eye on the consumer market at all times. But never both eyes (the other is on production). There is, thus, a strong product-quality orientation: The Vanguard recognize that companies make products and only the U. S. Treasury makes money.

• *The Vanguard Are Future-Oriented.* At Control Data, nearly $800 million was spent on PLATO, a state-of-the-art teaching machine that only began to make a profit after fifteen years of investment.

Arco invested billions on North Slope oil, waiting a decade before they realized a return.

Motorola uses ten-year technology forecasts as the basis for their five-year strategic plans.

Weyerhaeuser has stuck with a ten-year experiment with aquaculture—farming the sea—that is not yet profitable.

• *The Vanguard Provide a Sense of Ownership.* At Hewlett-Packard, every worker has a financial stake in the company. Managers are like the owners of small businesses. Every time a division reaches a certain size, it is split up into smaller units, none having more than a thousand employees. Similarly, Honeywell is solving the problem of insufficient advancement opportunities for managers by breaking up divisions, thus creating many more entrepreneurs and top managers.

Control Data goes into partnership with those employees who are willing to take a new product and develop it in a spin-off or joint venture.

At Motorola, every one of the company's 60,000 domestic employees is on a bonus plan in which he or she can increase monthly salary by up to 40 percent.

At Levi, risk taking and entrepreneurial behavior are re-warded—and even sewing machine operators get productivity bonuses.

The Vanguard pay philosophy for top managers was best stated by Malcom Northrup, CEO of Verbatim Corp. (which was on my list of the ten best-managed companies until it was acquired by Kodak in early 1985). I quote him, verbatim:

> Give no increases for poor performance. In fact, put it an-other way:
>
> Pay very poorly for poor performance,
>
> pay poorly for average performance,
>
> pay good for above-average performance, and
>
> pay obscenely for outstanding performance.

• *The Vanguard Are a Link with Entrepreneurial Small Businesses.* The entrepreneur knows that business consists of two basic activities: making and selling things. He also knows that the best way to make and sell things is to motivate employees to have pride in their work. The entrepreneur has no time for acquisitions, tax games, or portfolio management. There is time only for basics. Sticking to the basics, Lincoln Electric, Fel-Pro, Herman Miller, and Olga have become some of the most successful small-to medium-sized companies in America. GM, ITT, and other greats have steadfastly claimed that it was impossible to translate what these small companies do into big company practices. But now, Motorola—with the world's biggest employee participation plan—Hewlett-Packard—with employee stock ownership and productivity sharing—and Control Data—with their employee entrepreneurship program—are showing that the secrets of small business success can be captured by big businesses, too.

Not surprisingly, I thus discovered that the Vanguard do almost all the things one or another management theorist has recently associated with corporate excellence. If I were to stop right here, I would validate much of the current thinking about management. But stopping here would be arbitrary. For I can immediately think of several other common characteristics of success—sound financial controls, decentralization, commitment to technological innovation—that could also be included. Moreover, a large number of companies that wouldn't make anyone's list of great enterprises have many of these characteristics (and some even have them all). Thus, while these characteristics might be seen as prerequisites for excellence, they clearly don't satisfy the requirements for conferring the degree! (In the chapters to come, we'll nonetheless examine these important characteristics in greater detail, discovering in the process that there is more to running a great corporation than meets the eye.)

Tolstoy Turned on His Ear

To discover the elements of eminence, perhaps it would be fruitful to turn Tolstoy's proposition around. After all, it could be that the characteristics of corporate success are myriad, but the reasons for failure are few! Indeed, a strong case can be made that all unhappy companies are unhappy in the same ways—at least it would seem that corporations almost always fail when they do one or more of the following things:

• *The Old Guard Become Insensitive to the Realities of the External Environment.* RCA attempted to sell the nonflexible, mechanical, Selectavision videodisc recorders in the face of such patently superior technologies as flexible videocassette recorders and the nonmechanical laser disc recorders. General Motors attempted to sell big cars in the midst of an oil crisis. Texas Instruments attempted to market personal computers that were incompatible with most common hardware and software. These failures to be responsive to change in the environment led to enormous financial losses for all three of these companies (in the next chapter we'll explore how and why they lost touch with their customers and competitors).

• *The Old Guard Diversify Out of Their Expertise and, Thus, Lose Sight of the Basics.* In 1976, the board of stodgy Addressograph-Multigraph Corporation hired Roy Ash and charged him with changing the company from a failing old-line manufacturer into a high-technology challenger of IBM and Xerox. Ash was an excellent choice for the job. In fact, he is one of the most intelligent, honest, and diligent corporate leaders I have ever met. Ash warmed to the challenge and went on a high-tech acquisition spree, buying promising new companies like a Saudi sheik doing his holiday shopping at Harrods. When Ash discovered that his existing management team didn't know Silicon Valley from Carol Doda's silicone transplants, he fired some 80 percent of them.

During all this hiring and firing, he ignored the basics of making and selling things. Computers were being sold that had not been fully assembled. Traditional product lines needed to finance the new ventures were ignored. When Ash was relieved of his duties in 1981, his successor inherited a company that lost $250 million on $860 million in sales. A former employee joked that Ash's last words as they dragged him out of the executive suite were: "Keep up the firing until the morale improves." Like many corporate tales, the AM saga is open to many interpretations. Some observers lay the ultimate blame on the AM board for not giving Ash sufficient time to make his strategy work. Nonetheless, the corporate graveyard is full of CEOs who diversified out of their area of expertise.

•   *The Old Guard Make Facile Assumptions About the Future.* In the late 1970s, Exxon's economists produced a remarkable series of forecasts of long-term energy supply and demand. Their most important forecast was that the price of oil would continue to rise between the years 1980 and 2000 at roughly the rate it had increased after the Arab oil embargo in 1973. Since assumptions drive the behavior of corporations, Exxon planned to invest $20 billion on synthetic fuels (oil from shale and tar sands; natural gas from lignite). Significantly, these are fuels that would become economical in the late 1980s only *if* the price of oil continued to rise as the Exxon economists extrapolated. Therefore, the forecasts were good news, indeed, to Exxon's top management. After all, the world's biggest company needed big projects on which to spend their big profits. However, in 1978, several futurists suggested to Exxon's planners that the price of oil might actually *fall* for any one of four reasons: (1) conservation could reduce demand; (2) new oil discoveries could increase supply; (3) OPEC members could engage in under-the-table discounting, thus weakening the power of the cartel; or (4) in the long run, alternative energy sources (solar, wind, nuclear) might lessen the dependence on fossil fuels. Shouldn't Exxon do some contingency planning just in case one of these four alternatives were to develop? The futurists were politely shown to the door. Exxon went on to lose $1 billion on synfuels before finally abandoning the program in 1982. (Admittedly, a billion clams doesn't amount to much more than a rounding error on Exxon's balance sheet; but at most companies, it adds up to real money!)

• *The Old Guard Become Smug and Complacent.* In early 1975, a young IBM planner was given the rare opportunity to make a presentation before a group of that great corporation's top managers. He spoke about the long-term potential of the microprocessor—the computer on a chip—and about the high likelihood of the miniaturization of nearly the entire range of computers. He concluded his remarks by drawing two boxes on an overhead transparency; the big one he labeled "us," the small one he labeled "them."

He suggested that, to IBM, only the big box was a computer. But, to many small companies, the little box was *also* a computer. In fact, to many companies, the little box represented the future of the computer industry. He warned: "IBM must also learn to think of the small box as a computer if we are to be fully competitive in the future." According to one who was in attendance at the meeting, the young planner's talk was met by stony silence.

It is easy to see why IBM's top managers would not have taken easily to this argument, for it challenged their basic belief system. No doubt, they were able to reject it on the grounds that it was inconsistent with perceived reality. After all, IBM had some 60–75 percent of the nation's computer business—and almost all that business was in mainframes and other big computers. What did this upstart kid know? In IBM's eye, the small computer was the exception that proved their rule that big was an essential characteristic of computers. At best, small was merely a toy for "hobbyists" and other people working at home—none of whom were considered relevant stakeholders in the IBM scheme. IBM then turned their back on the small computer for some five years.

In the late 1970s, Apple and several other Silicon Valley firms successfully introduced personal computers and, in the process, turned the young IBM planner into a prophet. The interpretation of what happened next is quite controversial and must await further development later. The point here is that IBM missed the significance of small computers the first time around. And, had they delayed another two years in entering the market, probably even they could not have afforded the price of entry (assuming that, by then, Apple would have established the industry standard).

• *The Old Guard Become Overly Action-Oriented and Insufficiently Thoughtful.* "Do it, try it, fix it," is the hottest corporate slogan of the early 1980s. This zippy phrase captures the essence of how Old Guard managers like to see themselves: as fast, tough, decisive decision makers (à la Fredric March). Not long ago, I sat through a meeting of top managers at a corporation that once was great, but had recently fallen on hard times. The meeting went like the gunfight at the O.K. Corral—decisions were made bang, bang, bang—no questions were asked, no prisoners were taken. I later asked a manager who was present if the company's executives were always so decisive. He jokingly replied, "Most of us are new at our jobs, so we have to prove how smart we are."

It was a flip answer, but revealing nonetheless. For Old Guard corporations place high value on such quick, "macho" decision making. Managers prove their stuff by being tough, not by being thoughtful. The action-oriented executive is viewed as a "leader" —the manager who says "It all depends" is seen as wishy-washy. Studying an issue carefully is too close to what happens in universities—and every Old Guard executive knows that professors never *do* anything. Old Guard managers get impatient with the hard, time-consuming work of coping with ambiguous issues. That's why "Ready, fire, aim" is the way of life at the Old Guard. "Silver bullet" answers—simple ones that can be applied quickly to any situation—give the Old Guard manager a sense of virility, of purposiveness, of being in control, of earning his keep. Ideas are seen as incidental to this type of management; that is why basic questions about managerial philosophy are seldom asked at the Old Guard.

• *The Old Guard Repeat Past Successes and Ignore the Need for Change.* For generations, AT&T assumed that their prime objective was to serve the home customer. Indeed, they succeeded in installing a telephone in every American home. Then, the world changed technologically, competitively, and legally. The new AT&T now faces a radically different world—one in which their old assumptions are valueless—and they are forced to play catch-up with computers and other new technologies.

• *The Old Guard Think Short-Term.* A great success story of the postwar era is the California wine industry. They succeeded in getting Americans to substitute Chablis for coffee at dinner. Now, according to vintner Robert Mondavi, the industry has grown complacent, dropped research, and is not planning for a more competitive future. Says Mondavi, "California's wine industry is headed down the path taken by Detroit." Now, Italy—the Japan of viticulture—is eating (drinking?) into California's market share, and the little old winemakers from Napa are petitioning Washington to reduce foreign wine imports much as Detroit is protected by quotas on Japanese cars.

· *The Old Guard Behave As If the Only Purpose of a Corporation Is to Maximize Shareholder Wealth.* In the 1970s, Mobil became the nation's leading proponent of unbridled free enterprise for large corporations. In a long-running series of strident newspaper ads, Mobil took on the critics of corporations, speaking out against regulations, for lower taxes, against environmentalists, and for freedom of corporations to maneuver as they see fit. The essence of their argument was that the public interest is best served when corporations are free to maximize shareholder wealth. Mobil's position was undercut by their own behavior: While arguing for higher profits in order to acquire needed capital to increase the nation's supply of energy, Mobil used their oil profits to buy Montgomery Ward; while saying that the company's policy of serving only shareholders was in the public interest, Mobil threatened to move their headquarters offshore if they didn't get their way on a key piece of Congressional legislation; while arguing for deregulation, they lobbied against oil decontrol when it was clear that their competitors would stand to benefit from free competition more than they; while arguing that the oil companies know what is best for America in the field of energy, Mobil put all their eggs in Saudi Arabia, only to find themselves stuck with overpriced oil when the world suddenly found itself awash in crude; while arguing for media accuracy, Mobil deliberately misrepresented the neoliberal position on unions and welfare in one of their ads—thus alienating the last remaining group on the left that was not mindlessly antibusiness. Over the decade, Mobil became the national symbol of corporate greed and shortsightedness. They were viewed by most of their critics as an unpatriotic, unprincipled organization that served no constituency well, not even, in the end, their shareholders.

Clearly, the identification of common characteristics of failure can be rewarding. But the shortcoming of the exercise is that some great companies have made the mistakes listed above and survived, and some mediocre companies have committed none of these errors. Tolstoy backward is thus at least as useful as

Tolstoy frontward. But neither approach identifies the true source of corporate eminence. Moreover, if we pursued the exercise a bit further, we would find that some characteristics would appear on both the list of positives *and* the list of negatives! That is, traits that appear to be signs of excellence in one company may be signs of failure in another (or, more often, relevant traits in one industry but irrelevant in another). Here are a few examples of such paradoxical or eccentric characteristics:

•   *Single-minded Leadership.* Many contemporary theorists advocate that managers should concentrate on doing only one (or possibly two) things: "Be a Johnny One Note," they advise managers, "do one thing well."

Paradoxically, such single-mindedness cuts *two* ways! On the one hand, as the theorists claim, it provides clarity of vision and consistency of purpose. As we saw earlier, for generations AT&T was committed to a single goal: customer service. The corporation's founding father, Theodore Vail, had the foresight to see that, if American households had no complaints about telephone service, there would be neither a constituency favoring nationalization of telephones nor public support for antitrust action against the Bell monopoly. History shows that Vail's single-minded dedication to service had exactly the payoff he intended. Indeed, my colleague Warren Bennis has interviewed some ninety corporate leaders, and he is struck by the single-minded consistency of vision and purpose he found in them all. In particular, the trait seems essential among entrepreneurs, managers of small businesses, and managers of corporations in relatively static, noncompetitive industries.

On the other hand, single-mindedness can lead to the decline and even fall of a corporate empire. As we saw, AT&T's single purpose became inappropriate in a new world in which technological change—not customer service—was the overriding environmental concern. Mobil's single-minded commitment to serving one constituent (the shareholder) was appropriate until the Arab oil embargo of 1973 transformed energy into a public, as well as a private, concern. Singular marks of excellence are thus fine in ordinary times, but not enough in periods of fundamental transition. For example, Exxon has been declared an excellent company because its leaders write short, snappy memos. This is admirable, but it does not offer protection against public hostility during an oil shortage! That Teledyne is single-minded about maintaining a lean corporate staff is well and good—but it is of little use when a subsidiary is caught dumping toxic waste. And so it is with other singular characteristics of excellence. In large, multipurpose corporations, there are often *many* things necessary for success in the long run.

• *Skunk Works.* The "Skunk Works" is Lockheed's famous high-security facility where the company's best brains work on crash, top-secret defense projects for the federal government. That the level of innovation and productivity is higher at the Skunk Works than at Lockheed's lower-security, less-pressured research labs has led some observers to conclude that *every* company should have a skunk works—indeed, that *all* research and new product development should be done in skunk works. Lockheed managers disagree. ("Of course, if you take the best people, give them the most money, and tell them they are on a special mission, they will outperform the average people with less money who are doing less interesting things," one Lockheed manager told me, "but the things the average people do are just as important as the things the stars do—and there is no way to fool the average folks into believing they are working on crash, top-secret projects. Most R&D entails painstaking trial and error. Indeed, if you take a long-term view, the most significant developments come out of that kind of routine environment, not out of a skunk works.")

Nonetheless, IBM's success in creating their highly successful Personal Computer at a skunk works has propelled the idea to prominence. Examining what really went on at IBM during the development of the PC illustrates just how complicated an issue like skunk works can be. Let us pick up our IBM story at the point we left it earlier . . . when Big Blue decided they would have to enter the home computer business or risk becoming permanent nonstarters. In creating the PC, IBM did not draw on their own research nor on their own well-established structure for product development. Because the company had ignored small computers throughout the 1970s, there was simply too little in IBM's technological cupboard for the former, and it was too late in the game for the latter. They turned, instead, to a skunk works. Significantly, the IBM skunk workers achieved no technological innovation; instead, they masterfully assembled parts from several other computer suppliers. For instance, they got the microprocessor "brains" from Intel, the monitor from Matsushita, the floppy disk drives from Control Data, semiconductors from Motorola, the software from Microsoft, and then they named the handsome mongrel they created the *IBM* Personal Computer.

Many of those in American business schools who have studied this rushed, jury-rigged effort have hailed it as a model for others to copy, a *succès d'estime*. But could it be that skunk works can be signs of failure as well as success? After all, it was only because the regular IBM structure had broken down and had failed to prepare itself for the eventual shift to smaller computers that IBM was forced to break with tradition (and their usual business procedures) and establish a skunk works. IBM simply had no other choice but "to skunk it" if they were ever going to get into the personal computer business. While this process was no doubt resourceful and, ultimately, financially successful, is it a sign of excellence?

In the 1970s, Xerox had a similar experience. Several Japanese and American competitors started to make deep and rapid inroads into the theretofore Xerox-dominated copier market. Xerox's distributors sent panic calls to corporate headquarters for help. They needed a new product—and fast—to counter the growing threat. When Xerox's top brass met with their product development people to discuss the problem, they were informed that it would take about two years to get the next product from the design stage into full production. Xerox's top executives quickly calculated that in two years they would lose many of their best dealers to their competitors and, in the process, perhaps forever lose their overwhelming market share. They asked: Why will it take two years if the product is already designed? They got a long answer about work flows, testing, quality control, inventory buildup, supply bottlenecks, and so forth.

In a word, the problem was *bureaucracy*. Xerox had grown so large that, in the process, they had had to establish detailed development procedures to avoid chaos—procedures that now prevented them from meeting a real threat to their survival. Faced with no alternative but to create a skunk works in a loft some distance from corporate headquarters, Xerox executives ordered it done. Within some six months, a small team of leading technical people had the new product in full production. Xerox executives have had the modesty not to claim that their skunk works was a sign of their managerial brilliance; rather, they recognize that it would have been a sign of real excellence had Xerox anticipated the need for the new product, and/or been able to respond to the needs of their suppliers in a routine, nonpanicked, way.

In similar circumstances, IBM was able to throw together a team of brilliant people who, *faute de mieux*, were able to salvage the situation. The IBM PC was the silk purse that a crisis-management team created from a sow's ear handed to them by executives who had wrongly pooh-poohed the small computer business. Better IBM's managers had learned more quickly to think small!

In IBM's defense, it is argued that it was probably cheaper, in the long run, for IBM to have developed the Personal Computer at their skunk works than it would have been to do so through its normal research and product development procedures. Given IBM's relative lack of knowledge about small computers, and the amount of organizational resistance personal computer champions would have met from the established divisions of the company, I'm willing to concede the point. Yet, even if it turns out to have been cheaper, in hindsight, to have skunked it, is this a characteristic of eminence? This is not to condemn IBM. It is merely to call attention to the fact that no other high-tech company could have afforded to do what IBM did. (And, when IBM went back to the well a second time with the PCjr, even they were unable to recreate that old skunk magic.) Hence, while the PC was an industrial miracle, it is questionable whether the process by which it was developed should serve as a model for American industry in general. Moreover, if every corporation waited until the last minute and attempted to skunk it, where would the American economy be? That the Japanese succeeded, in the 1950–80 era, basically by skunking products invented in the USA, is no defense. Some of America's greatest competitive advantages are our risk taking, innovation, and scientific creativity. While skunking might be fine for a few extremely large corporations with billions to spend, it is questionable that it should be added to the list of traits of all eminent companies.

• *Being Nice to Employees.* This is the "one-minute" route to corporate excellence. We are told that employees are motivated by corporate demonstrations of love. Hardworking employees are to be honored in elaborate spectacles invoking ruffles and flourishes, speeches, slogans, campaign ribbons, hugs and kisses. Such half-truths are far more difficult to destroy than complete lies. While it is absolutely true that people like to be publicly recognized for their efforts, privately patted on the back, and at all times treated with kindness and respect (and there is no excuse for managers ever to do otherwise), forty years of well-monitored experience in industry shows that this is insufficient motivation for workers. In fact, workers are motivated by financial rewards for their ideas and efforts and by the opportunity to participate in the decisions that affect their own levels of productivity. Hugs are nice; but if forced to choose, most workers prefer cash.

• *Staying Close to Customers.* Without doubt, no company has ever succeeded by being insensitive to customers. The problem is that this truism is an inadequate guide to corporate behavior without a lot of caveats attached. As it stands—and as it is interpreted today by a growing number of business people and leading management consultants—staying close to one's customers means getting all of one's new product ideas from them (that is, abandoning basic research). But no customer ever asked Du Pont to invent nylon. There was no customer interest in the 1950s whatsoever in RCA's "farfetched" idea, color television. No computer user ever said to Texas Instruments, hey, why don't you guys try making silicon chips? And no frustrated camera buff ever sugggested instant photography to Edwin Land. While staying close to your customers is probably better advice than one or two of the ten commandments that come to mind, industries in high technology and commodities (and much of manufacturing in general) cannot rely on customers to provide all their new product ideas.

• *Being Run by "Left-brained" Engineers.* In 1980, two Harvard professors wrote that executives with backgrounds in finance had "managed" American industry into decline by ignoring production technology. In effect, the professors "discovered" that the Fredric Marches of the world had taken over industry. As engineers, the Harvard professors were acutely sensitive to the lack of knowledge lawyers, economists, and financial analysts bring to the complexities of technological change. Their criticism was well taken. Their solution—give the keys to the executive suite to engineers—is a bit more problematic. While some engineers have been excellent managers (we'll meet more than a few of them in subsequent pages), as a group engineers have been insensitive to the important marketing and human resource issues of management. In particular, engineers often have had problems dealing with emotional and ambiguous issues and with such difficult social issues as equal employment opportunity. Like finance folks, engineers too wear blinders—they just obscure different planes of vision.

- *Being Run by "Right-brained" Executives.* At roughly the same time the Harvard professors just cited were discovering the need for rational, structured, and scientific management, another school (centered mostly in California) arrived at exactly the opposite conclusion: What was needed in industry are emotional and intuitive managers. As we see in subsequent chapters, the leaders of the Vanguard are sensitive, open people who stand on no formalities with their employees and who occasionally play their hunches on big, strategic issues. But they also wouldn't be where they are without their highly developed left-brain skills and without their formal planning and analytical processes. It would seem that *both* the left and the right hemispheres of the brains of great managers are well developed.

And both the right and left arms of professors become developed from their ambidextrous gesturing while saying, "On the one hand . . . and on the other." Clearly, "It all depends" is an inadequate response to the question, "What are the characteristics of managerial eminence?" (It is such relativism that gives professors, politicians, and United Nations Secretaries General their bad reputations.) In this chapter we have only succeeded in illustrating that the currently vogue approach of offering an arbitrary set of characteristics of corporate excellence is as inadequate as the old financial rules of the 1950s and 1960s. But we still have not accounted for the obvious differences between great and mediocre companies. Something must account for the differences in performance between the former and the latter.

2.

THE CHARACTERISTICS
OF THE NEW MANAGEMENT

Not failure, but low aim, is crime.
—JAMES RUSSELL LOWELL

Corporate eminence is not only elusive—it is often illusory. Because management is an art and not a science, the public often mistakes the flashy performance of mediocre corporations for greatness. For example, great size is often confused with managerial excellence. Certainly, the very fact that a corporation has grown to enormous size is a sign that managers in the past did something right (and may still be doing so). But great size, in itself, is not proof of current (or future) managerial eminence. As we have seen, the world's largest oil company, Exxon, was able to lose a billion dollars on synfuels through managerial shortsightedness, and the nation's largest high-technology company, IBM, failed until the eleventh hour to enter the fast-growing personal computer business (and later was forced to spend tens of millions in a vain attempt to salvage their poorly conceived PCjr computer). And, as we shall soon see, the nation's largest manufacturing firm, General Motors, fumbled their early opportunities to establish a position in the small-car market and found themselves with the wrong product strategy in the energy-pinched 1970s.

Significantly, all three of these giants easily survived these episodes of mismanagement (errors that would have destroyed most of their competitors). Because of their enormous assets, commanding market shares, and high retained earnings, they have had the luxury to be followers rather than leaders, to buy market share through expensive advertising, to retain customers by way of their extensive service networks, and to hide their big mistakes in general. Indeed, I suspect that if one were to look closely, one would find that the quality of management at the chief competitors of Exxon, GM, and IBM is not significantly worse than at the headquarters of these industry leaders. Yet, their smaller competitors (Gulf and Sun in the oil industry, Chrysler and Ford in autos, and Texas Instruments and Digital Equipment in computers) have been in and out of serious trouble for years. This suggests a possible "law": If an organization is going to be mismanaged, the chances of survival are improved if they are the biggest company in their industry! This, of course, provides scant comfort to the managers of firms of less-than-gargantuan proportion (unactionable laws being of little use to those pursuing managerial eminence).

That a corporation is experiencing remarkable short-term financial success is also confused with managerial eminence. A player who hits a home run in his first major league game or runs for a thousand yards in his rookie season in pro football is certainly off to a good start to earning a niche in the Hall of Fame. But the truth is that most players who achieve such early success are ultimately remembered as flashes in the pan. In business, Wall Street analysts are particularly prone to confuse ephemeral profit making with sound management. Just yesterday, LTV, Equity Funding, Atari, and Recognition Equipment had their innings on The Street, only to wilt and fade like last season's rookie of the year now in a deep slump.

In this regard, there is a peculiarly American inability to distinguish between entrepreneurial success that comes from having a short-term monopoly based on a new technology and managerial success that leads to ensuring the long-term survival of a firm. Failure to make such an obvious distinction has recently afflicted financial analysts, business journalists, consultants, and professors who have been seduced into confusion by the initial successes of many Silicon Valley firms. The founders of these firms were hailed as geniuses in the press, in classrooms, and everywhere business is discussed. But the moment the market for personal computers matured, and an industry-wide shakeout ensued, many of these erstwhile geniuses found themselves in bankruptcy court. The loose management styles of these executives—advanced as admirable models of "right-brained" behavior by overly enthusiastic professors—turned out to be brainlessness, sloppiness, and a hindrance to change when it came time to meet new challenges. Indeed, short-term profitability is so often confused with good management that it seems necessary to point out the obvious: Firms are often profitable—occasionally for as long as a decade—even though they are poorly managed. This is true in high-tech companies (like Texas Instruments in the 1970s) and low-tech companies (like U.S. Steel in the 1960s).

Because of the failure to distinguish the good (or the merely lucky) from the greatest corporations, the denizens of Wall Street, the managerial professoriate, and the community of business journalists and consultants who set the standards for corporate eminence often hold up the wrong corporations as models for others to emulate. Today's models of corporate eminence neither break new ground nor do they attempt to raise business practices to a higher plane—indeed, they do not try to be the best. Instead, they enjoy the less demanding role of "nice guys" who accept rather than challenge the comfortable assumptions and standards of the day. Only in the field of business would it be news that the head of a major corporation pledged that his auto company "won't settle for anything less than the best cars, best protection, best service." So accustomed were Americans to seeing corporate leaders settle for second-rate quality, second-rate service, and second place to the Japanese that Lee Iacocca became a folk hero when he proclaimed: "We have one and only one ambition: to be the best. What else is there?" What else, indeed? What had Ford and GM (and Chrysler itself) been settling for for over a decade? Had the CEO of GM made a similar pronouncement in the 1970s, stockholders, employees, and customers would have died of shock!

While it is perfectly respectable, honorable, and praiseworthy to be an IBM, an Exxon, or a GM, it is nonetheless self-defeating in the long run for society to advance the *very good* as models of *the best*. The true standard of excellence is not met by a corporation that happens to capture an enormous market share. If corporations fail to use their resources to courageously advance technology and to improve the quality of life of employees and consumers, they must be relegated to the status of the very good. Hence, the crime of American management is not that so many corporations have failed to achieve lasting eminence (in any endeavor only a minority can be great), but that so few have tried. With only low expectations as standards, too few managers attempt to use the enormous resources at their disposal for the purpose of improving the state of their art. Instead, they are satisfied with the wrongheaded encouragement of those who fail to see the necessity of high aim if corporate capitalism is to endure and prevail. In this respect, today's so-called excellence is the enemy of greatness. For if all corporations aspire to only the mediocre standards of excellence advanced today, then the quality of all management will surely decline tomorrow. And, if that occurs, public support for the system will evaporate.

But my analogy is wrong, it might be said, for business is not an art, not even a profession. After all, art is a luxury, while business is a kind of "mean necessity" of life more akin to providing food, clothing, and shelter. But the preparation of food can be raised to an art, clothing can be finely designed and well made, and a home can be an architectural jewel. No doubt, business *can* be practiced at a low level, as it can be practiced with the kind of clever mediocrity that fools the undiscerning. But it can also be practiced as a profession—with care, commitment, and artistic integrity. That is the challenge Bill Holden placed before the Tredway board. And that is what the Vanguard corporations are about.

As I studied the ways of the Vanguard for nearly three years, looking for their elusive common elements, my notebooks became filled with examples of their programs, policies, and practices, many aspects of which they shared with traditionally managed corporations. But in rereading my notes many times, I began to see that certain words reappeared throughout the pages, words that suggested to me basic differences between the Vanguard and the Old Guard. Such abstract words as balance, integration, harmony, coherence, and justice seemed to underly the philosophy of management at the Vanguard and gave me a clue about what distinguishes these great companies from the very good.

As I read my notes over and again, it became clear that the Vanguard have four general characteristics in common:

1. They practice stakeholder symmetry.
2. They are dedicated to a high purpose.
3. They are committed to learning.
4. They attempt to be the best at everything they do.

Important, these are not rules, laws, or specific practices. Instead, they are general philosophical orientations that underlie all the various and varied activities of the Vanguard. In subsequent chapters, when we explore the specific management practices of the Vanguard, we find that these differ widely (and the reason why they differ is an important part of this book). But, by way of introduction, let us briefly review the commonalities among the Vanguard, the general characteristics of the New Management that I suggest account for their eminence.

1. STAKEHOLDER SYMMETRY

Traditionally, most companies have been managed with one obligation in mind: to maximize shareholder wealth. This is a clearly appropriate goal in small, family-owned businesses. It is *in*appropriate in large and publicly held firms that are social as well as economic institutions.

The Vanguard believe that shareholders are best served in the long-run when corporations attempt to satisfy the legitimate claims of *all* the parties that have a stake in their companies: consumers, employees, suppliers, dealers, special interest groups, host communities, government, as well as shareholders. In fact, the task of management is defined as resolving conflict between the competing claims of these groups. The top manager of a Vanguard company is neither a czar nor a servant of the shareholders; more accurately, he or she is a responsive politician who tries to provide some balance in the corporate response to competing constituencies.

This may sound terribly abstract and vague. Perhaps the clearest way to illustrate it is by reference to a company that for a long time ignored the need for stakeholder symmetry. That company is General Motors. In the late 1970s, GM got in trouble, in part, because they violated the principle of stakeholder symmetry. As we will see later, GM ignored the changing needs of suppliers, dealers, employees, customers, and the society of which the company was a part, ultimately losing social and marketplace legitimacy in the process.

In sharp contrast stands the behavior of the Vanguard. When I asked Robert Haas, the CEO of Levi Strauss, how an actual corporate decision by the Vanguard was different from those of the Old Guard, he offered me a candid account of a recent decision Levi managers were forced to make during the 1980–83 recession. Haas believes that "Adversity is the real test of your values," and that a corporation's greatness can best be gauged when they must make a decision that requires choosing between two valid and legitimate goals. He explained, "We found that we got in trouble a couple of times when push came to shove and we didn't stick to our principles." The "troubles" he alluded to were a price-fixing case and two incidents of overexpansion, one that nearly caused the corporation to lose their European business, and the other that lead to the first layoffs in the company's history. He explained that this latter incident occurred after one heady period of high demand during which the company had gotten carried away and pursued growth to the exclusion of other important values. The consequences: declining profits, labor problems, low morale, and poor relations with retailers. He explained what happened next:

> Finally, we had to go to the union and ask them for their help. We asked them to postpone a previously contracted raise for a few months until we could turn our business around. They agreed without any conditions. After the session with the union, we got to thinking about the raises that were coming due for the staff at corporate headquarters— *our* raises. We decided that it was unfair to ask blue-collar operators to accept a wage freeze if we didn't accept one ourselves. That decision to freeze our own wages was easy, in hindsight. But we realized that we had gotten out of the habit of thinking in terms of fairness, justice, and balance in our headlong rush to achieve maximum growth. The irony is that we couldn't achieve maximum growth without the other values—we needed good dealer relations and good employee relations to grow.

So what? One might object that even Haas admits this was a relatively easy decision. Maybe so. But within a month after Levi Strauss's executives denied themselves a raise, the top management of General Motors voted themselves an enormous raise hard on the heels of winning significant "give-backs" from their unionized employees. The subsequent outrage—from the union, from the public, even from shareholders—was so great that GM's executives were forced to eat crow and cancel their raises. When faced with similar circumstances, why did Levi Strauss behave in one way (the right way, I would argue) and GM behave in the opposite way? The difference, I suggest, is found in Robert Haas's commitment to what Levi calls their "Principles." According to

Haas, "The Levi Strauss philosophy can be stated in a phrase: *We seek to treat people with respect."* He explained to me how this philosophy informs all the firm's business decisions: "Throughout our history, we've honored a set of principles that define our character." He then ticked off examples for me, not from rote practice, but from the kind of memory that comes from living constantly and comfortably with an idea:

First of all, treating people with respect means encouraging and regarding employee initiative, teamwork, responsibility, and excellence. We believe it also means offering consumers high-quality products at good value, providing reliable, responsive and courteous service to our retailers, negotiating fairly with our suppliers, and encouraging responsible practices within our industry. We've argued for decades that it also means being exemplary citizens in the communities where we locate our facilities, observing the highest legal and ethical standards, and promoting social justice through responsible philanthropy. In short, it means giving our stockholders optimal long-term return on their investment by working diligently to meet our responsibilities to all our other constituencies. That's what we mean by respect for people.

Remarkably, he said all this without pretension. But, while listening to him, I started to think about the working conditions in many apparel manufacturing firms and found myself getting cynical. "It all sounds fine, Bob, but what does it mean to the 30,000 or so women who work for you, sitting eight hours a day stitching jeans behind a sewing machine? What does your respect mean for them?" Fortunately, Bob Haas is as good-humored as he is committed to his values. "I was wondering when you were going to bring that up," he laughed. "Let me tell you, it's not easy. These values are *goals*—ideals—to which we aspire. We're not there yet. We probably will never be. But let me give you one example of a way in which we *try* to live up to what we believe: our Community Involvement Teams."

To understand this program, one must appreciate three facts: First, Levi Strauss has one of the largest foundations among giant U.S. corporations (as measured by the percent of taxable profits given away). Second, the lifeblood of the company is their sewing machine operators, most of whom are women, most not terribly well-educated, and most from what is called "underprivileged" backgrounds—blacks in the U.S. South, Hispanics in the West, working-class Scots in the Highlands, Chinese immigrants in Hong Kong, and so on in 111 facilities in seventeen countries. Third, sewing jeans is a lousy job. Not lousy pay or benefits—Levi is a generous employer—but lousy in that it is repetitive, boring, hard on the eyes and fingers, tough on the back and neck. It is not the kind of job one would do if one were not well paid; it is not the kind of job one takes home at night because it is interesting or challenging; it is not the kind of job that causes a woman to wish it weren't so when her eight-hour shift is up; and it is not the kind of job in which time flies because you are having fun.

Haas explained: "We have a responsibility to improve the quality of the lives of all the people who work for us. We try to enrich their jobs—but there is a limit to what can be done to make sewing jeans interesting and fulfilling." So what has the company done to meet their self-imposed obligation to their employees? They have sought to *empower* these women. They have made them into philanthropists. By dividing up a considerable portion of the Levi foundation's cash among the company's various plants, and letting the workers decide who in their local communities should receive the contributions, the company has bolstered the status and self-esteem of employees (after all, the one person whose phone call is *always* returned is the philanthropist). These relatively disadvantaged employees, who just yesterday had little going for them, are now negotiating with the mayors of their hometowns. Here are women, many made shy and self-effacing by the experiences of their lives, now treated as equals by hospital administrators, school officials, and community leaders. No longer are they *just* sewing machine operators—they are influential, they are respected, and no doubt they have a small taste of that delicious feeling of self-importance the Carnegies, Rockefellers, and Fords felt when they engaged their considerable philanthropic egos.

"What are you doing, Bob?" I asked. "Is Levi a charitable institution? Is this paternalism? Is this just a clever way of getting employees to be more productive by being more committed to Levi Strauss?"

"Those are good questions. We worry about them constantly," Haas answered. While acknowledging a philanthropic responsibility, he denied vehemently that Levi Strauss was a charity:

"We're a business." While acknowledging a responsibility for improving the quality of the lives of his employees, he denied that Levi Strauss was paternalistic: "Nobody has to participate in the Community Involvement Teams; in fact, the majority of our employees probably don't." While acknowledging that such programs build employee loyalty, commitment, and, perhaps, productivity and product quality, he denied that was the reason why they are done: "This is simply the way we feel a corporation should be run. It is better for workers, better for communities, better for shareholders, and probably even better for our customers in the long run, if workers rather than managers make philanthropic decisions. It's simply better business to find ways to simultaneously serve all our constituencies' needs and interests."

Trying to find ways to simultaneously serve all our constituencies. In one form or another I heard something like that phrase on the lips of all the top managers of the great corporations featured in this book. When describing the philosophies of their corporations, the managers I have interviewed, like Bob Haas, used the language of politics more often than the language of economics. When describing the process by which they decide between two or more alternative corporate policies, they often drew metaphoric parallels to the process by which difficult actions are resolved in democratic societies.

Like other Vanguard leaders, Arco's former president, Thornton Bradshaw saw the role of corporate leadership in terms of *managing conflict.* He sought to create a consistent set of principles to guide the corporation's actions in their dealing with all their various stakeholders. I had not understood this about Bradshaw until 1977. In the spring of that year, I sat with him and some twenty Arco managers at the company's elegant training center overlooking the Pacific in Santa Barbara. At the closing session of the seminar, a young manager asked Bradshaw about the culture of the firm, and he replied:

> It must all be of a single fabric. From the company's social posture, through the way it treats its employees, to the care it takes in the artistic decor and style of its buildings, *everything* must manifest a commitment to quality, to excellence, to service, and to meeting the needs and aspirations of our owners, workers, consumers, and the broader society.

During the 1970s, the company's conduct was true to Bradshaw's principles. Arco was the industry leader in the fight for energy conservation. They abandoned billboard and product advertising and had exemplary records in environmental protection and occupational safety and health. In the public policy arena, the company shocked their industry by advocating the diversion of highway taxes to mass transit, favoring the windfall profits tax, and opposing California's Proposition 13 and the federal oil depletion allowance. Bradshaw defended each of these positions from the standpoint *not* of bleeding heart liberalism, but from a realism born of necessity. (In the case of the windfall profits tax, Arco wanted a *quid pro quo:* removal of federal oil price controls.) When he wrote an article in *Fortune* in favor of limited national energy planning, he did so as a capitalist who regrettably but realistically recognized the need for government to do some things that corporations couldn't do.

While on many occasions Bradshaw spoke out publicly and critically about excessive governmental red tape and unfair attacks on the industry by the media and the intelligentsia, he differed from others in the oil industry in that he acknowledged that wishing wouldn't make government, the media, or environmentalists go away. Moreover, he was willing to acknowledge when some criticisms by these groups were legitimate. And, as he said in 1979, he tried always to take into account the claims of all the corporation's stakeholders:

Every decision made at my desk is influenced by some, and at times many, of the following: the possible impact on public opinion; the reaction of environmental groups; the possible impact on other action groups—consumers, tax reform, antinuclear, prodesert, prorecreational vehicles, etc.; the constraints of government—DOE, EPA, OSHA, ICC, FTC, etc., etc.—and the states, and the municipalities; the effect on inflation and on the government antiinflation program; labor union attitudes; the OPEC cartel. Oh yes, I almost forgot, the anticipated economic profit, the degree of risk, the problem of obtaining funds in a competitive market, the capability of our organization, and—when there is time—the competition. When the government doesn't slice us up, Mobil, Texaco, Union are sure to try.

Here, Bradshaw uses the language and imagery of politics to describe his job. In many ways, this description sounds more like a passage from the memoirs of a U.S. President than it does a typical *Wall Street Journal* profile of an all-powerful and all-knowing corporate executive who, when making a decision, checks only the bottom line, then barks a command. It is also significant that, when explaining his managerial philosophy, Bradshaw does not quote the texts and cases from which he taught at the Harvard Business School. Instead, he is given to citing historian Arthur Schlesinger, Jr., a considered student of the Republic and our chief executive officers:

> With all its defects democratic pluralism retains a single advantage. That advantage is the capacity to correct its own errors. The political process is, in effect, a feedback system through which mistaken policy generates popular reactions that alter the policy. History is the record of the adaptation of institutions and values to changing material and moral circumstances. Rigidity is the enemy of adaptation, flexibility is its secret.

Bradshaw and his boss, CEO Robert O. Anderson, ran Arco with unflinching commitment to the principle that "Rigidity is the enemy of adaptation, flexibility is its secret." Throughout the 1970s, the company proved they could turn on a dime—out of shale into coal, out of foreign oil into domestic—and make a dollar in the process. All the while, they kept the corporation's policies in harmony with the needs of their employees, with the needs of consumers, and even with the needs of a chorus of corporate critics—environmentalists, consumerists, energy conservationists, and civil rights activists.

Like the President of the Republic, the CEO of a Vanguard corporation is not an authoritarian. The position is, in Theodore Roosevelt's famous phrase, a bully pulpit. The CEO leads not by direction but by example, persuasion, Socratic questioning, and by creating structures and opportunities in which the genius of his people may flourish.

This is not to say that the Vanguard corporations are headed by Carteresque executives. They are not like the former U.S. President who, according to Alistair Cooke, had "an accountant's temperament" which "made him see six sides to every issue and left him in the moment of decision like a centipede with all its legs wriggling but its body immobile." The chief executives of Vanguard corporations are not only more decisive than this, inherently their role has greater relative power than the U.S. presidency. But, in common with leaders of the democracy, they pay great heed to the wisdom of a "raucous assembly" of employees unafraid to speak their minds. Out of this tumult arises the raw material for effective—and decisive—actions. The Vanguard executives talk to all sides, listen to all sides, consider all sides—but are dictated to by no one side. Vanguard corporations therefore are free of the immobilization that often afflicts the nation as the result of the exercise of countervailing power by special interest groups. Thus, in many key respects—but not all—the philosophy of the pluralistic democracy and the philosophy of the Vanguard corporations run parallel.

2. HIGH PURPOSE

The "search for meaning" has become the leitmotif of modern times. Since workplaces have largely replaced the family, the church, and the community as the central institution of society, more men and women have turned to their corporate employers as the source of inspiration and purpose in their lives. So a base or unelevated purpose for the corporation is inadequate. Profit maximization is not enough. And such slogans as "Think" and "Progress Is Our Most Important Product" are seen as hollow by the sophisticated and educated employees of today—men and women who refuse to be manipulated. That is why a company that has as their highest goal (as one that has been recently called excellent proudly proclaims) "to ensure that our potato chips never get soggy on grocery store counters" cannot be thought of as a great company, even if they do make enormous sums of money in the short term. It is not that crisp chips are an unworthy business objective—I am as opposed to soggy Fritos as the next person—but, in the long term, the best employees will drift away in search of deeper purpose and more meaningful reasons to devote their lives to a corporation.

At the Vanguard there is commitment in word and deed to a higher purpose: These corporations exist to provide society with the goods and services it needs, to provide employment, and to create a surplus of wealth (profit) with which to improve the nation's general standard of living and quality of life. In this view, profit is the means, not the end, of corporate activity.

At Weyerhaeuser, where investments are made that won't—can't—reap returns for sixty years, the philosophy is "We do these things not for ourselves, or for our children, but for our grandchildren." At Control Data, where company policy is to build all their new factories in urban ghettos, to apply their advanced technology to help beleaguered small farmers, and to channel their financial resources to undercapitalized small businesses, the philosophy is "To address society's major unmet needs as profitable business opportunities."

Hence, the Vanguard have turned their backs on the most pernicious notion of recent management theory, namely, that "ideas don't count." This is wrong and dangerous and leads to the conclusion that all one need do to create an excellent corporation is to live by a company slogan or follow a set of rules—even if those rules lead to ends that employees as individuals would reject in their personal lives, or even if the sum total of those rules leads to no coherent philosophy or transcendent purpose. Ultimately, as Christ, Mohammed, the Buddha, Marx, and Thomas Jefferson all knew, people are governed and led by nothing else but ideas. A corporation must stand, steadfastly, for something worthy of the efforts of its many constituencies. A prime function of top management is to articulate with consistency and clarity a central governing idea, one that appeals to a noble or high human aspiration or purpose. In effect, great corporations must be governed by great ideas. For example: In the late 1970s, GM got into trouble, in part, because they violated this principle. As we will see later, GM stated proudly that they were in the business of "making money, not cars," all the while their employees, customers, and dealers were faced with a challenge from foreign competitors who, in sharp contrast, were in the business of making quality autos to bring jobs to their own shores. And American executives were "surprised" to learn that their Japanese competitors' employees were more loyal than Detroit's autoworkers!

The ideas that govern the Vanguard are found in simple, eloquent statements of philosophy that serve (much like the U.S. Constitution) as moral touchstones at times of difficult choice. Vanguard executives do not talk to their employees about the nitty-gritty of day-to-day operations—they leave that to the managers of their decentralized divisions—but rather about the great ideas in their "constitutions." The CEOs of the Vanguard lead neither by command nor control, but by repeated reference to the great ideas that govern their enterprises.

The Vanguard constitutions, vague and general as they may be, contain ultimate values to which all members of the organization can subscribe, a point of transcendent consensus in a dominion of competing claims. The most famous corporate constitution is Johnson & Johnson's credo. For those who are unfamiliar with the document, it merits a serious reading (the text is included in the extensive Notes and References that follow the last chapter).

Some things are obvious immediately on reading the J & J credo. First, it is an expression of the corporation's responsibilities to their major stakeholders. Significantly, the constitutions of all the Vanguard corporations (and all the runners-up like Johnson & Johnson) are stated in terms of a list of stakeholders followed by the corporation's responsibilities to each of them. Second, the responsibilities are not viewed as trade-offs—as either/ors—but as both mutually compatible and obtainable. Thus, balance and symmetry are incorporated in every one of these documents. What makes for a good corporate constitution? Albert P. Blaustein, a professor of law at Rutgers, is an authority on the various constitutions of the world. We might profitably examine what he has to say about national constitutions and see to what extent it applies to the constitutions of corporations:

> Virtually every successful constitution is a constitution of compromise. It aims at achieving equilibrium. Remember, a constitution is more than a structure and framework for government. It is in many senses a nation's frontispiece. It should be used as a rallying point for the people's ideals and aspirations, as well as a message to the outside world as to what the country stands for.

In Johnson & Johnson's credo we find "equilibrium" (moral symmetry among the competing claims of stakeholders), and we find a "rallying point" for the corporation's ideals (ideals around which J & J rallied during the Tylenol incidents in 1982, as we will see in Chapter Eight), and we find an expression to external constituencies of what the corporation stands for (a message to customers, investors, and potential employees).

But any corporation can put together such an assemblage of

words. If all of the Vanguard constitutions are similar, are they not, then, all fungible (and, hence, meaningless)? Not if the constitution represents the actual aspirations and practices of the company. Johnson & Johnson's credo emerged from the values of their founder, Robert Wood Johnson, and from the unique conditions and demands of the drug industry. Levi Strauss's principles are rooted in the values of their eponymous founder (the great-great-grand uncle of current CEO Robert Haas), values that are probably themselves rooted in Jewish ethics. The constitutions of the Vanguard thus arise from the values of their founders. What is significant about the Vanguard corporations is that there is congruence between the values espoused in their constitutions and the actual practices of these corporations. In distinction, some Old Guard corporations have high-sounding constitutions, but there is a contradiction between rhetoric and performance that belies their noble words.

Like J & J's credo, all of the Vanguard constitutions are sketchy. Does their lack of detail indicate that they are less-than-useful guides for behavior? In 1964, John Deere published their constitution, called the "Green Bulletin" (green being the color of Deere tractors). The loose-leaf booklet sat on the desk (or in the top drawer) of nearly every Deere manager I interviewed in the company. In its preamble, the Deere constitution says that "the statements in these Green Bulletins should be looked upon as approximations rather than complete and precise definitions." Thomas Gildehaus, a Deere executive vice president, explained to me that the purpose of the Green Bulletin is *not* to provide a list of ten commandments, but to convey "the cultural expectations" of the company:

> There is a broad sense of humanity in the series of Green Bulletins. They convey to managers that all decisions must reflect a balance between business and human needs. But, most important, the message is that we must lean to the human side when a difficult choice must be made.

The Vanguard thus differ from the Old Guard in that they recognize that a great corporation needs a stable core of moral values—an ethical gyroscope—at its center. The Vanguard recognize that a corporation cannot satisfy all stakeholders at all times and in all ways. For example, if only the needs of employees are considered, the corporation can rightly be said to be "giving the store away." If only the needs of the shareholders are considered, the corporation can rightly be said to be "exploiting workers," or "ripping off consumers." The Vanguard thus seek constantly to find a point of creative balance. Creative balance includes looking after shareholder interests in the short term while at the same time investing for the future. Creative balance means forming community involvement teams à la Levi. Creative balance means the reconciliation of apparent opposites which, it turns out, are seldom irreconcilable.

The trick in all this is that the point of balance is constantly shifting because the environment is constantly changing and because the needs of stakeholders are continually in flux. Too little responsiveness to such change leads to corporate paralysis, social illegitimacy and, ultimately, to corporate extinction. But if a corporation is too responsive, too driven by the market, it will become a prisoner of fads and the fickle fancies of some stakeholders. That is why a corporation needs a constitution—a gyroscope that provides stability to the ship as it plows forward through the stormy seas of change.

The constitutions of great corporations, like the constitutions of nations, are each different because each must reflect the unique values, experiences, and aspirations of the company's founders, employees, industry, and community. At the same time, each constitution is similar in that it reflects the core values of the greater society of which the corporation is a part, and each commits the company to meeting their responsibilities to their several constituencies. The latter is of central importance, because it is the commitment to meeting stakeholder needs that is the vehicle for corporate change. Without this vehicle, the constitution can become a deadweight. For example, because they overlook key stakeholders, the constitutions of many Old Guard corporations tend to make their managers prisoners of their past successes. Thus, effectively cut off from the most important source of change and renewal, the managers of the Old Guard become chained to outmoded assumptions. As the Levi Strauss example of top managers forgoing pay raises illustrates, long-term corporate success depends on the maintenance of basic principles while, at the same time, adjusting operating policy to meet the changing needs of stakeholders. This is a difficult thing to do. That the Vanguard manage the trick more often than not is one reason why I believe they are the places where so many informed business experts would want to work.

3. CONTINUOUS LEARNING

A fundamental point of this book is that there is no "right way" to manage all companies at all times. There is no monolithic theory or single set of rules that is appropriate in all countries, all industries, or all companies. In the absence of a single ideology that would magically solve the "problem" of management, the only alternative for a corporation is to become a "learning organization."

Eric Hoffer, the deceased sage of San Francisco's Embarcadero, summed up the spirit of learning in this way:

> In a time of drastic change, it is the learners who inherit the future. The learned find themselves equipped to live only in a world that no longer exists.

To remain a learning organization, a company cannot afford to succumb to the blandishments of an ideology or of easy answers. Flexibility, change, and responsiveness are the key to organizational survival. For a corporation to succeed in the long run, managers must abandon the search for the one right way to manage. Instead, they must adopt a learning attitude in which they constantly draw inspiration from changes in the environment and apply what they learn to the continuous recreation and renewal of the strategies and practices of their companies.

To understand this point, we must be clear about the differences in the philosophical assumptions of those who practice traditional management (the Old Guard) and those who practice the New Management (the Vanguard). To fully appreciate how and why the Vanguard learn, we will thus take a brief detour to Detroit where, for over a decade, American managers ceased to respond to changes in their environment.

In the late 1970s, General Motors got into trouble, in part, because they violated the principle of continuous learning. GM became complacent and arrogant, thinking they had "solved the problem of management" for once and forever. This led them to ignore rapid and revolutionary changes in the technological, social, and competitive environment, changes that ultimately eroded the company's profits and market share.

But the seeds of the problem were planted fifty years earlier. Recall that, by 1920, founder Billy Durant's seat-of-the-pants style of management had nearly done GM in. Across town, Henry Ford's Model T's were rolling off his famous assembly line in what, at that time, was the greatest production achievement in the history of industry. Old Henry had mastered the technique of uniform production and marketing ("They can have any color they want, as long as it's black.") and sold some 15 million of his Tin Lizzie's before production was finally halted in 1927.

But GM had a better idea! Shortly after succeeding Durant, GM's Alfred Sloan broke new ground by offering consumers a full line of cars with plenty of style: not just black cars, but blue and green, some with hard tops and some without. GM encouraged buyers to trade in (and up) every two or three years on ever bigger, roomier, more stylish—and more expensive—models. This product policy proved so successful that GM reduced their once-powerful chief competitor to the permanent status of an Avis: No matter how hard Henry Ford tried, he could never again become number one.

So successful was GM that they did not have to take the risk of becoming a truly multinational corporation; instead, they concentrated their efforts on dominating the world's largest auto market—the domestic market. As time passed, the North American market started to become saturated, and the rapid growth that made the company famous was no longer possible. At this stage, financial people took over the reins of the company from the marketers who had managed the growth phase of the business. The finance folks knew how to generate the quarterly profits necessary to keep stock prices high in the absence of spectacular growth. But whether under the guidance of marketers or finance men, the company was a success. The success was so great that the guiding principles that led to GM's early success were crystallized into operating assumptions for all subsequent generations of managers. Here, gleaned from the pages of *My Years with General Motors,* are some of Alfred Sloan's major operating assumptions (significantly, they remained as GM's operating assumptions as they entered the 1970s):

1. GM is in the business of making money, not cars.

2. Success comes *not* from technological leadership, but from having the resources to quickly adopt innovations successfully introduced by others.

3. Cars are primarily status symbols. Styling is therefore more important than quality to buyers who are, after all, going to trade up every other year.

4. The American car market is isolated from the rest of the world. Foreign competitors will never gain more than 15 percent of the domestic market.

5. Energy will always be cheap and abundant.

6. Workers do not have an important impact on productivity or product quality.

7. Consumer, environmental, and other social concerns are unimportant to the American public.

8. The government is the enemy. It must be fought tooth and nail every inch of the way.

9. Strict, centralized financial controls are the secret to good administration.

10. Managers should always be developed from inside the company.

There were many more assumptions, of course; some conscious, others inexplicit. But ten is a number with a fittingly Mosaic ring! Important, all these guiding assumptions were based on the pioneering policies that had made GM one of the most successful industrial organizations in the history of the world. By repeating what had made them successful in the past, the company became ever more successful. In turn, this reinforced the legitimacy of the operating assumptions. These assumptions then became unchallengeable—and unchallenged. Why challenge an idea with eternal validity? Only a fool would knock success.

Alas, nothing fails like success. While there is nothing intrinsically invalid about the company's operating assumptions, something happened in the 1970s that caused them to become anachronistic: The environment changed. Gasoline became expensive; the auto market became internationalized; the rising cost of (and time required for) retooling made it necessary to be a leader rather than a follower in the introduction of new products and new technology; consumer values changed from styling to quality; the size of families shrank; people could no longer afford to trade their cars in every few years; worker values and attitudes changed; successful government relations required cooperation rather than an adversarial spirit; the few "kooks" in California who bought Volkswagens and read *Consumer Reports* became an important segment of the auto-buying public. And much more. By 1980, the environment had changed so thoroughly that the brilliant assumptions created by Sloan to meet the exigencies of the environment of the 1920s were inappropriate.

Hence, GM's very success was at the root of its inability in the 1970s to innovate to meet the changing environment. Innovation requires the ability to read changes in the environment and to create policies and strategies that will allow the organization to capitalize on the opportunities those changes create. Innovation requires *learning*. Ironically, the most successful companies are likely to ignore environmental signals because it seems wildly risky to tamper when things are going well. For example, GM saw as clearly as any other company that, ultimately, people would want smaller cars. But, confound it all, they were *buying* big cars! The finance men who ran GM said, "Our stockholders will kill us if we don't go all-out to meet today's demand for big cars. What are we going to do, refuse to sell people the cars they want? We'll worry about tomorrow if it comes." And who could blame GM's managers for failing to anticipate and, later, quickly respond to a changed competitive environment? Who could expect of a successful company that they should alter their policies in anticipation of possible future changes in the environment? That's downright risky, isn't it? Besides, the government was sending crazy signals—keeping the price of gas low and, at the same time, exhorting people to conserve. Who could plan in an environment like that? Planning requires a predictable environment, GM's managers were quick to point out.

There were thus many reasons why GM could not innovate to meet the changed environment. First, they were succeeding in the short run. Second, the dictates of the stock market limited their options. Third, they were comfortable with doing what they had always done well. Fourth, they were in the business of making money, not cars. Fifth, and perhaps most important, there was the deadening hand of past success—Sloan's legacy—resting hard on the shoulders of GM's management, preventing them from learning.

Change is particularly difficult in large organizations. At places like GM, assumptions become engrained in the firm's culture. In fact, they spend millions of dollars in time and money socializing their managers book, chapter, and verse in the gospel according to their forefathers. They painstakingly create controls, structures, and incentive systems to support these assumptions. Hence, in order to change to meet a new environment, large corporations have to alter their entire management systems; they have to recreate themselves.

But such change is particularly difficult when there is no tradition of challenging the accepted premises of the organization. GM, from all accounts, was not a place where calling attention to naked emperors was prized or rewarded. I hesitate to cite John Z. DeLorean as an authority on this matter, but quote him I must. While DeLorean's business and personal behavior are questionable at best, he did at least one worthy thing in his life, so let me be charitable (if not prudent). What DeLorean did brilliantly was to dictate the second most important book ever written about GM, *On a Clear Day You Can See General Motors.* DeLorean's book documents the organizational reasons for GM's managers' inability to surface, let alone challenge, the outmoded assumptions by which they were held prisoner. In one of the most hilarious and telling vignettes in the book, DeLorean describes what he calls a "typical" meeting of the GM executive committee in which the top two or three managers would pontificate, while the remaining dozen or so executives present "would remain silent, speaking only when spoken to. When they did offer a comment, in many cases it was just to paraphrase what had already been said by one of the top guys." DeLorean writes that Richard Terrell, then vice chairman of the board, was "the master of the paraphrase," able to parrot the views of the chairman and big boss, Richard Gerstenberg. According to DeLorean, the following was typical dialogue:

GERSTENBERG: Goddamnit. We cannot afford any new models next year because of the cost of this federally mandated equipment. There is no goddamn money left for styling changes. That's the biggest problem we face.

TERRELL, after waiting about 10 minutes: Dick, goddamnit. We've just got to face up to the fact that our number one problem is the cost of this federally mandated equipment.

This stuff costs so much that we just don't have any money left for styling our new cars. That's our biggest problem.

GERSTENBERG: You're goddamn right, Dick. That's a good point.

This is cited neither to damn GM nor to praise DeLorean. Whether this hypothetical dialogue is accurate or not, it illustrates the essence of a behavior problem found in many large organizations. People in groups form fixed ideas—"collective representations" in the language of social anthropology—and all of the forces within the group conspire to protect those notions, no matter how outmoded or inaccurate they may be. American managers have fixed assumptions about the role of corporations in society, about how to manage people, about how to encourage productivity and so forth. Such assumptions—even when they are self-defeating—drive behavior. The central task of those interested in organizational change is to challenge those assumptions. Nationalization of corporations, industrial policy, regulation, or any of the other legalistic and punitive ways designed to bring about change in the economic and social performance of corporations are basically irrelevant. As the British, French, and Italian experience shows, there is no change in the behavior of managers after nationalization; they go on with their old philosophies operating under their old assumptions. Progressives in these countries now say, "Why bother with nationalization?" In Europe and America, the real key to change is to get managers to examine their basic premises and to adopt new assumptions appropriate for the future. As far as *giant* corporations are concerned, the issue is thus not one of ownership; it is one of beliefs.

Social anthropologists help us to understand how people in groups are capable of holding the most incredible of beliefs. To the anthropologist, that General Motors managers could embrace the idea that quality was unimportant to consumers throughout the 1970s is no more inexplicable than that Russian leaders believe the United States has *offensive* military designs on the Soviet Union. People in groups create an entire system of spurious evidence to act as bulwarks in defense of their basic assumptions. For example, one of the most illogical of social beliefs is witchcraft. Yet, the belief systems of entire cultures are based on this "superstition." Take the Azande of the Sudan— bright people like you and me who just happen to believe that sickness, death, and misfortune in general are neither scientific in origin nor the effects of bad luck (nor of Divine Providence). Instead, the Azande feel that all misfortune is caused by "enemies" who have bewitched them. If a Zande farmer's crop is destroyed by a pest, he looks neither to God nor to the local purveyor of pesticides; instead, he immediately consults an oracle to find out who cast a spell on him. E. E. Evans-Pritchard, the great British anthropologist, lived among the Azande, and he found it infuriatingly impossible to prove to them that the causes of most misfortune were natural. In fact, he was surprised to find that, "logically," the Azande were right! That is, they could explain the causal links between calamitous events, on the one hand, and the "spells" cast by their enemies, on the other.

Of course, the Azande had learned to avoid putting their entire belief system to a real test. For example, if Evans-Pritchard were to get them to test some specific aspect of witchcraft and it didn't work, they were always able to show that there had been some fault in the procedures used in that particular instance. (This is, of course, the good Western argument, "Well, this case is different," that we all use when confronted with a particular refutation to a fervently held generalization.) Evans-Pritchard wrote that, since the Azande belief system is circular, each particular objection he raised served only to strengthen their fundamental convictions:

> Let the reader consider any argument that would utterly demolish all Zande claims for the power of the oracles. If it were translated into Zande modes of thought it would serve to support their entire structure of belief.

What Evans-Pritchard found is that, *if* one accepted the basic assumption of the Azande, everything else followed logically. Accept witchcraft, and there were no logical holes in their explanations of death, disease, pestilence, flood, or drought.

Now, Evans-Pritchard was not interested in merely reporting the bizarre beliefs of an insignificant Sudanese tribe. That would have been an unworthy endeavor for a man of his learning and intelligence. He sought, instead, to identify elements basic to *all* human societies. He discovered that, to understand the behavior of any group of people, it is necessary to get down to the basic premises of their belief system—to root out their fundamental assumptions. These assumptions, these collective representations, are the glue that holds a group of people together, binds them in such a way that they can act purposefully. The ideas that people in a group hold in common—that all hold absolutely—allow for effective social, as opposed to less efficient individual, action. For any social organization to function, then, it is necessary for all its members to share a world view. In the words of another anthropologist, Michael Polanyi, "by holding the same set of presuppositions they mutually confirm each other's interpretation of experience."

A corporation is no different from a primitive tribe in this regard. Managers at GM were able, throughout the 1970s, to deny the need to produce smaller, higher-quality, more fuel-efficient cars because, as DeLorean might have written, "by holding the same set of presuppositions they mutually confirmed each other's interpretation of experience." DeLorean described the top managers of GM looking down from the fourteenth-floor executive suite of their corporate headquarters in Detroit upon the parking lot and adjoining streets below, and saying something like, Look at all those big cars! Who says people want small ones?

I suggest that the real tragedy of the fall of DeLorean was not the discredit he brought on himself, not even the negative image he provided of the American executive in the popular press and mind; rather, from the viewpoint of the American economy, the tragedy was that DeLorean provided an excuse for GM's top management to completely discount his many valid criticisms of their behavior and to slip smugly back into their comfortable old presuppositions. Since there is some truth to the notion that what is good for the largest U.S. manufacturer is good for America, John Z. DeLorean did all Americans a great disservice with his questionable behavior.

Of course, it will be argued that the problems of the American auto industry stem not from the belief system of Detroit's executive class, but from all sorts of exogenous factors—the cost of domestic steel, the value of the yen, the cost of fuel, the cost of U.S. labor and so forth. My point is not to deny the contributions of such factors to the plight of the U.S. auto industry; rather, I wish to suggest that the assumptions of auto industry executives *led* to some of these factors (overpaid labor) and set the stage for inappropriate *responses* to others (overpriced oil).

It will be further argued—particularly by those who advocate a national industrial policy—that the problem with the auto industry is endemic to all industries, and that we are merely witnessing the inevitable decline stage of a "life cycle" to which all industries are fated. There is some evidence to support the existence of such an "industrial life cycle" (even if the analogy to human life can be carried too far—death is probably *not* inevitable for organizations, and certainly, corporate lifespans are extendable in a way unknown to living organisms). Nonetheless, the problem of inappropriate assumptions can be found in all manner of industries, growing ones as well as declining (as we saw earlier with IBM's assumptions about computers always being big).

Misperceptions that arise from an orthodox world view may be at the heart of low productivity, declining innovation, and many of the other social, economic, and political problems besetting large corporations in America today. In fact, business organizations are no better or worse in this regard than any other major institution—political, social, or scientific. All institutions go through a period of believing the world is flat, even when the data establishing its roundness is plainly there before their noses. But how can a corporation go about the creative process of unblocking the habitual ways in which it views its operating environment and its own culture?

In Chapter Ten I review some techniques for unblocking organizational assumptions that are now being applied in several Old Guard corporations. The real trick, however, is to *avoid* the need for taking the cure for inappropriate corporate premises. The Vanguard corporations have discovered from the school of hard knocks that it is far better to practice preventive medicine. They have discovered that the way to avoid becoming a corporate Zande is to become a *learning organization*. And, since there is no static body of corporate knowledge to master—no set of rules or principles that will lead all corporations to success—the Vanguard have discovered that they must *learn continuously* from the changing environment. Their "teachers" are their many stakeholders. By listening to their many internal and external constituencies, the Vanguard continually test and revise their assumptions about the environment; by remaining sensitive to the changing needs of all their constituencies, the Vanguard institutionalize the process of change. As Calvin Coolidge once said, "Nobody ever listened himself out of a job."

An airline in California has the learning principle right when they say, "We don't take ourselves seriously; we take our competitors *very* seriously." In contrast, visit with IBM managers (as I have done twice recently) and one finds an organization that takes themselves very seriously, indeed, while they dismiss their competitors as second-rate. IBM has stopped listening, believing they have solved the problem of management and have nothing to learn from others. It is my guess that the obvious errors IBM made with the PCjr were attributable, in great part, to this complacency.

But visit Motorola, Weyerhaeuser, Honeywell, and Dayton-Hudson and you'll find managers busy challenging old assumptions, rethinking basic premises, revising, reading, questioning, learning, even *un*learning outmoded truths. At Motorola, a young middle manager came up to CEO Robert Galvin when I was with him. He said, "Bob, I heard that point you made this morning, and I think you were dead wrong. I'm going to prove it. I'm going to shoot you down." I was flabbergasted. In nine out of ten companies, the kid's career is kaput. But Galvin beamed proudly: "That's how we've overcome Texas Instruments as the world's largest producer of semiconductors!"

At Weyerhaeuser I've seen even middle-level managers list the corporation's assumptions about productivity, test them, and then challenge top management when the premises didn't square with reality. At Honeywell, the corporation's premises about future changes in the operating environment are revised and published yearly—*after* scores of people up and down the organization have had a chance to challenge them. At Dayton-Hudson the fear of group thinking is so great that decentralization has become practically a fetish. Heads of operating divisions are discouraged from talking with each other and are instead encouraged to talk with customers, suppliers, regulators, scholars, and community representatives. The company's central staff is kept smaller than that of a typical business a tenth their size to insure divisional independence from the orthodoxy of staff thinking.

In subsequent chapters we'll learn more about how these and the other Vanguard corporations encourage and reward learning. But the purpose of this digression has been achieved. In contrasting the Old Guard to the Vanguard, we see that corporate eminence derives not from any rules or techniques but is, instead, rooted in attitudes and assumptions. This brings us to the last of the general characteristics of the Vanguard.

4. HIGH AIM

Today, many management theorists propose narrow, even singular, goals for corporations; for example, persistent customer service, or active employee participation, or high-quality production facilities. To these theorists, excellent management consists of juggling one or, at best, two balls at a time. That's a necessary first step, but it's not juggling. In sharp distinction, the Vanguard manifest real coordination, balance, and dexterity. They do many things equally well. They manage to keep a whole array of Indian clubs, hoops, plates, beanbags, and medicine balls in the air at the same time! But more important is the Vanguard's dedication not only to do everything equally well, but to become the best at everything they do. To use words from Dayton-Hudson's constitution, there is a commitment *"to be premier in every aspect of our business."*

In my contacts with some two hundred large American corporations over the last fifteen years, one thing I find hard to explain (and harder to accept) is the cheerful willingness on the part of almost all of them to be second-rate. This trait runs counter to the American character and counter, one would have suspected, to the nature of people in groups. What self-respecting sports team, school, city, or state would admit that they were second-rate—and say they were perfectly satisfied, thank you, to remain that way? Precious few, I would guess. But, in over 95 percent of the large U.S. corporations I visit, I fail to find a commitment parallel to DH's "to be premier in every aspect of our business." When DH became the nation's leader in philanthropy, they didn't rest on their laurels; instead, they said, "Now we also have to be number one in ROI, number one in customer service, number one in marketing, number one in serving all of our stakeholders . . . number one in everything." Sure, they have a way to go: Sears, the industry leader, has fully three times DH's revenues. It might even take DH another fourteen years to catch up. So what? That's not so long. Eleven years ago, analysts told Motorola managers that they must be smoking funny cigarettes when they said they would one day be number one in semiconductors. "Look, Galvin," the analysts said, "seldom since World War II has any corporation overcome the leading company in their industry. Isn't Ford always number two behind GM, *Newsweek* always number two behind *Time*, Avis always number two behind Hertz, no matter how hard they try? Forget it, kid." But Galvin didn't forget his goal, not once in the eleven years it took Motorola to surpass Texas Instruments.

And that kind of dedication to being the best at everything is a common characteristic of the Vanguard. Deere & Company is known for having perhaps the world's strongest independent dealer network, but the company is also first in their industry in labor relations, in engineering, manufacturing technology, product quality, long-range and strategic planning, and ethical business practices.

Outside the Vanguard, I have found commitment to being the best in a few small- and medium-sized businesses, but seldom in a large U.S. corporation. For decades, GM was satisfied with being the *largest* corporation in the world—not once in the seventy-odd-year history of the company has their chief executive ever committed the company to being the *best*. Now, we find IBM falling into the same trap with their newly stated goal of becoming the world's biggest industrial enterprise (in terms of sales). All those owners of PCs who have struggled to obtain IBM equipment and software in recent months could tell the folks in Armonk that they are most likely to become the biggest if they rededicate themselves to becoming the best. Even in large companies that have one or two characteristics of excellence, there is satisfaction that that is enough. (At one giant enterprise that boasts of the excellence of their labor relations, I asked if their goal was to achieve the same level of excellence in their relations with their customers, dealers, and society. I got this answer: "We don't think we could do it, so why try? Besides, we're making great profits.")

That's the devil's proposition! If we can't be the best, why try? While there is nothing wrong with being number two; I suggest that there is something wrong about being satisfied with not being the best. At least, that's been my experience: In my long-lost youth, I was on a losing athletic team; the university where I work today is not ranked in the nation's top ten; and the new business magazine I recently started needs *only* 180,000 more subscribers to overtake the *Harvard Business Review!* Nonetheless, the goal of my team was always to be first; the goal of everyone at my university for the last thirteen years has been to become the best in the West; and I won't be satisfied until my magazine has the largest circulation of any university-based business publication. For the life of me, I can't understand why anyone would want to work for an organization that was satisfied with being second-rate or second-best at anything. No wonder the U.S. economy was in decline in the 1970s. James Russell Lowell, where were you when we needed you?

No doubt critics can cite shortcomings in the performance of each of the Vanguard companies. But, by God, they're out to beat the world and won't let up until they are the best at *everything* they do. It is that compulsion—plus the knowledge that all aspects of management must be integrated into a coherent whole —that I suspect has been behind the marked success each of the Vanguard has had over the last decade in significantly altering their cultures. Because each of the Vanguard has a chronic, healthy dissatisfaction with the level of their various achievements, they have *institutionalized* the process of change.

Leaders with Moral Courage

Which brings us to what may be the most important single point in this book: the four philosophical orientations just discussed do *not* depend on having a visionary, charismatic leader. Doubtless, a great leader facilitates organizational effectiveness, but great leaders should not be confused with those obsessive personalities who work seventy-hour weeks doing everyone *else's* jobs. Neither "take charge guys" with decisive "do it, try it" styles, nor manipulative cheerleaders with savior complexes and advanced degrees in psychobabble, are likely to be good for a company in the long term. Both create a kind of demotivating dependency which is, at once, unhealthy and undemocratic.

The myth of charismatic leadership arises from attributing the style of one breed of successful entrepreneur to all business leaders. While there is evidence that a number of successful entrepreneurs are visionary and egotistical workaholics whose organizations are, indeed, shadows of themselves, there is *no* evidence that such a rugged individualist has ever successfully run a large, complex corporation. Instead, the vast majority of effective professional managers are individuals who empower others and remove the roadblocks that prevent subordinates from being fully productive. But there is at least a third type of successful business leader, the type best-suited for Vanguard management. These individuals combine the best of the entrepreneur with the best of the professional manager: It turns out that entrepreneurs whose companies succeed in the long run are *also* excellent managers (we'll be learning about Olga's Jan Erteszek and Herman Miller's Max DePree in the next chapter) and that professional managers whose companies adapt to change *also* have entrepreneurial traits (as we will see when we discuss Dayton-Hudson's Kenneth Macke and Motorola's Robert Galvin).

Most important, the eminent entrepreneurs and managers discussed in these pages have in common a trait seldom mentioned in the literature on leadership: *moral courage.* These leaders may or may not have superior intellect, creativity, decisiveness, passion, vision, or charisma, but they all exhibit several types of courage, examples of which we'll become familiar with in the pages that follow. *The courage to change things when all is going well.* We'll see how it took courage for Robert Galvin to move relatively low-tech Motorola into competition with high-tech firms, courage for Jan Erteszek to institute employee stock ownership in Olga (then a small, struggling apparel company), courage for James Lincoln to offer employment security to Lincoln Electric employees as early as 1951, and courage for William Norris to move Control Data from the familiar computer hardware business into the untried area of computer services. *Courage to share power and authority.* We'll see how it took courage for Edwin Land to form a workers' committee in the 1950s to share in Polaroid's management decisions, and courage for Robert Galvin to involve all 60,000 of Motorola's domestic employees in the process of management. *Courage to hire subordinates who are likely to outshine oneself and to give them the freedom to make their mark.* We'll see how it took courage for Arco's Robert O. Anderson to hire and listen to the brilliant Thornton Bradshaw, courage for Robert Galvin to hire and listen to the brilliant William Weisz, and courage for the DePree family of Herman Miller, Inc., to abandon themselves to the wild ideas of a group of designers more sophisticated than themselves. *Courage to stick with one's values in hard times.* We'll see how it took courage for George Weyerhaeuser to reaffirm Weyco's responsibility to employees, communities, customers, and society in the midst of the worst financial crisis in the company's history, and courage for Levi's Robert Haas to offer generous severance allowances to employees (and costly long-term contributions to communities where they were shutting down plants) at a time when Wall Street was demanding the expedient course of cutting and running. *Courage to resist pressures for short-term actions.* We'll see how it took courage on the part of William Norris to stick with long-term investments in programs designed to solve social problems when the financial community was devaluing Control Data stock for so doing, and courage on the part of Honeywell's Edson Spencer not to abandon Honeywell's computer business when Wall Street was demanding it. *Courage to take unpopular positions.* We'll see how it took courage for Levi's Walter Haas to integrate his company's facilities in the South in the 1950s, and courage on the part of Arco's Thornton Bradshaw to speak in opposition to the self-defeating practices of the oil industry in the 1970s.

And, finally, *courage to be an innovative subordinate.* We'll see how it took courage for Prudential Insurance's Morton Darrow, a staff vice president with no real power base in the organization, to woo, cajole, and convince his peers and superiors to make Prudential an industry leader in employee participation, long-term planning, and community responsibility; courage for Norwest Bank's Douglas Wallace to reinterpret his relatively powerless job as one that addressed the key failings of the bank (and to successfully involve employees at all levels of the organization in overcoming them); and courage for James Renier who, while still a divisional manager, cast aside Honeywell's "command and control" culture and introduced human-centered management in the group he headed. These individuals remind us of something almost all people in organizations tend to forget: It is one's moral responsibility to do one's best even in a mediocre environment. Whenever we are in an organization, we each have the responsibility to educate our peers and superiors about what is the right and proper behavior (and to do so with humility, compassion, and tact, of course), to do what is right with one's own subordinates regardless of overall corporate culture, and to put one's job on the line when the alternative is to support policies that threaten the survival of the organization.

There are indications that now, as American business is regaining some of the lustre lost in the 1970s, employees at all levels in large organizations are again playing it safe, much like the "organization men" of the 1950s. From CEOs who seek only to keep their organizations on an even keel until they retire a few years hence, to middle managers who fear that any change will threaten their jobs, the first rule of management is again becoming, "Above all, don't screw up." I say "again" because such timidity was rampant from the 1950s through the 1970s. I encountered it firsthand in 1972 when I traveled around the country doing the research that led to the study, *Work in America*. At that time, I found only a handful of business executives who had the courage to try such things as quality of work life programs, profit sharing, pay for performance, statistically based product quality programs, and long-term forecasting and planning—all of which had been successfully demonstrated nearly two decades earlier. That almost all American industry has now begun implementing these concepts only serves to make my point: Knowing the right thing to do is relatively simple; having the courage to act on it is the true mark of leadership.

If we think back a moment to *Executive Suite*, we see that all of Bill Holden's fellow VPs (with the exception of March) knew as well as Holden what had to be done to save the Tredway Corporation. Holden differentiated himself from the others in only one respect: his *moral courage* to act on what he knew was the right thing to do.

So these are the four philosophical orientations of Vanguard management: stakeholder symmetry, high purpose, learning, and high aim (all of which are buttressed by the moral courage to stick with these principles in hard times). Significantly, the Vanguard corporations did not acquire these four general traits by succumbing to the easy answers offered by corporate and economic theorists. Instead, they have realized that corporations can survive and thrive only when they are responsive to changes in their external environments and when they constantly learn from those environments. They have faced the disappointing fact that, in social and economic affairs, there are no eternal truths. The Vanguard have discovered that success comes from the hard work of constantly aligning their corporate strategies with the ongoing process of social, political, economic, competitive, and technological change.

If this sounds difficult, well, it is. But who said that managing multibillion-dollar organizations with tens of thousands of workers should be simple? As Lewis W. Lehr, the CEO of the 3M Company says, "It's not supposed to be easy!" The good news is that it is not impossible. In each of the eight great corporations featured in this book, managers have mastered the art.

I see that I may already have given the wrong impression about the Vanguard corporations. They are *not* run like political democracies, with one worker, one vote. They are *not* paragons of virtue. They are *not* perfectly managed. They make mistakes. Sometimes regrettable mistakes. We can learn a great deal, indeed, from how they made their mistakes—and how they seek to avoid repeating them in the future. For as the classical dramatists knew, the most instructive moral lessons are drawn from the flaws of heroes and heroines. The guys in the black hats are predictably and boringly bad, and the goodie-goodie Miss Two Shoes of the corporate world are predictably and boringly complacent. Since perfection is unnatural in human affairs, we are thus not surprised to find that the Vanguard have failings and weaknesses. Applying the words of John Updike to the Vanguard, "They have the exciting difficulty of reality itself."

A Touch of Vinegar to Cut the Treacle

How, then, should the reader think about the Vanguard corporations? *As examples and nothing more.* It is important to keep in mind that this book is about the principles of the New Management, and *not* about the peculiar characteristics of any special set of corporations. Indeed, it is never fruitful to debate the virtues of the examples used to illustrate a general proposition. For example, while one may cite the works of Shakespeare to support the general proposition that "Reading is morally good for one," the proposition can be neither supported nor refuted by reference to the merits or shortcomings of *Hamlet.* Instead, logic requires that general principles be validated or invalidated only by direct analysis of the proposition in question.

Hence, while I am willing to go to the mat to defend the four key New Management *principles,* I have no stake in defending the Vanguard corporate *examples.* Indeed, I am just as comfortable (or uncomfortable) using illustrations from Hewlett-Packard, Borg Warner, Digital Equipment, Johnson & Johnson, and the "new" Chrysler recognizing that, like the Vanguard, none of these companies fully adheres to the principles I describe. Indeed, several of the Vanguard have recently backed off from the very principles that had made them great. Even at the Vanguard, there is a tendency to listen to the "get tough" advice of the house Fredric Marches when economic conditions become threatening. The Vanguard, like the Tredway Furniture Company, live with constant tension between the Marches and the Holdens who do battle within. That the Holdens carry the day more often in the Vanguard than in the Old Guard is the sole reason I cite them as examples. Lord knows I don't do so because they have achieved perfection. Levi Strauss, Control Data, Deere, Arco, and Honeywell have each recently resorted to various degrees of Old Guard behavior in bad times, and this not only caused their performance to further decline in the short term, it eroded their long-term ability to respond to changing conditions with flexibility and sensitivity.

No organization is all bad (including the Old Guard), and none is all good (including the Vanguard). While the Vanguard have a great many traits that make them worthy of emulation they, too, are far from perfect. In contests of corporate excellence, no organization deserves a score of ten. Here are some of the reasons why each of the Vanguard is only an eight or a nine.

Start with Control Data. The company's greatest strength, their brilliant CEO William C. Norris, is also their greatest weakness. For example, when it comes to strategic decision making, Norris often seeks no one's counsel, not even the advice of president Robert M. Price and vice chairman Norbert R. Berg. Price tells a fanciful but illustrative story about Norris calling a press conference to announce the development of a new, super product: A silk that warms you when you are cold, cools you when you are hot, and is cheap, durable, and biodegradable. While this announcement is being made (to the surprise of Price and Berg), they find themselves standing offstage frantically trying to urge two silkworms to mate, "And we aren't even sure if the worms are a male and a female!" Clearly, communication and consultation are not Norris's long suit.

Not only is Norris often autocratic, he is sometimes arrogant. While it might be said that the average, well-adjusted, "nice guy" ends up as a real estate agent or fourth vice president in a bank, Norris seems unnecessarily harsh in his dealings with others, particularly outsiders. Since top management establishes a model for behavior down the line, it is not surprising to find that CDC managers, in general, are not terribly participative, and most are arrogant in their dealings with external constituencies. CDC has a reputation for poor customer service and for having a bossy "we know what's best" attitude when dealing with their community-based "partners" in their City Venture projects. In general, the quality of CDC's communications with the outside world are middling to mediocre. Indeed, most Old Guard executives are more prompt and conscientious than CDC executives when it comes to returning phone calls and responding to an outsider's request for information.

While most of Norris's ideas have been farsighted, the execution of them has often been inadequate and, on occasion, down-right sloppy. Only recently has efficiency in operations been awarded the same attention as product innovation. Almost none of CDC's social-oriented programs has yet to turn a profit (although PLATO finally did so in 1983). While the corporation's willingness to wait patiently for market acceptance of an innovative product is one of their most admirable traits, they are none-theless remiss in their failure to attend to details that could facilitate earlier acceptance (for instance, it took CDC far too long to make PLATO courses available for use on personal computers). Even a slight increase in attention to customers, productivity, and operational details would make CDC more profitable (and, thus, able to try more of their marvelous ideas). To their credit, there is evidence of movement in this direction.

Ain't nobody perfect, not even Motorola (although they come about as close as any major corporation). The company has one shortcoming of which I am aware: With the exceptions of their public stand against the unfairness of Japanese competition and their efforts to rewrite outmoded unemployment compensation laws, Motorola exerts far less moral leadership in arenas beyond the confines of their corporate walls than do the other members of the Vanguard. Of course, one can't expect a company domi-nated by male engineers to throw themselves into Levi-style community involvement or Dayton-Hudson-like social giving. But one could reasonably expect them to be far better than average in terms of philanthropy and public service. One won-ders why a company that excels at almost everything they at-tempt doesn't make the small additional effort to round out their overall performance by being national leaders in the one area where they are now merely very good. In fact, I'm beginning to see some signs that they are doing just that.

Honeywell, in contrast, tries not only to do everything, but to do everything well. Their problem is one of execution, not of omission. In almost every area of management, Honeywell has considerable room to improve performance. For example, in employee relations, they lag behind their Vanguard peers in terms of employee participation in decision making and in profits. And, while top management now says all the right things, there is considerable room for more collaborative and less autocratic behavior at the top. (A company joke concerns a pep talk by vice chairman James Renier on the importance of self-esteem in effective management: "In conclusion, I want you turkeys to go out and get some self-esteem!") Honeywell has badly handled their computer business, failing to find a strategic niche that would provide a secure market share (let alone failing to find a growth position). I could go on detailing other shortcomings, but to do so is, in a way, unfair, for the company is in the throes of a complete culture change, and it is premature to judge the effects of that effort.

Much the same might be said of Weyerhaeuser, another firm in the midst of massive change. The company clearly had grown complacent in the 1960s and 1970s, letting plant and equipment deteriorate and allowing the central staff to act like cholesterol in the system (creating premature arteriosclerosis). Top management displayed the twin traits that brought down the Bourbons: autocracy and inattention to what was happening in the trenches. To their credit, Weyerhaeuser recognized these shortcomings and is acting forcefully and creatively to overcome them. The question remains, will they have the patience and fortitude to stick with their time- and energy-consuming change effort—particularly if economic conditions improve and remove the compelling force for change?

Of all American corporations, Dayton-Hudson probably has the strongest written commitment to excellence and the most comprehensive plan for achieving it. Given this, the few puzzling inconsistencies in their behavior stand out in greater contrast than they would in a lesser institution. Given DH's commitment to employees and communities, one wonders how they reconcile their hair-trigger release of faltering operations (they sold off their Plum's chain less than a year after they opened three pilot stores). Given the importance of the company's basic values, one wonders why they haven't made a greater effort to defuse these values in their decentralized operations. And, given their stated commitment to employees as stakeholders, one wonders why they have been slow to involve employees in decision making and in profit sharing.

The veneer of the Deere culture has its scratches as well (but, like DH, no serious dents). The company seems not to have provided sufficient leadership in the communities where they have a massive presence (if we compare the generous effort Cummins Engine has made to improve the quality of life of Columbus, Indiana). While Deere has the best relationship in the industry with the UAW, they still have not embraced their unionized employees as full corporate stakeholders. The company's excellence in farm equipment has not been as fully realized in construction equipment, where dealer relations and quality control are not up to company standards. There is some reason to question Deere's strategic decision to concentrate solely on the high end of the farm market, where their customers are at the mercy of the vicissitudes of federal wheat deals with the Soviet Union. Finally, one is struck by their curiously out-of-date decision to build colossal plants when all evidence today points to the fact that "small is beautiful" where manufacturing is concerned.

While Levi Strauss earns a strong eight on the scale of greatness, there is obvious room for improvement. The giant company has not fully solved the problem of how to manage effectively in an industry custom-tailored for fast-moving entrepreneurs. Levi has not won the hearts of their retailers (who are, perhaps, the company's most important *external* constituency). Internally, there is still a great deal to be done to further involve workers in decision making, and in managing staff conflicts with their operating divisions. And, most basically, there is the company's failure to do effective long-range planning (they failed to respond to the change in demographics that caused a decline in the age categories most likely to buy jeans and failed to effectively diversify into other forms of apparel—failures that led to massive plant closings and employee layoffs in 1984).

Finally, there is Arco, where the disastrous 1977 decision to acquire Anaconda for years diverted the attention of management as they engaged in the fruitless effort of trying to salvage that business. And, today, as the fortunes of the oil industry have declined along with the price of oil, there are those within Arco who wish to abandon the very characteristics of eminence that made them special in their industry.

Indeed, at each of the Vanguard there are those who are opposed to the principles of New Management and who use every downturn in profits, stock price, or the economy as an opportunity to lobby for a return to the "tougher-minded" practices of the Old Guard. What philosophy will prevail? That is the question. Indeed, the book is open on Arco, as it is on each of the Vanguard. All is flux in the life of a corporation . . . and sustaining greatness is probably harder than achieving it. There is little doubt in my mind that if I were to rewrite this book five years from now the list of Vanguard companies would be significantly different (based on the positive changes that appear to be occurring today at such Old Guard companies as GM and Kodak, I would not be a bit surprised to find that they had successfully made the transition to eminence; five years *ago* I would have included Polaroid, Xerox, Dana, and Cummins).

When I started the research for this book, the influence of founders Thornton Bradshaw and Robert O. Anderson was still strong at Arco. In the intervening years, as these men moved to retirement, I watched the company's commitment to public leadership noticeably wane. Business critic Milton Moskowitz, who once ranked Arco among the top five corporations in the nation, has demoted them dramatically and now says, "With the two architects of the company culture gone (or about to leave), the engineers are in control again." While I think such a judgment is premature, it well may be that before the print is dry on these pages, Arco (or any of the seven other companies) will have lost their Vanguard status. Eminence is a fragile state.

This sketchy overview of the Vanguard's shortcomings will be filled out in the chapters that follow (those readers desiring smarmy accounts of unblemished corporations are requested to look elsewhere). But how could companies with such glaring weaknesses ever be called the best-managed large corporations in America? Because the weaknesses of the next best companies are more fundamental (I briefly outline some of the failings of HP, Polaroid, Cummins, and Johnson & Johnson throughout the book). And, compared to the congenital afflictions of the Old Guard, the shortcomings of the Vanguard are mere surface blemishes. Most basically, the Vanguard deserve their status *not* because they have achieved perfection, but because they actively strive for it, and because they have institutionalized the mechanisms of change that force them to constructively address their weaknesses.

Life in the Vanguard corporations is neither simply good nor simply bad. It is like real life: It is simply complicated. It is sometimes rough and tumble and always marked by the tension of moral choice—an inescapable tension in a world fraught with differences of values, perceptions, and objectives and inhabited by people with human frailties. Because they are not perfect, the Vanguard companies are, in many ways, like the organizations in which most of us work. Because they are not unapproachable ideals, they can serve as *achievable* models of what the organizations in which most of us work can realistically become.

In the chapters that follow, we will see how adherence to the four general principles of the New Management permits the Vanguard corporations to achieve eminence in the absence of a monolithic set of rules about how they should manage day-to-day operations. Moreover, we see how commitment to these principles can enable a traditionally managed company to create the climate and attitudes necessary for the successful implementation of the best ideas offered by the current crop of management theorists—ideas that managers quickly abandon when it is seen that they are not the cure-all their advocates claim them to be. And, most startlingly, we see how those who lack the ultimate power in organizations—divisional and middle managers—can use these principles in a bottoms-up approach to corporate change, even without support at the top!

In a nutshell, here is what this book is about: Over the last few years, American executives have acquired most, if not all, of the pieces of an incredibly complex puzzle called "excellence in management." But they have not been able to put it together because of a frustrating complication: This is a strange kind of puzzle in that there is no one right way to assemble it. Since each company has different needs and characteristics, each company must fit the puzzle together in its own way. Thus, the puzzle can be coherently assembled in numerous ways. However, most corporations have failed, try as they might, to create their own coherence because they have instead been looking for a singular solution, the magic formula to make their organizations excellent. Because there is no such single model or ideology, corporations require, instead, *general principles*—a kind of key—that will allow them to see how the various parts of excellent management practices relate to the special and unique wholes they must each create.

Hence, the message of this book is both simple and complex: Simple, in that we will see by our analysis of the Vanguard corporations that there are no rules or laws of good management; complex, in that we will see by our analysis that what is at issue in management are *justice and legitimacy*—the same issues that are at stake in our democracy—and that these are achievable only when there is moral symmetry among the competing claims, objectives, and values of the relevant corporate constituencies, both internal and external. Creating that balance is the task of management. Moreover, creating that balance is the only hope for the survival of competitive, corporate capitalism. There is, thus, more at stake when we talk about how to run a business than the future of a single firm or industry; the issues with which the Vanguard corporations wrestle are the same issues that confront our democratic political/economic state.

Is There an Easier Way?

The lessons of the Vanguard obviously cannot be fully understood in a short course. They are not meant for the one-minute, one-hour, or even the one-semester manager. To create a great corporation worthy of a great society requires career-long dedication. Many managers have had their appetites for such a commitment whetted by recent discussions of corporate excellence. For the prospect of creating an institution that is productive, profitable, adaptable to change, and viewed as just and legitimate by society is truly exciting for those who see management as a profession and not just a job, for those who view the task of management as meeting the basic needs of society and not a frivolous activity dedicated merely to getting rich quick.

But a career-long commitment? Why should one want to do it? After all, most of the largest corporations don't accept the Vanguard philosophy. So can't a company be successful doing things the easier way?

In the short term, yes. But in the long run, low aim is self-defeating. The lesson of *Executive Suite*, of the Japanese challenge of the 1970s, of the recent failure of many old-line manufacturing firms is that long-term success requires managers to take the high road—and that the other path leads to unproduc-

tive, unadaptive organizations that will ultimately fail to meet
their obligations to employees, customers, stockholders, and society. While there is no doubt that, historically, single-goal management led to success, the evidence is building that traditional
management practices are likely to fail both economically and
socially in the future.

In the six chapters that follow, I review in some detail how the
Vanguard corporations meet their responsibilities to their various
stakeholders through observance of the four general principles
just outlined. Then, in Part Three, I examine the processes by
which the leaders of the Vanguard have recently transformed
their companies from traditional practices to the practices of the
New Management and how they are working to sustain their
newly acquired greatness.

PART TWO

HOW THE VANGUARD CORPORATIONS MEET THEIR RESPONSIBILITIES TO THEIR STAKEHOLDERS

3.

BUCKS AND POWER: THE EMPLOYEE AS STAKEHOLDER

Reporter: "Does your husband deserve
the $7 million bonus he just received?"
Wife of chairman of Ford Motor Company:
"How can I answer that
without sounding like Marie Antoinette?"
—REPORTED IN *New York Times*

Until quite recently, most large American companies did not consider employees to be significant corporate stakeholders. To Alfred Sloan, workers were nuisances who had to be bought off with unconscionable wages in order to keep GM's assembly lines running. To ITT's Harold Geneen, workers were mere adjuncts to the businesses he bought and sold like a Monopoly player on a roll. In fact, to most corporate managers, workers have been no more than "a factor of production"—*the* factor managers sought to eliminate through automation, and the first factor to be sacrificed during economic downturns (it has been standard operating procedure in most large corporations to lay off workers before cutting dividends or paring executive salaries). While lip service has been solemnly paid to "the folks who make up our corporate family," practice didn't come into line with this rhetoric until recently—even at the Vanguard. And, at the Old Guard, workers are still seen more as bastard stepchildren than as legitimate members of the corporate clan.

The shortfall between word and deed with respect to employees has been exacerbated by the fact that the countless articles and books about "the human side of enterprise" seem to arrive at different—even conflicting—conclusions about how to treat and motivate workers. In no other business area has fad been so prevalent, have so many half-baked theories been proposed, have managers been more willing to dabble with today's nostrum —only to move on to tomorrow's, frustrated that "nothing seems to work."

While there have been, literally, thousands of theories of work organization and employee motivation, they can nearly all be clustered under one of these four broad philosophical headings: (A.) Meritocracy, (B.) Egalitarianism, (C.) Behaviorism, and (D.) Humanism. Each of these theories reflects a basic, if often unstated, assumption about the nature of work and workers. For example, if one believes that there are real, fundamental differences in individual talents, abilities, and willingness to work— and that these differences should be acknowledged and rewarded accordingly—then one is likely to be attracted to meritocratic theories of work organization and compensation. In a meritocratic workplace, rich rewards go to those employees who are most productive, and those who fail the stiff competition to climb the corporate hierarchy wash out of the system. Historically, meritocracy has fit well with the nation's oft-stated (and more often violated) free-market principles. In particular, libertarian and other market-oriented economists tend to support meritocratic forms of organization.

Those who believe that a meritocracy is inherently unfair because the differences between individuals pale beside the overwhelming fact of their common humanity—and that this common bond of humanity entitles all workers to certain minimal rights—are likely to be attracted to egalitarian theories of work organization and compensation. Egalitarians believe that employees have a right to be protected against virtually every type of risk by numerous "entitlements" and limits on managerial discretion. Egalitarians believe that workers should have guaranteed job security and should be paid equally for equal work (and as close to equally as possible across different jobs). Trade unionists and socialist economists tend to support egalitarian forms of organization.

Then, there are those who believe that group order and group survival are more basic values than the freedom afforded in a meritocracy or the dignity afforded in an egalitarian workplace. Such people may well be attracted to behaviorist theories of work organization and compensation. Drawing on the intellectual tradition of John B. Watson's experimental psychology, and the philosophical commitment to efficiency found in the work of Frederick W. Taylor, behaviorism reached its clearest expression in the work of B. F. Skinner. Because behaviorists believe that human behavior is a response to environmental conditioning, employee performance is closely monitored and regulated and elaborate incentive schemes reward efficient and productive behavior.

Finally, if one believes that work should be an ennobling experience—and that the real purpose of work is to draw out the full potential of all employees—then one will be attracted to humanistic theories of work organization and compensation. Drawing on the diverse ideas of such scholars as the psychologist Abraham Maslow and the economist E. F. Schumacher, humanists believe that organizational policies and practices should be designed to enhance personal growth and development. In humanistic workplaces, employees play a central role in decision making.

Where Would You Want to Work?

There are, then, four extreme, alternative theoretical approaches to how organizations ought to be structured and how employees ought to be managed and rewarded. (Detailed descriptions of the practices found in all four types of companies are presented in the Notes and References.) Each of these four approaches is based on underlying assumptions about human nature and on consequent values about the purpose of work. The four schools of thought (and their underlying values) can be diagrammed graphically, as trade-offs, on a quadrant:

(A.) MERITOCRACY
(Merit and Freedom)

(D.) HUMANISM   (C.) BEHAVIORISM
(Quality of Life)   vs.   (Efficiency and Order)

(B.) EGALITARIANISM
(Security and Equality)

In which of these would you choose to work? A few years back, a colleague and I gave that hypothetical choice to an experimental sample of trade unionists, government officials, corporate managers, university students, and business professors. Not surprisingly, when forced to choose, the union officials *tended* to favor egalitarianism, the managers *tended* to favor meritocracy, and the students *tended* to favor humanism. But even more significantly, all three of these groups found so many things they were attracted to in the three other types of companies (the ones they did *not* choose), that they expressed resentment at being forced to pick one alternative to the exclusion of the other three. The professors and government officials shared in spades this unwillingness to choose; moreover, as groups they offered no clear pattern of choice at all. It would seem, then, that pure alternatives are attractive only to the theorists who design them and to the few ideologues who promote them. Most American workers and managers, in contrast, are not extremists and are not certain that any *single* school of thought offers the best approach to organizational effectiveness.

If you found *complete* satisfaction with any one of the four alternatives described above, you will be disappointed to discover the way work is organized and rewarded in the Vanguard corporations. The leaders of the Vanguard companies believe that their corporations will not be viewed as legitimate by employees if they are organized to maximize only one goal or value. They also believe that all four values are necessary if a corporation is to be productive in the long term.

The task of management at the Vanguard is to find ways to simultaneously satisfy these four competing, but equally legitimate, objectives. As we look at the Vanguard corporations we will see that they follow no single route to this goal. Each of these corporations responds in a way that reflects its peculiar size, history, industry, locale, and mix of workers and managers. We learn from the Vanguard that there is no one best place to be on the managerial quadrant, and that "getting as much of all four desirable outcomes as possible" does not mean being in the geographical middle of the quadrant, in a state of compromise, offering a little of each. It actually means breaking through the trade-off barrier by creatively designing work systems that permit the simultaneous realization of all four *necessary* objectives.

Small Company Examples

For decades, the leaders of several small companies have treated their employees as stakeholders, have sought to create symmetry among the objectives of individual merit, organizational efficiency, job security, and the quality of work life, and have found creative ways to effectively and fairly provide for worker participation in decision making and profits. Let us briefly examine the work systems at Lincoln Electric, Olga, and Herman Miller to see how they do it.

Lincoln Electric. Located in Cleveland, Ohio, this manufacturer of arc welding machines and electrodes has operated since 1934 on the principle of rewarding workers in cold cash for their efforts. It is not just "output" that is rewarded; creativity and entrepreneurial behavior are especially prized. Highly paid to start with, workers receive an annual bonus based on four criteria —output, quality of work, cooperation, and ideas to improve productivity. This bonus effectively doubles the annual income of the average employee. (In 1982 the company's 2,634 employees *each* received an average *bonus* of $15,640.) Workers at Lincoln are encouraged to find ways to eliminate their own jobs—and they get a promotion if they do. The firm guarantees at least thirty-two hours of work fifty weeks a year for each employee with two or more years of service. (No specific rate of pay is guaranteed; the employee must be willing to accept transfer from one job to another, as well as accept overtime work during periods of peak demand.) The company has not laid off a worker since 1951.

During the 1980–1983 recession, Lincoln employees went on a short workweek, but they never fell below 75 percent of their normal hours worked. One of the ways in which Lincoln deals with the vagaries of the business cycle is to "bank" new products during good times and release them on the market during a recession. Another method is to move employees out of production and into sales. During the recent recession, 51 production workers (and 14 clerical workers) were trained to sell the new products the company had just taken off the shelf. In 1982, these new salespeople brought in $10 million of new business.

Worker productivity at Lincoln is about 100 percent higher

than in U. S. industry in general, and the cost of their products has not greatly increased for several decades. Their secret has been cost reduction, which has averaged some $13 million per year for over ten years, much of which has come from eliminating supervisory personnel (who simply become redundant when workers assume responsibility for their own performance).

Lincoln employees with forty years of service can retire at *full pay* at age sixty-five. In 1982, the company earned $37.5 million on $468 million in sales (after paying out some $41 million in bonuses). Lincoln Electric stock is 40 percent employee owned (and over 40 percent more is held by retirees and members of the Lincoln family).

The Olga Company. This Van Nuys, California, producer of ladies' undergarments stands as an example of treating employees as stakeholders in an industry where they said it couldn't be done. Most of Olga's California-based competitors run little better than sweatshops in which women from Asia and Latin America toil in substandard working conditions for less than minimum wages. In contrast, the Olga Company not only pays better than union wages, but workers own shares in the firm and participate in profits. Moreover, they have a high degree of security against layoffs.

While profit sharing is a widely accepted practice in American industry, it is practiced with a vengeance at Olga. The Olga plan:

· Includes every member of the company.

· Is highly intensive (25 percent of pretax profits—after a 15 percent provision for stockholders' equity—is contributed to the fund).

· Provides for both profit and ownership sharing. One fifth of every year's contribution is used to purchase Olga shares for all participants in the program.

· Includes a "Profit Sharing Through Profit Caring" program, the objective of which is to improve profits through the ingenuity, imagination, and participation of all managers and line workers. In 1982, the project produced the equivalent of 33 percent extra pretax profit. Of these savings 25 percent are, in turn, put back into the profit-sharing fund. Coincidentally, the project also produces significant incremental results for the company and the participants. It helps to identify and properly recognize people of talent, imagination, and commitment—those who, in turn, qualify for increased responsibility.

Job security has been practiced in a few fast-growing domestic companies that have been relatively immune to the business cycle, and in a handful of old-line manufacturing firms like Fel-Pro and Lincoln, but nowhere has it been tested in such a boom-and-bust industry as ladies' garments. At Olga, there have never been significant layoffs in the forty years the company has been in business. Even in 1982, when their competitors were shutting down left and right, Olga merely went on short workweeks; no permanent layoffs were necessary. What is their secret? According to Jan Erteszek, who with his wife Olga started the company on a $10 investment shortly after they arrived in this country as immigrants from Poland, the answer is: "planning for full employment." Erteszek explains:

> You must decide that the primary purposes of your company are to provide customers with the high-quality garments they need and to provide workers with steady employment. Once you've decided that, then everything you do is subtly different from what your competitors will do if they start from a belief that all they are trying to achieve is short-term profit.

The first thing Olga does differently is to think of their employees as stakeholders, or "associates," to use their word. Says Erteszek:

> The people who work for us aren't hired hands. They invest their time, their efforts, and, in some cases, their lives, much as stockholders invest capital or managers invest knowledge. All three are investors. All three, therefore, have a *right* to share in the wealth produced by the company.

Erteszek sees investors, managers, and workers as engaged in a "common venture enterprise," each with reciprocal rights and obligations. One of the obligations of workers is to provide ideas for new products at what Erteszek calls "creative meetings," which are, in a way, design-oriented "quality control circles." Olga's designers—many of whom are from the working-class areas of the San Fernando Valley—creatively come up with designs that match and often outpace the professional haute couture designers of New York. It seems that no matter what the competition—foreign or domestic—tries, the Olga Company keeps growing, keeps earning a healthy profit, and keeps creating jobs for underprivileged minority women. In fact, the only setback occurred in the late 1960s, at the height of the counterculture movement, when it appeared for a brief, threatening moment that bras would go the way of corsets. But, within a year or two, women were back in harness, and the three thousand employees who worked at Olga were major beneficiaries of this return to form.

Today Olga has about $200 million in annual sales. In 1981, they were a leader in their industry as measured by return on invested capital, on income from sales, and on increase in sales. They achieved these results *after* 25 percent of pretax profits were contributed to profit- and stock-sharing plans.

Herman Miller. Located in Zeeland, Michigan, this company is one of the nation's largest producers of office furniture. Ranked about six hundredth on the *Fortune* 1000, with some 3,500 employees, Herman Miller is *almost* a big company. But it manages to *feel* small because of the amount of worker participation found in the firm. In the early 1950s, Herman Miller threw out their last time clock and fully embraced their employees as stakeholders. They installed a system of worker participation that is based on a network of interlocking elected committees that discuss employee suggestions regarding corporate plans, problems, and opportunities. The system is based on the Scanlon Plan, named after a steel union president in the 1930s. Joe Scanlon's idea was to define a simple measure of costs, then pay a monthly bonus to workers for reductions in costs resulting from their suggestions or efforts. At Herman Miller, employees start by negotiating goals with a committee at the next higher level. Goals are in four general areas: customer service, effective use of money, effective use of materials, and effective use of labor. If the workers exceed their goals they get a bonus.

To make this system work, the company makes it a point to share managerial information: One day a month is devoted to providing information to workers on productivity, profits, and the status of employee suggestions. The company also provides job security and a generous employee stock ownership plan (among employees with over one year of service, 100 percent are stockholders and 43 percent regularly purchase shares in addition to those that come as a benefit of employment. At the company's 1983 annual stockholder meeting, some 900 Herman Miller employees were in attendance along with some 200 nonemployee shareholders). Over the last decade, the company has experienced a 28 percent annual rate of growth in profits. In 1984, the company earned over $28 million on $402 million in sales. Herman Miller has become internationally known for the quality of their products (for example, the Eames chair), and for their high level of product innovation (for example, "the action office" and "the action factory," both developed around the concept of creating open areas in workplaces).

The company credits employee participation for these results. Says CEO Max DePree:

> Participation is not encouraged at Herman Miller simply because it appears to be more humane, but rather because working together has proven to be a successful way to run this business.

Significantly, the company publishes their "assumptions about work" and contrasts these to "traditional assumptions":

HERMAN MILLER ASSUMPTIONS	TRADITIONAL ASSUMPTIONS
Focus is on self-control and the authority of competence	Control is through the authority hierarchy
Emphasis on what is right, a problem-oriented approach	Emphasis on who is right, a power-centered scheme
Performance is self-expression and self-fulfillment	Performance is an act of obedience
Subordinates share responsibility	Subordinates are assistants
Power is held in reserve as derived from knowledge and skill	Power is exercised by those in authority

Motivation comes from the work itself	Motivation is supposed to spring from loyalty to the organization

In 1979, the company appointed a group of managers—and the employees elected a group of workers—to form a joint committee to "review and redesign" their twenty-nine-year-old Scanlon Plan. The company recognized that the plan wouldn't be effective if it wasn't viewed as legitimate by their workers. When the committee put their revised plan before the entire workforce, it got a 96 percent approval in a company-wide vote.

Visit any one of these successful, smallish companies and you will find that the employee is clearly a stakeholder. Visit Olga and you will find that Jan Erteszek treats the people who work for him with the same respect he treats members of his board of directors. I've seen him discuss the Olga "common venture" philosophy with immigrant Asian and Latin women who operate the company's sewing machines. Jan demonstrates his respect for all his "associates" by talking to them about serious issues; he motivates them by being visible in the company's several factories; he underscores their importance to the firm by rewarding them in the manner top managers and investors are rewarded. Jan Erteszek is no wild-eyed radical. He is a solid, churchgoing, conservative man who happens to believe that there is no place for class distinctions at work.

Visit Herman Miller and you will find a company in which workers participate in decision making and in corporate profits, and in which there is a model system of upward/downward communications. At Herman Miller you will find every employee is dedicated to producing the highest-quality goods and where the commitment to excellence is felt as strongly by shopfloor workers as by the company president. Visit Lincoln Electric Company— arguably the nation's leader in labor productivity for the last several decades—and you will find such a congruence of beliefs about company objectives between top management and production workers that the need for all middle managers and supervisors has been completely eliminated. Or, while you are in the Midwest, visit Fel-Pro, a supplier to the auto industry that manages to rationalize production to avoid the cyclical layoffs that plague their *only* customers (in sixty-five years, Fel-Pro has never had a layoff). These companies have become national leaders in profitability, productivity, and technological innovation because their top managers pay attention to the basics of marketing and production. But that isn't enough. In addition, they treat every employee as an individual with something to contribute to the company besides her time or his back muscles.

In looking at the work systems at Lincoln, Olga, and Herman Miller, it is seen that employees have more *rights* than do workers in most traditionally managed companies. But it is equally important to note that they also have greater *responsibilities.* Legitimacy, equity, and ultimately, organizational effectiveness, emerge from a balancing of rights and responsibilities. The two concepts go together like the twin pans on the scales of justice. That is the main lesson to be drawn from our brief small-company tour.

Throughout the 1970s, executives of many of the largest U.S. corporations rejected the examples of Olga, Lincoln Electric, Herman Miller, and Fel-Pro. They said it was impossible for the ITTs and GMs to learn anything from these small, superbly successful companies. The managers of large corporations—and haughty students and professors at the nation's leading business schools—claimed that it was impossible to translate the stick-to-the-basics philosophy of small companies into big company practices. But the world has changed dramatically during the last few years. Now, the likes of Motorola—with what amounts to the nation's largest Scanlon Plan—are demonstrating that the secrets of small business success can be captured by big business, too. Sometimes it makes good sense to reinvent the wheel.

Getting It Together at Motorola

Motorola, headquartered in Schaumburg, Illinois (not far from Chicago's O'Hare Airport), have probably done the best job of any *large* U.S. business at giving employees a significant stake in the corporation. Moreover, they have institutionalized change processes more thoroughly and successfully than any large company of which I am aware. The company has built into their culture the things that make the high-tech companies of Silicon Valley such attractive places to work—with the added advantages of being an established corporation that has proved capable of adapting to changing markets and technologies and able to survive adversity with their principles intact (and workers' jobs secure).

Prior to 1970, Motorola was a relatively low-tech company with about a quarter of their business in consumer electronics—mainly car radios and Quasar televisions. The company is probably still best known for their art deco tube radios that were ubiquitous features in big autos during the second quarter of this century (Motor + Victrola = Motorola, in case you didn't know). Historically, the company turned in a steady but unspectacular growth in sales of about 15 percent per annum. That would satisfy most corporate leaders. But in the late 1960s, the company's CEO, Robert Galvin, decided that the technological future lay not with car radios, and not even with color TVs. The future was with higher-technology products, such as semiconductors and microprocessors. While Intel, Texas Instruments, and others appeared to have had a big technological jump on Motorola (and what appeared to be an insurmountable lead in terms of the sophistication of their engineers and scientists), Robert Galvin characteristically decided to "bet the company" and attempt to make Motorola number one in semiconductors, as well as in two-way communications where they were already number one. Galvin did it without flash or flair. To be accurate, Motorola is a plodder—a patient and thorough tortoise in a field of jittery and self-confident hares. While most of the high-strung, impatient, high-tech companies view *next year* as an eternity, Galvin laid out a detailed *ten-year* plan for transforming Motorola.

What must be appreciated is that Galvin did this *pro*actively. There was no crisis at Motorola; the company and the industry appeared to be in good shape. Galvin did something highly unusual for an American executive—he anticipated the need for future change even though the company was not in any imminent trouble. Many of the details of how he accomplished his change must await development in subsequent chapters (suspense being such a precious quality in works of nonfiction, I shan't expose my punch line prematurely).

Galvin saw that his plan could only be realized through the active support of *all* of Motorola's employees. In fact, in the 1960s, Galvin saw that to get the support he needed, he would have to involve as many of his people as possible in *creating* that plan (another critical point that must, perforce, await development in Chapter Nine). As the Motorola plan developed, it became clear to top management that a centralized, highly directive corporate structure would not produce the kind of commitment, effort, and innovation needed to succeed. To more fully engage Motorola's managers in his mission impossible, Galvin radically decentralized the company, creating many new "presidents" in the process, each with a small entrepreneurial business to run as he saw fit (as long as the actions of each complemented and abetted the thrust of the overall corporate plan). Galvin created an incentive system for these managers that made them feel they were the "owners" of their businesses (including a generous bonus pool that rewarded innovation, risk taking, and superior performance).

But that wasn't enough. Certainly, it wasn't enough to remain competitive with the Japanese who coveted the same markets Motorola planned to enter. By the 1970s, Galvin and his managers realized that, to compete with the Japanese, Motorola would need high productivity and high-quality goods. They also realized that they, Motorola's managers, could not achieve those objectives by themselves. What was required was employee dedication at all levels to high standards of quality, productivity, cost control, inventory control, customer service, and delivery. They realized that they needed a system that would turn out well-designed products—products with low cost, high yield, and high reliability. Their goal was nothing less than perfection—*zero defects*.

To beat the Japanese competitors at their own game, would Galvin and his managers have to mimic them? Not on your life! Instead, Galvin went to his roots, to the management principles established by Motorola's founder, his father, Paul Galvin. Under Paul Galvin, Motorola had pioneered some fairly "radical" employee practices. In 1947, Motorola started a profit-sharing fund into which the company placed 20 percent of pretax earnings. In the 1950s, Motorola jettisoned their last punch clock, putting all workers on an honor system. At about the same time, Motorola created an employee advisory committee that reported directly to the board of directors and separate employee task forces to review such subjects as benefits (to insure that workers got what they needed, and not just what managers wanted to give them). Motorola workers were also among the first in a large U.S. corporation to gain a measure of job security: A decision by the CEO was (and still is) needed to fire any worker with ten years or more service in the company. Significantly, the burden of appeal is on the manager who wishes to do the firing, and *not* on the worker. All of this seems to have set well with Motorola employees. In five decades, only one union election has ever been contested in a Motorola plant, and that was in a bargaining unit with only 20 workers (the union lost 17–3).

The Motorola PMP

Throughout the 1970s, the engine of change at Motorola was what they called their Participative Management Program (PMP). It is misnamed. For it is not a "program" at all; rather, it has become synonymous with the way they manage at Motorola. Building on the highly participative style of founder Paul Galvin, Motorola's managers have created a system in which employees now have a greater stake in Motorola than Japanese workers have in the best-run corporations in Japan. Even if the latter point is found to be overstated, it is no doubt the case that working conditions at Motorola are better-suited to American workers than would be any Japanese alternative. As one Motorola employee explained to me, "Like the Japanese, we play softball and volleyball on the excellent facilities the corporation provides for us. But, *un*like the Japanese, we play when *we* want to, not on cue!"

The Motorola system of worker participation is not much simpler to describe than it was to create, for it was not easy to devise a system in which employees could all legitimately feel they have a say in management. To begin, it was recognized that it would be impossible for all Motorola's 60,000 domestic employees to function effectively if they each acted as individuals. For purposes of coordination, then, Motorola employees have been grouped into teams of some 50 to 250 workers. Each employee shares in a common bonus pool with his or her other team members. The idea is that the people in each pool will be responsible for their own performance—as measured by the production costs and materials use that are controllable by the team, by quality, by production levels, by inventory of stock and finished goods, by housekeeping standards, and by safety records. Whenever an idea proposed by a team leads to a cost reduction, or to production that exceeds a target, all team members share in the gains through bonuses that can amount to 41 percent of base salary (the average varies between 8 and 12 percent).

This system is similar to the Scanlon plan that has been successful for three decades at Herman Miller (described earlier). The genius of the Motorola system is that it has been made to work in a very large corporation. A key element in this successful translation of a small company idea into big company practice is Motorola's intricate process of communications. Each working team has one of its members on a steering committee at the next higher level in the company, (which, in turn, has a member on another committee at the subsequent higher level). The steering committees perform several critical functions:

1. Coordination. A steering committee will act on ideas that come from a working group that require cooperation with one or more other working groups.

2. Lateral Communication. A steering committee will disseminate the ideas or practices of one working group to other groups, thus facilitating organizational learning.

3. Downward Communication. A steering committee will insure that each work group has all the managerial information it requires to do its job.

4. Upward Communication. Since each steering committee is linked to the next level steering committee (which, in turn, reports to top management), shop floor issues reach Motorola executives after going through only four levels in the hierarchical chain (this is an extremely "flat" organizational structure for a company with 95,000 workers).

5. Control. A steering committee negotiates output standards and measures of performance with the work teams that report to it. This is a continuing process in which trust is built by clearly establishing the performance criteria by which work teams will be measured in advance of the evaluation process.

6. Evaluation. Based on the negotiated measures of performance, a steering committee evaluates the record of the work teams that report to it, and allocates rewards based on a prenegotiated formula.

This system is clearly designed for manufacturing and production workers. Recently, Motorola has augmented it with a parallel plan for professional, clerical, marketing, research, and other staff people. These employees are also organized into teams and also partake in a bonus program based on performance measures appropriate to their tasks.

The entire system is buttressed by Motorola's "I Recommend" plan. In this system, every work area in the company has a bulletin board on which employees can post questions or recommendations. The questions and recommendations can be either signed or anonymous. Either way, the supervisor responsible for the area is required to post a reply within seventy-two hours. (In those cases where it is impossible to obtain an answer that quickly, the supervisor must post the name of the person who is working on obtaining the information, along with the date by which a final answer will be posted.)

Results of the PMP

Since initiating the PMP, Motorola claims significant productivity improvement, the exact percentage of which is meaningless for several reasons. First, some parts of the company have been involved in PMP for many years, while a few parts have only recently been phased in. Second, any overall figure homogenizes what are, in reality, quite different levels of performance, as well as confusing production with staff results. Third, overall productivity is devilishly hard to measure in any large, diversified organization.

Nonetheless, it is relatively easy to measure productivity at the level of any single work group, and that turns out to be the best way to evaluate the results of Motorola's PMP. For example, a worker in Fort Worth, Texas who assembles radios discovered that about one of every ten screws she would drive in with an air gun would break. Now, in most companies, the worker would simply throw the faulty screws away and be done with it. In exceptional cases, the worker might bring the matter up with her supervisor who, in turn, might then call someone in the purchasing department, who then might call the screw vendor and complain. Lots of steps, lots of mights. At the Fort Worth plant the Motorola employee called the vendor *herself*. After that initial conversation, her work team got together with the vendor and they collectively solved the problem. It turned out that if the screws had proper heat treatment they wouldn't break. What happened at Forth Worth is true self-management. The problem never went to a higher level. Layers of managers were kept out of the loop, and many opportunities for slipups were avoided. A solution was reached far faster than had it been approached bureaucratically. The company saved money, and the workers shared in the savings in their next monthly bonus.

When a group of Motorola secretaries joined the PMP, they were at first skeptical that they could find such ways to increase their own productivity. Then one of them had a bright idea: She said, "Let's pool all the inventory of supplies that each of us has squirreled away." By the time they had unearthed all the staplers, paper clips, rulers, envelopes, typing ribbons, scissors, and sticky tape they had each hoarded, they found enough supplies *on hand* to last the year without reorders. Small stuff in this case. But it adds up when everybody is doing it, and when constant productivity improvement becomes a way of life in a company. And, in some areas, savings can be enormous. For example, gold is used in the production of Motorola's semiconductors. Before the PMP, something like 40 percent of the gold used was wasted. After two months of analysis, Motorola employees identified some fifty spots in the process where the gold was being lost. Ultimately, they reduced the waste to zero.

Other PMP results are equally impressive. The company reports:

- A substantial increase in machine throughput (which in some cases made possible as much as a year's postponement of investment in additional equipment).

- Major improvements in safety and cleanliness.

- Reductions in staff levels through attrition. (As vacancies have occurred through natural turnover and retirement, employees have said, in effect, "You don't have to hire a replacement —we'll share the added work." And share *themselves* in the fruits of their increased labor productivity.)

- Cooperation between shifts has improved. (For example, workers now leave notes for people on the next shift, which helps to keep equipment running continuously.)

- Turnover is decreasing (as jobs become more interesting, fewer people quit in search of greener pastures).

What is the secret to the PMP's success? Part of it is that rarest of all free commodities: common sense. The PMP simply encourages better communication at all levels and between all levels, and this better communication gets people working together toward common objectives. The system also increases the visibility of management through the constant standards reviews. These reviews show that management cares and create a climate of trust and openness. The PMP also links cause and effect in the minds of workers through a fast and fair system of feedback (there is a weekly posting of performance records). In essence, employees end up understanding what their piece of the business is and how it contributes to the grand corporate scheme. As a result, Motorola employees tend to make more "rational" decisions—and without the need for constant managerial coercion.

Assumptions, Assumptions, Assumptions

If Motorola's PMP is merely common sense, why haven't other companies done it? The answer is that many have tried. In fact, many companies have bits and pieces of this type of management going on here and there in various divisions. Motorola is unique only in that they have made participation the cornerstone of their culture. They have institutionalized participation to an extent known only in such small companies as Lincoln Electric, Olga, and Herman Miller. The reason why they have done so (when others have not) is, according to Motorola's chief operating officer William Weisz, because "of our set of assumptions about human behavior." Significantly, in Motorola's employee handbook on PMP, the discussion of the system *begins* with an elucidation of the company's assumptions about workers and work. Here's my summary of Motorola's assumptions:

1. Employee behavior is a consequence of how they are treated.
2. Employees are intelligent, curious, and responsible.
3. Employees need a rational work world in which they know what is expected of them, and why.
4. Employees need to know how their jobs relate to the jobs of others and to company goals.
5. There is only one class of employees, *not* a creative management group and a group of others who carry out orders.

6. There is no one best way to manage.

7. No one knows how to do his or her job better than the person on the job.

8. Employees want to have pride in their work.

9. Employees want to be involved in decisions that affect their own work.

10. The responsibility of every manager is to draw out the ideas and abilities of workers in a shared effort of addressing business problems and opportunities.

There is nothing terribly controversial in this litany of premises about workers and work (those familiar with the writings of Douglas McGregor will spot the influence of his famous "Theory Y" assumptions about the nature of man). What is remarkable is that, among the many thousands of large U.S. firms, only a handful have bothered to surface their own assumptions about employees. To my knowledge, none of the Old Guard have explicitly confronted what they believe about workers and work. But if they did, I suggest that they would find they believe something like the following:

1. Workers are paid to do, not to think.

2. Workers have little to contribute in terms of ideas that will improve productivity.

3. The sole reason people work is to make money.

4. Workers are all alike.

5. There is one best way to manage workers.

6. The function of managers is to manage; the function of workers is to carry out orders.

7. Employees do not want to accept responsibility for the quantity or quality of their own work.

8. Capital and management are the major sources of increased productivity.

9. Worker participation, profit sharing, stock ownership, and the like are softheaded at best, socialistic at worst.

10. Given any opportunity, workers will goof off; the role of the supervisor is that of a policeman to keep workers in line.

Clearly, this is *post hoc* reasoning. I've started with the kind of work systems one finds in the Old Guard, and worked backward to the kinds of assumptions that would have caused these systems to have been created. It seems reasonable to conclude that the systems found in the Old Guard—systems based on authoritarian discipline and adversarial relations—would stem from premises in which the worker is seen as a necessary evil, a cost of doing business, a mere factor of production. Certainly, if one thought of workers as corporate *stakeholders,* one would never have created traditional work systems.

In short, within Motorola's walls, there is satisfaction of multiple objectives. There are rewards for merit, incentives for efficiency, guarantees of security (more about this in the next chapter), and opportunities for personal growth, and job satisfaction. Significantly, there is *balance* between these. Motorola is no hang-loose Silicon Valley-type firm in which workers go barefoot and jump into the company hot tub whenever the stress of three hours of uninterrupted work becomes unbearable. Motorola is not a Marin County-type firm in which pot-smoking employees vote out management in the name of "industrial democracy." Motorola treats people with dignity without losing discipline; it provides a high quality of life without sacrificing order; and, most important, it shares money and power fairly without degenerating into anarchy.

Bucks and Power

I was recently at one of the Vanguard corporations when a famous consultant received some $10,000 for telling a group of top managers that all that was required of them was to praise their secretaries and to reduce stress by "giving employees lots of candid feedback." After the talk, one manager told me "that was the best ten grand this company ever spent." Why? *Because it got him off the hook.* If he just treated his people nicely, nothing more was expected of him. He would not have to address the two necessary ingredients involved in giving employees a stake in the company: money and authority.

For participation to be effective and legitimate, two things must occur: First, employees must participate in the decisions that affect their own work. Second, employees must participate in the financial rewards that come as a result of their efforts.

Participation in decision making without participation in financial gains is viewed as illegitimate by workers who see all the fruits of their efforts reaped by others. And participation in financial gains without participation in decision making is seen as illegitimate by workers who are powerless to influence the things that determine the size of their paychecks. Thus, if treating employees as stakeholders is to be anything more than meaningless rhetoric, it all comes down to the two most sensitive issues in management: *power and bucks.* As the Motorola case illustrates, the task of management is to find the appropriate ways to share those scarcest and most jealously guarded of all organizational assets. For too long, management theorists have attempted to shield corporate executives from this painful fact of life.

4.

VANGUARD EMPLOYEE PRACTICES

> Unity of thinking is not thinking at all.
> —COMMENT BY AN ANONYMOUS POLE
> AT AN EXHIBIT OF SOVIET ART.

It is what a company does—and not necessarily what it says—that ultimately makes the difference between organizational effectiveness and ineffectiveness. Important, it is not simply in their constitutions that the Vanguard treat their employees as stakeholders; the Vanguard manifest their commitment to employee rights and responsibilities in all aspects of management. In this chapter, I analyze a few specific examples of Vanguard employee practices. We find that the Vanguard provide:

- Stakeholder status for unions
- Employee stock ownership
- A fair measure of job security
- Lifelong training
- Benefits tailored to individual needs
- Participation in decision making
- Freedom of expression
- Incentive pay (discussed in Chapter Seven)

Union Relations

None of the small, excellent companies described in the previous chapter is unionized. In contrast, most large American manufacturing firms have at least some organized employees. That is another reason why this book is not about the country's best-run companies—instead, it is about the Vanguard (all of which, with the exception of Motorola, have at least minimal union representation). Significantly, the unionized Vanguard corporations have sought to build cooperative relationships with their unions. It has not been easy. By nature, union/management relations are adversarial. By nature, union officials are suspicious of corporate managers. Now, it is not that the Vanguard managers return this hostility with love. The Vanguard are merely realistic. Unions are like parents. Once you've got them, for all practical and ethical purposes, you can't get rid of them. Without the possibility of divorce, the only alternative is accommodation. Most unions are like Jewish mothers (and Irish fathers) in that they take extreme pleasure in making that accommodation as trying an experience as they can make it. Unions love to be wooed, only to then reject the signs of affection. They love to remind managers of past offenses (again, like mom: "Remember that time when you were eight years old?"). And they love being suspicious and paranoid almost as much as they love being caustic and insulting. Getting along with unions requires the patience of Job, the insight of Freud, and the skin of Jumbo.

That fairly well describes Weyerhaeuser's top management. In the early 1970s, Weyerhaeuser became one of the first unionized corporations to experiment with worker participation. It was a painful experience, marked by squabbles between the local union and their international representative, and between two of Weyerhaeuser's several unions. The upshot was that Weyerhaeuser soon had another distinction: They were one of the first major corporations to *abandon* a worker participation experiment. Characteristically, Weyerhaeuser's top management accepted the blame for this failure. Says William Ruckelshaus (for several years a Weyerhaeuser vice president): "We didn't have the willingness to see the effort through thick and thin. We made the mistake of seeing it as an experiment."

But Weyerhaeuser is a learning organization. Nearly a decade later, the company encouraged mill and plant managers to reapproach the union about employee participation (the company realized that if top managers took the initiative, union leaders would smell "manipulation"). Doubly wary after the previous ill-fated attempt to build cooperation, union officials predictably responded like cornered porcupines. While pulling the quills out from his hand, the manager of one Weyerhaeuser mill hit upon a creative way of reducing the obvious skepticism of the union. Since union officials mistrust all manner of corporate, university, and consultant types, it was obvious that there was only one group that they did trust: unions. Why not fly Weyerhaeuser's union officials around to meet those few trade unionists in other industries who had tried cooperation and found they liked it? Let unionists sell the union on the mutual advantages of worker participation, was the Weyerhaeuser manager's creative insight. And it worked. It worked not only because the union officials had a change of heart, it worked because the corporation started to treat the union as a legitimate corporate stakeholder. Once the corporation took the initiative to transport their union officials to meet other unionists and assumed the responsibility for inviting union officials into meetings from which they were previously excluded, the stage was set *on both sides* for cooperation.

The first test of the new relationship came at a Weyerhaeuser mill in Snoqualmie Falls, Washington. As background, one must understand that, in purely economic terms, Weyerhaeuser probably shouldn't be in business in the Northwest. The real profits in the wood products industry today are to be made in the South (Georgia-Pacific, for example, has abandoned the Pacific—it's all Georgia now). But Weyerhaeuser made their mark in the Northwest and they are determined not to abandon the area that gave them so much in the past. But, in 1980, the company could no longer justify keeping the sixty-six-year-old "Sno Falls" mill open. When you are losing money on every tree you cut, you can't make it up in volume! So, the company reluctantly shut the mill and laid off 150 workers.

After being shut down for nearly a year, Sno Falls was reopened thanks to a joint union-management effort. The problems at the mill were clear for all to see: It was overstaffed and the equipment used was ancient. The plant managers approached the union leaders with a proposal to change the product mix in the mill, to reduce the numbers of both salaried and union workers, and to increase worker participation. The plan entailed equalizing the rates of pay among union workers (who had theretofore jealously guarded their job-wage classification differences) and getting the union to throw out rules that prevented workers from moving from one job to another as needed for efficient plant operation.

Weyerhaeuser started the ball rolling with a 31 percent reduction in the number of supervisors (after all, they felt workers should become largely self-managing, so why not indicate to the union that they meant business?), and the union responded by agreeing to a 37 percent reduction in the number of workers (simply ending featherbedding and overspecialization took care of this). The remaining supervisors were retrained to act as "facilitators"—trained to help workers and to get information for them, rather than to act as policemen. But if workers were going to have to work harder—and if they were going to share in decision making—it was only fair that they also share in the financial results of their efforts. According to George Van Vleet, the Weyerhaeuser manager responsible for Sno Falls, here's how gain sharing was arranged:

> Before the closure, the mill's highest production was 23,500 board feet per hour. In our negotiations, we figured the mill could survive if 24,000 board feet per hour were cut for twenty straight days in a ninety-day period. So we offered workers a challenge. We promised them a $50 bonus each to hit that 24,000 mark, $75 to hit 25,000, and $100 for 26,000 board feet per hour for twenty days running. That first day, they fell on their can. But from then on, they hit 29,000 board feet per hour. And I'll be damned if they didn't get that $100 bonus in the first eighteen days. After a year of operation, workers hit 31,000 to 32,000 board feet per hour pretty consistently. One eight-hour shift set a record with 39,000 board feet per hour.

A year later, the mill was turning out 30 percent more product with 30 percent fewer employees than before the shutdown. Today the union official at the mill sees his role as making sure that supervisors follow through on suggestions made by workers. Supervisors see their role as making sure workers have all the information needed to do their jobs. And, while union and management still have their differences (lambs lie down with lions only in myth), both parties are united in the desire to keep the mill open.

At John Deere, unions are as much a way of life as they are at Weyerhaeuser. Almost before they knew what was happening, the company was unionized in the 1945–47 postwar blitz of the Midwest by the United Auto Workers. Significantly, Deere has continued to treat their organized workers with much the same respect and dignity they afford their nonunion employees. When one visits a Deere facility, there is little of the adversarial tension one feels in such other UAW-represented companies as GM, Ford, or International Harvester. While most auto plants are nearly paralyzed by restrictive work rules, grievance filings, and a we/they attitude that prevents the cooperation needed for effective operations, Deere facilities are marked by relatively relaxed union/management relations. The climate is due, in part, to a healthy incentive system that rewards workers for high productivity. But the main part is the attitude of the corporation towards the union. One UAW official explained to me, "Our relations with all our employers are rough; but I'd say Deere is far and away the best of the bastards." Scant praise, perhaps, but on the shop floor it translates into high productivity. Paradoxically, by not responding in kind to some of the unkind actions of the union, Deere has maintained the loyalty of its work force. One Deere worker told me: "In Detroit, most UAW people think of themselves as members of the Autoworkers first. Their main loyalty is to the union. Here we think of ourselves as Deere employees. Only at contract time do we think about the union." This climate should be contrasted to the antipathy found at Deere's chief competitor, International Harvester, where a hard-ball-playing management got comparable treatment from the union in return, in the form of a debilitating, long-term strike.

Treating the union as a stakeholder seems an obvious thing to do, but most managers can't swallow the pride needed to pull it off. They believe that they prove their virility by staring down the union and making the other fellow blink. The idea is to embarrass or humiliate the union—but such little "victories" end up being Pyrrhic because the unions are past masters at retaliatory humiliation.

At Levi Strauss, the attitude is different. The company makes no distinction between their union and nonunion employees. Hence, if they decide to offer a benefit to their white-collar workers, the union members also get it without the need to bargain for it (and vice versa). At GM, the philosophy has always been just the opposite: The corporation has done everything in their power to distinguish the "class" differences between blue-collar and white-collar, between union and nonunion employees. At Levi, the notion of the union as stakeholder is taken to the extreme of making the union look good. When Levi managers decided that their sewing machine operators deserved to share in profits because "they are the ones who produce the goods," the managers met with union officials to discuss the Levi plan. In effect, here's what they said to the startled union officials: "If you *insist* on opening the contract in midterm to provide profit sharing for operators, we will accept your demand." Later, when Levi needed a postponement in a contracted raise in order to weather a recession, the union readily agreed. Contrast this with the "I'm alright, Jack" attitude of the UAW when GM needs concessions.

Honeywell operates in the Levi style. When Honeywell planned to conduct an employee attitude survey, they first met with Teamster officials to get their ideas about what items should be included. Then, they voluntarily shared the results with the union—even though Honeywell was, in effect, giving the Teamsters potential ammunition that could be used against the company at bargaining time. In union relations, it is the little things a company does that count in the long run.

Stock Ownership

Making every worker into a capitalist is the Vanguard's creative way of meeting the workplace needs of merit, efficiency, equality, and the quality of life *simultaneously.* Employee stock ownership is supportive of traditional capitalistic theories of motivation: If you own a "piece of the action," you are more likely to work harder than if you are a mere "hired hand." Employee stock ownership increases efficiency by encouraging workers to cooperate with their fellow owners—and puts the greatest of all productivity incentives (peer pressure) on those who don't carry their own weight. Employee stock ownership increases equality by closing the gap between management and labor, between owners and employees, between the haves and have-nots. Finally, employee stock ownership is consistent with worker participation in decision making. When workers are owners, participation is not a *privilege* granted by management; rather, it becomes a right and an obligation.

It has taken some twenty-five years for American managers to see that it is necessary to bring the assumptions about property and motivation found within industry into sync with the assumptions about property and motivation in our capitalistic economic system. Around the nation, as corporations were threatened by economic failure during the 1980–83 recession, many managers returned to the traditions of the American system in a last-ditch attempt to save their companies: As part of the federal bailout of the Chrysler Corporation, employees assumed up to 20 percent ownership of the firm; to save Eastern Airlines, employees traded pay cuts for 25 percent of the carrier's stock; at the Weirton Steel Works, 6,000 employees purchased the plant from the National Steel Corporation for some $585 million; when the Great Atlantic & Pacific Tea Company announced it might have to shut down twenty Philadelphia A&P supermarkets, approximately 1,000 store clerks swapped pay cuts in exchange for a significant share of store ownership; and employee ownership has even come—indirectly—to General Motors (In 1981, 1,200 workers bought a bearings plant from GM for some $53 million). All told, between 1973 and 1983, some sixty corporations in deep financial trouble were purchased by employees. According to the Conference Board, only two of these employee-owned companies failed; and at least 50,000 jobs were saved during the decade.

The shame of the matter is that American industry seldom gets the idea to cut employees into the action unless faced with bankruptcy or intolerable losses. In the light of study after study showing a strong correlation between employee ownership and profitability (that is, employee-owned firms are more profitable on the average than investor-owned firms; and the greater the percentage of employee ownership within a firm the more profitable it is likely to be), it is remarkable that corporations have for so long ignored the facts before their eyes. Again, it all comes down to a matter of basic premises. Workers simply have never been thought of as capable of being, or entitled to be, substantial owners of corporate stock.

Corporations who have not waited until the last rites before "getting religion" on employee ownership have fared remarkably well. For instance, the corporate success story of the early 1980s, People Express Airlines, is employee owned. All 4,000 People Express employees are stockholders (on the average, each holds about $55,000 worth of stock). All are on a profit-sharing plan (with bonus potential of 50 percent of total pay). Significantly, all full-time employees have the title of "manager" and all assume an array of duties (even pilots make reservations and schlep bags four days each month). The company has the lowest cost per seat-mile in the industry and the greatest increase in stock value. They turned a $2.1 million profit in the last quarter of 1983, while the eleven largest airlines were *losing* a combined total of $619 million!

Most of the Vanguard companies have employee stock purchase plans in which the employer pays anywhere from 15 to 30 percent of the cost of a share of company stock, with the employee picking up the rest. In addition, most of the Vanguard have, or are in the process of forming, employee stock ownership plans (ESOPs). Among the Vanguard, Levi Strauss takes employee stock ownership the most seriously. Indeed, the desire to increase employee ownership was a major factor in the company's decision to "go public" in 1971. Since companies with over 500 shareholders are treated as "publicly held" by the government (whether shares are traded publicly or not), Levi found itself up against the legal "ceiling" with 480 employee shareholders in 1970. The company decided that, since the benefits of private ownership were soon to be lost anyway as they made stock available to more employees, why not kill two birds with one stone by raising badly needed capital *and* spreading employee ownership at the same time? As a condition of their public offering, the company insisted that 126,000 shares of stock be sold to employees free of broker commissions. By the end of 1971, some 20 percent of Levi stock was held by employees. Today, almost all Levi domestic employees are stockholders. On several celebratory occasions—for example, when the company reached the two-billion-dollar sales mark during the 1970s—the company gave stock to all full-time employees. They also grant shares to mark each employee's five-year anniversary of service.

While the other Vanguard companies all have one form or another of employee stock ownership programs, it is not the case that all are equally committed to the idea. Indeed, Control Data's CEO William C. Norris is downright skeptical about the whole notion. When I put the issue to him directly, he quickly put forward three thoughtful objections to the practice: First, he said there was no evidence that employees desire ownership. Second, he said there was no evidence that employees fully understand the complexity of ownership. And, third, he questioned the advisability of making the financial security of employees dependent on the vagaries of the stock market, the ups and downs of which are only tangentially related to company performance. While I believe Norris's first two points can be refuted by reference to the information presented earlier, his last point is not an easy one to refute (in fact, it is the primary argument used by labor leaders, a group traditionally opposed to employee stock ownership). It is an issue that worries even as great an enthusiast of employee stock ownership as Levi Strauss' CEO, Robert Haas. When I once asked Haas what the trading price of Levi stock was on that particular day, he replied:

> I'm one of the largest shareholders in this firm, so you'd think I'd be checking the stock listing daily. But I don't. I hold my stock whether it goes up or down, so it doesn't make any difference to me personally what Wall Street is up to. But there is an important reason for Levi management to care about stock prices, and that's our responsibility to employees who own shares. If we take actions that drive down the price of our stock, we adversely affect their future financial security. That's a big responsibility . . . one that makes employee stock ownership (and public ownership in general) a mixed blessing.

Not even the best of ideas is perfect, it would seem.

Job Security

And not the best of companies is "perfect," either. For example, none of the Vanguard corporations offers their employees an ironclad guarantee of lifelong employment. Such a guarantee is impractical given the volatility of markets and industries (who can predict when semiconductors will outmode manual widgets?). Such a guarantee is also unwarranted for those who have many employment options (highly mobile professional workers, managers, journalists, doctors, and lawyers are like tenured university professors in this regard—they often develop degenerative "root rot" as a side effect of job security). At issue, then, is not the provision of a sinecure for all employees; rather, the challenge accepted by the Vanguard is to provide greater security for those at the lower levels of the organization who have the fewest job options (particularly middle-aged and older workers who have devoted their entire careers to one employer).

Like Olga, Lincoln Electric, and other great, small companies, the Vanguard are learning to plan for steadier and fuller employment. They are challenging the common assumption that industry must always "respond to the business cycle," quickly laying workers off when demand slackens and rehiring them as soon as orders pick up. Almost all of the Vanguard are now establishing long-term plans that they hope will lead to steady employment.

Vanguard managers are experimenting with several tools to achieve this end. Many are adopting tighter hiring policies. One top manager of Weyerhaeuser explained the new philosophy like this: "In the past, whenever demand increased, we'd start staffing up left and right. We'd justify this by saying, 'This employee is only costing us $35,000 per year.' Now we will say, 'Over the course of this person's career, the dollar investment will amount to well over two million dollars.' It will be much tougher to justify a multimillion dollar investment than a few-thousand-dollar one." In another spirit, some companies are offering employees a new kind of "social contract." In effect, they are saying, "We'll guarantee you a job, if you agree to work overtime and on weekends during the booms and agree to work sharing and pay cuts during the busts."

That corporate behavior toward employees is driven by managerial assumptions can be nicely illustrated by comparing the ways in which Texas Instruments and Motorola respectively handled the employment effects of the 1980–82 recession. At TI, where the employee is *not* viewed as a stakeholder, the company laid off over 3,000 people in their semiconductor business. Motorola weathered the same slump in demand without significant layoffs. When the crunch came, Motorola was able to avoid morale-destroying layoffs because it had been planning since the severe recession of 1974–75 for that eventuality. That earlier recession and the pain of the layoffs involved had been an eye-opener for Motorola. Says COO William Weisz: "We decided then and there that we weren't going through that experience again. We learned our lesson." Motorola then introduced a program of "work sharing." Workers were informed that when demand for semiconductors fell (as it inevitably would given the boom-and-bust nature of our economy), that the problem would be met through reduced workweeks rather than through layoffs. For example, when the crunch came in the early 1980s, instead of laying off 10 workers out of a hundred to meet a 10 percent reduction in demand, all 100 workers were assigned to work a four-day week every other week.

As a result of such work sharing, Motorola was able to keep many thousands of regular employees on the payroll in their Arizona semiconductor division who otherwise would have been laid off. Moreover, in anticipation of the layoffs, Motorola had lobbied for the reform of Arizona's unemployment compensation laws to permit workers to collect partial benefits when they were only working part-time. Motorola's workers were therefore only minimally affected financially by the reduced workweek. And, now that demand has again been picking up, Motorola is finding that workers are willing to put in overtime to help the company meet it. Work sharing thus gives Motorola tremendous production flexibility. Motorola can cope with increased demand without putting on new capacity (which quickly becomes *excess* capacity when the economy turns down). In effect, Motorola can handle substantial swings in demand while maintaining the same level of employment and capacity. And, since Motorola is not losing skilled workers who might drift away to other employment during a prolonged recession, transitions are fast and smooth when production is shifted to a higher gear.

In contrast, the layoffs at TI were accompanied by a loss of skilled employees, a reduction of morale among those who stayed on, a ragged transition back to full production, and problems of quality control while new workers learned their jobs. The bottom line is that Motorola has overtaken TI as the world's largest manufacturer of semiconductors.

Among the Vanguard corporations, Control Data has gone furthest with their plans for eventual employment stability. It has created "rings of defense," the first of which is a long-term R&D strategy in which new products will be regularly introduced (the best defense against layoffs is growth and the ability to introduce attractive new products during business-cycle troughs). The second ring is turnover (encouraging attrition even during good times, being careful not to replace retired workers whenever possible, and so forth). The third ring is the judicious use of part-timers. (Control Data has employees who work from nine to three in order to care for school-age children, others who work from three to six after school, some who just work weekends, and still others who work two- and three-day weeks. All of these people give the corporation tremendous flexibility in meeting fluctuating product demand.) The fourth ring is the use of contractors. (During good times, the company contracts out work that is not labor intensive and pulls such work back in-house during business slumps. Importantly, this policy doesn't simply transfer CDC's employment problem onto the shoulders of others. CDC will not pull back from a contractor *if* it is (a) dependent on CDC for more than 25 percent of its business, (b) a minority firm, or (c) a workshop for the handicapped.) The fifth ring of defense is subcontracting with prisoners (whose bed and board is guaranteed even during depressions). The sixth ring is the use of intercompany transfers (moving people from one division into another—for example, retraining production workers to reprogram mainframe products for use with personal computers). The seventh ring is offering summers off without pay (some 10 percent of CDC workers *volunteer* to do so in order to be with their kids or teacher-spouses). The eighth ring is *voluntary* time off without pay (many people *prefer* four-day workweeks or would like to take a minisabbatical). The ninth ring is *in*voluntary days off (the company has closed plants for a week over the Fourth of July and again at Thanksgiving; it has also offered four additional holidays—two paid and two unpaid). Faced with the need to lay off the equivalent of 4,800 workers in the 1980–83 recession, Control Data made their first attempt at implementing this strategy and ended up having to lay off only 600 (for a saving of 4,200 jobs). In 1985, however, they were forced to lay off workers because they ignored a tenth ring: competitive products and high productivity.

In *My Years with General Motors,* Sloan proudly recalled how GM made money during the Great Depression—even though they put tens of thousands of people out of work in order to do so. In his *General Theory,* Lord Keynes examined the consequence of such layoffs, when multiplied across the economy as a whole, and concluded that the net effect of many unemployed workers with little or no expendable income was to reduce the level of "aggregate demand" for goods—thus compounding the depth and duration of the Depression (and making recovery nearly impossible without massive government stimulation of the economy).

Without engaging in a consideration of the pros and cons of *The General Theory,* I believe it is useful to consider the possible effects on a depression *if* the many Sloans of American industry were to keep their people on three- or even two-day weeks. Certainly the two or three days of pay those workers would earn (and then spend) would do more to increase aggregate demand than the zero days of pay they would receive from the Old Guard. One wonders what the net macroeconomic effect on the 1980–83 recession would have been had even one half of American corporations followed the lead of Motorola and Control Data and utilized "rings of defense" to minimize layoffs. At a minimum, it could not have made matters any worse and would certainly have alleviated a great deal of human suffering and insecurity.

Why haven't other companies planned for full employment? Again, the answer lies in the basic premises of management. American corporations—like American institutions in general—are imbued with the devil's proposition: If the ideal can't be achieved, it is better not to try at all. That is, if a proposed legal reform won't eliminate the problem of crime completely, it is better rejected. If a proposed school reform won't solve all the problems of education, it is better to stick with what we have. And if we cannot achieve *complete* job security, it is better not to do anything about the issue at all. Certainly that has been the reasoning in Detroit. I suggest that if the Big Three had altered their assumptions about the necessity for layoffs, they might have reduced unemployment in the auto industry by as much as 50 percent during the miserable on-again, off-again 1973–83 decade. But their reasoning went that, since lifetime security was impractical, *any* effort to reduce layoffs was impractical.

In contrast, when managers are truly committed to full-employment strategies, the idea tends to become more practical: Abbott, Data General, DEC, Delta, Eli Lilly, Hallmark, Hewlett-Packard, IBM, Upjohn, and Wrigley are ten large U.S. corporations that have found it possible to completely avoid layoffs. In a recent study of two dozen such "full employment" companies, Fred Foulkes discovered that they all use imaginative corporate strategies to buffer themselves against the kinds of abrupt environmental changes that would compel layoffs. For example, HP regulates their environment by limiting the number of governmental contracts they will accept (when Uncle Sam cancels a contract, there is a kind of finality that throws people out in the street). Lincoln Electric moderates fluctuation in demand for their products by striving to be the low-cost producer—hence, gaining some of the benefits of market regularity enjoyed by monopolists. Almost all full-employment companies carry very little debt, since the absence of debt gives a corporation tremendous flexibility in planning for full employment. The inescapable conclusion to Foulkes's study is that where there is a will, there is a way.

A related assumption—equally unsupportable—has been that manufacturing jobs must flow to the source of cheapest labor. If labor is cheaper in Taiwan, then televisions must be made there. If labor is cheaper in Hong Kong, then garments must be made there. This premise rules economic thinking in America. One can see the effects of the idea on the behavior of managers: In the 1970s, General Electric added 5,000 jobs to their payroll. But they did so by creating 30,000 jobs abroad and *eliminating* 25,000 here. A sound strategy in the eyes of GE, perhaps, but is it sound for GE's American workers, or for the U.S. economy as a whole? Let us examine the premise a little closer. GE (and, indeed, most of the U.S. electronics industry) has moved production of many consumer products abroad, claiming that these cannot be made here economically. Ironically, when the Japanese moved production of these same products to the United States, they have been able to outstrip the runaway U.S. producers while using American labor! Robert Reich and others who have studied the issue claim that no American manufacturer has been able to defeat concerted foreign competition by manufacturing products abroad for the domestic market.

The Vanguard operate under a different premise. Motorola, Levi Strauss, and Honeywell believe in manufacturing products in the countries in which they will be sold. Levi makes their jeans in some eleven countries, but almost all the jeans that are sold in America are made in America. Nearly all U.S. corporations could do the same. But if they start with the premise that "it can't be done," it is as clear as night follows day that it can't and won't. Instead, if one starts with the premise that "it can be done," human ingenuity will usually find a way. As Olga's Erteszek says, "If you start with the premise of planning for full employment, then everything you do as a corporation will be subtly different."

Career-Long Training

The Vanguard place training extremely high on their agendas. At Control Data, training is the company's number-one priority. Motorola, Honeywell, Levi Strauss, and Dayton-Hudson are also labor-intensive businesses in which, because human capital is the source of all productivity gains, the constant renewal of employee skills receives the attention of all corporate managers at all levels (and not just the time and effort of human resources specialists). As one Motorola manager explained to me:

> The steel industry got into trouble because they let their equipment become obsolete. In high technology, brainpower becomes obsolete faster than equipment. That's why we are committed to continually retraining everyone to keep up with change.

The Vanguard back their commitment to training with dollars. At Levi, a significant part of the annual merit evaluation of managers is based on how well they train people. The typical manager is expected to cross-train at least two people per year and to take responsibility for mentoring one younger person. The company even creates "training jobs"—lateral "promotions" for managers in which they may broaden their skills while waiting for the opportunity for a true, vertical promotion.

Even capital-intensive Atlantic Richfield takes training seriously. Over the last five years Arco has brought all of the company's upper-middle-level managers to their elegant training facility at Santa Barbara on the California coast. During a two-week session of intensive discussions, Arco managers learn about the company in seminars led by other Arco managers and about general business problems affecting Arco in seminars led by outside consultants. The corporation spends about $1.5 million a year on this program (and on its follow-up one week "graduate course"). The purposes of the Arco seminars are twofold: First, to prepare people who have been educated as specialists (often people with narrow, technical backgrounds in engineering, geophysics, chemistry, and metallurgy) for broader management responsibility; second, to enculturate Arco's future leaders with the company's unique values. Important, to enculturate does not mean to indoctrinate. There is a significant and subtle difference that is honored at Arco between coercive learning on the one hand and voluntary socialization on the other. At the Santa Barbara seminars, Arco people learn to openly debate issues. They discuss cases that concern past incidents in which Arco clearly fouled up. The purpose of these case discussions is *not* to come up with the "right" answer. Rather, it is to teach Arco managers to anticipate consequences, to look for creative alternatives, and to apply ethical principles in dealing with difficult matters. One could profitably contrast this with what reportedly has gone on at IBM's Sands Point Management Training Center. According to MIT's Edgar Schein, IBM managers have been given a case and then graded on how close they came to "the IBM solution." Their grades were subsequently sent back to their supervisors. This is more a process of intimidation than a process of voluntary enculturation.

Practically speaking, not all corporate values can be voluntary. One that must be shared by all employees, particularly in a service industry, is customer service. American employees, imbued as they are with a philosophy of a class-free society, are frustratingly resistant to the idea of serving *anyone*. This means that bank tellers, salesclerks, receptionists, hashers in hamburger joints, and all the other proud Americans who will "serve no master" need a little introduction to the need for a service ethic. Since they can't be successfully indoctrinated, they must be shown why they must serve customers with a smile, why they must be helpful, and what the economic consequences of sloppy service are. In addition, they can also be encouraged to find ways to serve customers more effectively (and be rewarded for doing so). This requires lengthy and well-designed training. But, ironically, the best training is in manufacturing where jobs are relatively easy to learn. In service industries, young kids are commonly released on defenseless customers in hotels, restaurants, and stores with only the most cursory preparation.

An exception is Peter Burwash, International, the innovative king of resort tennis. This small company may well be a forerunner of a class of entirely new service organizations. For starters, each employee undergoes a full month of training. At the end of that time, he or she is prepared to be the manager of his or her own little business. To prevent the burnout that comes from constant attention to carping customers, once a month each Burwash tennis pro acts as a customer in another Burwash program.

In addition, to get everyone enculturated to the idea of service—to make it second nature—Burwashers practice "lateral service." This means that they practice serving each other with the same quality they serve the public (at a minimum, this puts an end to schizophrenic behavior). The company is a true learning organization in which all employees are encouraged to come up with new and better ways to service customers. New ideas are treated as opportunities for employees to expand their authority. The corporate response to all their ideas is invariably: "Great! Go do something about it."

The issue is different at Honeywell where hardheaded scientists often have problems dealing with soft, human, and vague strategic questions. James Renier, Honeywell's president, argues that the company's electrical engineers, solid-state physicists, and computer scientists often get into trouble when messy human values "contaminate" their ordered and quantitative worlds. Here's how Renier describes this process:

A typical example is a young man who graduated from a good school with good grades in electrical engineering . . . Six months into the job, he gets the idea that things are not quite what he had expected. He finds he is involved in a lot of stuff that is not really engineering. He is given assignments for which he sees little value. Something he calls "politics" is apparently a big force in decision making. People in marketing, who don't know a diode from a differential equation, seem to be calling all the shots . . . He did not know that in the real world you can't separate technology from human instincts, prejudices, and foibles. And these are much harder to grapple with than anything encountered in his technical training.

Renier, himself a physical chemist, has been responsible for creating a unique course to help technical people to develop their potential and to gain understanding of human issues in the workplace. The eight-day course includes subject matter that deals with communication, counseling, coaching, motivation, and group processes. Some 250 Honeywell engineers go through the program annually.

Like Motorola, Honeywell is engaged in the process of moving up the technological ladder to higher levels of sophistication. This requires not only better training in human relations and management but, obviously, continuing technical training as well. Honeywell now offers all their employees a full range of courses, balancing both the technical and human sides of the business. They have a catalogue of training programs that reads like the bulletin of a good-sized private college. Unlike many companies that treat training as fluff or a nice employee perk, Honeywell does not view training as separable from their basic business concerns. For example, at the company's Aerospace and Defense Group Training Center, the director, Tom Brown, sits down twice a year with the operating divisional managers and they jointly design a curriculum that meets the strategic concerns of the business. Watching this process over a period of three years, I was fascinated to find that these bottom-line-oriented managers continually told Brown that the greatest payoff comes from courses that teach supervisors and managers how to treat employees as stakeholders. Balance between technical and human factors is thus a secret to Brown's highly successful training center. Another secret is creativity. Brown continually invents new ways to deliver his products and to make learning a part of the daily routine of Honeywell managers. One of his most original ideas is *Newstapes*. Modeled after the format of National Public Radio's "All Things Considered," Brown's *Newstapes* deal with a smorgasbord of managerial and scientific news, including interviews with famous management gurus and with Honeywell managers who have introduced innovative programs that are worth disseminating. Each month, Brown prepares a professional-quality, one-hour tape and sends copies to the 300 top managers in the company (who accept the tape with the understanding that, once they have listened to it, they will pass it on to a subordinate who will, in turn, pass it on to another subordinate —and so on down line, until thousands of Honeywellers have been reached on freeways from Minneapolis to California by new ideas worth considering).

Honeywell is, of course, one of the nation's major manufacturers of computers—and computer technology is utilized in every aspect of their business from aerospace to space heating. Therefore, "computer literacy" has a special meaning at Honeywell, so special that the company decided that it would be best if *every* employee (executives, salespeople, secretaries, production workers) were to be familiar with the marvelous new technology that was becoming the core of all their businesses. To this end, Honeywell arranged with computer dealers for an attractive discount on computers for all Honeywell workers. The company then offered interest-free loans to make the purchase of a computer possible for every Honeyweller who wanted one. What is most remarkable is that Honeywell themselves do *not* make a home-type personal computer. So intent is Honeywell to have their people learn about computers that they are willing to subsidize the purchase of the products of other computer companies—some of whom are competitors in Honeywell's computer lines. Honeywell is a true learning organization.

Control Data is, if it is possible, even more serious about training than Honeywell. So serious, in fact, that Control Data went into the training business themselves some ten years ago. CDC have developed training programs for their employees that they then turned around and sold to other companies, and they have developed training programs for sale to others that they then turned around and made available to their own employees. At Control Data, training is not something that occurs off the job, in a classroom, or after hours—it is *integrated* into every one of the 60,000 CDC jobs around the world. The chief vehicle for delivery of training programs is PLATO—the teaching machine that provides flexible, individualized, computer-based instruction. You can't study poetry, ethics, or philosophy (or learn the kinds of things that are in this book) on PLATO—but any subject that can be learned by drill can be taught on a PLATO terminal. You can learn accounting or mathematics or French or how to fly an airplane (American Airlines uses PLATO to train its pilots). Most important, PLATO can be used to retrain production workers to deal with such new technologies as computers and robots.

PLATO is at the center of a remarkable change in labor/management relations that is occurring at General Motors. In the past, whenever GM introduced new, laborsaving technologies, they would extrude the existing work force and bring in younger, better-educated, nonunion personnel to install, program, repair, and monitor the machines. The unionized workers were not seen as permanent stakeholders in the firm, so why not get rid of them? In the past, the UAW would therefore resist the introduction of new technology, afraid that the new machines would take away their members' jobs. But recently, the UAW negotiated a contract with General Motors that sets aside ten cents per hour from each paycheck for training. Increasingly, blue-collar workers—many of whom haven't seen the inside of a classroom for twenty to thirty years—are being retrained to operate electronic robots and other high-tech equipment. In 1983, General Motors retrained about 2,000 of its manual workers at a Fisher body plant using computer-assisted, *individualized* learning. In 1984, a massive retraining program was a central provision of the UAW-GM contract that broke with the tradition of adversarial labor relations in the auto industry. Ironically, it took the nonhuman technology of CDC's PLATO computers to transform GM's workers into stakeholders!

Flexible Benefits

One of the most prevalent of unexamined managerial assumptions about workers has been that they *are all the same*. The result has been a monolithic design of jobs, a singular career path, and a uniformity of benefits and working conditions within most large corporations. Clearly, such sameness is easier to manage than diversity, so this system has had the not-inconsequential secondary benefit of making the jobs of managers easier.

The Vanguard start with a different propositon: They assume that workers are all different—that each individual has unique aspirations, wants, needs, and, moreover, that these change during the course of each person's life and career. Starting from that premise, the Vanguard attempt, as far as possible, to offer workers a diversity of tasks—each requiring different levels of skill, ability, effort, creativity, and length of time for completion—and a concomitant spectrum of rewards and incentives. Then, the Vanguard make it possible (through such techniques as job posting) for workers themselves to select jobs that meet their individual needs. In addition, to meet the many and varied types of family responsibilities workers have, the Vanguard allow employees to tailor their own working conditions and career paths as far as this is practical.

Control Data's PLATO is a quintessential example of a system that provides such diversity, choice, and flexibility to workers. Working at individual terminals, each worker begins at her own level of knowledge as determined by pretesting. From that point, a student studies at his own pace, taking only courses that he or she needs. CDC has another program, called HOMEWORK, that allows employees with long-term disabilities to be financially independent by working at home on a computer terminal (or to be retrained at home). For workers who simply desire the benefits of reduced travel or flexible working hours, CDC offers WORKSTA-TION, an alternative work site program that enables people to work at home or at a satellite location. Recognizing that the quality of one's work life is related to the quality of one's personal life, CDC has created the Employee Advisory Resource, or EAR. This twenty-four-hour telephone hot line has proved so success-ful that it is now used by over 40,000 workers at 125 organiza-tions in Minnesota. Workers suffering from emotional difficulties, from marital discord, from trouble with co-workers, and from disputes over company policy can call at any time and get infor-mation or help.

Control Data argues that these—and other related individual-ized employee benefits—have had a tremendous impact on the company's performance. Between 1977 and 1982, Control Data's employee turnover rate declined by some 13 percent, lateness dropped by 46 percent, sick leave was down by 16 percent, and productivity (based on revenue per employee) rose by 46 per-cent.

Control Data's boldest departure from traditional, individual-ized management practices occurred in 1968 at a company bind-ery in a depressed, minority section of St. Paul. There, the com-pany pioneered an innovative job-sharing system for some 250 part-time workers in which two traditionally hard-to-employ groups—young mothers and teenagers—were given fruitful em-ployment. The mothers work from 9 A.M. to 3 P.M. while their young children are in school, and the teenagers work the second shift, after school, from 3 P.M. to 6 P.M. While the bindery is nonautomated, it is as profitable and productive as automated binderies in the area. So successful was this experiment that CDC has since built several other inner-city plants.

Part-time employment is one of the fastest growing labor force trends in America and not just at CDC. Over 20 percent of American workers are part-timers, yet the number of part-time positions available still falls far short of meeting the growing demand for such jobs. But as good as part-time work is for many people, it is not, in itself, a panacea to the problems of job inflexi-bility. While part-time jobs clearly respond to the increasing de-sire of workers to spend more time in family, leisure, and recreational activities, they do *not* offer the kind of job security, career ladder, or fringe benefits associated with full-time work.

Dayton-Hudson is one of the few large corporations to squarely face the dilemma of part-time work. This is not, I hasten to add, because DH has always treated employees as stakeholders. The truth is nearly the opposite. Remember that the Vanguard are *not* perfect. Their excellence derives not from perfection but from their willingness to recognize and attempt to honestly address their *im*perfections. Only recently has DH come to accept full responsibility for their part-time employees. They were *forced* to do so by the fact that at least 50 percent of their workers (at B. Dalton, Mervyn's, Target, and the other DH chains) are now part-timers, and they forecast that figure to rise to 75 percent by 1990. DH simply could no longer hide from the consequences of demograpic change. And the change was not just in the hours their employees were working; it was, according to one DH executive

> . . . a change in the kinds of people we were hiring. These were smart, educated people. Many were single parents. They came to us because we had a reputation of serving the communities in which we were located, and because we offered flexible hours. We now know we are providing the jobs of the future, the jobs a growing minority want. The challenge is: "How can we make these jobs better?"

To find some answers to that question, the top management of Dayton-Hudson went on a two-day retreat at which they concluded three things: (1) Store managers will take advantage of part-timers if there aren't sufficient controls. Hence, a top executive in the company was charged with writing guidelines to protect part-timers from arbitrary managerial decisions; (2) Part-timers don't share in the overall spirit of the company. Hence, efforts were initiated to involve part-timers more fully in the company's most significant benefit of employment—philanthropic activities; and (3) Honesty is the best policy. Hence, the company prepared a ten-minute film introducing potential employees to the company in which *both* the pluses and minuses of part-time work were candidly examined. These are obviously only first steps, but they are more steps than other corporations have taken to deal with the important phenomenon of part-time work.

The essential benefit of part-time work is, of course, more time away from the job. Indeed, pay for not working was a central demand—and key problem—of work in the 1970s. Deere & Co. plowed fresh ground in this regard in their 1973 contract with the UAW. The agreement provided "bonus time off" for workers with good attendance (and for thirty-year workers who didn't want early retirement). For example, the company gave workers one half hour of paid time off for every forty hours of perfect attendance. In some respects, this was a marvelous benefit for those who were tired of assembling plows. Yet, what kind of signal does it send to workers about the meaning, importance, and economic utility of their jobs when they are paid *not* to work? (One could argue, I suppose, that it is no more counter-productive than the government paying farmers *not* to use Deere equipment to plant crops. But two sillies don't make a sense.)

Consider an alternative to the Deere/UAW approach: Levi's Community Involvement Teams are also an employee benefit in which people are paid for time not working. As described earlier, these teams are composed of employees who elect their own officers, identify the needs of their communities, and develop projects to meet those needs. Employees are given a small amount of paid time off to plan and to administer their projects. In effect, the release time from the tedium and stress of work is applied to *useful* ends. The same principle is found in Xerox's sabbatical program for workers who wish to spend a year doing public service. The programs differ, however, in that only a minuscule percentage of Xerox workers take part in this program compared to the thousands of Levi employees who are members of the CITs. This is not to say that greater participation makes the Levi program necessarily better than Xerox's (in fact, employees at Xerox who have *not* participated in the public service leave program also consider it an important psychological benefit, finding comfort in knowing the *option* is there if they should ever want to use it). The point is that time off is more justifiable economically and psychologically if it is put to useful ends.

Sabbaticals are great benefits for workers, but their main limitation is cost. Indeed, there is nothing more costly than to pay an employee not to work. There are basically three justifications for doing so. First, to help people recover from stress or to head off burnout. To this end, the most innovative approach I have heard of is found at Chapparal Steel. Robert Townsend offers an intriguing description of how the system works. Instead of offering sabbaticals to top managers—who can run off to unwind and refresh themselves at some sunny spa—Chapparal addresses the stress problems of *first-line supervisors*. Townsend writes of Chapparal's approach to foremen burnout (in which supervisors pass on their boredom to their workers) that:

> One way to beat this is to have five foremen for every four turns. By rotation, one foreman is available each thirty days to work on projects with the general foreman, superintendent, or even top management. This is a sort of working sabbatical. When he goes back to his turn, his filter is backwashed and he passes his enthusiasm along to his people.

The second rationale for sabbaticals is to enhance the personal development of workers. Since 1977, the Wells Fargo Bank in San Francisco has offered three-month "personal growth sabbaticals" to employees who have been with the company for at least fifteen years. While on sabbatical, Wells Fargo employees receive full pay, earn vacation time, and retain their fringe benefits. The third rationale for sabbaticals is to retain skilled workers. Tandem Computers offers six-week sabbaticals every four years. Keeping people as long as four years in the highly competitive Silicon Valley labor market is a real accomplishment (half of Tandem's employees have been with the company less than six months). The sabbatical trend in Northern California was started ten years ago by another Silicon Valley company, Rolm, which offers leaves to employees who have six years of service. At Rolm—at least at the time they were acquired by IBM—full-time employees have the option of twelve weeks' leave at full pay or six weeks at *double pay* (even part-timers are eligible—they get pro-rated sabbaticals—something that DH might consider).

Such programs are incredibly costly. Indeed, on every benefit from coffee breaks to pensions, employers are spending more than ever before. In 1983, employers spent about $480 billion, up from $390 billion in 1979, according to the U.S. Chamber of Commerce. During the 1970s, the cost of total benefits, on the average, went from $39 per employee per week to $117 (a 197 percent increase over the decade; in comparison, average weekly earnings rose at a slower 123 percent clip). Significantly, fringe benefits appear to have risen *faster* in the Old Guard than in the Vanguard. If it is benefits you want, go to work for Mobil, IBM, Du Pont, or, especially, Kodak. Here's a smattering of what Kodak offers employees:

Supplementary Group Life Insurance Plan
Savings and Investment Plan
Retirement Income Plan
Medical Assistance Plan
Occupational Death Insurance
Basic Health Care Plan
Dental Assistance Plan
Extended Health Care Plan
Family Protection Plan
Long-Term Disability Insurance
Group Life and Survivor Insurance Plans
Holiday and Vacation Allowance Plans
Eye Examinations
Square Dancing Lessons
Ice Fishing
Table Tennis Tournaments

In addition, some 34,000 Kodak employees (and 5,200 retirees) are members of the company's Kodak Camera Clubs, which provide free use of darkrooms, free use of equipment, and a discount on film. About the same number of employees and retirees belong to the Kodak Park Activities Association that sponsors sport and entertainment activities and offers discount vacations. In Kodak's hometown, Rochester, N.Y., there is a 300,000-square-foot building with a cinema (offering first-run movies at lunch) and a bowling alley. There is also a company store, a company savings and loan, and eleven softball fields. Why does Kodak do all of this? A candid Kodak executive told *Business Week:* "If we didn't, people might quit." That, and "keeping up with the competition," are the primary premises upon which most corporate benefit programs are based.

The Vanguard start with three different assumptions: (1) Benefits should reflect the core values of the corporation (that's why Levi Strauss came up with their Community Involvement

Teams); (2) employees should have the freedom to choose among an array of benefits to get the mix that is right for themselves (Herman Miller pays the same amount in adoption costs for employees as the company's insurance plan pays for natural births; Honeywell has introduced "cafeteria benefits" in which workers can pick and choose, trading vacation days for orthodontia or whatever benefit meets family and individual needs); and (3) the system must be based on participation rather than paternalism. Clearly, Kodak offers a package of benefits that would knock the sandals off the typical worker in Osaka, but that isn't enough. Paternalism is no longer working in America. The Japanese way of golden handcuffs, company stores, company songs, and cradle-to-grave uniform social benefits has failed to inspire in Kodak employees the motivation and creativity needed to meet increasing competition and changing technology. While Kodak smothers employees in the benefits of corporate socialism, they do not treat them as individuals, they do not trust them to choose what benefits are right for themselves, and, most important, there is no participation in any significant decisions that affect the work life of Kodak employees. That last fact is the primary reason why nearly great Kodak, IBM, and J&J are not among the Vanguard.

Participation

Like many corporations, Minneapolis's Norwest Bank was recently faced with a gap between managerial expectations and corporate performance. Top management would announce a new policy and then wait in vain for it to be carried out; in turn, tellers and lower-level managers had little idea what top management expected of them. Into this communications void strode Douglas Wallace, an ordained Protestant minister who had the good fortune of having had neither a formal business education nor actual business experience in which to pick up Old Guard assumptions. Nonetheless, from his experience developing young leaders at the YMCA at the University of Minnesota, he had formed a couple of his own ideas about people in organizations. First, he felt that in any organization a little participation in decision making was better than none, and that a lot of participation was better than a little. The second thing he believed was that you can't start off with a lot of participation—that is impractical in a large organization. But he had a theory that allowed him to bridge his two beliefs, to wit: "Five percent of the people in an organization, if they work in a concerted way, can affect the culture of the entire system." Hence, if he could build a habit of participation in a few, he felt it would spread to the many.

In 1978, Wallace was given a chance to test his theory at Norwest when he was appointed vice president for social policy. Now, that is not exactly a powerhouse position from which one could be expected to leverage cultural change—but it was plenty for Wallace. He sold the bank's top management on a program that would involve Norwest employees in formulating policy on social issues affecting the bank. Specifically, he won the commitment of top management to form a task force composed of sixteen employees, representing a cross-section of bank functions and levels. He promised that the team would produce a report on the first topic chosen—the role of the bank in revitalizing older neighborhoods—within a year. Top management agreed to receive the report from the task force in a face-to-face meeting, to take it home to read it, and then to meet with the task force again within a month to discuss their response to the report. During the year, the task force met weekly. They interviewed as many other bank employees as possible and brought in outside experts to "testify" before the task force. Meeting half on bank time and half on their own time, the task force produced its first report as promised. Top management met with the task force, read the report, and met with the task force again—all as promised. The surprise came when top management then put into place almost all the major policies recommended by the task force. In subsequent years, using a different task force each time, Wallace's teams have produced reports in a variety of areas of future concern to the bank.

These issues have included "Individual rights in the corporation," "Protection of privacy of the bank's constituents," and "Work and the family." The bank's top management has found that "employees are a rich source of information and insight on social issues." But, more important, they have found that opening up the communication channels in the bank has led to improvement in the bank's overall performance in their most critical area: customer service. As employees started to participate in managerial decisions, they came to identify with the needs and goals of top management—they came to understand why and how to better carry out the company's mission. In turn, top management learned from their employees about aspects of the bank's culture that needed to be changed if the company were to grow and thrive in an era of increasing bank competition. Wallace's five percent theory is being validated in snowy downtown Minneapolis.

Significantly, Norwest's compensation and benefit plans are paltry in comparison with Kodak's. But, for most Americans, being treated as an adult is preferable to the most generous paternalism. Kodak's culture creates a sense of destructive psychological dependency—as surely as welfare does the same to inner-city families. Consequently, most Americans would choose participation over paternalism. That is not to say that some would not choose paternalism (after all, hundreds of thousands of Americans volunteer to serve in that most "socialistic" of all U.S. organizations—the military) but rather that the vast majority wouldn't, and those who would are unlikely to be the most energetic, innovative, or productive workers.

Ideally, of course, workers should not have to choose between generous benefits and participation. That's where the Vanguard come in. Leaving the Norwest Bank and crossing Minneapolis in the direction of the airport, one arrives at suburban Bloomington, where Control Data has successfully implemented a form of participation that parallels and complements their excellent benefit program. If a CDC employee finds himself or herself in conflict with a supervisor or with corporate policy, he or she can appeal to a corporate ombudsman. This independent individual will then draw together a "peer panel" composed of a random cross-section of CDC employees. The panel is empowered to make recommendations *directly* to top management for the resolution of the conflict (or, for a change in policy). Interestingly, since establishing this recourse to justice and equity, CDC has seen a reduction in the very conflict that had made it necessary to create the ombudsman. The institutionalizing of this process apparently encourages people to find ways to resolve conflict at the locus of the problem.

Participation came to a third Minneapolis company, Honeywell, when surveys showed that employees felt the company was too authoritarian. James Renier, then a division president, felt that this was a problem because the company had, as we have seen, recently set for itself the demanding goal of moving into areas of higher technology. Renier could not see how this could be accomplished without full employee support and effort. Renier then called for "Democracy of the Workplace" at Honeywell:

> When I say Democracy of the Workplace, I don't mean voting on who will be boss, or what products will be manufactured. I simply mean the establishment of a climate and work rules that respect the dignity and ability that people are assumed to have, according to the democratic principles that Americans claim to hold sacred . . . We have a history of defending these principles. We have made them work in this country. They have brought us the respect and, in some cases, the envy of the other countries of the world. But too often, here in our own country, the ideals of democracy have stopped at the factory gate.

To achieve the changes he sought, Renier argued that Honeywell managers should discard their old assumptions about workers and accept the following four new ones:

1. People want to do a good job.
2. Each employee knows how to do his or her own job better than anyone else.
3. Employees deserve to be recognized as intelligent, responsible people who can contribute to decisions that affect their work.
4. People need information so that they can better understand the goals and problems of the organization and make informed decisions.

Renier's "conversion" to workplace democracy was not immediately followed by a flood of other Honeywell managers anxious to take the baptism of participation. As we will see in a later chapter, it took Renier nearly ten years to win over the majority of his peers. But inside Honeywell today one finds examples of top managers putting programs in place that are based on Renier's four assumptions. One of the first Honeywell converts to participation was Warde Wheaton, head of Honeywell's Aerospace and Defense Group. He took seriously the notion of sharing information with employees and, since 1981, has been publishing an *Employee Annual Report* that tells what products the company makes, how much money they make on those products, where the profit comes from, and where it goes. There are chapters describing company breakthroughs in innovation and productivity, major business opportunities and threats, and human resource plans.

But the primary mode of participation at Honeywell is quality circles. Honeywell created its first quality circle in 1974, and circles have since spread gradually throughout the company, to where there were some one thousand in place in 1984. Honeywellers have a quiet stick-to-itiveness that keeps them committed to making a good idea work long after other companies will have abandoned similar efforts out of boredom or frustration. And there have been plenty of good reasons at Honeywell to justify abandoning quality circles. Like everywhere else quality circles have been tried, their record at Honeywell has been mixed. There are examples of fabulously successful circles: workers finding ways to reduce the cost of circuit panel boards from $55 to $21; workers instituting their own quality standards and reducing the rejection rate of a product from 65 percent to 15 percent; workers voluntarily enrolling in school to prepare themselves for the introduction of the next generation of technology; and workers developing several new methods for wiring aircraft instrument panels, then deciding for themselves which was most efficient, applying it to the job, and ultimately reducing the time needed to prepare a panel from thirty hours to less than fifteen. There are also examples of quality circles that never meet, those that do meet but bicker, and those that can never decide what they should be doing or why.

Honeywell knows why some of their circles succeed. Success stories are almost all due, in large, to the active training of supervisors and middle managers who are taught to act as "expert consultants" to workers, *not* as directive authoritarians. In the words of Renier, "If 25,000 workers decide they are going to do something productive, the role of managers is to get out of the way."

The dysfunction found in many Honeywell circles seems attributable to the absence of profit- or gain-sharing. When workers at Honeywell develop ideas that reduce costs or increase productivity, they do not share directly in the fruits of their efforts (as they would at Motorola or any company with a Scanlon plan). As good as Honeywell's top managers are, they nonetheless have had a blind spot on the subject of gain-sharing that has kept a fairly successful ten-year effort to increase participation in decision making from bearing full fruit. Their blind spot is an ideological *idée fixe*, a basic premise about what is right and wrong, that neither facts nor reason could budge for years. Finally, however, after years of badgering by staff people, Honeywell's top managers reluctantly authorized two "experiments" with gain-sharing in 1983 and committed themselves to the broad dissemination of the practice if the experiments prove successful.

As this incident illustrates, Honeywell's quality circles have had an impact on the culture of the corporation that has spread far beyond the factory floor. As workers have gotten into the habit of participation, they have put pressure on higher levels of management for deeper, organization-wide changes. Workers have identified roadblocks to productivity that extend beyond the scope of their little circles. They have sent messages up the organization that the basic productivity roadblocks have to do with company pay and promotions policies, product strategy, and a host of other top management concerns. Over the last few years, in response to change at the bottom, Honeywell's top management has had to engage themselves in a process of overall organizational renewal—thus offering another demonstration of Douglas Wallace's theory that a small number of people can, indeed, change the culture of an entire organization.

To the credit of Honeywell's CEO, Edson Spencer, and President James Renier, they have responded positively in most cases to the upward pressures for change. In contrast, most Old Guard managers put up real resistance to forces for change that come bubbling up to the executive suite from the basement. For example, on two occasions when General Motors' quality circles at Tarrytown, New York, started to become productively self-managing, the reaction on the part of top management was to limit the scope of authority of the circles by confining participation only to those factors completely under the control of the group. Even when it was shown that the technologically out-of-date Tarrytown operation could be made competitive through employee involvement, GM managers retreated out of fear of losing their authority. While GM wanted the additional productivity and commitment of workers, they did *not* want them to share in the rights and responsibilities of management. This was demonstrated most clearly in 1978 when GM opened a new plant in

Oklahoma City. This nonunion, highly automated plant was to be the place where GM showed the world they had the stuff to outperform the Japanese. One of the first things GM did was to divide the Oklahoma City work force into small teams. But, instead of giving the teams the rights and responsibilities of self-management, GM told the workers that the only authority they had was to police their own attendance. It came as a surprise to no one but GM's managers when the workers balked at this inauthentic participation and proceeded to vote in the UAW.

Getting just the right balance between rights and responsibilities is no mean task. While the lack of trust on the part of GM's managers led them to give workers insufficient rights, Polaroid erred on the other side by creating a system in which workers had too many rights and too few responsibilities. It has been forgotten by many chroniclers of worker participation that Polaroid was the first large corporation to treat workers as stakeholders. In the 1960s, Polaroid's practices rivaled those of Olga, Lincoln, and Herman Miller and exceeded even today's performance of the Vanguard. One illustration of how Polaroid's brilliant lead in worker participation was bungled and squandered is the sad tale of the company's employee committee. Some thirty years ago, Edwin Land decided that the company should have an elected board of employee representatives that would advise top management about the concerns of the work force. Anticipating the two-tier boards that would soon develop in Europe, this idea was pathbreaking and clearly responsive to the need for worker participation. But Land was always better at creating managerial ideas than at carrying them out. Instead of making the committee truly a worker's panel, he freed the thirty-six elected workers from their jobs, making them into full-time professional "legislators." Eventually, they lost touch with their constituents and, like all good politicians, turned their greatest energies to the task of being reelected. Moreover, because the employee committee had no formal powers, the only way a representative could influence policy (and impress the electorate) was to gripe as loudly as possible and to take an obstructionist position against every management initiative. Soon, the employee committee became as irresponsible, irascible, and as posturing as any university faculty senate.

Polaroid's permissiveness undercut a rare opportunity for meaningful participation. If the members of the employee committee had simply been sent back to work (at least part-time), had their terms of office been limited (to prevent reelections), and had the powers of the committee been formalized in a constitutional process, Polaroid might still be the nation's leader in treating employees as stakeholders. This is not to generally condemn Polaroid's treatment of workers (at their worst, Polaroid is a better place to work than GM at their best), but to suggest how difficult it is to strike a creative balance between rights and responsibilities—even with the best of intentions. Johnson & Johnson is another example of a very good company that can't quite get the hang of appropriately treating employees as stakeholders. In their credo, J&J has all the ingredients of balance and symmetry, but in practice there is little meaningful worker participation. Some companies are thus like those countries that have wonderful constitutions and all the structural trappings of just government—except for the actual day-to-day practice of democratic pluralism.

I suggest that the missing ingredient in such companies is basically an ethical blind spot. Even the Vanguard have difficulties from time to time in making clear distinctions between what they say they do and what they actually do. Ultimately, commitment to balancing worker rights and responsibilities requires the explicit exercise of moral judgment. When I asked Walter A. Haas, Jr. (Robert's father, who headed Levi Strauss when the company's Community Involvement Teams were instituted) what the rationale was for forming the teams, he said, "It was simply the right thing to do." When I asked Jan Erteszek why he believed that every one of his "associates" had a right to share in Olga Company's profits and ownership, he answered: "Because it is the morally right thing to do." And when Honeywell's Renier was asked why he stayed with the goal of participation through ten years of less-than-enthusiastic support from his fellow managers, he replied:

> If we help people develop into the best they can become, and if we enable people to make their maximum contribution on the job, we will get the innovation and productivity we seek. But I suggest to you that even if it did *not* get more productivity, or make the company more secure, or improve profits, it would *still* be worth doing. It would be worth doing simply because it is the right thing to do.

The ethical nature of the issue is brought to light explicitly in a Norwest Bank document that contains two columns, "What employees can expect from the company" and "What Norwest expects from its employees." Rights are in one column, responsibilities in the other. Hewlett-Packard's constitution, "The HP Way," puts the company on record that workers and managers share the responsibilities for defining and meeting company goals, share responsibilities for personal and career development, and share responsibilities for shouldering the burden during economic downturns (through reduced workweeks, reduced salaries, and so forth). At the same time, both parties share in the rights of stock ownership, profits, and job security.

As Honeywell's Renier puts it, "When the going gets tough there is, perhaps, a temptation to forget the ethical side of operations—but, in so doing, we forget the foundations of success." In 1983, Renier visited with the top management of another Vanguard corporation, Atlantic Richfield, and discussed Honeywell's decade-long experience with worker participation:

> Since the early 1960s, we have heard that workers are different today—they care only about themselves, they have no real interest in their jobs, they are not concerned about the company. But I think we are beginning to understand today that people do *indeed* care, that they want to be successful, and they want to achieve company objectives when they are parallel with their own job objectives. I think we have learned that we should worry a little less about the Work Ethic in America and think a little more about our companies' employment ethics.

> The challenge is to pick up the ethics of democracy, dust them off, breathe new life into them, and install them in the workplace. Think of it as an ethical undertaking. That will insure that programs like quality circles, participative management, and quality of work life help our people achieve their objectives and do not degenerate to mere manipulation.

Individual Freedom

As Renier suggests, treating employees as stakeholders can easily degenerate into paternalism, even manipulation. True participation is the only known antidote to paternalism. It is therefore not an insignificant fact that IBM has probably done the *least* of all major U.S. manufacturers to implement genuine worker participation. Even GM was experimenting with work teams and quality circles as early as 1971. But not Big Blue. IBM has never been able to find a way to reconcile real participation with their cherished paternalism. And they won't find it. Participation is simply so inconsistent with IBM's need for employee conformity that the two values would come into conflict, and one would have to go. As we see at Honeywell, genuine participation shakes a corporation to its roots, ultimately causing a complete change in culture. That is too much of a risk for IBM to run while they are comfortably ensconced at the top of every financial analyst's list of excellent companies. Change at IBM must thus await some sign of failure.

To be fair, paternalism is a seductive condition. There is nothing quite like the comfort of the corporate womb, whether at IBM or the U.S. Army. Paternalism can even be clothed in the glamorous values of the new left. For example, Tandem Computers has evolved a "Marin County" culture. There are classes in yoga, modern dance, and oriental philosophy, and lots of the other good things of California life. As one who personally likes hot tubs, white wine, quiche, and jogging, who am I to knock these values? But what about those poor, benighted souls who aren't into the touchie-feelie, let-it-all-hang-out Aquarian culture? What happens to the Tandem employee who likes to take his modest pleasures in private with his family over roast beef and milk, and not in the hot tub drinking *Glugg* with a dozen scantily clad co-workers?

Defenders of companies like IBM and Tandem argue that it is not paternalism that is at play, but the provision of a strong sense of "community." It is argued that workers find a total community in which all their social and economic needs are addressed a welcome alternative to the condition of "alienation" in modern society. While this does seem to be the case for some people, one of the prime lessons of anthropology is that people in "total communities" find them stultifying and that as soon as there is an option for freedom in the big city, most people will take it. This is a difficult issue. Personally, I long for a sense of community, but I wouldn't trust even myself with the power to force *my* sense of community on others.

The problem exists on the right, too. In that most American of all corporations, the professional football team, efforts to instill conformity also come a cropper. The Dallas Cowboys—the IBM of the NFL—are imbued with a born-again Christian fire that manifests itself in prayer meetings and a prohibition on cussing. While their culture of conformity has had some undeniable success, it has also led to the ostracism of a few great players who didn't fit the Cowboy mold. It is significant to note that the team with the best long-term record in professional sports—the Oakland-cum-Los-Angeles Raiders—is noted primarily for picking up players with reputations for being individualistic at best (and malcontents at worst) and integrating them into the team by tolerating their eccentricities and need for freedom.

Fortunately, as the Raiders example illustrates, bureaucracy is not the only alternative to paternalism. In the corporate world, Borg-Warner is also attempting to find a middle ground. As Borg-Warner attempts to change their culture to create a "commonwealth" with their people, they have been careful to reject the temptation of IBM- and Tandem-like paternalism. Throughout the process of change, Borg-Warner's CEO has continually stressed respect for the dignity of the individual. He says there will be no "company-type" at Borg-Warner:

> We're not looking for a generation of corporate clones. We mean it when we say we value individuality, differences in thinking and style.

Indeed, the major shortcoming with the current fuss about "corporate culture" has been the wrongheaded insistence on creating a single, "right" culture within a company. But if one starts from the premise that all people are different, then this monolithic approach to culture is clearly inappropriate.

In light of this, one might say that the American system, as a whole, works well to meet the differing needs of individual workers, because it offers a spectrum of alternative corporate cultures. Since an individual who would feel comfortable at ITT probably wouldn't feel comfortable at Kodak, the American system leaves this individual free to choose between these employers (and many, many others). While our pluralistic, competitive system is clearly preferable to the monolithic Soviet or Japanese systems that offer little variety among the cultures of their various enterprises (and precious little opportunity for individuals to choose among them), our system isn't the only alternative, nor necessarily the best. For there are two serious limitations to our current system: First, the amount of choice people have among employers is, in fact, greatly limited by the constraints of unemployment and by limited information. Second, once one gets into a Tandem or an IBM, the worker has only a single choice (to conform or get out).

The Vanguard have a better idea. At the Vanguard, individuals are free to express their personal values (within the limits necessary for purposeful human cooperation). For example, at Arco one top manager is the head of the right-wing Libertarian party, while another top manager is a noted civil rights activist. While the first of these individuals probably wouldn't survive in the leftish totalitarianism of Silicon Valley, and the second probably wouldn't survive in the right-wing totalitarianism of Mobil (and neither would survive in IBM's faceless land-of-the-well-modulated-voice), no one at Arco seems to think twice about the activities of these two highly visible individuals—even when they sometimes make rather controversial public statements. At the Vanguard, such personal freedoms as how you dress, how you vote, and who you sleep with are held sacred.

Among other things, that makes the Vanguard good places to work for minorities, women, and all other groups who feel some sense of discrimination in American society (for example, at Levi Strauss, 33 percent of all executives and managers—and 51 percent of all professionals—are women, and 18 percent of all executives and managers—and 30 percent of all professionals—are members of minority groups). Although the very top decision makers in the company are still white males, Levi is addressing this issue with as much sincerity as any company of which I am aware.

Translating such sincerity into action is not always easy. For it often entails treating people differently, which goes against the grain of organizations in general. (Traditionally, sameness of treatment has been taken as a sign of fairness. Recall the television reporter who, in the early 1960s, asked a black player "How does [Green Bay Packer coach] Vince Lombardi treat Negroes?" "Like dirt." "Is he a racist?" "No man, he treats *everybody* like dirt.") Dayton-Hudson has been a leader in breaking with the Lombardi mode (which was, by the way, far fairer than the discriminating mode found on most sports teams of the era). For example, when DH's Karol Emmerich became the first high-level executive at the company to request a three-month maternity leave, the company signaled their support for her by promoting her to be corporate treasurer. Treating a manager *that differently* requires real sincerity.

Arco was one of the first heavy industrial corporations to voluntarily publish the numbers of women and minority workers employed at various levels of the company. In the beginning, this was a rather embarrassing undertaking, since the boxes at the top of the matrix were all filled with zeros. Clearly, the company had far to go. And top management knew it. In the early 1970s, they set rather ambitious affirmative action goals for themselves. This was not entirely unheard of in corporate life at the time—after all, the government was breathing down every corporate collar it got its hands on (and nothing generates virtue more surely than the threat of litigation). But it was out of the ordinary when Arco announced they would evaluate all managers annually on how well they recruited and promoted women and minorities. True to their promise, the company generously honored managers with the best affirmative action records with that noblest and most liquid of all rewards: cold cash.

Significantly, Arco has stuck with this effort, even when the breath of the feds turned tepid during the Reagan administration. In fact, women and minorities are starting to move up the steep managerial ladder. Granted, the numbers of those on the top rungs aren't all that impressive (unless you compare Arco's record to that of other heavy industrial concerns), but the company now has a woman officer (she's a senior vice president) and a woman director (in 1982, Hanna Gray, president of the University of Chicago was appointed to the board). No minorities have made it to the very top yet, but their numbers are growing in middle- and upper-middle management.

Nonetheless, Arco is under almost constant criticism by women and minority group members who are dissatisfied with the pace of affirmative action promotion. In defense of their record, Arco claims they are a meritocracy in which *all* people must prove themselves at each level before they will be promoted to the next. The company points out that most of the men at the top have spent their entire careers working their way up; blacks and women must now do the same. Arco says that it would be unfair and demoralizing to leapfrog blacks and women over qualified white men. Just be patient, they say, and in a few years one will see that the women and minorities who have recently entered the ranks of middle management will have moved up the hierarchy at the same pace as white men.

Merit schmerit, say the critics. White men always cite the danger of promoting "unqualified" blacks and women, as if all the men in the top ranks were superachievers, or even marginally qualified. The critics ask: Why is a marginally competent white male less a threat to the meritocracy and to corporate efficiency than a marginally qualified woman or black? The critics contend that meritocracy isn't working in the first place, or there wouldn't be those who are undeniably losers among the white males at the top. So why not just call off the sham, and promote a few women and minorities who are at least—if not more—qualified than some highly placed men?

And so the argument goes—with some truth on both sides—a conflict of values, perceptions, and personal interests. At Arco issues of equality are treated much as we treat them as a nation, with honest confusion and ambivalence. Significantly, this argument is very much in the open at Arco where nothing—it seems —gets swept under the rug.

And freedom of expression on corporate matters is equally cherished at Arco and the rest of the Vanguard. Freedom to express different ideas about corporate policies, practices, and strategies is not only protected, it is *nurtured*. The Vanguard see the differences among their employees not as a constraint, but as a source of innovation, change, and vitality. The Vanguard have learned that not only are differences of opinion among their employees a valuable resource, but that such useful differences will not flourish in a monolithic culture. Pursuing one set of values will simply stifle all those who have different values. That is why the Vanguard are organized to provide rewards for merit, incentives for efficiency, guarantees of security, and opportunities for personal growth. Whatever the employee is seeking from work, he can find it in such an environment; and whatever the employee can bring to the job, she will have the opportunity to share it in such an environment.

In summary, treating employees as stakeholders is not a case of doing something *for* the employee at the expense of the organization. Treating employees as stakeholders entails no costs to others. In fact, it is the other way around: As we see in this chapter, treating employees as stakeholders works to the benefit of customers, dealers, suppliers, local communities, and shareholders. Hence, there is no trade-off necessary between people and profits. In the following chapter we find an equally significant complementarity: Corporate profitability is in the long-run interest not only of owners but of *all* corporate constituencies.

5.

PROFITS AND THE ART OF CHINESE MANAGEMENT

One doesn't set out just to make money.
The thing is to do something right
and one hopes to do well out of that.
—LORD WEINSTOCK,
CEO of General Electric of Great Britain

The "J&J Credo," Johnson & Johnson's famous corporate constitution discussed in Chapter Two, lists the company's responsibilities to their five prime constituencies: (1) customers, (2) employees, (3) J&J's managers themselves, (4) local communities, and (5) shareholders. Periodically, J&J managers convene to discuss the meaning and significance of the credo. Importantly, these exercises are something more than ritual incantations of the corporate litany. One of the greatest strengths of J&J's CEO, James Burke, is his enthusiastic encouragement of managers who dare to challenge the received wisdom. Burke's commitment to the credo does not preclude entertaining motions for revisions of, or amendments to, the revered document. To demonstrate that he didn't bring the credo down from Mt. Sinai on stone tablets, Burke has videotaped for general corporate distribution debates about the relevance and usefulness of the credo, tapes in which top J&J managers are shown being more than a bit iconoclastic. In one of these tapes, a skeptical executive can be seen reviewing the company's list of responsibilities, and then challenging Burke that J&J, in practice, may give highest priority to shareholder obligations:

It's like juggling five balls. Four of them are white, the fifth one is bright red. I know I'd better not drop that red one. But can I fumble the others? I don't know for sure.

The Red Ball

The importance of that red ball—profit—and its relationship to the other balls managers attempt to adroitly juggle should be central to any serious discussion of the art of management. To discuss corporate excellence without examining the role of profit in a firm is tantamount to discussing the quality of autos without making reference to their engines. Clearly the role of profit is controversial—and that is why most recent popular accounts of managerial practices have ducked the issue. But the Vanguard managers do not skirt it. In their constitutions, each of the Vanguard companies explicitly states what the role of profit is in their various firms. Significantly, what they have to say about profit differs greatly from both of the two most frequently expressed views on the subject.

There are two commonly held premises about profit. Corporate critics on the left assume that profit is inherently evil, inevitably ill-gotten, and always antisocial. In sharp contrast, most traditional economists and Old Guard managers assume that profit maximization is the only legitimate purpose for a corporation. While both of these extreme views are refreshingly astringent, one finds that, like Listerine, they are more cosmetic than useful. In fact, if one examines the role of profit in the Vanguard, one cannot help but conclude that profit is a terribly complex concept that defies ideology and cant.

Left-wing Assumptions About Profit

Believers in the demonology of profit naively assume that it is the handmaiden of capitalistic corruption, the fuel of entrepreneurial exploitation, the essence of avarice, an unnatural invention of the industrial revolution foisted on humankind by the likes of Adam Smith, J.P. Morgan, and Marc Rich. These critics should visit China or Yugoslavia. In those Communist countries, managers of state-owned and worker-owned enterprises respond to the profit motive in much the same way as do American managers of privately owned firms. It is interesting to note that there is no word in Chinese for management, but the Mandarin word for profit is as Chinese as their word for tea. On a recent tour of Chinese factories, I asked the heads of some eight state-owned enterprises the following question: "Why are you concerned with making a profit?" Here is a summary of their answers:

If there is no profit, we must lay workers off or reduce their wages.

Without profit, our retirees will be hurt because we will not be able to replenish their pension funds.

The state needs some measure by which to evaluate if we are meeting the needs of consumers; profit is clearly the best single measure of performance.

We need profits in order to invest in the plant and equipment we will need in the future. In this way, profit should be seen as a *cost* of doing business. Only the Gang of Four see it as an immoral surplus.

It is difficult for unprofitable enterprises to borrow working capital. Not even state banks will loan money they don't expect to get back.

We use our profits to support community schools, worker housing, and hospitals.

If we are not profitable, we must cease production. If that happens, the suppliers who depend on us and the dealers who sell our products may also go out of business. And the consumer who has bought our product will no longer be able to get parts and service. Lots of people depend on us to stay in business.

To me, these Communists sounded an awful lot like capitalists (which isn't surprising, since capital is needed to fuel any advanced economy, regardless of its nature). Perhaps I was asking the wrong question. So I tried to serve them up a nice fat, left-handed slow ball they could belt into the proletarian bleachers: "But how *much* profit?" The managers were nearly unanimous in the surprising answers they gave: "As much as we can make," they answered with apparent glee. "Why so much?" I asked. They replied, variously:

Because we need a great deal of capital.

Because our workers need jobs and houses.

Because we must increase the standard of living of the Chinese people.

In effect, the Chinese managers told me that one couldn't have too much of a good thing. This was clearly Eastern logic. Being a good Aristotelian, I had the advantage of knowing about the Golden Mean: "Come on," I asked, "aren't there some limits? Aren't there some things you won't do to increase your profits?" The Chinese thought I had really come off the Great Wall with that question. Nonetheless, they patiently explained that, in order to increase profits, one would *not* do such things as break the law, sacrifice the quality of a product, skimp on future investment, reduce safety in their plants, cheat suppliers, or gouge dealers. I figured I had one more question before they got completely irritated, so I shot the works: "Why not?" I asked. "If profits are so important, why not maximize them in all instances?" One manager answered the question in the style I had expected, but so seldom found, in the world of the Buddha and Confucius: "Because profits are like breathing. You must breathe to live; but you don't live to breathe." I quickly translated: "Do you mean that profits are not the *purpose* of an enterprise?" He smiled approvingly, apparently pleased to find that even big-nosed occidentals were educable.

From this brief encounter with communism, I concluded that the American left has the Chinese reds outflanked on the issue of profit: While in favor of life, U.S. lefties are categorically opposed to breathing (and willing to exercise the power of the state to curtail excessive respiration).

Old Guard Assumptions About Profit

Similarly, the right-wing's probreathing, antilife position on profits would seem equally absurd from the point-of-view of the Chinese. This position is stated clearly and succinctly by the Confucius of monetarism, Milton Friedman. In his famous dictum, Friedman says, "The one and only social responsibility of business is to increase its profits." Friedman's major point—that business folk have no right to engage in philanthropy with corporate funds because such activity is both theft and undemocratic—raises a serious issue that must, perforce, await its considered demolition in a subsequent chapter. But his minor point—that profit maximization should be the sole goal of corporations—is what is truly representative of the Old Guard way of thinking about profits. For example, U.S. Steel's chairman, David

Roderick, in a (conscious?) echo of Alfred Sloan nicely translates Friedman's position into a managerial rule: "The duty of management is to make money. Our primary objective is not to make steel."

How is one to think about this proposition? Clearly it has merit. As we have just seen, even Communists accept the necessity of profit. No rational person, I suspect, would say that it is Roderick's duty to *lose* money. And it would be equally as irrational to state that U.S. Steel should keep piling up ingots, rods, and beams that no one wants to buy. Thus, at one level at least, both parts of Roderick's position are unassailable.

Indeed, the shortcomings of Roderick's view are not apparent until one examines the implications and consequences of his assumptions. It is in the "therefores" that must logically follow from his statement that we find its inherent limitations. For example, because it is Roderick's duty to make a profit, he assumes that it is also his duty to abandon the production of steel if that activity becomes unprofitable (or even if it becomes less profitable than producing silicon chips or chocolate chip cookies). That, in effect, is exactly Mr. Roderick's position, for it was originally stated as a defense for his company's diversification out of steel. Now, if Famous Amos were to discover that his cookie business was on the skids, it would make perfect sense for him to change his line of goods to croissants or gourmet pasta. Wally Amos is free to do as he will with his business because (a) he is the sole owner, and (b) the product he makes is not vital to national survival. Mr. Roderick simply does not have the same freedom as Mr. Amos. In clear distinction, Roderick manages a publicly traded firm with a social charter to produce a resource necessary for national self-sufficiency and defense. The major stakeholder at Famous Amos is the famous one himself; at U.S. Steel we are *all* stakeholders. (As this was on its way to the printer, Famous Amos was acquired by a larger corporation.)

While the managers of U.S. Steel have explicit responsibilities to their shareholders—responsibilities I enumerate later—at a higher level of abstraction, the nature of the ownership of the corporation is irrelevant. Now, this is not to advocate nationalization; rather, I wish to call attention to the broader role that giant, publicly held firms play in the economy. As the Lord Corporation's CEO Donald Alstadt once explained to me:

If, heaven forbid, there were a Marxist coup in this country, the effects wouldn't be apparent in the nation's largest corporations. Years after their nationalization, IBM would still look like IBM and it would still be making and selling computers, and GM would still be making and selling cars and even run by the same cast of managers. What this tells you is that the basic purpose of these large corporations is not to serve the needs of their shareholders, but to serve national social, economic, and technological needs. Why did the U.S. Government move to guarantee the bailout of Lockheed several years ago? To protect the company's shareholders? Not on your life. The government acted because the purpose of Lockheed is to act as the nation's prime repository of national security technology.

Therein lies the error of Roderick's thinking. He sees no strategic role for U.S. Steel in meeting the needs of U.S. society. Moreover, his mistaken premise that his basic role is to maximize profits for shareholders is the very same assumption that led his predecessors at U.S. Steel astray in the 1950s and 1960s. Throughout this period, U.S. Steel executives paid unrealistically generous dividends and attempted to keep quarterly profits high —all at the expense of reinvestment in the modern technology the company would come to need in the 1970s in order to remain competitive in world markets (technology that, in hindsight, would have made it unnecessary for Roderick to consider diversification out of steel in the 1980s).

It is clear that Roderick's assumptions about profit have made it impossible for U.S. Steel to meet their obligations to society (we need domestic steel for defense), to employees (the company is shutting down domestic facilities and, thus, exporting jobs), to customers (the rising price of domestic steel has been passed on to the hard-hit auto industry), and, ironically, even to shareholders (their profits, dividends, and stock prices are, today, far from attractive). But what help can one offer to Roderick? How should managers of such large corporations think about the role of profit and about their responsibilities to shareholders?

Vanguard Assumptions

As we turned to the Chinese to challenge the assumptions of the left, we now turn to the Vanguard to challenge the assumptions of the Old Guard. George Draper Dayton, the founder of what would become today's Dayton-Hudson Corporation, said the following in 1932: "Shall we agree to start with the assumption that success is making ourselves useful in the world, valuable to society?" To this day, like the other Vanguard corporations, Dayton-Hudson sees their raison d'être as providing the goods and services society needs and providing steady, long-term opportunities for employment. Importantly, this does *not* mean that Dayton-Hudson is casual about profits. The company's lengthy constitution, "Management Perspectives," starts with a chapter on "serving society," but moves on quickly to several chapters about how that goal will be achieved through productive and profitable business practices. The document is explicit about the importance of the bottom line: "Growth in earnings and return on investment are the two most important measures of our financial performance." The constitution goes on to state that return on investment is "the most comprehensive and illuminating *single* performance measure available to us." The company computes ROI by multiplying return on sales (earnings per sales dollar) by investment turnover (investment dollars per sales dollar). The two ratios that constitute ROI are applied to all of the divisions of the company in an objective, quantitative evaluation that would have pleased Harold Geneen in his toughest days at ITT.

And the payoff to DH's stockholders has been great. Dayton-Hudson are the fastest-growing retailers in America. While Sears, Montgomery Ward, and J. C. Penney have all stumbled recently, Dayton-Hudson has sailed right along, surpassing even red-hot K Mart on most common measures of financial success. Where DH *differs* from their competitors is that they have adhered to founder Dayton's view that their enormous profits are the means to success, not the end in themselves. In the words of the DH constitution: "The business of business is serving society, not just making money. Profit is our reward for serving society well. Indeed, profit is the means and the measure of our service—but not an end in itself." This is not a mere rhetorical flourish. For

example, DH's careful delineation of ends and means leads them
to contribute to the communities that host their stores approximately 5 percent of their taxable income, which is by far the
highest percentage of any large U.S. corporation. (The *Fortune*
1,000 average a little under 1 percent. Cummins Engine also
allocates 5 percent, but as they have been only profitable sporadi-
cally in recent years, their pledge has not been backed by big
bucks.)

But sorting out ends from means is not the only critical distinction made by the Vanguard in regard to profits. Also important is
their distinction between stock *investors* and stock *speculators.*
Unlike the Old Guard, the leaders of the Vanguard show disdain
for the latter. While Mr. Roderick and the leaders of the Old
Guard continue to equate these two types of shareholders, Weyerhaeuser, Levi Strauss, and Control Data have historically made
it clear that they have responsibilities only to the former. The
Vanguard's responsibilities to their *investors* are fourfold:

1. To provide long-term growth of equity (that is, to increase
    the overall value of the corporation).
2. To provide a steady and competitive return on investment
    (profits should cover the risks of investors).
3. To manage operations as prudently, efficiently, and pro-
    ductively as possible (it is irresponsible to put other peo-
    ple's money at risk).
4. To treat investors as if they were the actual long-term
    owners of the firm (that is, as people who are concerned
    with the future viability and continuing survivability of the
    enterprise).

Even with this commitment, Vanguard corporation stock is
devalued by Wall Street. Motorola, Honeywell, Control Data, and
Weyerhaeuser are not Wall Street favorites and, while Atlantic
Richfield, Levi Strauss, and Dayton-Hudson have had their innings on The Street, they are by no means the darlings of stock
analysts and brokers. The reason for Wall Street's indifference to
the Vanguard is that no one has ever gotten rich quick in their
stock. Quick is the operative word. The time frames of stock
analysts and Vanguard managers are radically different. To the
former, time is measured by a stopwatch; the latter use a ten-year
calendar. In addition, analysts live in the past while the great

managers live in the future. Stock analysts sit in their offices and pore over numbers that are no more than figurative representatives of the *past*. They fail to understand that even four good quarters running says little of certainty about the *next* quarter (and nothing about the next few years). To the great managers, the last quarter is ancient history. To stock analysts, the last quarter is the future!

That they sit in their Wall Street offices also explains why stock analysts are typically ignorant about the true quality of corporate management. They don't get out and visit corporations (except to attend the sanitized, annual "dog-and-pony shows" that all corporations tailor to the limited interests of stock analysts), and they don't visit plants and talk to workers to discover how well-motivated and committed the people are who have the ultimate responsibility for delivering on a company's promises. All the analysts know is what their numbers tell them and what they read in the business press—periodicals written by people with the same myopic perspective as the analysts themselves.

Look at any profile of a corporation in the *Wall Street Journal*. Who is the journalist's source of information? Nine times out of ten it is a stock analyst (analysts have plenty of time for chat and, hey, the free publicity is great). Business journalists too frequently mask their pristine ignorance of their subject by reporting exactly what they are told by their sources, unprocessed by trained intelligence. (Few business journalists have degrees in business or economics, and few have ever worked for anything but a newspaper or magazine, so how are they to know?) In turn, stock analysts faithfully read the articles in which they are quoted and then pronounce themselves "informed." In this closed loop, neither journalists nor analysts risk having their basic assumptions challenged, and both can point to printed evidence that supports their understanding of reality. While the business press is anxious to dramatize minute changes in quarterly earnings and the intrigue behind personnel shifts in the executive suite, they shy away from challenging such basic premises of traditional management as "corporations have responsibilities to stock speculators." This system would do little damage if it weren't for the fact that managers also read the business press and, in the process, have the premises of the Old Guard reified in print. (This is not a blanket condemnation of the business press. Most of the journalists who write for *Fortune*, *Business Week*, and the New

York *Times* are informed, responsible professionals willing to dig deeply into stories and ask tough questions. They also care about *management* and understand that that subject is not synonymous with *finance*—a distinction that the *Wall Street Journal* often fails to make.)

The untested assumptions of the business press, stock analysts, and the like have willy-nilly been applied to the Vanguard and other excellent companies, and these companies have come up wanting. For example, in 1979, *Forbes* criticized Honeywell's 9.6 percent return on its investment in computers as "less than what Honeywell could have gotten if the money was invested in CDs." Now, the Vanguard aren't perfect, and Honeywell has made mistake upon mistake in the handling of their computer business. But the *Forbes* reporter could not understand the difficult technical, managerial, and strategic reasons why Honeywell's computer business wasn't taking off; instead, the reporter played the dummy for some Wall Street ventriloquist. The journalist mouthed a favorite assumption of the Old Guard (see Roderick earlier), of finance professors, and of stock analysts, to wit: "If you get 14 percent in the money market, then you are throwing money away if you start a business that only returns 12 percent." This is the kind of logic that wins journalists praise from Dow Jones (and gains tenure for finance professors). It is also the kind of logic that gets businesses and the economy in trouble.

What would happen if every American company that wasn't making a 14 percent return cashed out their businesses and put the money in the bank? If, indeed, the purpose of a business is to make the highest possible profit, that is the "rational" thing to do (moreover, it is the "responsible" thing—remember that management's fiduciary obligation to shareholders is to profit maximize). In fact, during the 1970s, when few corporations were earning more than they could make in the money market, many did stop investing and did stop introducing new products. A result was a net decline in the productivity of the economy and a loss of markets to foreigners who kept turning out new products even when it was "uneconomical" to do so. (Fortunately, there were enough American entrepreneurs and enough corporate managers who believed they were in the business of making products and not just money that the entire U.S. economy didn't collapse.)

What happens when a firm plays out the "therefores" of the

Sloan/Roderick/Friedman/ *Wall Street Journal* dictum to its logical conclusion? The Mennen Company did just that. The rational and prudent owners of that company paid out the considerable profits from their firm and socked them away safely in the bank. They took no risks, introduced no new products, and made no new investments in plant or equipment. Instead, they milked the profits earned by Mennen Skin Bracer (the industry's leading after-shave lotion at the time the owners started this strategy). In the short term, the strategy worked exceedingly well. The high interest paid by the money markets brought in a higher return than could have been garnered in the short term from the expensive process of developing and marketing new toiletry products. And Wall Street responded to the company's exceptionally high dividends with salivating enthusiasm. But, in the long run, the company went into decline.

Today, Skin Bracer has barely 3 percent of the market, the company has from time to time teetered close to bankruptcy, and the Mennen family may end up with no business to pass on to their heirs. (In a less dramatic but basically similar fashion, the managers of U.S. Steel pursued the Mennen strategy in the 1960s and 1970s.) Ironically, it is the most faithful shareholders—the real investor/owners who hold onto their stock for the long haul —who suffer most when managers attempt to satisfy the short-term speculators (who have no lasting interest in, nor loyalty to, the corporation). This is a point that has continued to escape (1) Wall Street analysts, (2) business journalists, (3) finance professors —and the managers of the Old Guard who are prisoners of the collective scribblings of this Gang of Three.

Meeting the Real Needs of Shareholders

Paradoxically, there is no way for a corporation to *directly* meet its responsibility to shareholders (when managers attempt to do so, they end up paying out their "seed corn" in dividends). In practice, corporations can only meet their responsibilities to shareholders *indirectly* by meeting the needs of their other constituents. Nonetheless, it is assumed by the Old Guard that when managers resist the legitimate claims of employees for fairer wages, resist the demands of consumers for safer products, resist the requests of suppliers for long-term relationships, and reject the pleas of dealers for a larger share of profit, they are acting in the interest of shareholders. Doubtless, managers do act in the interest of shareholders—and all stakeholders, in fact—when they resist *il*legitimate and *ir*responsible demands. But meeting the *real* needs of society is seldom detrimental to shareholders in the long term. Profit, as the Dayton-Hudson constitution says, is "our reward for serving society well."

This Vanguard view is at odds with the prevailing opinion among financial analysts that there is a trade-off between profit and meeting the needs of corporate constituents. On this score, no corporation has suffered more at the hands of the financial community than Control Data. The company's strategy is clearly stated in their annual report as "Addressing society's major unmet needs as profitable business opportunities." The *Wall Street Journal* has called this strategy "far out" and vilified William C. Norris, the company's CEO, as being "eccentric" for pursuing it. The sway of assumptions is, indeed, powerful: The likes of Mr. Roderick are the corporate heroes of the *Wall Street Journal.* While failing to meet the needs of customers, employees, shareholders, and society, the Rodericks of the world win the *Journal*'s encomiums, while Mr. Norris is considered "eccentric" for serving society. Why? Because Mr. Roderick's principles are no threat to the *Journal*'s unexamined premises about profit, while Norris creates an advanced case of cognitive dissonance for the periodical's editors. William C. Norris is not a socialist out to destroy the capitalistic system—the *Journal* could cope with him if he were. What the *Journal*'s editors find so unsettling is that he is a crusty conservative (he seeks to replace nonprofit public sector social services with private, for-profit social services) who argues that the future of capitalism depends on serving society and not just shareholders. That kind of talk can't be answered by mindless reference to the gospel according to Milton Friedman. What does the CEO of Control Data mean by serving the needs of society?" Norris explains:

> Let me emphasize here that I am *not* talking about just altruism or huge increases in government spending or the reordering of priorities. What I *am* talking about is more efficient utilization of existing technological resources, achieved primarily through widespread cooperation, motivated by profit and the recognition of wider responsibilities.

Specifically, Norris feels that there is money to be made by applying Control Data's computer knowledge, financial resources, and human talent to the major unsolved problems of society. He goes on:

It is evident that jobs can be taken to poverty-stricken areas; education and training can be made responsive and affordable; disadvantaged and disabled people can be trained and placed in meaningful jobs; small businesses can be helped to start up and grow and create more new jobs; poverty-stricken urban and rural areas can be revitalized; and public services privatized. And all these actions can be accomplished efficiently and, in the long run, profitably through broad-based cooperation.

Mirroring the *Journal*'s disdain for such an approach, the financial community has consistently undervalued Control Data stock, even in the years when the company has been among the leaders in profitability among big computer manufacturers (Control Data is the nation's leading manufacturer of such computer peripherals as disk drives). Norris has spent over a decade vainly trying to explain his philosophy to security analysts, and the best he has gotten out of them in return is the claim that "Control Data's good work constrains profitability." Interestingly, Norris has also been a special target of the left who portray him as a wolf in sheep's clothing, profiting from illiteracy, poverty, and social misfortune in general. Norris answers these criticisms:

No one objects to a reasonable profit on a can of beans. Why should there be objections to making a profit meeting special needs of disabled persons?

Indeed, Norris's experience at Control Data helps to resolve a persistent and puzzling dichotomy in the thinking about profit. Traditionally, the role of management has been to do well (for stockholders). More recently, critics have argued that managers shall do good (for society). Norris and the Vanguard show that it is possible to do well and to do good at the same time. Even more important, Norris shows that one can do well *by* doing good.

The Control Data story highlights the central fallacy of both the left and the right in seeing profit as an either/or issue. To the left, profit comes at the expense of society. To the right, the needs of society can only be met at the expense of shareholders. The

Vanguard put the lie to this trade-off fallacy. Indeed, the Johnson & Johnson executive who raised the question about dropping the infamous red ball went on to offer an alternative to either/or thinking about profits.

> . . . I know I'd better not drop that red one. But can I fumble the others? I don't know for sure. *But I think the answer is balance.*

The Answer Is Balance

Here's the real answer: At the Vanguard, *all of the balls are red!* At the Vanguard, managers learn that they must not drop any of their many responsibilities. This imperative was brought home to Levi Strauss managers when the company recently broke with tradition and fired a top manager. Now, firing someone for anything short of a capital crime is unheard of at the maternalistic Levi Strauss (would a mother cast out her child?). But there it was, in plain sight, a manager was fired. Significantly the manager was among the company's most successful in terms of the profitability of his unit. He was recognized across the entire corporation as a hotshot pants producer. Nonetheless, he was fired because he had mistreated employees, because he had created a sweatshop climate of fear in his organization. A top executive of Levi explained the firing to me:

> We wanted to send a clear, unambiguous message to everyone in the company that abusive behavior would not be tolerated. If this individual couldn't get away with it, it would be obvious to everyone in the company that no one could. We don't like to fire anyone and don't plan to make a habit of it. In fact, had this individual been a lower-level worker or one with a mediocre track record, we would simply have transferred him to a staff job where he couldn't do any damage. But he was well known in the industry, so future employment was no problem for him. So we felt justified in making an example out of him, in telling all our employees that no matter how much money you may be making for the company, there are some things you just can't do.

There are many other instances in which Levi Strauss has made it clear that they see no distinction between the color of the balls managers must keep in the air. Throughout the 1960s and 1970s, Levi chairman Walter A. Haas, Jr., maintained, "The moral position usually turns out to be good business." What is significant is that Levi acts on their principles. Early in the 1980s, after the company experienced their worst quarter since the Depression, then-CEO Robert Grohman went to New York to announce to Wall Street that the company was introducing a plan to share economic gains with their sewing machine operators. A securities analyst asked: "Will this further depress your earnings?" Grohman replied, "In the short term, you bet. Since people are our most important asset, the more we pay out, the better for us in the long term." It may have been an obvious point to a Vanguard manager, but it was difficult for a stock analyst with a financial background to comprehend (and it took courage on the part of Grohman to make the point so forcefully). The analyst could not understand how it could be good for Levi shareholders if employees got a bigger chunk of profits. To Wall Street, the interests of capitalists and labor must always be mutually antagonistic.

While the notion that the goals of shareholders and workers are at odds still holds sway in the financial community (and among the new left), the essential compatibility of the two was recognized long ago by some leaders of organized labor. Samuel Gompers got it right when he said, "The worst crime an employer can commit against the worker is to fail to make a profit." It says something about Motorola that, when its chief operating officer went to the Big Apple to explain Motorola's philosophy of sharing profits with workers, he quoted Gompers several times in his talk. Here is what Motorola's William Weisz had to say:

Profit is important not simply because a company greedily wants to make money, but a profit is important because of *what it does for people.* Profit gives a company (which, after all, is basically just a big group of people) the ability, through the distribution of that profit, to raise the standard of living of the people associated with the company. Whether it is in salaries or profit sharing to employees, in dividends to the stockholders or the increasing price of its shares on the stock market that only occurs if a company is successful and profitable, whether in educational assistance, suggestion payouts, or patent awards, the source is always profits. Without the earning of profit we could have none of these. But equally important, out of that profit we must invest continuously in new plants, tools, materials, and receivables in order to maintain our share of the business, and to grow. If a company starts losing its share of the business and does not make these investments, it starts losing position ever more rapidly. The companies who do increase their share, at the losing company's expense, can now make lower cost products because of their volume. They can invest more in engineering or improved services to make their company step out in front. It is a snowballing situation where soon the company that does not make a profit and reinvest much of it in the business in order to serve the customer will have to shut its doors and put *all* its people out of work. Obviously, a company that sustains a loss may substantially hasten this final result. Business history is filled with these situations. And so, Samuel Gompers knew that in our competitive society, to *protect the jobs* of the working people, companies must operate efficiently and be profitable.

Where have we heard these arguments before? Funny, Weisz doesn't look Chinese! While Weisz's logic would seem unexceptionable to Shanghai executives, Wall Street has nonetheless taken some exception to the Motorola practices that are based squarely on what Weisz preaches. In 1982, the *Wall Street Journal* offered more than a hint of criticism of Motorola for their "risky decision" to buy Four-Phase Systems, a computer maker whose acquisition made it possible for Motorola to meld their existing technological strength in communications and semiconductors with computers. While other American corporations were walking away from direct competition with the Japanese, Motorola was investing heavily to take on Nippon in the growing field of semiconductors, telecommunications, and office automation. How did Wall Street react? Motorola stock lost 10 percent of its value during the week the Four-Phase purchase was announced. And, although Motorola did better than their competitors during the hard times of 1980–82, Wall Street was still not impressed. Instead, Wall Street analysts stuck with flashy skyrockets like Texas Instruments—right to the bitter end. Motorola, it was said, had a "low price earnings ratio." But the P (stock price) in a P/E ratio is nothing but a measure of the confidence of Wall Street. Investors were, in effect, frightened by their own shadows! ("Not fair," an investor friend of mine argued, "we discounted Motorola because of its relatively low earnings." And how did they measure earnings? "By ROI," he answered. I suggested that, if Motorola's ROI was relatively low, it had to do with the high level of investment (the I). When a company is moving into higher technology and developing a new line of business, a high level of investment is an indicator of preparation for a lucrative future. "Maybe so," the analyst replied, "but we've got to go with the hard data about the here and now.")

It is not my intention in this chapter to score the stock market. Rather, my purpose is to call attention to the deleterious effects that result when the assumptions of financial analysts are applied to the management of corporations. When corporations accept the dominion of short-term financial premises, they do like U.S. Steel and skimp on investment, or they do like GM and ignore the needs of the company's many stakeholders (the careful service of whom builds real profitability for long-term investors).

Weisz puts the lie to the left-wing notion that profits are evil or socially irresponsible. To the contrary, profits are the "irreducible minimum" of business activity, in the words of Olga's Jan Erteszek. Without profit, none of the important contributions that Weisz, Erteszek, and Chinese managers make to their societies would be possible.

Profits are not only *means* to higher ends, they are also a *measure* of performance. There can be no doubt that profitability, over time, is a key indicator of how efficiently a corporation uses resources. And, over time, it is probably true that stock prices reflect this efficiency. To believe otherwise is to be mindless. My point is that single-minded and short-term obeisance to the goals of profit and stock price distorts the behavior of managers and causes them to fail to meet their responsibilities to investors (and all stakeholders) in the long term. For example, in 1984 when ITT finally did what they should have been doing for a decade— making heavy investments in their American telecommunications business—Wall Street responded by devaluing ITT stock by about a third. In response, one clear-minded partner at Goldman, Sachs & Co. told *BusinessWeek* that "I don't think any company can afford a long-term investment today unless its managers own 51 percent of it."

Indeed, Old Guard managers have gotten the message and internalized it. Fearful of alienating The Street, they engage in such survival tactics as investing in acquisitions instead of start-ups, reducing research expenditures, trimming capital spending, buying back company stock, increasing short-term debt, and abandoning investments in such slow-to-reap natural resources as timber and oil.

What is remarkable about the Vanguard is that they eschew the common assumptions about quick profit that would win them the easy approbation of the financial community. Instead, they courageously pay the price of short-term disvaluation in order to do what is right for owners in the long run. One further example: In March 1978, *Forbes* ran a sarcastically critical article about Weyerhaeuser, arguing that while all the other forest product companies were booming, "Weyco" was not. An invidious comparison was drawn between the leadership of George Weyerhaeuser and Georgia-Pacific's CEO, Owen Cheatham (Dickens would have loved that name). *Forbes* contrasted G-P's high profitability with what they disdainfully called Weyco's "mystique and complacency." The article captures in pluperfect fashion the supremacy of unexamined financial reasoning in the business press (I quote it at some length in the Notes at the end of the book).

Weyerhaeuser, by thinking about future generations, was said by *Forbes* to behave irrationally and irresponsibly. Indeed, if one uses net present value (the holy writ of corporate finance) as one's sole criterion for investment, it is virtually impossible to defend Weyco's reforestation efforts. For the costs of site preparation, replanting, fertilization, spraying, and thinning—most of which occur sixty years before harvesting—are so large that even if one assumes mind-boggling rates of appreciation of timber value, the returns are not competitive with a middling CD. The unstated premise of the *Forbes* article was that the role of the corporation is to meet the short-term financial desires of investors. The "therefores" then follow from the financial premise as naturally as great trees from little pinecones grow, *viz:* Weyerhaeuser was wrong not to cut and run, wrong not to go into debt, wrong to remain loyal to the Northwest, wrong to invest in research and in maintenance of timberland, and wrong to put timber technology ahead of financial thinking. Almost every article one reads in the

Wall Street Journal (and too often in *Forbes,* even though the publishers and editors there know better) reflects this kind of thinking. It is no wonder, then, that with such constant reinforcement, the majority of American managers have come to accept such assumptions. They accept them, in fact, even when experience puts the lie to them. By 1982, Georgia-Pacific was in deep trouble. In the face of enormous losses, their CEO was forced to step down. Weyerhaeuser, in contrast, remained steadily but unspectacularly profitable and, because of their careful reinvestment and reorganization, was poised to capture market share during the recovery. Did *Forbes* print a retraction? Did finance professors change their assumptions? Did Wall Street sing the praises of Weyco? Is the Pope Chinese?

Mutual Advantage

Too much of the nation's thinking about profit is rooted in the assumptions of a bygone era. To this day, the financial community reflects the premises of railroad baron William H. Vanderbilt who, when asked by a reporter if his plans to shut down an unprofitable New York-to-Chicago train would inconvenience the public, replied, "The public be damned; I'm working for my stockholders." While Vanderbilt may have had good reason to shut down the line, his logic broke down in his conclusion that he could serve his shareholders in the long run if he failed to serve the public. The trick to understanding the role of profit is to see it in the light of serving all constituencies and not as antagonistic to the interests of everyone but shareholders. Profit is not an either/ or proposition. As F. Scott Fitzgerald once wrote, "The test of a first-rate intelligence is the ability to hold two opposed ideas in the mind at the same time and still retain the ability to function."

Vanguard executives score in the top percentile on Fitzgerald's test. The Vanguard have all been exceptionally creative in turning the pursuit of profit to the *mutual advantage* of all corporate stakeholders. Here is an excerpt from the John Deere constitution:

Mutual advantage is the soundest basis for any relationship entered into by the John Deere organization with any individual, group, or organization. The result on both ends of any relationship must be beneficial. The measure always is long-term self-interest and conscience, not short-term gain. Our organization seeks its own interest through others by assisting them to gain some measure of their own legitimate interest.

It might be argued that the Vanguard are only able to pursue mutual advantage because they are relatively free of stock market pressures for short-term gain. That is, unlike most large, publicly held firms, ownership of the Vanguard tends to be controlled by one individual or family, who are thus able to resist Wall Street's demand for immediate financial gratification. While it is true that William C. Norris at Control Data, Robert Galvin at Motorola, the Haas Family at Levi Strauss, the Daytons of Dayton-Hudson, and the Weyerhaeusers (and related families) at Weyerhaeuser all hold significant blocks of stock in their companies, I do not believe that this fact fully explains their balanced attitudes toward profit. There is no doubt that the philosophies of those companies were formed by individuals (and families) who exerted strong leadership during their companies' formative years, but ownership is neither a necessary nor a sufficient explanation of their extraordinary behavior. It is not *necessary* because Honeywell, John Deere, and Arco are today free from the influences of any individual owner or hereditary voting bloc and these companies, too, believe in mutual advantage. It is not *sufficient* because many companies have been under the control of a single family (Du Pont, Mennen, Ford, to cite only three), yet have still behaved as if short-term profit maximization were the sole corporate goal. While I do not deny that having working control of a company through ownership greatly facilitates the implementation of a Vanguard philosophy, such control does nothing to explain why only a few such owners are drawn to the philosophy.

Rather than being an instance of noblesse oblige, I believe that clear thinking about profit derives from a CEO's premises about the purpose of the corporation. If he or she believes that the sole responsibility of a corporation is to maximize shareholder profit, then the therefores that follow from that assumption will inevitably preclude the adoption of a Vanguard philosophy. Vanguard leaders, for whatever deep-seated psychological reason, simply start from another place. Says Donald Alstadt, CEO of the Lord Corporation: "Profits are like health. You don't live to be healthy; but you must be healthy to live." Funny, he doesn't look Chinese.

6.

PRODUCTIVITY AND INNOVATION: THE CONFUSED AND CONFLICTING ASSUMPTIONS OF AMERICAN MANAGERS

To make headway, improve your head.
—B.C. FORBES

In the previous chapter we saw that the Vanguard make money the old-fashioned way: They pursue profitability as both an obligation to all their stakeholders *and* as a reward for serving them well. For an executive to be able to hold these two seemingly contradictory ideas in mind at the same time requires impressive mental agility. Thinking clearly about the role of profit is no mean trick—and the Vanguard are among the few who manage to do it consistently and with dedication.

But thinking clearly about profit is child's play compared to thinking clearly about productivity and innovation. Here, the Vanguard also stand out from the crowd. They achieve enviable levels of both productivity and innovation from their workers, managers, and machines. Since productivity and innovation are the handmaidens of profit, the Vanguard do not make distinctions between the pursuit of the former and pursuit of the latter but, instead, pursue all in a single, unified effort. Vanguard managers have manifest faith that a productive and innovative firm is destined to be profitable in the long run. Here are some examples of the Vanguard's activities and achievements in innovation and productivity:

- Between 1974 and 1983, Deere & Co. invested some $2 billion in the most up-to-date manufacturing technologies. Their "factories of the future" now make them one of the most productive heavy manufacturing firms in America.

- Motorola combined heavy investment in new technology, generous rewards to productive workers, an innovative product strategy, and a daring public challenge to the Japanese in a successful bid to become the world's leading producer of semiconductors and a major exporter of high-tech electronic products.

- Dayton-Hudson was the first retailer with the Ivy League look in the 1950s, the first with Carnaby St. and madras in the 1960s, the first with Mao suits in the 1970s, and the first in a fully enclosed suburban mall (in 1956). Today, they are innovators in chain bookselling and upscale discounting.

- In 1983, Levi Strauss announced their "President's Sweepstakes," a contest with $3 million at stake to support the best new product ideas of employees. Within the space of a year, the company went from their worst quarter ever to their best —attributable, at least in part, to employee new product ideas.

- Weyerhaeuser, the forest industry leader in research, pioneered tree farming, aquaculture, and such technological innovations as a hydraulic jack that makes trees fall *uphill* when they are cut (thus saving some $20 million annually in smashed-up timber).

- Honeywell encourages innovation and productivity by constantly dividing and subdividing operating units. In the process, they turn scores of managers into entrepreneurs—in effect, making them bosses of their own little companies. The people who work for those little companies come to know all their co-workers and managers personally. They come to identify with the goals of the unit and to feel they have a personal stake in making it more productive.

- Arco's solar division is a world leader in photovoltaics, providing Californians with some nineteen megawatts of electricity at three futuristic power facilities. Arco also is the first major U.S. firm to install two-way video teleconferencing—a $7 million system that links the corporation's far-flung operations in a single, cost-effective, telecommunications network. That is probably *not* an Arco executive sitting next to you on a transcontinental flight.

- Control Data Corporation has created joint partnerships with dozens of their employees (and scores of outside entrepreneurs) in a successful effort to marry the innovative dynamism of small businesses with the assets of a large corporation.

How have the Vanguard achieved these things? It wasn't easy. And we won't be able to understand what they accomplished until we understand why. If we were to jump directly into a description of what the Vanguard do, we would not learn the secret of *why* they came to do it—which is the most crucial thing any manager who wishes to increase innovation and productivity must understand. For the poor performance of American corporations is not caused by any lack of knowledge of what to do (pick up any issue of the *Harvard Business Review* and one will find a half dozen unexceptionable descriptions of what excellent companies do to increase corporate performance). The key issue is *why* the leaders of the Vanguard have been willing to do the things that will increase innovation and productivity while their competitors have failed to do so. (This failure is all the more remarkable given the fact that the knowledge of what to do is equally at the disposal and command of all American executives —after all, the *HBR* is not a "limited-circulation" publication: A thirty-dollar check will get any manager into the club.)

If knowing what to do is not the problem, it seems safe to assume that low levels of productivity and innovation are attributable, instead, to a matter of differences in the basic assumptions managers hold about the sources of productivity and innovation. That is, if an executive believes that capital is the basic source of corporate performance, she will devote her efforts to the improved utilization of capital. If an executive believes that engineering is the basic source of corporate performance, he will devote his efforts to improving engineering processes. Hence, whatever methods managers choose to become more productive and innovative will be a function of their basic beliefs about the ultimate source (or sources) of corporate success. Again, this is an instance of behavior being driven by unexamined premises. To state the matter precisely: Innovation and productivity are to be found in the *heads* of managers.

What Managers Think
About Innovation and Productivity

If the Vanguard respond to the need for improved corporate performance in ways that are different from the Old Guard, the reason for the difference must be rooted in differing perceptions of the problem. Therefore, if we wish to understand why the Vanguard are more innovative and productive than other companies, we need to understand the differences in the ways managers think about corporate performance.

In 1981, I undertook a year-long study to see if I could uncover what managers were really thinking about innovation and productivity. Tired of pure speculation, my premise was that a little data—kept in its proper place, of course—was unlikely to do great harm to the cause of business research. But where should one start such an examination of the collective corporate psyche? Keynes offered a clue in his oft-quoted line: "Practical men, who believe themselves to be quite exempt from any intellectual influences, are usually the slaves of some defunct economist." Why not see which academic scribblers were influencing business executives? Why not distill the wisdom of the major schools of thought about the causes of industrial decline to see to what extent corporate managers bought into each? In doing just that I quickly discovered that, even given the high level of nit-picking, infighting, and squabbling found in academia, the experts on industrial performance could be roughly divided into four theoretical schools (if one were willing to do a little trimming here, some paring there, and overlook the leftovers on my study floor). Here is a brief summary of the theories of each of these four schools that were advanced in the late 1970s, followed by the evaluations of each by several groups in the business community:

The Antigovernmentalists. While disagreeing among themselves on many issues, such noted economists as Murray Weidenbaum, Herbert Stein, Arthur Laffer, and Milton Friedman argued forcefully that inappropriate governmental policies were the prime cause for the decline in the performance of American industry that began in the mid-1970s. According to these economists, the worst of these policies were the increasing, costly, unpredictable, and mutually incompatible regulations that created an uncertain, sometimes even hostile, environment for entrepreneurs. A "new class" of regulators—who were too seldom held responsible by any cost/benefit analysis of their actions—led industry away from healthy risk taking and into the unproductive arena of "defensive" research.

Federal tax policies—particularly in the areas of capital gains, investment tax credits, depreciation rates, and income tax—provided too little incentive for innovation. Similarly, antitrust policies discouraged needed cooperation in research and export activities and sometimes "punished" successful companies who had earned substantial market shares as the result of their technological superiority. Other areas of serious concern to these economists were patent policies which offered inadequate protection to inventors and restrictive trade practices that kept American products from being able to compete freely and fairly in world markets. Finally, these economists were critical of an unofficial "industrial policy" that favored the propping up of dying industries over the encouragement of dynamic ones. In short, they saw adversarial governmental activities providing a less-than-fertile ground for the seeds of industrial innovation and productivity.

To what extent was this argument accepted outside the small school of economists who propounded it? To evaluate the potency of the argument, I polled 156 corporate managers, entrepreneurs, and scholars and asked them to estimate the percentage of the decline in the performance of American industry that they felt was explained by the antigovernmentalist line of reasoning. Here are the averages of the estimates made by these three groups:

PERCENT OF DECLINE EXPLAINED
BY THE ANTIGOVERNMENTALIST ARGUMENT:

Managers' Estimate	32 percent
Entrepreneurs' Estimate	41 percent
Scholars' Estimate	20 percent

In essence, the top managers I polled (there were seventy-five of them in my sample, from seventeen of the fifty largest U.S. corporations including, as a "control," several from two of the Vanguard—Deere and Arco) felt that governmental policies were responsible for nearly a third of the decline experienced by U.S. industry. The entrepreneurs I polled (there were sixty-one of them—all young presidents of small-to-medium-sized companies) felt that the government was responsible for nearly half the problem. And the twenty scholars I polled (each of whom had recently published a major study of innovation and/or productivity) felt that governmental policies were accountable for only a fifth of the problem.

The Structuralists. Such authors as Lester Thurow, Robert Reich, Ira Magaziner, and Amitai Etzioni advanced the theory that the decline in industrial performance was caused by shifts in the underlying structure of the American economy. While members of the structuralist school disagreed on many specific points, in general they argued that America, like Britain in the 1920s, seemed to be reaching its "climacteric." The authors suggested that heavy industries in the U.S. were at the "mature" stage of the industrial life cycle, which made them very costly to revitalize.

In general, these authors argued that America reinvested too little in the 1960s and 1970s to allow the country to make a rapid, significant turnaround in the 1980s. During this period, the country spent too much on defense and consumption and too little on productive investment and industrial R&D. Moreover, during this transitional period, a major part of the economy evolved into a postindustrial system in which service and knowledge industries came to dominate—and where improvement in productivity through the introduction of innovative technologies was far more difficult to achieve.

During this period, the country also became dependent on foreign oil, which contributed to chronic inflation. As inflation became indexed into the system, this increased the costs of (and decreased the potential profit yields from) reinvestment. Yet, even under such conditions, labor unions demanded more money for doing less work—ironically, this was particularly the case in industries with declining innovation and productivity such as steel and autos.

Members of the structuralist school argued that, if American industry had had adequate incentives to produce for foreign markets, there might not have been such a deleterious long-term impact on our industrial system. But the enormous size of the domestic market kept managers uninterested in exports.

The structuralists also argued that there was a severe training gap in America: In the old and dying industries, there was a surplus of soon-to-be unemployable workers; in the new and growing industries, there was a shortage of highly trained workers. The structuralists suggested that the active "manpower" programs of our foreign competitors avoided such a mismatch and this put the United States at a decided comparative disadvantage.

Finally, smaller firms—which are frequently the sources of the most radical innovations and the creators of most new jobs—were for many years hampered by unfavorable access to capital.

To what extent was the structuralist argument accepted as a valid explanation of the decline in the performance of American industry? The experts I polled tended to agree that the argument explained between a fifth and a quarter of the decline:

PERCENT OF DECLINE EXPLAINED BY THE STRUCTURALIST ARGUMENT:

Managers' Estimate	24 percent
Entrepreneurs' Estimate	22 percent
Scholars' Estimate	22 percent

The Organizationalists. Such authors as Robert Hayes, William Abernathy, William Ouchi, Thomas Peters, Robert Waterman, Anthony Athos, and Richard Pascale argued that the decline in the nation's industrial performance was due to the policies and practices that make up the organizational culture in the majority of large corporations. To these observers, staff groups (legal, financial, and accounting) appeared to be stifling the innovation of line managers rather than working with them to develop strategies for meeting external economic and regulatory challenges. In an apparent role reversal, staffs became decision makers and line managers worked for them. Hence, in many corporations, merger and acquisition activities took precedence over investment in R&D or in new plant and equipment, and over longer-term efforts to improve process technology. In such a climate of "administration by the numbers" the managerial inclination was to strive for short-term profitability rather than long-term growth. The separation of management from ownership and the generalist rather than specialist orientation of professional managers further reinforced short-range thinking. In addition, American industry had lost sight of its consumers: Dedication to service and quality had become a low priority in too many large corporations.

According to the organizationalists, corporate reward systems also encouraged behavior that was short term, safe, and conservative. The "punishments" for entrepreneurial failures—even when they were beyond a manager's control—were much greater than the rewards for successful risk taking. Additional sources of discouragement for the innovator included the hurdles and delays associated with too many levels of approval needed for developing a new product (or implementing a change in manufacturing processes or administrative practices).

The organizationalists also argued that, unlike the Japanese, American corporate managers were insensitive to "people issues." Corporate leaders had overlooked the latent potential of the human resources they strangled and stifled with authoritarian rules and excessive controls.

While the organizationalists disagreed among themselves on many key issues, they did agree about the bottom line: American industry had met the enemy and, like Pogo, discovered, "They are us."

To what extent was this line of argument accepted? Significantly, the scholars I polled were far more willing to lay the blame on management practices for the decline in the performance of industry than were those in business willing to place it on themselves:

PERCENT OF DECLINE EXPLAINED
BY THE ORGANIZATIONALIST ARGUMENT:

Managers' Estimate	21 percent
Entrepreneurs' Estimate	16 percent
Scholars' Estimate	38 percent

The Culturalists. This was an extremely diverse group of authors including Christopher Lasch, James Fallows, Daniel Bell, George Gilder, Barbara Tuchman, and Daniel Yankelovich who, while agreeing on nothing in particular, agreed in general that the decline in industrial performance was due to basic, underlying shifts in American society and culture. As a result of growing affluence, rising expectations, the impact of television, the women's movement, the trauma of Vietnam, and other social forces, there were new values in place in America. These values—while not entirely antibusiness—were nonetheless more concerned with the quality of life than with economic efficiency, more concerned with consumption than production, and more concerned with instant personal gratification than with long-term sacrifice for the good of the whole society. This was coupled with a growing mood of pessimism about the future.

Compounding these changes in values was an educational system that had faltered badly. While the typical Soviet high school graduate pursued three years of calculus, her American counterpart could not do simple algebraic calculations. Reading and writing skills declined, and the ability to speak foreign languages was all but extinct. A "clean hands" society was created that degraded production and industrial work and favored white-collar and professional employment. Fewer bright youths chose careers in engineering and science, more became lawyers and accountants. Nor were demographic trends of any help. An aging population (with few opportunities for promotion) further eroded the incentives critical to change or innovation.

In general, the culturalists believed there was a decline in discipline in American society as the result of challenges to traditional beliefs and practices. Instead of the traditional American entrepreneurial spirit, there was a psychology of (1) entitlement, (2) zero risk, and (3) narcissism that was conducive to neither productivity nor to innovation. (I'm a reformed culturalist myself. I keep the phone numbers of two other members of Culturalists Anonymous on my bedstand should I get the urge in the middle of the night to give a talk about changing social values!) To what extent was the culturalist argument accepted by the panel? As we see below, all three groups of respondents rated this the *least* convincing of the four theories they considered:

PERCENT OF DECLINE EXPLAINED BY THE CULTURALIST ARGUMENT:

Managers' Estimate	18 percent
Entrepreneurs' Estimate	16 percent
Scholars' Estimate	11 percent

One of the most obvious things to emerge from this survey is, of course, the clear differences in premises found among the three groups I polled. Corporate managers, entrepreneurs, and scholars see the same world in three quite different ways. Life is like a ball game: Where you sit determines what you see. This fact can be demonstrated even more clearly with reference to another aspect of the same 1981 survey. To further define the major impediments to innovation and barriers to productivity, I asked the 156 members of the panel to rate each of sixty items according to its negative impact on the performance of U.S. industry. While the ratings were in themselves interesting, even more surprising were the vast differences in the relative rank orderings of the managers, entrepreneurs, and scholars:

CAUSES OF THE DECLINE
OF AMERICAN INNOVATION AND PRODUCTIVITY

	CORPORATE MANAGERS' RANKINGS	ENTREPRENEURS' RANKINGS	SCHOLARS' RANKINGS
The diversion of funds for reinvestment away from the private sector due to high taxation.	1	1	15
Top managers being evaluated more on short-term profitability than successful long-term policies.	2	17	1
The uncertainty or unpredictability of government regulatory policies.	3	3	12
The current level of incentives for Americans to save and invest.	4	4	8
Scarcity of capital for new product development, plant, and equipment.	5	5	9
Bureaucratic resistance to change arising from the large size of organizations.	6	*	16
The current regulatory practices in environmental-, worker-, product-, and consumer-safety areas.	7	2	26
The difficulty of institutionalizing change in large, complex organizations.	8	*	6
The necessity for "defensive" research (e.g., antipollution devices) at the expense of	9	11	37

more "productive" research as a response to regulatory policies.

The traditional American entrepreneurial spirit giving way to a psychology of entitlement, zero risk, and narcissism.	10	8	38
Uncertainty of payoff on innovations because of current inflationary trends.	11	10	11
A managerial emphasis on "administration by the numbers," return on investment, and other financial and accounting controls.	12	37	3

Others:

Top managers come from nontechnical fields, such as finance, accounting, or law, and hence lack hands-on experience in production.	24	36	4
Lack of concern for process/technology innovation.	25	15	2
The nature of training received by young managers in American business schools.	49	38	5

(* indicates question not asked of entrepreneurs)

In general, corporate managers tended to see the causes of the decline in industrial performance as a combination of organizational and governmental impediments while entrepreneurs saw the causes as being almost purely governmental. At a minimum, a reading of this data should cause one to foreswear ever again treating business as a monolith. There are clearly two separate classes of business people in America: (1) the owner-entrepreneurs who are classic free-market individualists and (2) the professional managers who, while they buy into laissez-faire economic attitudes to a significant extent, have these beliefs greatly tempered by the realities of bureaucratic existence. This "class" difference can be seen most dramatically in the third part of my 1981 survey. Here, I asked the panel to consider some fifty possible actions that could be taken to enhance the performance of U.S. industry. The panelists estimated the degree of positive impact each action would have. The actions that corporate managers felt would have the most positive impact are compared with the rank orderings of the entrepreneurs and scholars as follows:

SOURCES OF IMPROVED CORPORATE PERFORMANCE

	CORPORATE MANAGERS' RANKINGS	ENTREPRENEURS' RANKINGS	SCHOLARS' RANKINGS
Greater organizational incentives for individuals to "champion" new ideas.	1	4	6
Managerial compensation systems greatly altered to reward individual merit, risk taking, and performance, rather than seniority or overall company performance.	2	7	7
Increased emphasis on evaluation of long-term performance of executives.	3	16	2
Increased investment tax credit for R&D expenditures.	4	1	11
Movement away from "zero-risk" toward "acceptable risk" in personal, social, economic, technological, and regulatory domains.	5	10	26
Greatly increased incentives for saving and investing.	6	2	5
Increased corporate basic research expenditures.	7	19	8
More rapid depreciation rate.	8	6	16
Reduced capital gains tax rate.	9	9	17
Reduction of disincentives/penalties for managerial risk taking.	10	14	10
Increased research expenditures on process technology.	11	23	1
Change in business school curriculum away from financial and accounting bias toward planning, entrepreneurship, and production skills.	12	17	3
Reduced corporate income tax rates.	13	3	12

Other:

Reduced influence within the corporation of people with narrow backgrounds in accounting, finance, or law.	24	35	4

Now, consider the two sets of responses together. What do we learn about the relative attitudes of the respondents concerning the causes and possible cures of economic decline? Talk about egotism: The entrepreneurs said, in effect, "Get the government off our backs and we'll make this old economy swing." Talk about *mea culpas:* The corporate managers said, in effect, "We accept responsibility for having created organizational systems with negative rewards for productivity and innovation." Talk about *mea culpas and egotism:* The scholars not only blamed themselves for teaching managers the wrong things, they confidently predicted that improved business education would lead to better industrial performance.

And talk about further complications and confusion: When I broke down the responses of the corporate panel, first by industry (oil, chemicals, manufacturing, and so forth), and second by job function (production, engineering, planning, finance, marketing, and general administration), I found that the views of managers were greatly influenced by both the business they were in *and* the nature of the job they held. That is, oil folks disagreed greatly with those in manufacturing over both the causes and cures of industrial decline and, even within the same company, marketers and engineers didn't exactly see eye to eye, either! And, curse the day statistics was invented, there were also great differences in opinion among corporate managers based on their age and educational backgrounds. (Gender, alas, was no problem: Unfortunately, there weren't enough women in high positions in these companies to do a statistically valid breakdown by sex.)

Now, the trouble with this kind of research is that you end up with reams of data, but what do you have? What is one to make of these findings? For our purposes, I think there are at least five useful conclusions that can be drawn from the evidence:

First, and most obvious, is that business people disagree greatly among themselves about the issues of innovation and productivity: Entrepreneurs disagree with corporate managers, marketers with finance folk, engineers with MBAs, the young with the old (and business scholars not only disagree with all of the above, they disagree among themselves, as well). It would seem that these differences are rooted in a reality that is many-faceted (obviously, impediments to innovation in the drug industry *are* different from those in heavy manufacturing) and are rooted in different world views (entrepreneurs draw their basic assumptions from free-market economics, corporate types are more likely to base their premises on organizational theories).

Second, and drawing on the first, it seems logical to conclude that no one of the four schools of thought (or no one of the three groups polled, or no one of the four demographic groups into which corporate managers were split) has a monopoly on truth. There is no reason to assume that one view of innovation and productivity is right to the exclusion of all the others. It is more reasonable to assume that, from their unique vantage points, each has caught a valid glimpse of a reality that is too great and too dynamic to be captured and understood by a single theorist, group, or company.

Third, the practitioners' responses provide a reality check on facile scholarly theorizing. For example, when the corporate managers considered the potential impact of some fifty actions on the performance of industry, the top eleven actions they ranked had to do with either improved incentives for individual managers or increased financial incentives for corporate investment in new technology. The managers thus zeroed in on two items—monetary rewards and technology—that were totally ignored in all five of the bestselling books on management published in the early 1980s: *Theory Z, The Art of Japanese Management, The One Minute Manager, In Search of Excellence*, and *Corporate Cultures*. This is not to imply that financial rewards and technology are the sole keys to improved innovation and productivity, or to imply that the other factors identified in the bestsellers are *un*important. Rather, it is to say that any single-dimensional perspective is likely to be limited and likely to overlook one or more important element of reality. (For example, Robert Hayes and William Abernathy's famous article, "Managing Our Way to Economic Decline," hit the technology theme right on the head; but it missed completely the human factors that were so well covered in the five bestsellers just mentioned.)

Fourth, and related to the third point, it seems reasonable to conclude that: If innovation has a technological side, then a marketing-oriented strategy is unlikely to be successful on its own; if productivity has a human side, then a technology-oriented strategy is unlikely to be successful on its own; if productivity and innovation both have marketing dimensions, then even full attention to technology and people will be insufficient to generate adequate corporate performance. Hence, the main conclusion I draw from this data is that productivity and innovation are complex, multidimensional issues that have been oversimplified by economic, social, and organizational theorists. Instead of the various narrow, unidimensional approaches advocated by the mixed bag of experts, I suggest that improved corporate performance requires a *balanced, multidimensional strategy*.

Fifth, that is exactly what the Vanguard do (as we are now more fully prepared to understand as we turn to an examination of their practices in the subsequent chapter).

7.

PRODUCTIVITY AND INNOVATION: THE PRACTICES OF THE VANGUARD

> Big ideas are so hard to recognize, so fragile,
> so easy to kill. Don't forget that,
> all of you who don't have them.
> —JOHN ELLIOTT, JR.,
> former chairman
> Ogilvy & Mather International

What do the following have in common:

- innovation
- quality
- productivity
- participation
- technology
- financial rewards
- profitability?

In most traditionally managed companies, these words would constitute nothing more than a laundry list of business concepts. In contrast, at Motorola they form a coherent, inseparable whole. Here is how these concepts are linked in the Motorola philosophy. To begin, Motorola's prime goal is to be the world's leading company in their industry. In the late 1960s, the top management of the firm became convinced that the only way they could become the industry leader was to produce high-quality products at competitive prices using state-of-the-art technology. In effect, they would have to be in the right markets at the right time with the right products. To accomplish that, they realized they would have to use their physical, financial, and human resources as efficiently and as effectively as any of their competitors.

In the eyes of Motorola's leaders, Robert Galvin and William Weisz, none of this need entail black magic, luck, or the application of Colonel Sanders's secret recipe. Instead, they saw it would take hard work. Ultimately, the company would need a managerial system in which there was a clear, complementary relationship between technology, organizational structure, and rewards. If they created such a coherent system they assumed that high profitability would inevitably follow. Nothing was left to chance. Even the development of new technology was planned—in effect, innovation was seen as a management function just like any other.

At Motorola, picking the right technology starts with a "technological road map," a forecast of basic technologies ten years into the future, with interim technological milestones, product "destinations," and clearly delineated routes to those destinations. Significantly, the preparation of the road map is not the task of Galvin and Weisz—it is the shared responsibility of people at every level in the company. All employees with technical knowledge are involved in generating the initial forecasts and are involved in implementing the plan that will be based on those forecasts. Semiannually, a cross-section of top managers meets to review the road map, to question its basic concepts and assumptions, and to challenge the methods or strategies that have been developed for reaching the goals of the plan (or destinations on the map). In this fashion, almost everyone in the firm participates in the innovative activity of new product creation and development.

Once they know *what* they are going to produce, Motorola then turns to how to produce it in a way that insures high quality. What is quality? To Motorola, quality is a subjective and changing measure applied by customers. If customers say a product is high quality, then, as far as Motorola is concerned, it is a high-quality product regardless of its objective physical attributes. Because customer satisfaction is at the heart of Motorola's philosophy, improvements in product quality will, by definition, improve profits. Since customers typically define quality as getting a product on time, with no defects, and at a competitive price, *quality*

in the eyes of consumers is usually synonymous with, and inseparable from, *productivity* in the eyes of Motorola employees.

How does Motorola improve quality/productivity? Internally,
productivity depends on five factors:

- The design of the product
  —The concept should be simple
  —Production should involve the lowest-cost methods avail-
  able
  —There should be zero defects
  —The product should be reliable
  —The product should be easy to maintain
- The use of the finest tools and the highest possible level of
  automation in manufacturing the product
- Continuous challenging of the policies, procedures, and
  practices used in making the product (and these should all
  be as simple and as understandable as possible)
- Constant and clear communication upward and downward
  about all of the above, and
- The continued and authentic participation of employees at all
  levels in the design and implementation of all of the above.

The latter is accomplished, of course, by the Motorola Participative Management Program (described in Chapter Three) in
which employee teams set targets and standards and are rewarded by monthly cash bonuses for achieving or exceeding
those standards.

The single most important element in this system is Motorola's
ability to link their production workers with their customers.
Here, in summary, is that link: Workers receive *financial rewards*
for their *participation* in product *innovation* and in the *productive* manufacturing of state-of-the-art *technology* that generates
high *profitability* because customers perceive that Motorola
products are high in *quality*.

The Motorola system pays off. The quality and dependability of
their semiconductors has made them the supplier of choice
among manufacturers who purchase high performance microprocessor chips (for use in computers and all sorts of other electronic devices). This technological edge is nothing new at Motorola: Since the company's beginning they have been innovators.

Motorola produced the first: walkie-talkie, commercial car radio, two-way FM car radio, portable TV, rectangular color TV tube, and TV that utilized semiconductors. What is remarkable is that the company has been able to consistently replenish their technological cupboard. In 1981, they became the first company to offer a completely integrated "cellular" mobile phone system composed of electronic exchanges and switches, telephones, and software—all of which are produced by Motorola.

Looking back to the previous chapter, one can say that Motorola has evolved a balanced, complex, multidimensional approach to productivity and innovation that is responsive to the concerns of:

—*Culturalists*—Motorola addresses the "new values" of workers, overcoming their "selfishness" by involving them in managerial decision making and holding them responsible for the quality and quantity of their own work;

—*Organizationalists*—Motorola creates rewards for entrepreneurial behavior, long-term thinking and customer service; and

—*Structuralists*—Motorola places as a prime goal the capture of world markets through investments in the latest technology.

But what about the concerns of the *antigovernmentalists?* Motorola speaks to these, too. The company's balanced approach to productivity and innovation is rounded out with an active program that encourages the development of appropriate federal industrial policies—policies based on sensible legislation and on equitable and reciprocal international trade policies. Motorola is a corporate leader in the effort to reform the nation's trade policies. Importantly, it is not necessary to agree with either the stand they have taken—or the methods by which they have chosen to publicize their position on governmental matters—to appreciate the differences between Motorola's approach on the one hand, and Mobil's on the other. While Mobil was attacking the government's tax policies for draining capital away that the energy industry needed for oil exploration, Mobil was at the same time investing their own capital in Montgomery Ward—a company that, to all the world, appeared to *use* energy rather than produce it. In contrast, while Motorola criticized the government for making it difficult to compete in international markets, the company made certain that none of their own failures to penetrate foreign markets were due to their own managerial shortcomings. That is, Motorola made certain that they were without fault before they began casting brickbats.

Given the company's remarkable record, one might expect them to appear on all those lists of excellent companies. That they have never made any such list is, I believe, due to the fact that they dare to transgress at least three of the "laws" of the currently dominant organizationalist school of management, specifically:

- Organizationalists often claim that excellent companies are "right-brained." That is, the leaders of great companies are not supposed to engage in formal strategic planning or in structured programs for improving productivity and innovation. Motorola, as befits a company of left-brained engineers, does everything in a precise, planned, rational, and structured way. For example, Motorola has a raft of midlevel technical committees composed of cross-sections of all corporate divisions. These committees are at the heart of formal efforts to plan for (and disseminate) productivity and innovation efforts. They have a manufacturing council, a purchasing council, an advanced automation council, and so forth, that meet regularly in seminars in which members deliver scientific papers designed to generate discussions about corporate performance. The original idea for such committees was developed at GM under Alfred Sloan; but, within a few years, GM's committees had been captured by powerful central staffs and, thus, their power was emasculated. In contrast, at Motorola, the committees are vital, active, influential, virile, and, especially, *cerebral* in a very formal, left-brained way.

- Organizationalists claim that all excellent companies "stick close to their customers." That is, since ideas for new products are generated by marketing departments, there is no need for formal research and development activities. In contrast to this wisdom, Motorola is a research-based firm that starts with the technology and *then* asks how it can be configured to meet consumer needs. That doesn't mean they don't do market

research, which they do and do well, but that they are not
slaves to it. Remember that key word, *balance*.

· Organizationalists claim that all excellent companies reward
productivity with "symbolic acts"—banners, balloons, campaign ribbons, and showers of affection. In contrast, Motorola
rewards productive and innovative behavior with cash.

I highlight these differences not to argue that right-brained,
marketing-oriented firms that go in for symbols and hugging
must always fail to elicit productivity and innovation. To make
such a claim would be to fall into the either/or trap that has
ensnared the organizationalists. In fact, Motorola does many
right-brained things (Robert Galvin is an open, supportive,
nondirective leader who likes to play his hunches); Motorola
often sticks close to customers (the company has been called the
most reliable producer of microprocessors by their corporate
clients); and Motorola does many important, symbolic things to
demonstrate concern for all employees (there are no executive
dining rooms, washrooms, or the like; *every* employee, including
Galvin and Weisz, wears a name tag at all times, and all Motorola
people, from janitors to the CEO, are called by their first names).
These things are clearly important. But, by themselves, they are
not hallmarks of excellence; in most cases, they will not elicit high
levels of productivity in the absence of planning, technology, and
financial rewards for performance. To pretend otherwise is to
base one's conclusions about the source of excellence on a biased,
limited sample of companies, or to curry the favor of Old Guard
managers by telling them they needn't do the hard and, to them,
distasteful work of creating a balanced system that includes (1)
planning, (2) technology, and (3) financial rewards for innovation
and productivity. Precisely because these three factors have received short shrift by the organizationalists, let us look at the
relationship of (a) money and (b) technology to innovation and
productivity in the Vanguard (reserving the role of planning for a
later discussion).

Pay and Other Financial Incentives

Financial rewards is the most ideological issue in corporations. On the one hand, there are those who believe in pay for performance. On the other, there are those who believe in equal pay for all employees at the same level. Few organizations manage successfully to bridge the gap between these two poles of thought. Instead of finding a creative mean, most corporations opt to follow the path of least resistance and end up standardizing pay in a rigid system that looks embarrassingly like the Federal Government's Grade and Pay Scale. It is ironic that the most unabashedly free-enterprise nation in the world accepts pay systems that could have been designed by Olaf Palme's Swedish bureaucrats!

Ironic, but understandable; for it is frustratingly difficult to design a reward system that is both equitable *and* motivational. Companies experiment with pay for performance only to drop the idea like a hot spud when employee complaints of "favoritism," "unfair treatment," and "subjectivity" lead the entire typing pool to hit the sidewalks in protest. It is simply easier to pay all those disgruntled folks the same amount and be done with it. But is that fair to those who work harder or better than the others? Doesn't equal pay kill off the incentive to excel?

My colleague, Edward Lawler, has shown that this dilemma is not unbridgeable. Indeed, it is only a dilemma if one insists that the gap between pay for performance and equity must be bridged with a single span. Lawler (who has consulted in most of the Vanguard and runner-up companies) shows that the great companies solve the problem by using a wide variety of pay systems—they are, to use his words, "shot through with incentives" for productivity and innovation. For starters, the Vanguard distinguish between *compensation* (the monthly pay you get for faithfully putting in your time on the assembly line or behind a desk) and *incentives* (the rewards you are not entitled to but come only as a result of extra effort). For example, every Motorola employee is fairly *compensated* (they are all paid competitive salaries), but all domestic employees are also eligible for a variety of *incentives* (profit sharing, the 40 percent bonus pool, and cash rewards for such things as suggestions, patents, product breakthroughs, and getting a new plant on-line).

The Vanguards' secret is getting the right mix of rewards and making certain that their incentive systems complement the overall objectives of their organizations. Lawler's research leads to the conclusion that corporations get the behavior that they reward. For example, a few years back a researcher at Gillette came up with the idea of using two blades instead of one in safety razors. The researcher developed a prototype of such a razor and turned it over to the corporation. While Gillette went on to rake in scads of moola on the Trac-II system, what did the researcher get for his efforts? His usual monthly paycheck. A company spokesman explained in a *Time* interview that Gillette didn't owe the researcher a plug nickel. After all, he was paid month in and month out when he didn't invent anything, why should he get a bonus for simply doing successfully what was in his job description?

Certainly, Gillette *compensated* him even when he didn't come up with any good ideas; but what *incentive* did he have to come up with more? The bigger question is what message did the company send to all other Gillette employees when the researcher failed to get a bonus? What is the likelihood that other Gillette employees will reach out in an attempt to excel? Will the company be able to attract (or retain) the most creative people (people who can go elsewhere and be rewarded for their ideas)?

Throughout the 1970s, pollsters found remarkable consistency among the responses of working Americans to two interrelated questions:

- When asked if they could work harder if they tried, between 70 percent and 80 percent of American workers would reply, yes, they could be more productive.
- When then given a list of reasons why they are not more productive, roughly 75 percent of workers would indicate that "all the benefits of harder work go to management and owners and not to workers."

The inability of managers to see this connection between pay and performance is demonstrated time and again. In 1981, the U.S. Chamber of Commerce polled a cross-section of American workers and asked them, "How should good ideas for improving productivity be encouraged?" The largest percentage of workers (42 percent) believed that money was the best incentive. In contrast, only 33 percent of the executives who were polled favored monetary rewards. Instead, fully 51 percent of the executives felt that workers would be most inspired by "personal recognition" (speeches, praise, balloons, battle ribbons). Only 26 percent of the workers polled found such nonmonetary awards effective as incentives.

The managerial misreading of what workers want apparently comes at some considerable cost to productivity. In 1983, the Public Agenda Foundation conducted a national poll in which only 22 percent of American workers said they saw any link between how hard they worked and how much they were paid, and an alarmingly high 73 percent conceded that they personally exerted less than full effort because there was no such link.

There is, then, a deep gulf between what managers assume workers want and what workers say they want. Managers have bought into the convenient "just be a nice guy" philosophy of the sixty-second school of management ("Here's all you've got to do folks: Give'em praise!"). Misperceptions have consequences. This philosophy reinforces the worst inclination of many managers: greed. When smiling and friendly managers fail to reward workers for their efforts, this in turn reinforces worker perceptions that it is senseless to work harder because managers will just exploit them. Of course, the best idea is for managers to give their subordinates both cash *and* praise; but if they are forced to choose, they should send money.

At Arco, Honeywell, Levi Strauss, and Motorola top managers are struggling to develop pay systems that complement the values stated in their constitutions. It is becoming clear that workers see the differences between what is said rhetorically and what is rewarded in practice—and they are wise enough to respond to the latter. Moreover, the issue of pay for performance is not confined to lower levels in the organization. The behavior of managers, too, is governed more by the direction of the carrot held in front of their noses than by the orders being barked by the person holding the stick. For example, while one of the nation's largest construction companies has always encouraged engineers to be cost conscious, they nonetheless used "cost plus" billing with their biggest clients (when Saudi Arabia is your customer, cost plus is the only way to fly). Since engineers were rewarded based on the amount of their "billings," this system instilled a lack of concern for getting things right the first time (after all, the cost of second and third tries would be picked up by the customer). That was fine with the Saudis, but it ultimately got them into contract difficulties when their client was a small company or a public utility to whom cost and quality control are crucial. The lesson is that managers get the behavior they reward.

If the goal of a pay system is to provide incentives for innovation and productivity, the *least* effective scheme is straight profit sharing (in which all employees receive the same fixed percentage of overall corporate profits). Kodak has such a plan that annually pays about $2,000 per employee. If Kodak does well, every employee does well (even poor performers), and if Kodak does poorly, every employee does poorly (even outstanding performers). Such pay systems are common in the Old Guard (GM's managers participate in a similar system). Interestingly, Kodak also has a bonus plan that, on average, annually pays about fifty *cents* per employee for ideas that contribute to performance. Again, Kodak is generous to a fault with an inappropriate benefit and chintzy in an area where they could get some potential payoff.

Hewlett-Packard has gone further than any other large corporation in tying managers' rewards to their efforts to live by corporate values. H-P's constitution outlines their obligations to eight different stakeholders. Putting their money where their mouth is, the company evaluates all managers annually (for both pay and promotion) on how well they met the needs of those eight stakeholders. There is thus no ambiguity about objectives, no sense of contradictory signals, no confusion over what the company wishes to accomplish. (Similarly, at Dayton-Hudson a set percentage of the annual performance review of managers is allocated to how well they meet social objectives. Levi does the same for employee development, and Arco rewards those who meet affirmative action objectives.)

The difficulty, of course, is that there is no one right way to reward people, no ideal compensation system. Each corporation must discover the right forms of rewards and the right measures of performance for their particular business needs. All of the Vanguard have their own mix of: *awards* (Arco gives $5,000 prizes for special effort), *equity sharing* (Levi distributes shares of stock when the corporation passes important performance milestones), *merit pay* (Motorola measures managerial performance over as long as a six-year time frame), *gain sharing* (Motorola gives bonuses for reduction in waste and increases in productivity), and *profit sharing* (20,000 Levi employees are part of a plan that during good times has paid out the equivalent of a week's pay to each employee per quarter).

Within the last year or so, Arco has developed one of the most sophisticated compensation systems in industry, one that addresses all four of the major concerns of employees and organizations discussed earlier. In addition to rewarding *merit* with their $5,000 bonuses for technical excellence, they provide *security and equality* with close to the highest level of average pay and benefits in American industry, they meet *quality of life needs* with a generous Employee Stock Option Plan, and they encourage *efficiency* with a touch of Skinnerian behaviorism ("Comfort Bucks," which are certificates exchangeable for cash that are distributed randomly to employees who are behaving productively).

And, as there is no single correct mix of rewards, there is no single right way to measure performance. There are clearly wrong ways, however. Corporations like ITT and GM—with pay systems in which people, groups, or divisions must compete with each other destructively—are patently unfair *and* ineffective. In overresponse to this problem, some American theorists have opted out of the measurement business completely and now advocate a Japanese-style system in which everyone at the same grade level is paid equally. This system is also unfair and ineffective. First, there is now considerable doubt whether the Japanese do, indeed, pay workers equally. (Even on mainland China, industrial workers are on a bonus system and can earn up to three times their regular salaries based on how hard they work and on the contributions of their ideas to productivity improvement. Some Communist managers apparently know more about economic motivation than do many American capitalists.) Second, even if it were true that the Japanese paid everyone equally, it would be irrelevant. In America, workers *want* pay for performance. It is the responsibility of American managers to respond to the desires of their major stakeholders—particularly when doing so is consistent with the broader values of capitalist society and the need for improved productivity and innovation.

The best argument managers use against pay for performance is that "workers may say they want it but, when we try it, they cry 'foul.' " When one studies such situations, one invariably finds that workers object not to the principle of pay for performance but to the particular way in which the principle has been administered. The only system of pay for performance that will be widely perceived as fair is one in which the participants in the system identify the measures themselves by which they are to be evaluated. Lawler's research shows that members of a typing pool, researchers in a laboratory, or divisional presidents are capable of designing *accurate* measures of their own performance. More important, members of a work group can also agree that the criteria they designed are *fair*. Significantly, a person who was not a member of the group would not be able to identify better measures than those actually doing the work. And an outsider's measures would not be viewed by the group as being as legitimate as their own measures. Finally, if the group is evaluated by its own measures it cannot later complain that such measures were arbitrary, subjective, or otherwise unfair. Thus, the creative way to bridge the ideological gulf between pay for performance and equity is to have the workers being evaluated participate in establishing the measures by which they will be rewarded. If this is done well, it will be found that the real objections to pay for performance are rooted in the methods of measurement and not in the end of rewarding productivity and innovation. As Motorola has discovered, a participative gainsharing plan can lead to greater cooperation between managers and workers as all come to work toward the same goals and reap the fruits of their common efforts.

Let's now turn to the second most slighted subject in recent discussions of innovation and productivity: technology.

Deere's "Factory of the Future"

The Wilson Learning Corporation of Eden Prairie, Minnesota, publishes a colorful and appealing poster in which organizational performance is graphically represented as a bicycle, the front wheel of which is "people," and the back wheel "technology." In the Wilson poster, none of the bicycles have front wheels, symbolizing the undeniable fact that American managers over the last three decades foolishly ignored the human factor in their businesses. In overreaction to this managerial error, many consultants are now selling bicycles with no rear wheels (search as one might, the word "technology" is hard to find in any of the five management bestsellers of the 1980s). The problem is that bicycles without rear wheels have no mechanism for forward propulsion—they lack the productive drive of technology. This is no better than a bicycle that lacks the steering power of the human mind. Wilson's point is that all bicycles must stand and move on two wheels. It is a message that has been absorbed at the Vanguard—these companies are as balanced on two wheels as any in America.

Like the concepts "innovation," "productivity," and "pay for performance," "technology" is also hard to define. Let us call it "the systematic application of scientific knowledge to practical tasks" (with the understanding that "scientific" includes all organized and replicable knowledge, both quantitative and qualitative). The reason why most recent books on management pay scant attention to technology is because management professors know nothing about it (for example, of the 140 professors of business at the USC business school where I work, only four have any background in technology, and only one—not me—can lay claim to being an expert). And technology frightens the hell out of most managers (who were educated, after all, by that very same technologically illiterate mob just mentioned).

The state of most managers' knowledge of technology is frozen at about the level of Eli Whitney's great idea that, if parts could all be standardized, they would be interchangeable. This led to the introduction of efficient mass production of manufactured goods (as opposed to the slow and expensive process of making things one by one). Beyond that, all most managers know about manufacturing technology is that it is complicated, it creates a constant demand for costly reinvestment, and that it often involves unionized workers. To learn more, managers know they would have to visit a hot, noisy, and grimy factory where they would not only get their Brooks Brothers suits soiled, they would get grunted at (at best) by people who are supposed to be *their* employees. Is it any surprise that so many managers come to the conclusion to shut the factory down and acquire a burger chain?

At Deere, they had a different idea. Until 1970, Deere & Company's "mass produced" tractors were built mostly by hand in an odd collection of grimy, sixty-year-old brick factories spread over half a square mile near the center of a sleepy Iowa town (improbably named Waterloo). The factory, like many manufacturing operations, had grown a little like my Uncle Fred's house—add a bathroom here, a bedroom there. At the beginning, an entire tractor was made in one building but, as tractors became more complicated (and bigger), additional steps in the manufacturing process—and the introduction of new, complex tools—necessitated adding a new wing, building a new plant, and all manner and sorts of other "amendments" to the original facility. By the late 1960s, building a tractor had become a miracle of orchestration, a cacophonous symphony involving thousands of workers, engaged in hundreds of different tasks, making thousands of parts in a score of different buildings.

A miracle, yes, but to Deere it seemed like a far too complex and inefficient process. A tractor is built up from its basic parts—gears, drive shafts, axles, and the like. In the old Deere Waterloo works, for example, a slug of uncut steel would be sent to a man on the second floor of Building A operating a hobbing machine, and he would start the process of turning that piece of metal into a gear. When he was finished with it, another man would transport the hobbed piece of metal to a worker on the fifth floor of Building B, who operated a drilling machine. When she was finished with the proto gear, it would be transported to the first floor of Building C for grinding, then back to Building A for cleaning, and then shipped to the assembly building where it was stored in a "crib" (a giant parts supply room). An assembly worker in need of a gear was at the mercy of a materials handler who lined up at the crib, waiting his turn to give the inventory manager an order, which, when filled, he would take back to the assembly worker.

If one mapped the path of a part as it moved around the old Waterloo plant, the path resembled that of an errant Ping-Pong ball bouncing from here to there as men and women dragged it back and forth in various stages of preparation. Then, when the part was put into a transmission or a hydraulic system, workers would drag that assembled component to where it would be bolted into a tractor chassis. If one had walked by the old Waterloo plant, one would have seen tractors in various stages of completion being schlepped from one building to another until, finally, they would come to a hot and stinking building where they would all be painted a glorious gleaming green (the shade of fresh alfalfa). The tractors would then be finished and, as any Iowa farmer would tell you, they were the best damn tractors in the world. The production process may not have been textbook neat but, by God, it worked!

In the early 1970s, business was going swimmingly for Deere & Company. The CEO, William Hewitt, was in the process of turning Deere, traditionally a domestic producer of farm equipment, into an international manufacturer as well. Hewitt was also enlarging Deere's product line from farm machinery into construction machinery—smack into the bailiwick long-dominated by the big, yellow monsters of Caterpillar Tractors. Around about that time, engineers in the grand, new Eero Saarinen-designed Deere headquarters in Moline, Illinois, had a daring idea: Deere could build the factory of the future, an automated factory with wondrous machines, with efficiencies beyond anything yet realized. And not just new machines here or there, but an entirely new *system*, starting with the design of the tractor right on down to fueling her up! The old Waterloo works had reached its capacity and had become unmanageable—what with a foundry, an engine works, a transmission plant, and what-have-you all at one location. It was obvious that the company would have to do something to both expand production and to break it down into more manageable units. But who would have expected such a bold plan from the country slickers in Moline? When others were retreating from manufacturing—conceding markets to foreigners and diversifying into "cleaner" white-collar businesses— Deere decided to remain the best at what they did so well. Hewitt was not an engineer, but he instinctively understood the importance of engineering and the significance of the grand scheme being laid before him. He asked: How much would this cost? Oh, it will drive our total capital expenditures to some two hundred million a year for, say, ten years. That will take every penny we've got, it will depress earnings, it will drive us perilously close to the edge . . . It's risky, Hewitt said, but we've got to do it.

In 1974, Deere bought a corn farm, a big one, on the outskirts of Waterloo. That's where they would build their factory of the future, in the midst of working farms, to symbolize the company's tie to the soil. The factory opened in 1981. Forget about assembly lines, forget even about robots, forget everything you've ever seen in factories or heard about them. This one is different. Not just that it is clean, quiet, and well lighted. Not just that it is architecturally pleasing sitting out there, across the field from several classic red barns with silos and all. Not just that the bloody place is twenty-four times the size of a football field (and several stories high, to boot). Not just that there are few people to be seen on the factory floor. No, what strikes you most is the *lines*. The factory looks like one of those Piet Mondrian paintings, all color and geometry. Geometry, especially. The interior of the factory is dominated by vertical lines running from the floor to the ceiling, and horizontal lines connecting them all in an eye-catching grid. Thin pipes, beams, pillars, girders, rails . . . the only thing like it was one of those German factories designed by Walter Gropius in the early part of the century, one in which the skeleton of the building—stark, naked lines—was exposed on the outside. But this is the *inside* of a factory, not the exterior. (The outside is clean and smooth and white.)

The inside of the new Deere Waterloo Tractor Works is dominated by the geometric pattern of a 68-foot high-rise stack of some ten thousand storage bins—wire cages that look like shopping carts. All the parts used in assembling a tractor are stored in these bins. Like a giant Rubik's Cube, this structure is puzzling. How do they get parts out of a bin that's up there on the top and over there in the middle? And where is the crib manager and the queue of workers waiting to get their parts?

The answer, one discovers, is that a computer finds the part, directs an automated hoist to retrieve the bin that it is in, delivers it to a waiting "robocarrier" (a computer-controlled cart), and this carrier transports the part to the worker who had requested it by simply punching a number on a terminal at his workstation. (The robocarriers strike terror in the visitor's heart. Seemingly hundreds of them are gliding about at all times, unmanned, going their own ways at the breakneck speed of 135 feet per second, each carrying up to a 4,000-pound payload. One would, indeed, break your neck if it hit you. But you are shown that a robocarrier is a smart little devil. Stand in its way, and it stops dead in its path.)

Gone, then, are people dragging parts around. Gone are people going up and down elevators to get parts out of the storage crib. Gone are workers standing around in queues waiting for parts. At this plant, computers "talk" to each other and coordinate the delivery of parts—and they arrive just in time for assembly. There are miles of guide-wire paths that the robocarriers run along, miles of conveyors and monorail tracks—all those lines!

The system saves the workers' time and labor. And it saves the company money: Deere now needs to have only about 50 percent of the inventory required by their competitors.

Another source of increased productivity is reduced set-up time. The plant is unlike the typical assembly operation in which identical products are produced by men and machines engaged, over and again, in the same repetitive tasks. Instead, nearly every tractor built at Waterloo is different, *customized.* Farmers are finicky folk. One wants a 15-gear transmission, another will pay less and get fewer. One wants a closed cab, another wants fresh air. The Waterloo Tractor Works can turn out some five thousand different tractor configurations, customizing each without the time and cost of retooling, without so much as stopping production to remind a worker that the next tractor needs a stereo tape deck.

This system is called "flexible manufacturing" and it is to the historical development of manufacturing processes what computer-assisted instruction (à la PLATO) is to the historical development of teaching. When Eli Whitney invented the "American Method" of assembly based on standardized parts and standardized products, could he ever have guessed that one day manufacturing would evolve to the point where his *mass* production would also be *customized* production? Eli, you've met your Waterloo!

Please, it is not the case that Deere's engineers invented all of the methods utilized in their marvelous system. Rather, Deere has had the audacity to bring together various state-of-the-art technologies developed elsewhere and to combine them in innovative ways that increase their productivity through synergistic coordination. Here are some of the techniques Deere is using:

Computer-Assisted Design and Engineering. Deere spends more than 4 percent of their annual sales on research and development—about 50 percent more than the average for the entire machinery industry. The lion's share of Deere's R&D is spent at their spanking new Product Engineering Center (also near Waterloo) where 125 people with advanced professional and technical degrees lead an even larger team of technicians and assistants in designing, developing, and testing engines, transmissions, hydraulic systems, and electronic components. In cold rooms, hot rooms, sound rooms, wind tunnels, and other chambers of horror,

Deere engineers and scientists will take a tractor and freeze it, broil it, blow on it, bump it, shake it, pound it, and twist it, all to the end of producing the highest quality product possible. The lab is also the "conscience" of the firm on safety and environmental issues, paying close attention to such factors as operator safety, noise levels, pollution emissions, and so forth.

While the lab sits in the middle of a cornfield, it has the air of a sophisticated university campus (indeed, some 40 employees are pursuing master's degrees in engineering while on the job). The lab is among the nation's leaders in the industrial application of computer-assisted design and computer-assisted engineering. Deere engineers now do their drawings on computer screens. The computer then generates design specifications which it feeds to machine tools, instructing the tools what to make and how to make it. The computer is also used to search through Deere's inventory of some 250,000 parts, looking for an existing part that can be used in a prototype product, saving the expense of designing and making a new part.

Group Technology. Better utilization of parts is a key to almost all of the increases in productivity that Deere has realized in the last decade. "Group technology" is an approach to improving productivity based on identifying the underlying commonality found among "families" of parts. Deere has developed a system for scientifically clustering parts based on their shapes and functions. By rationalizing parts in this way, the company has been able to: achieve greater standardization across product lines (they can now use tractor parts in construction vehicles, for example); reduce the total number of parts in their inventory; get greater economies of scale in production (making more each of a smaller variety of parts); and avoid reinventing a part when an existing one would work just fine.

Group technology also leads to reduced costs by minimizing materials handling and by allowing common tools to make an entire family of parts. For example, prior to the introduction of group technology, only 7 percent of the parts used in one Deere manufacturing department were made completely within the confines of that department. In the past, a part from this department would be sent to the first floor milling department, moved to the fifth floor for drilling, sent half a mile away for grinding, then back to the original department for cleaning and shipping.

Now, using group technology, 72 percent of the parts used in this department are made from beginning to end within its walls. The savings—as measured by schlepping, storing, inventory, lost parts, and quality—are enormous.

Focused Factories. When Deere opened its new assembly facility out in the cornfield, this permitted them to reorganize the cluster of old factories in downtown Waterloo. Deere then redesigned them and turned them into the component works of the future. Deere engineers rationalized operations, creating "factories within a factory," each responsible for the complete production of a single component (for example, transmissions, hydraulics, gears). In this way, workers came to feel they were part of a small company (the largest having 3,000 employees), instead of working in a single big, impersonal factory with 14,000 workers.

Within each small factory, operations were further broken down into "cells." Here is how a cell is different from a traditional manufacturing department: In the production of gears in traditional plants, for example, a slug of metal was moved around from machine to machine, from a worker turning a lathe, to another working a hob, to another on a shaper, to another on a shaver, and, finally, to one operating a mill. This process would employ five workers on five different machines (and at least one other worker to transport the part between them). By grouping the production of gears into a single "cell," three operators now run their own little cluster of two lathes, three hobs, three shapers, a shaver, and a milling machine. And, by bringing the machines into close proximity, it is now possible to move gears automatically from one machine to the other, thus eliminating the need for transportation. All of this sounds simple, but it cost $15 million for Deere to improve the efficiency of just the production of three sizes of gears—that is, only three parts of the thousands that go into the making of a tractor. That's why the entire Deere transformation cost $2 billion.

Flexible Machinery. Because numerically controlled machines permit rapid retooling, they have become increasingly popular in American industry. But Deere goes one step further by linking dozens of numerically controlled machines together through a common computer. The computer not only constantly reprograms each machine to do different tasks, it rationalizes the overall systemic efficiency of all the machines by directing parts and work to each machine at the proper pace and in the optimal amount. This system eliminates both machine idle time and long queues of parts.

Robotics. It is curious that one of the nation's most advanced manufacturing operations utilizes the services of only a very few of those machines most commonly associated with futuristic production. Robots are unloved by Deere engineers for two reasons: Robots weld, but Deere's high-quality tractors are bolted together; robots work on high-volume assembly lines, but the manufacturing of tractors is a low-volume business. But robots also do dirty, unsafe work—like spray painting—and it is in such jobs that Deere employs a few of these mechanical workers, saving the lungs of dozens of *real* workers.

Deere has been able to introduce the factory of the future without having workers pay the price of the transition. Through careful planning, there have been no layoffs as the result of automation. (Thousands of Deere workers *were* laid off as the result of the severe 1980–84 depression in the farm industry, but not as a result of technology. Indeed, because of low demand for tractors, the Waterloo plant never, in its first three years, operated at more than 50 percent of capacity.) The jobs of many workers have also been upgraded. For example, workers who once drove forklifts have been retrained and they now operate complex machines. In addition to finding their tasks more interesting, workers also appreciate the cleaner, quieter, lighter work environment and the much improved amenities (cafeterias, dressing areas) off the shop floor.

Significantly, one problem Deere has with this marvelous system is that it complicates pay for performance. Historically, almost all of Deere's workers have been on an incentive system that rewards output. Now, in many cases, machines do all the labor—which is fine with the workers—but the machines are *also* responsible for work quality and quantity—which isn't so fine. In the factory of the future, automation makes it difficult to measure and reward the contributions to productivity of individual workers. To put some incentives back into the system, Deere is now experimenting with group rewards à la Motorola and with profit sharing and other alternatives to traditional piecework. Why do they care about employee incentives if machines make the tractors? Because, while the machines may do all the *labor,* they do not do all the *work.* There is still plenty of brainwork left. This is work that, if it isn't done well, is costly to repair. For instance, a bored worker who neglects to monitor the maintenance schedule of machines can cost the company tens of thousands of dollars in downtime. It is no wonder that Vanguard managers often say that the two key variables in corporate performance are technology and human motivation!

One other problem that Deere may or may not have with their factory of the future is with the colossal size and scale of the undertaking. Deere went ahead and built the giant Waterloo facility in the midst of a trend toward small manufacturing plants. In the 1960s and 1970s, Pratt & Whitney and General Electric both built giant plants in which to assemble jet engines— and both quickly learned that they could not make these mammoth facilities anywhere near as productive as their much smaller plants. As a result, both companies—and hundreds of others that soon followed—adopted a "small is beautiful" manufacturing philosophy to avoid the diseconomies of scale that result from workers feeling like ants in a giant colony. Deere, instead, gambled that they could create the sense of smallness that motivates workers by stressing teamwork and their factory-within-a-factory concept. They reasoned that, if demand picked up and if there was a major shakeout in the industry (which, in fact, occurred when International Harvester went out of the tractor business in early 1985), they could capture the economies of scale of fully integrated production. In addition, through sound management, Deere has made the Tractor Works break even while operating at only 40 percent of capacity. Nonetheless, the risk is great. Not only did Deere lock themselves into high overhead, they locked themselves into the relatively small expensive end of the tractor market (one couldn't build small, cheap tractors profitably in Waterloo). In this regard, Deere has a possible failing in common with the two giant leaders of the Old Guard— IBM and GM—both of which are addicted to manufacturing megalomania, which is the most likely cause of any future failures they may experience.

This future vulnerability not withstanding, what is the bottom line at Deere? Does all of this effort have a payoff? Between 1971 and 1981, Deere's sales went from $1.5 billion to $5.4 billion. (During that period Deere's earnings were higher than the average for *high-tech* companies!) Beginning in 1980, Deere weathered the worst farm depression in fifty years without experiencing a losing year, while their chief competitors International Harvester and Massey-Ferguson were driven to the brink of bankruptcy. Deere boosted both capacity and efficiency during the farm depression of 1980–84, even though they were already the low-cost producer in the industry. They emerged from the depression poised to move from a 40 percent share to 60 percent of the domestic market for farm equipment.

Deere proves that it is possible to be innovative, productive, and dynamic in a sleepy, mature, cyclical, and highly competitive heavy manufacturing business. If Deere can do it, why not U.S. Steel or Chrysler? Why did Deere find the way to become fully competitive in world markets (the Japanese don't dare take them on in anything but the small tractors that Deere has no interest in producing) while International Harvester, Massey-Ferguson, and, in fact, almost all of the largest North American manufacturers did not?

There is nothing magic or exotic about what Deere accomplished. Automated materials handling, automated inventory management, group technology, customization, focused factories, flexible machinery, and computer-assisted design, engineering, and manufacturing—none of these ideas was invented by Deere. Yet Deere invested in them—even in bad years—while others did not. Why? The answer, according to James F. Lardner, Deere's vice president of manufacturing development, is none other than differing *managerial assumptions:*

> If our foreign competition can recognize the advantages of these technologies and has been willing to accept the risks involved in adopting them, why haven't American companies done the same? Our present concepts of organizational structures, manufacturing management qualifications, and financial-analysis-and-control systems used to evaluate investment—all of these stand in our way.

For example, traditional financial analysis causes managers to miss out on new technologies because "hurdle rates," "discounted cash flow," and other cost-accounting measures are ad hoc. That is, they may be appropriate for analyzing the value of single machines, but they are not useful in evaluating an entire *system* in which, when a critical mass is reached, unheard-of economies may be realized. Applying traditional analysis, there is no financial justification for replacing a conventional $175,000 numerically controlled machine with a $350,000 computer-controlled machine. Only if one can see the whole of production as a *system* with long-term benefits will one be able to see the justification for the greater investment. Hence, the desire for short-term profit maximization will cause managers to skimp on the investments that will insure long-term profitablity.

Most American managers simply don't understand production technology, don't understand the long-term opportunities presented, for example, by a system that allows for the cheap manufacture of small batches of goods. It is no wonder, then, that in the United States 34 percent of all machine tools are twenty years old or more (as opposed to 24 percent in England, and 18 percent in Japan). It took American managers some twenty years to be able to understand the advantages of numerically controlled tools; now these same technological illiterates are resisting the move to flexible manufacturing and, worse, they are having their predilections reinforced by the currently ascendant school of consultants who tell them the future is in marketing *not* in manufacturing. As Deere's William Hewitt recognized, the future is, in fact, to those who think *systemically:*

> We have no special advantage that cannot accrue to any other company. The primary way we can maintain and advance our position is through better planning, design, engineering, fabricating, distributing, selling, and servicing—through better work on the part of John Deere people and groups.

That's what productivity and innovation are all about in the end: a balanced system of people and machines—bicycles with two fully inflated wheels.

R&D Where You'd Least Expect It

When we think of high tech, we tend to think about companies in the Silicon Valley, along Boston's Route 128, in North Carolina's Research Triangle—and not about a tractor factory in Waterloo, Iowa. But, in fact, we see that the process technology used at the Deere Tractor Works is far more sophisticated than the hand assembly used in making many computers. While we're engaged

in destroying myths, let's consider two other improbable technological leaders: Weyerhaeuser and Levi Strauss. For there's high
tech in the timber and pants businesses as surely as John Deere
uses the latest technology to make big green tractors.

Weyerhaeuser has outspent their nearest competitor by about
two to one in research and development activities over the last
decade. In 1978, Weyco opened a $40 million research center
near their headquarters in the Washington woods. Weyco's scientists are now using genetic engineering to find ways to stimulate
plant growth; they are using computer-assisted graphics to find
the most efficient way to cut up giant logs; and they are using the
latest in chemical engineering to extract and purify cellulose.
These efforts are paying off: In 1950 nearly 80 percent of a tree
was wasted; today, Weyco uses over 96 percent of every tree they
cut. Nearly everything—roots, leaves, stumps—is now turned
into useful products. Even sawdust finds its way into such things
as fireplace logs, oils, and paper. And whatever is left over is
efficiently burned, making the company's milling operations
nearly energy self-sufficient. Not even the hot water used in
making paper is wasted: It is recycled and used to nurture baby
salmon in an adjoining Weyco hatchery.

As we have seen, Weyco was the first company to farm trees (as
opposed to the old cut-and-run method that left millions of acres
of the Northwest as barren of growth as Telly Savalas's pate). The
company now spends about $150 million annually on reforesta-
tion. To speed up the rate of tree growth (few tree farmers live
long enough to harvest the crops they plant), Weyco built enormous greenhouses in which to cultivate seedling Douglas firs. A
waste of dough, said Weyco's competitors, just wait 'til the first
housing recession and they'll be stuck with acres of unused
greenhouse capacity—that'll fix those do-gooders. Sure enough,
demand for lumber declined as the federal government coped
with inflation by causing a depression in the housing industry.
What did Weyco do? They used their greenhouses to raise seedling grapevines for the booming Washington State vineyards.
Weyco's scientists were able to produce grape stalks with large,
fibrous roots that greatly increased the survival rate of these
valuable plants. Weyco sold 60,000 grape cuttings the first year
(and 200,000 in the second year) of operation. And, while such
Weyco competitors as Macmillan Bloedel, Georgia-Pacific, and
Crown Zellerbach listened to the popular but facile advice from

consultants ("Don't invest in R&D, just get close to your customer"), Weyco's scientists went on their dreamy way and engineered thinner, lighter, and stronger particleboard and flake-
board that opened entirely new markets for the company.
Throughout the recession, Weyco continued to invest in R&D, in
new products, and in new plant and equipment, while their
competitors played it safe and tried to maximize quarterly earnings by minimizing investment. In 1984, Weyco emerged from
the recession as the industry leader—indeed, as the only wood
products company not deeply in the red. While it was as
countercultural for a wood products company to go high tech as
it was for a tractor company to do the same, the payoff in both
cases was enormous.

Similarly, it is easy to be the technological leader in the apparel
industry. Most of the folks in the "rag trade" devote all their
attention to marketing and none to R&D. These companies see
themselves as being in "the fashion business." In sharp distinction, Levi Strauss says that their business is "product innovation."
Product innovation includes process R&D (Levi invented a semi-
automatic "pocket closing" machine); fabric R&D (Levi developed a high-quality cotton and polyester denim); and market
research (the company has found that customers want "durability, washability, comfort, breathability, and warmth" from Levi
products). Says CEO Robert Haas, "We want to be *first* in our
industry in these three aspects of product innovation, and *second*
in fashion." The company is also the industry leader in the use of
computers: Their Terminal Order Entry System allows salespeople to plug into any phone and place an order with a central
computer. This speeds up delivery and reduces inventory. The
judicious use of technology contributes to Levi's ability to compete with foreign and domestic manufacturers—competitors
who often run sweatshops while Levi pays fair wages.

Weyerhaeuser and Levi Strauss are technological leaders in
industries where R&D is considered an arcane, even bizarre,
activity. Moreover, in industries where technology *is* considered
important, Vanguard members Arco, Honeywell, CDC, and Motorola are near the top in terms of technological input (measured
by expenditures for R&D and new plant and equipment) and
technological output (measured by product innovation and labor
and capital productivity). Still, I would not claim that the Vanguard are the best across the board in all technological applica-

tions. In one small experiment, Digital Equipment Corporation has done something that no American corporation has dared to do: allow workers to alter the basic nature of technology being used in a plant. Some fifty-seven DEC employees recently designed their own factory to make the guts of a computer. The workers were given carte blanche to take apart the assembly line, modify machines, and alter production techniques to find ways to make the computer component as efficiently as any competitor, domestic or foreign.

The lesson here is that technological superiority entails more than spending vast sums on R&D. Xerox, GM, and many other struggling industrial giants spend as much, often more, than the Vanguard on research and product development. The problem in those companies is bureaucratic resistance to the innovations of their researchers. In the Old Guard, change is seen as disruptive of business routine. In contrast, Vanguard managers see change as the flywheel that keeps their business moving. Hence, they embrace the innovations of their engineers and researchers —and workers.

Thus, even when coupled with pay for performance, a commitment to technological leadership is an insufficient guarantee of high productivity and innovation. In reality, the vehicles that carry the Vanguard forward have more than two wheels (it turns out that life is always more complex than the models we create in order to describe it). Corporate performance requires more than a bicycle—it requires something on the order of complexity of a space shuttle with dozens of support systems that complement a corporation's pay and technology policies. Consider just two examples: At each of the Vanguard companies, one also finds (a) an openness to new ideas, and (b) a willingness to take risks.

Openness to New Ideas

There is a natural resistance to all things new. Particularly in organizations, there is a tendency toward the "herd instinct" that forecloses an honest appraisal of a fresh perspective or a new idea. This instinct was first identified by Wilfred Trotter, who wrote:

The mind likes a strange idea as little as the body likes a strange protein and resists it with similar energy. It would not perhaps be too fanciful to say that a new idea is the most quickly acting antigen known to science. If we watch ourselves honestly we shall often find that we have begun to argue against a new idea even before it has been completely stated.

Imagine, then, that you are a Control Data manager in 1963 and you have two new ideas: One, you want to make disk drives for computers (when the world is quite pleased, thank you, using tapes for memory storage); and, two, you want to sell these drives *not* directly to customers, but rather to other computer manufacturers (when every expert "knows" that it is self-defeating to make parts for competitors who will, in time, produce their own and leave you out in the cold). Imagine your surprise, then, when your boss authorizes you to go ahead and implement your idea. And imagine what all those experts who knew better in 1963 say twenty years later when Control Data is the industry leader in the production not only of disk drives but of *all* peripheral equipment for sale to computer manufacturers. If you can't imagine them saying anything, you are probably right. Because the one thing the mind likes less than a strange idea is evidence that staying open to new ideas is a central ingredient in long-term business success.

Interestingly, the roadblocks to organizational innovation parallel the roadblocks to individual creativity. In *The Act of Creation*, Arthur Koestler described and documented the genesis of the greatest scientific inventions. Koestler concluded that creative progress occurs through the unblocking of familiar ways of viewing the nature of things. Habit is the stumbling block. Even the greatest of minds will stare a fact in the face for decades, but reject it—literally, fail to see it—because it didn't fit into their preconceptions of the order of the universe. Koestler noted that, in the original manuscript of Copernicus's *Revolutions of Heavenly Spheres*, the great astronomer had written the following:

> It should be noticed, by the way, that if the two circles have different diameters, other conditions remaining unchanged, then the resulting movement will not be a straight line, but what mathematicians call an ellipse.

But Copernicus—having hit upon the true shape of planetary orbits—was unable to accept the fact. He crossed out the passage,

Koestler wrote, because "Copernicus was an orthodox believer in the physics of Aristotle and stubbornly clung to the dogma that all heavenly bodies must move in perfect circles at uniform velocities."

The pattern repeats itself throughout history: Kepler "discovered" gravity—only to reject it later. Galileo refused to see the comets before his eyes in the telescope because all heavenly bodies must, in his world view, move in circles while those "optical illusions" persisted in traveling in elliptical orbits. And the brilliant mathematician Poincaré "had held all the loose threads in his hands" of the theory of relativity, yet he would not face the consequences of where his data led him and, thus, failed to make the discovery that a "lesser" mathematician, Einstein, would make years later. Similarly, the theory of evolution and the theory of the subconscious had been "created" many times before Darwin and Freud—but were not "seen" as important. Koestler called this age-old problem "snow blindness."

When Plutarch anticipated Newton's First Law of Motion by roughly six hundred years, the great minds of Europe failed to note his accomplishments, so blinded were they by the Aristotelian view of the universe. Koestler explained why this is so:

> One of the conspicuous handicaps is the conservatism of the scientific mind in its corporate aspect. The collective matrix of a science at a given time is determined by a kind of establishment, which includes universities, learned societies, and, more recently, the editorial offices of technical journals. Like other establishments, they are consciously or unconsciously bent on preserving the *status quo*—partly because unorthodox innovations are a threat to their authority, but also because of the deeper fear that their laboriously erected intellectual edifice might collapse under the impact. Corporate orthodoxy has been the curse of genius from Aristarchus to Galileo to Harvey, Darwin, and Freud; throughout the centuries its phalanxes have sturdily defended habit against originality.

Indeed, even once-open minds slam shut at the first blush of success. Bell Labs invented the transistor, then closed their minds to its potential applications. Texas Instruments developed the semiconductor, then couldn't figure out what to do with it. Kodak invented simple, one-step amateur photography, but couldn't see a future in instant photography. Rigidity and inflexibility follow almost every corporate success *unless* something is put in place to institutionalize the nurturing of new ideas. Control Data's Norris is one of the few corporate leaders to address that fact of organizational life. In the past, he was personally open to the idea of disk drives, open to moving from hard technology into computer services, and open to developing teaching machines. But he saw that innovation which is dependent on a single personality is a perishable commodity. So Norris established CDC's "entrepreneur assistance program" that to date has helped some 60 employees go into partnership with the corporation.

Normally, when an employee gets a good idea he will try to sell it to his employer and, if the employer has a closed mind on the subject, the employee will quit and go into business making the product himself. A classic case of this: When Bill Gore worked for Du Pont he discovered that a plastic he was working on would be an ideal coating for electric wires. Du Pont greeted the idea with a yawn, Gore left the company, went into business for himself, and got very rich, indeed (in a later chapter we see what Gore has done to make certain that no employee with an idea in W. C. Gore and Associates ever gets the corporate cold shoulder). At CDC, Norris made the same mistake that Du Pont made with Gore: Norris failed to nurture Seymour Cray, CDC's chief computer maven. Cray left CDC, started his own company, and soon was outdoing his former employer in the supercomputer field. The "entrepreneur assistance program" is Norris's attempt to insure that that mistake is never made again. In order to retain entrepreneurial people who would normally quit the corporation, CDC provides them with capital to start their own company (retaining a 49 percent nonvoting minority interest in the firm). Says Norris "If we got involved in giving these entrepreneurs advice, we'd just screw 'em up." CDC promises to buy out the entrepreneurs when the fun goes out of the enterprise during the routine production stage of the business (when corporate marketing skills become more important than entrepreneurial enthusiasm). This program both defies the logic and the law of corporate R&D. The law says that an employer "owns" the ideas of all employees that are job related (even if the employer develops the ideas after work hours in his own garage). Norris says it is not worth pressing the point in the courts. He avoids patent and copyright suits, concluding that it is better to encourage people to develop their ideas than to stifle them with legal and bureaucratic maneuvers.

In 1984, Norris's policy was put to its ultimate test when Control Data spun off what had once been their core business—super computers. Worried that CDC would lose their key scientific people as computer hardware became a smaller and smaller part of the company's overall business, Norris decided to give these people an entrepreneurial stake in the operation by letting them run their own business. This act was tantamount to King George III having granted the American colonies their independence when Jefferson and his buddies said they'd like to see if they could make a go of it on their own!

Levi Strauss has a similar attitude and approach. Robert Haas's philosophy is to encourage anyone who wants to build an entrepreneurial operation within the corporation. He explains:

> We only have three rules. First, the entrepreneur must submit a plan. Second, the business must be run in a manner consistent with the Levi corporate principles regarding our stakeholders. Third, whatever the entrepreneur does, we shouldn't be embarrassed if we learn about it in the S.F. *Chronicle* some morning.

Levi USA President Peter Thigpen's biggest worry is that the large size of the corporation will suffocate employee initiative. After all, the company was started by an immigrant who had the strange idea to make pants out of tent canvas! Thigpen says, "A couple of years ago, such a strange idea coming from a Levi employee would have suffered bureaucratic strangulation. Imagine if the little old Bavarian had come in with an idea for something called 'jeans.' We had gotten to the point where we'd have required him to compile a 250-page marketing report!" In order to break out of this mentality, Thigpen created the $3 million "President's Sweepstakes" in 1982. The money goes to promote the best new product ideas sent to top management. The first winner was "Two-Horse Jeans" (prewashed denims with leather patches and copper rivets) which ran up $20 million in sales in the first year.

Herman Miller uses a variation on the same theme. Max De Pree, the company's current CEO, says that a major factor in the company's success was that his father, D. J. De Pree, "had the strength to abandon himself to the wild ideas of others." For nearly fifty years, Herman Miller has attracted many of the world's greatest designers to their headquarters in Zeeland, Michigan, a tiny, frosty town with no bars, no pool halls, and no theaters. A paragraph from the company archives tells how D.J. got great designers to come to Zeeland:

> He did it by inviting designers to come to a place where they could have a free hand—a company in which design is as important as sales or production. D.J. promised that no design would be changed without the designer's participation and approval. There would be no reliance on market research; the company would not be concerned with what was already popular. If designers and top management thought something was good, it would be put into production. D.J. and the early designers made one very important decision, one that it took a lot of courage to make, and they stuck with it: They decided that there was a market for good design.

Such designers as Gilbert Rhode, Charles Eames, and Robert Propst came to Zeeland and created, among other things: the sectional sofa, the Eames chair, stackable molded plastic chairs, the wall-attached desk, and the "open office." And the De Prees never once said, "Hey, don't you guys know that all great product ideas come from customers?"

As much as an open mind is central to the process of innovation, organizational openness in general is needed to lend courage and confidence to those who would dare to be original in their thinking. Indeed, one of the things my graduate students have frequently commented on when studying the Vanguard is the impressive amount of freedom these companies offer their employees. My students frequently say they are pleased to find that there is no such thing as "the Arco man" or "the Levi woman." In general, my students are attracted to places like Arco and Levi where managers and workers are marvelously varied in attitudes, beliefs, dress, life-styles, politics, and interests. In short, the students feel they could be loyal to a company that would allow them to retain their individuality.

When my students study companies like IBM and Hewlett-Packard, their reactions tend to be a mixture of (1) admiration, and (2) "But not for me." Very few of my students are conformists, few want to be "organization men." Most of the men and women I see in class—the next generation of corporate top management—are attracted by the prospect of discovery, change, and experimentation in their careers. They want the entrepreneurial freedom to take risks, question long-standing assumptions, and try something new.

At the end of each semester, I poll my students on their reactions to the companies we have studied. First I ask them which are the most prestigious companies in which to work (IBM and Hewlett-Packard almost always top this list). Then, I ask them where they would most want to work (IBM and Hewlett-Packard don't make the top ten). When I asked one student who had studied Hewlett-Packard why she wouldn't want to work there, she told me about an interview she had with a manager who had recently quit the company:

> He told me, "You can't imagine how stultifying it is to work at a place where they are convinced they have all the answers. Even though I must admit they *do* seem to have a lot of the answers, it is simply more rewarding and more exciting to work in a place where you can try things out for yourself." I kept getting responses like that from people who knew Hewlett-Packard well. I guess it was H-P's complacency and uniformity that ultimately turned me off.

That so many of my students rank the Vanguard in the top dozen of places where they want to work reflects, I believe, a set of values that is increasingly common in America. To my students, companies like Levi and Arco mirror what is most attractive to many young people about the direction our nation is taking. The Vanguard seem to "fit" with the kind of crazy, mixed society we are becoming—an uneasy amalgam of freedom, humanism, entrepreneurialism, and corporate security.

Significantly, the kind of security they find at the Vanguard is not paternalism, but the sense that workers are free to be themselves—and that they are safe to take risks. At Motorola, there is one statement by founder Paul V. Galvin with which every employee is familiar: "Do not fear mistakes. Wisdom is often born of such mistakes. You will know failure. Determine now to acquire the confidence to overcome it. Reach out."

Willingness to Take Risks

Levi's Peter Thigpen could well be expected to play it safe. After all, in 1972, he let his propensity to take risks get a bit out of hand. Fresh out of the Stanford Business School, Thigpen took off like a meteor in the Levi organization. By age thirty, he was in Brussels heading the company's booming European business. Jeans were all the rage at the time—every French and German teenager wanted to look like John Wayne. Since Levi could sell more jeans than they could produce, Thigpen ordered more produced, and produced fast (even if it meant skimping a bit here and there on quality). Then, suddenly, Europeans took a fancy to bell-bottoms and Thigpen was stuck with tens of thousands of pants and other "unfashionable" apparel he couldn't unload (not even the Russians would buy it). As a consequence, the company took a $12 million write-off in 1973 (and their stock price plummeted by some $43). Walter A. Haas, Jr., then the Levi CEO, flew to Brussels with a team of experienced people who quickly put the business back in order. Haas also demoted Thigpen. Thigpen asked Haas why he didn't fire him. Haas replied, "Pete, we've put a lot of money into your education. Now we want to get a return on all the tuition we've paid." In 1984, Levi got their return on their investment: Thigpen is now number three in the company. The message was clear to everyone in the corporation. Levi is the kind of place where risk takers are not punished if they fail.

All great managers know that innovation involves taking risks —but that people won't take risks if they are punished for failure. The greatest corporate leaders don't even see losing (on a calculated risk) as a failure. Said Edwin Land, who failed almost as often as he succeeded in his long career at Polaroid, "Lots of companies put a great premium on avoiding mistakes; here, we put a great premium on being able to make mistakes." Polaroid's secret was to learn from their mistakes. For example, Polavision was the company's costliest product flop, but Polaroid's scientists were able to later apply the technology to their 35-mm slide "autoprocessor"—the company's biggest new product in years.

Land's risk taking included taking risks on unlikely people. In his famous "pathfinders" program he would take promising young people off the Polaroid assembly line, put them in the corporation's laboratory, and turn them loose as researchers working alongside trained scientists. Why would Land do such a risky thing? Because such people were not burdened by the established scientific assumptions that often act as barriers to creativity. Land often found that fresh—even unschooled—perspectives served to unblock the path to innovation.

Johnson & Johnson's entrepreneurial climate is enhanced by their tolerance of failure. James Burke, the current CEO, tells this story about his biggest failure, and about General Robert Wood Johnson's reaction to it:

> When I failed with Arestin (a children's cold remedy), the General called me in and told me that I had cost the company a lot of money. But he said that was okay because if I wasn't making mistakes, I wasn't making decisions. He told me just to not make the same mistake twice.

Important, risk taking at the Vanguard is not the same as the macho, "do it, try it, fix it," decision making at the Old Guard. At the latter, the premium is on being fast at the draw (no matter who might get hit by stray bullets); at the former, the premium is on wide-scale participation in the process of idea generation, and in nonpunitive learning from calculated mistakes and well-planned experiments.

One final example: Control Data's Norris has become so convinced that large corporations restrict the innovation needed for technological progress that he has built on the company's internal "entrepreneurial assistance program" by adding a venture capital firm that invests in small companies owned by outside entrepreneurs. Norris's explanation of the difference between large and small companies might stand as a summary of the Vanguard position on innovation:

> Failure of large companies to be more innovative is partly a function of our growing, no-risk culture. Innovation means doing something new, often at great initial expense, first in development and later in start-up costs of manufacturing and marketing. The rising cost of innovation, investor pressure for immediate earnings, and greater uncertainty of an unstable economy have increased the tendency of large corporations to avoid the risks associated with truly major innovative products or services.

Innovation and risk taking are ways of life for the small-business person. They are unavoidable in starting a business and achieving profitable growth in a highly competitive environment dominated by giant corporations. In short, a small business innovates, takes risks, or dies.

The Keys to Production and Innovation

Pay for performance, technological leadership, openness to new ideas, and a willingness to take risks—these are four elements central to the high levels of productivity and innovation found at the Vanguard. But even these four key characteristics do not begin to describe the culture of productivity and innovation found at the Vanguard. These elements are merely parts of a much larger whole—a highly integrated system that also includes these other equally essential elements:

- The commitment to long-term profitability through sensitivity to stakeholder needs discussed in Chapter Two.
- The employee participation in profits and in decision making discussed in Chapters Three and Four.
- The strong consumer orientation described in the next chapter.
- The long-term planning horizon analyzed in Chapter Nine.
- The institutionalized change mechanisms described in Chapter Ten.
- The decentralized corporate structure described in Chapter Eleven.
- The moral courage and spirit of cooperation with other institutions described in Chapter Twelve.
- And the integration of all of these elements as described in every chapter of this book.

Productivity and innovation are thus like the issues of profitability and employee participation discussed earlier. They are inseparable parts of a complex whole that, when taken together, constitute the New Management.

8.

THE CUSTOMER:
SERVICE NOT SUBSERVIENCE

Beat your gong and sell your candies.
—CHINESE PROVERB

In the early 1980s, American consumers got fed up and decided not to take it anymore. For over a decade, the quality of service had deteriorated in the nation's shops, department stores, government agencies, and other loci of the optimistically named "service sector." When the nadir was reached in the late 1970s, rudeness, incompetence, and inefficiency were the norms of service (particularly among younger workers in large cities). Where once "You are welcome" was the anticipated response to a "Thank you," now the customer was lucky to get an "OK," or even a grunt of acknowledgment. Service stations quit offering service and became, simply, gas stations (pump your own, pay for that map, what windshield?). A letter would take a week (if it arrived at all) to make its way from New York to Washington. Hot meals were no longer available on most trains, and the quality of Amtrak's other services ran from tepid to frigid.

And, if the quality of service was bad, the quality of American manufactured products was perhaps worse. The big three domestic automakers peddled cars that were mechanically unreliable, expensive to operate, and, too often, unsafe at any speed. Fenders would crumble like cardboard in a five-mile-per-hour collision, and the "fits and finishes" of cars gave drivers and passengers fits: plastic knobs, plastic handles, plastic armrests, plastic everythings literally fell apart in one's hands. It seemed that nearly every product had to be returned: The odds were that his new long-playing record was warped, her expensive appliance wouldn't operate as advertised, and their kids' bikes (shoes, toys —you name it) would fall apart in a week.

So the American consumer got mad and then got even: She bought a Japanese car, he sent his mail by Federal Express, they both flew rather than take the train. The depth and breadth of the reaction to poor service and shoddy products led almost all observers of American business to offer the same sensible advice to corporate managers: "Get closer to your customer and pay more attention to quality." That this advice was as original and as profound as "Wear your boots and overcoat in a snowstorm" made it no less valid and no less necessary. Sometimes we need to be reminded of the obvious. Clearly, making high-quality products is a business essential. For that reason, quality is inviolable at the Vanguard (Levi's famous jeans have become such a symbol of quality that a pair hangs in the Smithsonian, right down the hall from such other symbols of durability as Mr. Ford's Tin Lizzie and Mr. Remington's rifle). And customer service is equally essential to business success and equally respected at the Vanguard (Deere & Company, for all their high-tech wizardry, keep "one foot in the furrow," right in there with their farmer customers).

Product quality, customer service—no company has ever gone broke from dedication to the simple truth that these two factors are at the heart of the activity that is called business. But simple truths are nothing more than simple truths, and one cannot build an entire theory of corporate excellence on such a limited base. Yet that is what numerous scholars have attempted to do. In understandable overreaction to the quality gap of the 1970s, many famous American professors and consultants have argued that *the* way to counter the Japanese trade offensive is to increase the quality of American products. This leads directly to the introduction of "statistical control" methods in manufacturing. And, in understandable overreaction to the services gap of the same era, other professors and consultants have argued that *the* secret to corporate success is to "get closer to your customer." This leads directly to the introduction of sophisticated market research. While statistical controls and market research are both extremely useful techniques, each by itself—and even both in combination —are insufficient responses to the complex quality/service problem of American corporations.

The more thorough response is to make the customer a corporate stakeholder. That's what the Vanguard do. And, as we now see from examples of their behavior, in so doing the Vanguard remain both quality conscious and close to their customers. *But, in addition, the Vanguard do many other essential things for their customers.* For example, they reach out to create goods and services that will greatly enhance the quality of their customers' lives—products so advanced that customers often haven't even imagined them, let alone demanded them.

Service Not Subservience

"One must be market-driven" is the most dangerous conclusion of those who embrace the simple truth of customer service as the be-all and end-all of corporate excellence. Not that the idea is wrong, but that it is simplistic (it is right to wear your overcoat and boots in a storm, but that won't get you an "A" in algebra). Worse, to the disciples of excellence, being market-driven means getting one's new product ideas *only* from one's customers. This is taking a good idea to excess. While there is no doubt that customers can offer their inchoate feelings about what they would like ("Gee, I'd like a faster computer"), if silicon chips haven't yet been invented, customers can't tell a company that silicon chips are what they need to speed up their computing. Hence, if TI had been a market-oriented "excellent" company in the late 1960s, we'd still be using transistors and not semiconductors in computers. And no customer ever asked for nylon, jet planes, color TVs, or a Polaroid camera.

At best, market-driven behavior leads to improvements in existing products: Frito-Lay listens to their customers and then produces low-calorie junk food; IBM listens to their customers and puts cordless keyboards (invented by another company) on their baby computers. Good stuff, perhaps, but hardly the essence of excellence. Writes George Gilder:

> Like the politician in the thrall of "public opinion" who lives always in the past, demand-oriented businesses rarely create new goods, for there is no measurable demand for what is not already familiar. The market surveys are mute on most innovations.

Hence, market-driven behavior leads to continuity, not to creativity; to the conventional, not the experimental; and to modifications and improvements, not to advancements and breakthroughs. Perhaps the most market-oriented firm in America is 3M. A frequently told joke about the company is "If Thomas Edison had worked for 3M he wouldn't have invented the light bulb, he would have developed a bigger candle." Other quintessentially market-driven firms in America during the post World War II era included the big three automakers. When Lee Iacocca was president of Ford, he was asked about the significance of the then-emerging front-wheel drive technology. Iacocca pooh-poohed the idea, noting that the consumer "can't see it. I say, give them leather. They can smell it."

Presumably, Mr. Iacocca has learned a thing or two about the sources of corporate excellence since changing employers. Sadly, most of the other leaders of the Old Guard have not, for they are enthralled by today's hottest management precept, to wit:

> Being market-driven is the ultimate source of excellence; research and new product risk taking are irrelevant.

The consequences of this philosophy were summed up by Du Pont's senior vice president of research when he raised a hypothetical question with a *Business Week* reporter: "Why risk money on new businesses when good, profitable, low-risk opportunities are on every side?" Thus, Delaware's once-great leader in science and technology, the company that created nylon, has now been reduced to a defensive posture in which they use their resources to buy an oil company in order to reduce risk.

Contrast the attitude of Du Pont with this statement from Hewlett-Packard's constitution:

> In considering entry into any new field, the important criterion is whether H-P can make a real contribution by providing something new and needed—not just another brand of something already available. To meet this objective, H-P must continually generate new ideas for better kinds of products . . .

At this point, it is important to reiterate a central theme of this book: balance and symmetry. It is *not* the case that customers are served only by radical innovation and *not* the case that they are *un*served by minor improvements in existing products. There is no doubt that evolutionary improvements are an essential aspect of customer service. And it is *not* the case that consumer-oriented firms are invariably inferior to research-oriented firms. For example, a few years back I bought a Cromemco "state-of-the-art" personal computer (it was a fast-witted creature that would seemingly chew up twice the data processed by an IBM personal computer at half the price). The problem was that Cromemco software had a serious glitch that made the computer incompatible with any decent printer available in Christendom. After several frantic, pleading phone calls to the Silicon Valley headquarters of the Cromemco computer jocks ("Hey, man, we're too busy with our research to mess with a little problem like that"), I sold the offending machine and bought a nice, slow, expensive, reliable IBM that Big Blue's service people keep running like a charm. Of course, what I *really* needed was a company with Cromemco's research brains and IBM's service brawn. The answer, again, is balance. An executive who talked clearly about the virtues of balance—virtues that his company promptly abandoned—was Pat Haggerty, TI's former chairman, who once wrote:

> . . . Too often in this technological age we associate innovation automatically with research and development . . . But the fact is that critical innovation . . . may occur in the *make* and *market* functions as well as the *create* function. Further, effective innovation is the integral (that is, the sum total) of innovation in all three of the categories: create, make, and market.

It is in that balance between creating, making, and marketing that the customer is best served. And it is failure to achieve (and hold) such balance that has helped to bring former Vanguard companies Kodak and Polaroid down a notch to being merely good.

Kodak Kapers

Until recently, Kodak had something like 90 percent of the domestic color film market and 60 percent of all the world's total film business. By any traditional measure of profitability, productivity, or progressive management philosophy, Kodak was a marvel—a star sapphire in America's corporate diadem. But Kodak got big, real big, and more than a bit bureaucratic along the way. And the once predictable world in which they operated also started to change: Suddenly, the Japanese were aggressively challenging Kodak on their own turf; the decades-long growth in demand for film started to slow; and new, electronic technologies were beginning to make inroads in the theretofore chemical- and mechanical-based field of photography.

What could Kodak do to respond to these challenges? What any market-driven company would do: introduce a new product that is a marginal improvement over their existing products. Now, a common complaint of photographers had always been that, with traditional cameras that use roll film, one can't advance the film fast enough to take a rapid sequence of pictures. Being a consumer-oriented company, Kodak responded with the much-ballyhooed "disk" camera that allows rapid-fire exposures. But, whoops, for the first time in the long and successful history of the company, the "new product" ploy didn't work. Clearly, it would have worked in normal times. A consumer-driven strategy almost always works when it is business as usual. *But these were unusual times.* For the first time, consumers had a real choice in terms of alternative camera technologies—for example, they could buy videocassette recorders or 35-mm cameras that were as fully automatic as Kodak's lesser-quality line of Instamatics. Consumers thus greeted the disk camera with a barely concealed yawn.

How could this have happened to a once-great American institution? Why, Kodak was to photography what General Motors was to cars! Therein lay the trouble. After dozens of years of leading in creating, making, and marketing film and cameras, Kodak started playing it safe in the 1960s. They adopted the IBM/GM/Du Pont approach to new product creation and development. Instead of risky pioneering, Kodak would wait until the field was tested, then enter proved markets by buying technology or "designing around" existing patents. This way, they would come up with a cheaper, mass-produced, brilliantly marketed, but technologically inferior product. (The classic example of this is when Kodak muscled in on Polaroid's technologically superior instant cameras, after having waited on the sidelines for a decade while Polaroid absorbed most of the research and development costs.) Clearly, such a strategy can work. As GM and IBM have proved, if one has sufficient muscle, late entry is often no handicap. And, if the late entrant happens to be a corporate behemoth the size of Kodak and IBM, consumers often benefit from getting a cheaper, simpler product that is backed by a first-rate service organization. But they probably will not get a *better* product. As IBM's personal computer illustrates, the technological state of the art may be frozen by the marketing-oriented strategy of a giant corporation.

And, sometimes, the cost to consumers and society of big company muscle can be enormous. For instance, in the 1950s Kodak muscled into Technicolor's motion picture business with cheap, easy-to-use color film. Almost overnight, Hollywood switched to Kodak film. Unhappily, Technicolor film was a higher quality product. Technicolor dyes didn't fade, but Kodak's washed out and went sickly yellow in a matter of years. Remember that classic Rodgers and Hammerstein film *Carousel* starring Shirley Jones and Gordon MacRae? Seen it lately? No? You're not likely to, either. Like many other film classics, it has faded to the color of legal writing paper (just like your old Brownie "color" snapshots of the same era).

And Kodak, too, have come themselves to suffer from their unbalanced approach to serving customers: Ignoring the create function and putting all one's eggs into marketing only works when there is a lengthy product life cycle. But if products are being made obsolete in less than a year by technological change, market muscle does a company little good. Today, by the time Kodak flexes, their faster and more agile Japanese competitors have often scored a knockout punch. For example, as technically unexciting as the disk camera may be, Kodak nonetheless spent $300 million to bring it to market. A former Kodak employee explained in a *Fortune* interview, "The people at Kodak are hardworking but bureaucratic . . . if you came up with an idea, it would be five years before you saw the product." In the case of the disk camera, six years to be exact. And for all their time, money, and mighty labor, Kodak produced an unglamorous mouse that sold for only slightly less than a new, fully automatic Japanese mini 35-mm camera.

The problem at Kodak wasn't simply bureaucracy. It was also inappropriate assumptions. Kodak's costly decision to enter the instant photography business is a case in point. According to *Fortune*, when Polaroid finally broke its dependence on Kodak as its supplier of negatives, Kodak assumed that

. . . by producing its own film, Polaroid could lower its costs; if it then cut prices, instant photography might become more competitive with Kodak's business. Or, alternatively, if Polaroid held prices high and started earning the pretax margins of 60 percent and up that efficient film manufacturers realize, it would soon be very rich indeed. The most visionary schemes of Edwin Land, the genius who had founded Polaroid, might begin to look plausible. The company might even develop a marketing organization rivaling Kodak's.

In either case, Kodak assumed it had to enter the business. Instead of making the decision based on their own strengths and interests, they jumped into the instant photography field in order that Edwin Land would not succeed in *his* dream.

An even more costly decision has been to stay out of a field in which they have some potential expertise. For twenty-five years Kodak's leaders assumed that they could *not* make a competitive 35-mm camera. Moreover, they should not do so because such cameras were "specialized products" that appealed only to the elite of professional (or deadly serious amateur) photographers, while they (the Rochester democrats) were in the business of serving the masses. In fact, the real challenge was to find a way to bring the superior quality of 35-mm cameras to mass markets. Indeed, that is exactly what the Japanese were up to while Kodak was futzing around with the disk camera. It is my guess that, given six years and a $300 million investment, Kodak could bloody well have produced a decent, automatic 35-mm camera instead of an inferior disk camera. Important: The reason why Kodak blew this opportunity is that they listened subserviently to their existing customers—folks who simply couldn't imagine themselves using one of those old, complicated 35-mm cameras. Now the Japanese have given them new, simple 35-mm cameras and Kodak's old customers are discovering the joys of professional-quality photography.

Kodak's immediate response to all of this has been to throw up their hands and then throw in the towel: Instead of moving into new technologies by recruiting people from outside the company with fresh perspectives, Kodak is now marketing Japanese products under the Kodak brand name. Oh, once proud Rochester, how could you do this to your customers and to your nation?

Ironically, Kodak's chief domestic competitor is in much the same pickle—but they got there by pursuing almost exactly the opposite strategy. At issue then, as we now see, is not the right or the wrong strategy, but striking a proper balance between the extremes.

Pugnacious Polaroid

No follower was Edwin Land. He said,

> Our company has been dedicated throughout its life to making only those things which others cannot make . . . We are alone because at each stage of invention we ask if what we plan is ten times harder than anybody else can do and twice as hard as we can do . . . We deliberately choose to have very few products but to make them important.

Land was always as good as his word. Instead of making a minor modification in an existing product, he would reach out for the new and, in the process, make his entire product line obsolete. That took guts. And it worked time and again until Polaroid simply got too big for that small-company ploy (no company with 18,000 employees can afford to shut down their entire business for a six-month product changeover). Land's genius and his weakness was that he ignored the consumer market and acted like a small-company entrepreneur even when his corporation had become a giant. He was, perhaps, 50 percent right in adopting this strategy. Clearly, every success Polaroid had was attributable to Land's guts-out willingness to make what *he* knew the public should want.

His biggest failures were also attributable to the same strategy. The Polavision fiasco, for example, set Polaroid back some $68.5 million in 1980. Like RCA's videodisk recorder and Kodak's disk camera, Polavision was simply the wrong product at the wrong time based on inappropriate assumptions about technology and consumers. While the world was getting ready for electronic videotapes, Edwin Land was creating a chemical-based instant movie system. He ignored the alternative technology; he didn't test the market; he didn't see that home movie sales were declining; he was holed up in the lab oblivious to the world around him. Significantly, most observers miss the point of this sad story. Ergo, they say, "Stay out of the lab and get into bed with the consumer!" Naw, that's not the moral. Had Land just stuck his fool head out of the lab from time to time, had he listened to the advice of a couple of his most sage lieutenants, had he just not been so single-minded, he would never have made such an obvious error. But that doesn't mean he should have been a slave to the market.

Historically, Polaroid ignored the signals they were getting from customers who found such instant cameras as the Pronto cumbersome and the quality of pictures inadequate. Polaroid ran all over their dealers, treating them like delivery boys, not like stakeholders. All Land cared about was the scientific "beauty" of his product. This was wrong. But so, too, was Kodak's approach. When Kodak finally decided to get into the instant picture business, they answered Polaroid with the Handle. This was a technological dud that grew like a deformed monster from the egg of that tired old marketing question: "What product will sell?" Both Polaroid's Pronto and Kodak's Handle left a lot of disgruntled consumers. Clearly, neither Polaroid nor Kodak understood what Levi, Deere, Dayton-Hudson, and Johnson & Johnson know about customers and quality.

Vanguard Practices

Dayton-Hudson. One of the most successful marketing organizations in America, DH succeeds in the cutthroat world of retailing that has recently witnessed the extinction of W. T. Grant, Korvettes, Arlan's, and Fed-Mart, and in which Montgomery Ward survives only by virtue of Mobil's deep pocket, and where even such well-managed companies as J. C. Penney's and Sears have had their rough moments of late. How does DH do it? By serving their customers well. They do a lot of what upscale competitors like Bloomingdale's and Neiman-Marcus do well (classy ads, museumlike store layouts), and a lot of what their best downscale competitors like K Mart do well (clean, well-organized stores, great prices). DH is also a master of the Madison Avenue arts: The week before they opened an experimental new discount chain (the experiment flopped), they took out eye-grabbing, full-page ads in the Los Angeles *Times* featuring a nearly nude couple with the caption, "We Can't Take It All Off—Yet."

While there is thus a lot of Hollywood hype involved in the retail business, the real secret to DH's success is to be found in their Midwest virtues. They have a simple, seven-word statement in their constitution that explains their principles concerning customers and quality: "No deception. No shortcuts. No gray areas." The DH constitution explains what that ethical code means in practice:

- Our customers have the right to expect us to act on their behalf; to choose merchandise with care—and sell goods that are as good as they look.
- The public has a right to expect honest communications—in press releases, in advertising, in all promotional techniques.
- We're "in stock" on advertised items. We scrupulously avoid techniques that trick the customer into the store—and lead to disappointment.
- We conduct every aspect of our business as if the public were looking over our shoulder.

And they mean what they say: 98 percent of the time the merchandise they advertise will be available in any given store; 90 percent of customer complaints are handled on first contact; there is a clear, no-questions-asked returns policy; their Target Stores division applies safety standards to the toys they sell that *exceed* federal standards.

While any one of these traits may also be found at a competitor, DH alone combines them all. Even more impressive is DH's ability to harmoniously blend their responsibilities to consumers with the claims of their other stakeholders. For example, when a Minneapolis art museum asked DH to sponsor a blockbuster show that would put the institution in the gravy, the company creatively used the occasion to serve consumers as well. The exhibition of paintings from Amsterdam featured *De Stijl*, "the style" of stark, geometric designs and bright colors that swept Holland between the two World Wars (remember Piet Mondrian in the previous chapter?). DH put examples of *De Stijl* on their shopping bags, in their store windows, and in their ads. Significantly, increases in the number of customers using their stores were exceeded only by the increases in attendance enjoyed by the museum. On one level, this is just clever exploitation of an opportunity to do well while doing good. But when one studies the broader pattern of corporate behavior, one finds example after example of DH uniting customer and community interests. In one store or another, they have offered seminars on the changing role of women and the problems of the aged, and they have offered free EKG tests and child care. Even when there is no direct commercial involvement, DH finds a way for consumers to benefit from their numerous community activities (recall that DH leads the nation in corporate philanthropy). Importantly, DH knows that a strong tie to consumers and to communities is the key to institutionalized change. By treating customers and communities as stakeholders, the company is able to monitor social, economic, and technological as well as fashion changes— and better serve all their constituencies in the process. For example, in 1983 DH sponsored a major conference on the problems of Hispanic Americans. DH managers in attendance used the event as an impetus to redirect corporate policy to better serve Spanish-speaking customers in the Southwestern states.

There is nothing casual about Dayton-Hudson's commitment to serving customers through monitoring change. For example, the company has a formal Trend Marketing system that permits them to chart product changes through five distinct stages:

- *Experimental testing,* when buyers stock up on a small quantity of a new item.
- *Incoming,* when the "test item" starts catching on.
- *Pre-peak,* when the item's popularity is still growing.
- *Post-peak,* when the rate of growth begins to decline.
- *Outgoing,* when the customer has lost interest.

This system allows buyers to have sufficient inventory when demand for a product is high (but supply is likely to be short) and to have low inventory when consumer demand can be met by reordering at a lower cost. Most important, it permits profitability on both sides of the demand curve by keeping inventory in line with demand. At DH, a market orientation is therefore something far more disciplined than "keeping in touch with one's customers."

Different Strokes at Arco, Control Data, Honeywell, and Motorola

Dayton-Hudson also has one other trait that sets them apart from the companies that merely stick close to their customers.

DH believes in "competitive pricing"—that is, good, old-fashioned, market capitalism. This is in sharp distinction with the practices of GM and IBM, whose strategies are predicated upon positioning their products at the top of the line where profit margins are greatest. Don't get me wrong, there is nothing intrinsically invalid about this (after all, it is also at the heart of the Deere and Olga strategies). But a problem arises when one tries to take the strategy and turn it into a "rule." That is, while we are likely to agree that Neiman-Marcus is an excellent company that succeeds by occupying the high end of their market, shouldn't we also agree that K Mart is equally excellent occupying the low end of the same industry? To argue that only top-of-the-line companies can be excellent excludes many successful corporations from that status. It is also anticapitalistic in that it excludes companies like Arco who serve customers through price competition.

In 1983, Arco abolished their credit cards and returned price competition to the oil industry for the first time in a decade. (Significantly, the first competitors to cry foul were those archdefenders of capitalism, Mobil Oil!) Through a combination of fortuitous factors (a glut of relatively cheap North Slope oil), clever planning (the most efficient refining capacity in the oil industry), and a creative marketing innovation (eight hundred "mini-markets" that allowed dealers to sell gas at no profit and still make money overall), Arco was able to serve consumers in the only way possible in a commodity business: by lowering the price of petrol at the pump. Not only did consumers benefit, but stock owners did too: While only seventh in sales among oil companies, Arco was fourth in profits in 1983.

Terrific. But what about the company's obligations to credit card holders? It is issues like this that make running a company hard work. Clearly, there was no simple right or wrong approach to the complex choice between serving consumers in general by offering lower prices, or serving credit card holders in particular by offering convenience and a line of credit. Indeed, it is not totally inaccurate to say that one could list almost everything that Arco—or any company—does on both sides of the managerial balance sheet. Anything of significance that a corporation does will be to the credit or debit of some stakeholder. What matters, ultimately, are the issues of long-term balance and *how* a decision is made.

In this instance, Arco's CEO William Kieschnick listened to the marketing and financial people who wanted to do away with credit cards in order to maximize efficiency and short-term profits; he listened to the planners who wanted to build short-term profits so they wouldn't have to cut back on their ambitious long-term investment program; he listened to the people from public affairs who worried about damaging the company's reputation for integrity; he listened to the people in consumer affairs who worried about the possibility of alienating loyal customers; and he listened to the operating people who needed to keep refineries boiling away as close to capacity as possible. Now, Kieschnick should not be confused with Solomon in his decision style. It is not even the case that he listened to everyone who should have been heard (he didn't consult the gas station owners on the front line, for example), and he didn't give equal weight to all parties (when push comes to shove, he tends to favor the folks who talk dollars over those who talk social sense). Nor is it the case that everyone at Arco was pleased by the decision. *But everyone with whom I spoke felt that the decision-making process had been fair.* Out of the tumult of disagreement, the decision, right or wrong, was thus legitimated.

Although Arco is dedicated to serving customers well, they don't always succeed. Remember the good old days when you would roll into a *service* station and they would give you a free map, wash your windshield, check your oil, pump gas *for you*, and let you use a (usually) clean restroom? And remember when you had engine trouble there was someone at the station who actually knew what was going on under the hood? Arco executives argue that people don't want these things anymore; they want cheap gas. Hence, they have given us gas stations, not service stations. Moreover, Arco executives argue that they can't whip their self-employed owner/dealers into line to keep the restrooms clean. Why is it that Colonel Sanders can get his franchisees to provide a high standard of service, and Arco can't work the same trick? The answer to this question is complex and probably has much to do with the fact that the road to the top in the oil business is by way of finding and drilling oil, not by selling gas. Not all functions are equal in a great corporation, and marketing comes up short in the oil industry.

Clearly, serving customers as stakeholders is no easy feat. As at all the Vanguard, Arco managers find themselves in constant debate about how to best balance the conflicting needs of all their constituencies.

Serving customers is clearly a complex issue that defies easy generalization. DH relies heavily on market research as we see above. But listen to Control Data's Norris:

> One of the nice things about our company is that we don't waste money on market research.

Control Data maintains an ambivalent attitude toward their customers. On one hand, CDC's booming computerized lottery business has succeeded by providing a wide variety of services to state governments at low prices. Yet, CDC does not do formal market research (Norris says that everything they need to know about customer needs can be found in the newspaper). This apparent contradiction (working closely with customers yet not soliciting their input) appears to stem in part from a certain degree of Edwin Land-like arrogance. Rather than ask customers what their needs are, CDC determines what they are and then sets out to fulfill them. Supporters of this strategy argue that this is the only way that CDC could have introduced the innovative programs and concepts that they brought to market during the last decade (the argument is that customers often do not know they need a particular service). In contrast, CDC's critics claim that, once these programs are initiated, they would be much more likely to succeed if the company worked closer with customers. Again, the truth is probably somewhere nearer the mean than at the extremes.

One complicating factor is that many CDC programs are very long-term in nature. Thus, traditional market research may not be as appropriate as it would be with other products or in other industries. Unlike every other mainframe computer company, CDC's long-term strategy is to provide customer services rather than hardware or software. Some of the most innovative of CDC's computer service businesses include: Arbitron (the world's largest radio and TV rating system), Ticketron (the computerized box office and lottery business), Cybersearch (a nationwide employment agency), and Technotec (an international technology exchange). An underlying assumption behind CDC's switch from computer hardware to these computer services is that the latter offer greater opportunity to provide added value to the customer. CDC's president Robert Price explains:

The basic characteristic to understand is that adding value to something takes time and money. It does require front-end investment, but we're prepared to do that because once you get there you have something that creates barriers to competition. The more value we have added, the more things that belong to us, the harder it is for competition to come in and take a market away . . . When you look at value added you see a different problem: You have to be patient; you have to be willing to wait for the long term. But once you get there you have something.

This nonmarket-driven strategy allows CDC to charge a higher price for its products which, ironically, gives them a characteristic of traditionally defined "excellence" in spite of themselves! Nothing, it seems, is all black or white.

Levi Strauss. Levi's traditional 501 jeans (named after the lot number of an early batch of denim) are as unique a part of American culture as peanut butter, Broadway musicals, and comic strips. James Dean and Marlon Brando made jeans *de rigeur* for angry young men in the 1950s. By the 1970s they were the symbol of apple-pie Americanism: Jimmy Carter wore them while he was President (even *that* didn't ruin their appeal—a further testament to their durability). Today, jeans are a part of our national costume for both men and women, worn by our Olympic athletes in the summer and winter games. Significantly, none of this came about as the result of advertising (although Levi has since gotten very sophisticated in their ads). Rather, Levi built a better pair of pants and the world beat a path to their door. (Ironically, Levi was making a special attempt to get closer to their customers in late 1984 when the bottom dropped out of the jeans market. Levi got so close, in fact, that they contracted a kind of "marketing myopia" that left them with short-range acuity but blind to the long-range demographic change in which the baby-boomers grew out of their jeans!)

Levi's slogan, "Quality never goes out of style," is constantly on the lips of their managers. In the 1970s, the slogan was put to the test when Levi managers shut down production for ten days in one of their largest factories when quality wasn't up to snuff. Levi will sacrifice quality for no person or cause: During World War II the company refused a federal order to skimp on the weight of denim (jeans, of course, had been declared an "essential product" for the war effort).

Of all American mass-produced goods, only the Model T has been as clearly linked as jeans in the minds of customers with quality, durability, dependability, and value for money. Says former Levi CEO Robert Grohman, "Our dedication to quality is unqualified." In an era of expensive designer jeans and cheap copies from Hong Kong, such a commitment doesn't come without a price. Says Levi USA's President Peter Thigpen, "All things being equal, people won't buy Levis. Our answer to that: Don't make them equal!"

Being the best requires both a formal commitment to quality—*and* practices and procedures to back it up. In 1967, Levi established a department of product integrity. This inhouse consumer advocate is empowered to stop production and even close down a plant in the face of severe quality problems. In addition, there is a product safety committee with similarly awesome powers. Such systematic concern for consumer protection is all the more remarkable given the antediluvian state of apparel industry practices. Along with publishing, the apparel industry remains in a preindustrial time warp. There are some 15,000 apparel companies in the U.S., approximately 14,998 of which are run in the unprofessional (often unethical) fashion characterized by Jack Lemmon in *Save the Tiger*. With the exception of Levi and Olga (and perhaps one or two others), most of the entrepreneurs in the rag trade play it fast and loose with customers and employees and manage to succeed by "making deals."

Levi's comprehensive commitment to quality (in the broadest sense of that concept) precludes making deals. Quality not only refers to products, but to the nature of Levi's relationships with all their stakeholders, including retailers. "What we do for one, we do for all" is the company's ethical standard for retailer relations. As this runs counter to the practices of the trade, it often leads to criticism of Levi Strauss from retailers who are looking for an easy competitive edge. When CEO Robert Haas was asked why Levi wouldn't make deals, he replied:

I would never want to be in a position like Richard Nixon, having to remember what I said to the last person. I also wouldn't want to be a retailer who always wonders if he got the best deal, or if the guy across the street did better. While it may be aggravating to some, we want our customer to know he's getting a fair shake. We deal with Sears and Penney's in the same way as our traditional accounts. Pricing, terms, conditions, and marketing programs are all the same.

Like Dayton-Hudson, Levi Strauss is in a business where advertising is a prime marketing tool. Like DH, Levi runs extremely creative media campaigns. (James Dean fans love the allusion to *Giant:* "Travis, you're a year too late!") And, again like DH, Levi has an ethical code that prohibits dishonest and misleading advertising. The ethics committee of the corporation's board of directors previews all Levi commercials to insure that they are compatible with both the quality of their products and the company's desire to be exemplary corporate citizens. They will not advertise on programs or in magazines with excessive violence or sex (such as *Playboy)* and they eschew celebrity endorsements.

This doesn't imply corporate perfection. In the late 1970s, Levi Strauss got sloppy in their dealer relations. Bob Haas recently explained:

> Up until the last five years, our relations with customers was fantastic. This has slipped due to divisionalization, arrogance, and complacency which comes with growth. We forgot the retailer—the middleman. We didn't make an effort to maintain a dialogue with our customers. Now that this deficiency is recognized, there are plans to correct it. But, once that trust is lost, it's difficult to regain.

In an attempt to regain that trust, Levi is attempting to provide clients with "one-stop" service in which managers act as "account sponsors," fielding dealers' complaints and mediating service problems that arise among their corporate divisions. To get closer to these clients, Levi top executives now work as salespeople in the stores of their major accounts. In 1983, for example, Peter Thigpen worked behind a retail counter at a Miller's Outpost store for three days getting a feel for the operations and problems of one of Levi's major accounts. Thigpen says that the way for giant Levi to stay close to their consumers is to "be big, act small." That's how they do it at Deere, too.

John Deere. What has made Deere a great corporation in an industry where most are mediocre? Spending a million dollars a day on R & D, treating employees as stakeholders, engaging in sophisticated long-range planning—these are all critical factors. Equally important, Deere has kept "one foot in the furrow" by making their five thousand dealers stakeholders in the corporation. John Deere's goal is to make all their dealers rich. In the United States, the typical Deere dealer nets around $200,000 in a good year, and many are millionaires. During the farm depression of 1980–84, over two hundred farm equipment dealers went belly up nationwide—but only a dozen or so of these were Deere dealers. (To put this in perspective, recall that Deere has over half of all the U.S. farm implement business.)

Besides money, Deere offers their dealers three things, all of them invaluable. First, Deere offers a commitment to quality that goes back to their founder, a Vermont blacksmith who invented a self-cleaning plow that didn't require constant stopping to clean mud off the steel blade. John Deere said, "I wouldn't put my name on a plow that doesn't have in it the best that is in me." That commitment is still there: In 1983, Deere shared (with Levi Strauss) *Quality Magazine*'s annual "Quality Recognition" award.

Second, Deere offers dealers what may be the most efficient parts distribution system in American industry. Twenty-four hours a day, seven days a week, Deere stands ready to ship a part (and guarantees forty-eight-hour delivery). They argue that there is no reason why an $80,000 combine should stand idle for want of a $50 part. Most dealers carry inventories of some 150,000 parts and most are linked to Deere headquarters by a computer. (Deere has even developed a portable computer that can be used in the middle of a field to diagnose tractor ailments.)

Third, Deere offers dealers a square deal. The company is quick to extend credit to dealers, offers them reasonable terms for purchase, and never forces inventory on them during bad times. Sounds like common sense? It is, but contrast it to the way General Motors treats their dealers. During bad times, GM pushes inventory on their dealers, balancing the corporation's bottom line by making dealers buy scads of unsalable cars. Since the days of Sloan, GM has had an adversarial relationship with their dealers; at Deere, the situation is opposite. Says Deere's Tom Gildehaus:

To the extent dealers do well, we do well. But the rule is that decisions at the margin should go in their favor.

That is what Deere means by "mutual advantage." Deere's CEO Robert Hanson explains:

When you visit our plants, you come to understand that it takes tremendous assets to generate a dollar's worth of sales in this business. The money we have tied up in unsold inventory further adds to that burden and reduces our ability to reinvest. We have always financed that inventory for our dealers. From time to time, we talk about lessening that burden by transferring it onto the dealers the way our competitors do (and the way it is done in the auto industry). But we never do it. Every time the idea comes up, it fails the test of "mutual advantage." In dealing with our customers, the ultimate question is this ethical test: Is it mutually advantageous?

It was that ethical test that led Deere to extend credit to farmers during the Great Depression—even though it took as long as ten years to collect in some instances. The company did the same in the minidepression of 1980–84, infusing enormous sums into their Credit Corporation (while their competitors were engaged in the self-defeating business of contracting credit lines). That is what comes of thinking of customers as stakeholders.

Product Quality at the Vanguard.

Early in the century, Honeywell managers dumped five thousand switches into Long Island Sound when it was discovered that they were of poor quality. By contemporary standards, this was an environmentally questionable act but, by the standards of the day, it was a remarkable expression of commitment to quality. Significantly, the story of the Great Long Island Dumping is still told in Honeywell's many divisions. Managers constantly refer to the story to remind employees of Honeywell's continuing dedication to product quality.

Motorola's commitment to quality is symbolized by their goal of "zero defects." While perfection is unobtainable, the company believes that striving for it is the best way to serve their customers. Motorola managers reinforce the attitude of quality consciousness by constant reference to an important statistical fact: In a circuit with one hundred components, each of which is 99 percent effective, there is only a 37 percent probability that the circuit will perform! The moral: While 99 percent reliability is "good enough" for some competitors, zero defects is the only acceptable standard at Motorola.

At Herman Miller the commitment to quality knows no limit. Managers constantly quote Charles Eames on the value of "good goods." Product quality is underscored by a concomitant dedication to quality in the design of Herman Miller factories, offices, and corporate artifacts. Even Herman Miller's annual reports are works of art. Instead of the typical slick, expensive, unimaginative annual reports that are issued customarily by large corporations (the intents of which are [a] to show solid upper-middle class affluence and [b] to offend no one) Herman Miller takes artistic and substantive risks with their reports. For example, one recent report had a slip jacket that contained an accordion foldout set of postcards picturing Herman Miller employees at work with "handwritten" messages on the back of each from the workers to the shareholders.

The interiors of Herman Miller factories are light and airy, with large windows through which production workers can view their natural surroundings, and are designed by the best architects (much as Herman Miller products are designed by the best furniture designers). In Bath, England, the award-winning Herman Miller factory blends into the cityscape of Britain's most beautiful Georgian city. Now, who else would have even have thought to put a factory in Bath (that's like putting a factory in Washington D.C.'s Georgetown or New York's Greenwich Village)?

It is not accidental or happenstance that the headquarters of almost all the Vanguard corporations are architectural gems. Weyerhaeuser's headquarters sit halfway between Seattle and Tacoma in the middle of a 500-acre forest with a view of Mt. Rainier in the distance. (Given the execrable Washington weather, it is considered a good year when they see the mountain twice!) The main building is situated on a 10-acre lake that is a preserve for swans and Canadian honkers. Designed by Skidmore, Owings and Merrill, and opened in 1971, the rambling, five-story building is the equivalent of a thirty-seven-story New York skyscraper (if it were stacked up instead of spread out). The executive offices are in red oak and white oak, and all are "open" —not even the biggest boss has a closed, private office.

In 1964, Deere opened their famous Saarinen headquarters on a 1,000-acre "campus" near Moline, Illinois. The buildings are built of glass and unpainted steel and have been allowed to rust to the color of fall leaves (or a newly plowed Midwestern field). The insides of the buildings are open, multistory greenhouses—jungles of figs, yews, and coffee trees smack in the midst of an area known for its harsh winters. Everything about the building is functional (an adjoining lake and fountain are used to cool off the building on hot summer days).

One of the Deere buildings houses a grand, three-dimensional *art trouvé* mural that tells the history of farming in America. Nearby is a Saarinen-designed auditorium (it is really a theater) that rivals Berlin's great symphony hall in design (if not in scale). In the lobby, there are subdued original paintings by Grant Wood to remind the viewer of where she or he is. Why go to all this expense? Deere's former CEO William Hewitt was determined to inculcate in every Deere employee an understanding of "how good we really are." Hewitt felt that the quality of Deere tractors must be manifest in the quality of all aspects of the corporation's spiritual and material culture. Hewitt explains:

> Our buildings have added a new dimension to our business, an additional pride in what we are about. In many fundamental ways they have raised the sights of all the people both in and outside our community who in one way or another are affected by Deere & Co.

In 1981, Levi Strauss moved to a new 8.2-acre "campus" (known by the locals as L.S.U.) at the foot of San Francisco's Telegraph Hill. Half of the land is given over to a public park and plaza overlooking the Bay Bridge and the Ferry Building. Levi constructed their new building in the style of neighboring brick buildings of historical note (which were renovated as part of the overall project). Significantly, Levi Strauss decided to build this architectural jewel shortly after moving into a new, high-rise office building. In the multistory building, with employees on many different floors, Walter A. Haas, Jr., felt that top management was losing touch with their people, meeting them only by chance in the elevator. Says his son Robert about the new building, "We belong on the ground, no higher than treetop level."

In general, at Vanguard offices one will find fine works of art, marvelous plants, and quiet, comfortable places for employees to gather to enjoy both (and to talk about common business problems). Significantly, five of the Vanguard companies refer to their headquarters as "campuses." And those that don't qualify for such a grand title compensate in other ways: Arco led in the urban development of downtown L.A. when other companies were retreating to the suburbs. And Honeywell, situated in one of the few rundown areas of Minneapolis, decided to stay put and revitalize their neighborhood rather than run to more affluent suburbs. In staying, they converted an enormous two-acre parking lot into a beautiful park for both employees and community residents.

Hence, quality is made palpable at the Vanguard by all manner of physical manifestations—including excellence in design and architecture. The settings of the Vanguard factories and offices serve as constant reminders to employees of corporate dedication to quality in all its physical, social, and psychological manifestations. Moreover, the design of offices, factories, and artifacts serves notice to consumers and society of the Vanguards' commitment to being the best at everything they do. The architecture of Vanguard buildings not only *fits in* with their environments—they *improve* the quality of life of their surrounding communities.

In effect, no distinction is made at the Vanguard between different kinds or levels of quality—everything is aligned, all is of a piece, as consciously and as well composed as a Beethoven symphony. This means that the Vanguard are not merely concerned with the external or superficial quality of their products. In addition, the concept of "good goods" includes the intrinsic value and usefulness of the product itself. A Weyerhaeuser middle manager explained to me, "Making and selling things that answer to basic needs—like housing—gives us a better feeling about ourselves than if we were making, say, cosmetics." Robert Hanson, CEO of Deere, echoes that sentiment,

> We are proud because we are engaged in a necessary kind of business. What we do is essential to the economy, to the quality of life, to life itself both here and abroad. We're in the business of feeding the world. Personally, I wouldn't get that feeling if I were marketing bubble gum or soda pop.

Hanson, like other Vanguard executives, is quick to point out that he is not making an elitist or invidious distinction between

Vanguard products and the products of others. After all, almost all products are useful to consumers (or they wouldn't buy them) and even necessary to at least some people. But treating the customer as a stakeholder is a far clearer endeavor when one is providing energy, clothing, food, or furniture than when one is selling cigarettes, whiskey, sugar, or caffeine. Junk-food purveyors may be good companies, but should they ever be thought of as excellent if their products are unhealthful for children? Nowhere is this subtle distinction made clearer than at Johnson & Johnson.

Johnson & Johnson
(Tylenol and the Credo)

Superficially, it might be argued that J&J is living proof that corporate success comes from "getting close to customers." The financial press credits J&J's CEO, James Burke, with turning the company around by emphasizing the marketing function. Indeed, J&J's new-product strategy will often parallel that of IBM and other market-driven companies: J&J will listen to their customers and make the incremental improvements needed to better serve them. While a marketing orientation is thus undeniably a great part of J&J's success, it is only a part. As we have seen in the previous chapter, J&J is also a leader in basic research. And, on still closer examination, one finds that J&J's leaders themselves claim that their success can be ultimately traced to their balanced approach to serving customers, an approach that goes far beyond responding to their demands for improvements in existing products, even far beyond basic R&D, to include ethical responsibilities for customer welfare.

J&J's response to the tragic Tylenol incident highlights what it means to treat customers as stakeholders. For many years, Tylenol had been a moderately successful aspirin substitute for children. Then, in the 1970s, J&J decided to put the product into direct competition with aspirin, Bufferin, Anacin, and the other "adult" analgesics. Through superior marketing, Tylenol became the bestselling U.S. drug in 1978. Tylenol was in the process of burying its leading competitor (Bristol-Myers' Datril) when tragedy struck in September 1982: A psychopath laced Tylenol capsules with cyanide and killed eight people. J&J's response was in sharp contrast with the recent behavior of other large corporations who had found themselves suddenly faced with potential legal liability in similarly tragic situations. The corporate norm of the era was to stonewall, to deny responsibility, to attempt to place the blame on someone else, and to refuse to cooperate with the public or the press. In contrast, even before J&J had full information about the cause and extent of the crisis (and long before they could assess their legal liability), they stepped forward to assume moral responsibility. They immediately withdrew thirty-one million bottles of Tylenol (with a market value of $100 million); they set up a toll-free hot line to handle calls from the public; they opened channels of communication to the health-care community; and they responded to all press queries with honesty and candor.

Not only was such a response unusual for a corporation, it ran against the current of behavior that society had come to expect from public figures and large organizations. Whether it was Richard Nixon and Watergate, GM and the Corvair, or Hooker Chemical and the Love Canal, the public had grown to expect an official denial, followed by stonewalling on the facts of the incident. Accepting responsibility and saying one was sorry was the passé response of the "old morality." Perhaps the saddest instance of the new morality was the attitude of the A. H. Robins Company, manufacturer of the Dalkon Shield, an intrauterine contraceptive device that has prompted some nine thousand claims against the firm from women who have suffered serious and, on occasion, fatal infections from the Shield. When Federal District Court Judge Miles Lord made his remarks on approving a $4.6 million liability suit against the company, he censured top management for not only failing to accept responsibility for the infections, but failing to withdraw the product from the market while they engaged in (a) legalistic maneuvering to get the company off the hook and (b) political lobbying to get Congress to forgive any punitive damages that might be imposed. Said the judge:

> It is not enough to say, "I did not know," "It was not me," "Look elsewhere." Time and again, each of you has used this kind of argument in refusing to acknowledge your responsibility and in pretending to the world that the chief officers and directors of your gigantic multinational corporation have no responsibility for its acts and omissions.

The ability to make an authentic apology, to admit responsibility, to censure one's own wrongdoings, is a sign of self-confidence, of life. J&J's remarkable comeback after the Tylenol incident is illustrative of this vitality. Within hours of the fatal poisonings, J&J's executives were accepting responsibility—and taking an enormous financial loss—*even when they were not guilty of any wrongdoing.* In response to a crisis, instead of withdrawing into a protective shell, the company opened up. They even opened their strategy sessions to the prodding—and often combative—eye of CBS reporter Mike Wallace and his "60 Minutes" crew. They stood naked in the light to be judged by the public. As a result, J&J emerged from the crisis as a champion of consumers. By early 1984, they had regained *all* of their market share. It is instructive to contrast J&J's actions with the stonewalling not of the A. H. Robins executives—for no responsible corporate leader would defend such immoral acts—but with the less flagrant behavior of GM's managers in the Corvair affair and Ford's managers in the Pinto affair. (Both of which won some considerable sympathy from Old Guard executives.) And it is equally instructive to contrast the consuming public's response to these same incidents (both the Corvair and Pinto precipitously lost market share and were soon after taken out of production).

The cynic might say that the difference in these corporate crises was merely J&J's clever marketing response as opposed to the ham-fisted response of the automakers. For example, Jerry Della Femina, the advertising whiz kid, said at the time of the Tylenol killings that any ad person who could save Tylenol "could turn water into wine." A year later, with Tylenol's market share nearly fully recovered, Della Femina was somewhat apologetic in a New York *Times* interview: "The next thing I want them to do is to take those loaves of bread . . . If they were so good with water, let's see what they can do with bread." But Della Femina's original error was *not*, as he suspected, in failing to attribute divine powers to J&J's marketing folks; rather, his error was in seeing J&J's recovery as a *marketing coup.*

There is no doubt that marketing played a part in the Tylenol comeback. But clever marketing could never have concealed a cold corporate heart. J&J could only remarket Tylenol because their leaders had done the right thing. Had they instead stonewalled and sought to scapegoat, no amount of clever advertising would have so quickly regained the public trust. Could the

Dalkon Shield be successfully remarketed with all the help in the world from Madison Ave.? No, Jerry, the secret was not to be found in advertising, it was in the vitality of J&J, in their commitment to the public not as mere customers, but as true stakeholders. Nor is the Tylenol incident "isolated." When J&J was doing research to develop a "morning after" birth control pill, the company held discussions about the morality of the product with philosophers, ethicists, and theologians. One can only imagine what the reception would be at IBM or GM to a proposal for a similar undertaking.

It all comes back to the Credo. Recall that the first line of the Credo reads, "We believe our first responsibility is to the doctors, nurses and patients, to mothers and all others who use our products and services," and recall that, since 1975, Burke had been leading employees in a series of "Credo challenge meetings" in which the underlying meaning of their responsibilities to stakeholders had been vigorously debated. As a result, according to Burke, when the Tylenol crisis hit, they knew immediately what to do. They didn't even have to refer to the Credo. They did the right thing because serving customers as stakeholders had become a corporate way of life. It was as if the people who had died, the people who were buying Tylenol, and the people who feared that they might be next, were the children, families, and friends of J&J's executives. It was not them vs. us. *Everyone* was us. As such, J&J executives knew immediately and surely the right thing to do.

If making the customer a true corporate stakeholder can give certain guidance in such an extreme situation, imagine how easy it is for J&J managers to know what to do in their far simpler, workaday activities of creating and making quality products and serving customers well.

Yes, But Does It Sell?

The limitation to the kind of argument I have just made is that it can be cynically dismissed by the Della Feminas and financial analysts of the corporate world as a kind of "do-goodism that constrains profitability." Fair enough. How can one measure the payoff of treating consumers as stakeholders and not mere customers? Let me try with this not insignificant fact: Weyerhaeuser, Honeywell, Johnson & Johnson, Motorola, Levi Strauss, Herman

Miller, and Deere are among the very few large American corporations to have made major inroads in Japanese markets where
quality is next to godliness.

Alas, not even stakeholder status for consumers is sufficient for
achieving corporate greatness. Formal strategic planning is also a
necessary requirement, as we see in the following chapter . . .

PART THREE

HOW VANGUARD LEADERS CHANGE, LEAD, AND SUSTAIN THEIR ORGANIZATIONS

9.

MINITRENDS: PLANNING AND STRATEGY AT THE VANGUARD

Most organizations reflect the uneasiness of transition for they were built upon certain assumptions about man and his environment. The environment was thought to be placid, predictable, and uncomplicated. Man was thought to be placid, predictable, and uncomplicated. Organizations based on these assumptions will fail, if not today, then tomorrow. They will fail for the very same reasons that dinosaurs failed: The environment changes suddenly at the peak of their success.

—WARREN BENNIS

Psst . . . wanna buy some expensive advice? Come outside to a dank and dreary backstreet where you will find a long line of gentlemen, each eagerly awaiting the chance to reach inside his raincoat and pull out a plain brown envelope containing "the secret to successful strategic planning." Among these infamous purveyors is one Michael Porter who, for a fee, will tell you that the secret is to concentrate on your markets and products. Through a vigorous analysis of market structure, he will show you how to position yourself in one of three sure-to-be-successful ways: as the low-cost producer, as the highest-quality producer, or as the occupier of a neat little niche. Doesn't turn you on? Try the wares of the next peddler. He is from the Boston Consulting Group and he will reveal, before your very eyes, an enticing little matrix depicting stars, wildcats, dogs, and that old favorite, the cash cow. Follow his advice and divide your company into "business units," then manipulate these units the way a stock speculator handles a portfolio of investments. The man from BCG will show you how to milk the cows, dump the dogs, and latch onto rising stars (all in the service of maximizing return on equity). Too hard core? The next itinerant salesman is Japan's Kenichi Ohmae —he's into "soft" planning. "It's all in the mind," he says. He'll even teach you to "think like an entrepreneur." Just pay close attention to his "strategic triangle" comprised of three C's (the customer, the corporation, and the competition). Through Zen-like contemplation of the relationship of these three C's, you will discover your zone of "relative superiority." Listen to Ohmae and learn how to exploit this area aggressively—just as they do in the exotic Orient! But the raciest line of goods is offered by the twins standing over there under the street lamp. When they open their raincoats, they reveal . . . nothing at all! "Don't plan," says the daring duo from McKinsey, Thomas Peters and Robert Waterman, "planning is an irrelevant waste of time." The secret, they whisper, is to be found instead in the culture of the enterprise.

Well, you get the picture—even if we didn't stop to examine such wares as Planning, Programming and Budgeting systems, Management by Objectives, Issues Management, and the host of other goodies concealed under the raincoats of folks from such salacious-sounding organizations as A. D. Little, SRI, the Hay Associates, and the Management Analysis Center.

By the way, that person who walked past the whole lineup without making so much as a single purchase was a Vanguard CEO. Don't misunderstand his behavior: All the Vanguard companies plan. They just have little need for prepackaged techniques because they each plan in their own unique ways. They each have their own style, use their own mix of methods, and, hence, present us with no single, imitable plan or technique. Nonetheless, strategic planning at the Vanguard companies centers around three general *processes:*

First, the Vanguard start by exploring the world around them. They know that *prior* to planning they must understand the political, social, economic, technological, and competitive context in which they will be doing business in the future. Therefore, they scan their environments in order to identify the opportunities and risks they face. Significantly, they do *not* attempt to predict the future. Instead, they try to create alternative scenarios of how external change might occur and of how relevant business conditions might evolve.

Second, the leaders of a Vanguard company articulate a strategy (or set of strategies) that seems appropriate for the firm given their interests and relative strengths, and given the way (or ways) they think the environment may evolve. As my friend Lewis Perelman points out, the word strategy derives from the Greek word *stratego*, a combination of *stratos* (army) and *ego* (leader), and comes from the head of the company. A good military strategy is always comprised of contingencies (a field commander will not go into battle with the idea of slavishly adhering to a single plan). Vanguard strategies are similarly flexible, nonmechanical, and entrepreneurial. The source of this flexibility is continued responsiveness to the corporation's stakeholders. Moreover, Vanguard strategies are concerned with big ideas ("What do we want to be when we grow up?" and "How much diversification is too little, and how much is too much?"), and not with tactics (which are left to the captains and lieutenants who manage decentralized divisions).

Third, the Vanguard attempt to get everyone in the organization involved in carrying out the plan. The purpose of full participation in operational planning is *to integrate all the parts of the corporate system—strategy, capital, human resources, reward systems, structure, marketing—into a coherent and manageable whole*. And that is the most important point made in this chapter.

While this all might sound fairly straightforward and textbookish, in fact, the Vanguard approach to corporate planning is highly unusual. Let's leave those pandering fellows in raincoats out in the cold and visit the Vanguard corporations to learn how they each do these four common things in their own, special, uncommon ways.

Futures Research

Meet Tony Finizza of Arco, Dave Willis of Deere, and Larry Schrenk of Honeywell. They are corporate futurists, and darn good ones (I've worked with some three dozen heads of long-range planning over the last decade, and I'd put these three near the top of the list of those active in the game). Before you get the wrong idea about these fellows, none is a corporate Nostradamus who attempts to predict the future by reading crystal balls, tarot cards, or goat entrails. The first thing they will tell you about the future is this: "It can't be predicted." Nor do they employ the scandalously useless technique found in the bestseller, *Mega-*

trends. The author of that weightless tome pretends to predict the future (his *first* mistake) by a careful examination of newspaper clippings (his *second* mistake).

A minute's thought puts the lie to his silly scheme: Imagine that you were in the megatrends business between 1918 and 1928 and you diligently clipped articles from newspapers and filed them away according to subject matter. You assured your corporate clients that, by counting the number of mentions of various subjects, you could monitor the direction of the future and thus help their companies position themselves for the decade of the 1930s. The ten years prior to 1928 were, of course, ones of incredible prosperity. Now, what signs would you have picked up in the newspapers that would have prepared your clients for the Great Depression (and its aftermath, including the New Deal)? An unusual set of circumstances? Not at all. The unexpected is the *norm*. Alvin Toffler, another pop futurist, basically used the same megatrends technique in doing research in the late 1960s for his bestseller, *Future Shock*. He carefully monitored *current* trends of the 1960s and completely missed the major social change of the 1970s—the women's movement. Example upon example could be adduced to demonstrate that trend extrapolation is only a slightly more useful guide to the future than star gazing. (The *third* mistake is made when Old Guard managers gobble up the gobbledygook of the pop futurists.)

Messrs. Finizza, Willis, and Schrenk are in a different business. No predictors they. But if the future cannot be predicted, why study it? While humans cannot predict most future events (with the exception of scientific prediction of natural phenomena), they can *shape* or influence the direction of the future. More directly, they can prepare themselves and their organizations to better cope with a range of probable and possible outcomes. In corporations, this is called futures research.

There are basically two kinds of futurists—exploratory forecasters and policy forecasters. A navigational analogy is useful in differentiating the two. An exploratory forecaster can be thought of as a sailor in a crow's nest who scans the horizon for things that might upset a ship's course. The sailor looks for signs of storms, icebergs, other ships, and even examines passing flotsam and jetsam for subtle indicators of trouble in the distance. Similarly, an exploratory forecaster attempts to identify signals in the environment that are likely to alter the course of a corporation, nation, or the world. The exploratory forecaster typically examines shifts in demographics, technology, resource use, economic patterns, and social behavior. In corporations, such people are often called environmental scanners.

In distinction, the policy forecaster is more akin to a ship's navigator. She identifies the many possible routes (and outlines for the captain the advantages and disadvantages of each) for arriving at a specific destination. She says, "If we steer this course at this speed, we'll arrive in port in four days." Similarly, the policy forecaster identifies the consequences of various alternative means for achieving a specific corporate objective. For each option, she will attempt to identify not only the immediate economic effects, but also higher-order consequences to help decision makers choose the most effective and appropriate policy. In corporations, these folks are often called long-range planners.

Both these forms of futures research reflect a tension between the need for forecasting accuracy on the one hand and the clear constraint of unpredictability on the other. In effect, Vanguard corporate futurists like Finizza, Willis, and Schrenk seek to improve the quality of forecasting and reduce the number of potential surprises, all the while recognizing that they can never fully do either. A quick review of three key futures concepts, (1) If/What?, (2) Unintended Consequences, and (3) Probability, illustrates some ways in which Vanguard futurists deal with this tension:

If/What? One way to reduce the number of surprises is to raise the question, If/What? For example: Suppose the issue that concerns the Vanguard forecaster is the future supply and cost of fossil fuels. The forecaster might ask the following kinds of questions: *"If* a superbattery is developed, *what* would the consequences be for the future supply and cost of fossil fuels?" *"If* people substitute communications for transportation by working at home with a computer terminal, *what* would the energy consequences be?" For a thorough analysis, it would be necessary to raise dozens of such questions. Using this exercise rigorously, the future would not be predicted, but the quality of the forecasts might be improved, and the number of surprises reduced.

Unintended Consequences. The social science concept of unintended consequences is central to futures research because it helps the researcher to anticipate problems. For example, in hindsight one can readily see that some unintended consequences of the introduction of the automobile included: highway deaths, increases in teenage promiscuity, urban sprawl, and the dependence of America on oil-producing nations. Consequences can be direct (cars cause an increase in accident-related deaths) or indirect (cars create demands for freeways; freeways then lead to urban sprawl). Some indirect consequences can be traced to the fifth or sixth order. For instance, when doctors in the San Francisco Bay Area reviewed mortality data for a ten-year period, they discovered an unexplainable, single, dramatic, short-term decline in deaths in 1973. Ultimately, they were able to explain the decline as a sixth-order consequence of Arab-Israeli hostilities. What? While this might seem farfetched at first blush, here is the causal link that the doctors traced: (1) Arab-Israeli hostilities increased, which led to (2) an embargo by Arab countries on the sale of oil to the United States, which led to (3) a gas shortage in the U.S., which led to (4) less driving, which led to (5) less air pollution, which led to (6) fewer deaths of infants and others (such as emphysema victims) who are highly sensitive to air pollution. A goal of Vanguard corporate futurists is to *anticipate* such causal links.

Probability. Vanguard futurists seldom make predictions, but they do make forecasts in terms of probability. That is, they will *not* predict that "Nuclear fusion will provide at least half of the nation's energy in 2025." But they might say "There is a 40 percent *probability* that nuclear fusion will provide at least half of the nation's energy in 2025." Further, corporate futurists seldom make forecasts *themselves*. Rather, they offer a probabilistic synthesis of the forecasts provided to them by specialists in the area they are studying. Hence, they are more likely to report that "The median estimate of a panel of twenty nuclear physicists is that there is a 40 percent probability that fusion will provide at least half of the nation's energy in 2025."

At Deere, Dave Willis has experimented with a computer model that combines dozens of such expert forecasts into countless alternative scenarios that top managers then analyze to sharpen the way they think about the future. Through such repeated exercises, managers come to understand the complex ways in which events and trends are interconnected and in which possible future developments might affect Deere's long-term strategies. The purpose of the exercise is *not* to predict the future or to develop *a* plan—rather, it is to get managers involved in thinking about the future and participating in the process of planning. Unfortunately, such mind-stretching exercises make even managers as sophisticated as Deere's uncomfortable and thus haven't yet won full acceptance as part of the formal planning process.

In sum, Vanguard futurists Finizza, Willis, and Schrenk are engaged in both exploratory and policy forecasting involving analyses of If/What?, Unintended Consequences, and Probability. Such thinking clearly distinguishes Vanguard planners from their counterparts in the Old Guard. For example, in the late 1970s, Exxon used forecasts generated by their economists as the backdrop for their corporate plans. Recall from Chapter One that Exxon considered only a *single* trend—a straight-line extrapolation that depicted the price of oil as rising between 1975–2000 at the same rate it rose between 1970–1975. This naive extrapolation led Exxon to invest (waste, as it turns out) nearly one billion dollars on synthetic fuels.

The whole planning process was different at Arco. To start with, Tony Finizza asked all manner of experts within Arco and without for the best ideas about how the energy future might develop. He then tested dozens of scenarios to refine a set of three that Arco executives found realistic enough to use in their strategic planning. In Finizza's three scenarios, the price of petroleum was high in the first, low in the second, and in the middle in the third. Arco executives then took these three scenarios and asked the following questions about each:

- What is the probability that this scenario will occur?
- What would have to happen (what path of critical events would have to occur) for this scenario to come true?
- If this scenario were to occur, what would the consequences be for the nation, the oil industry, and Arco in particular?

The executives decided that the probability of each of the three scenarios was too great (and the consequences of each too important) to dismiss any one from their plans. Therefore, they developed a strategic plan in which Arco's refining capacity was rationalized in such a way that the company could be profitable under *any* of the three contingencies. As a result of implementing this plan, Arco was the only major oil company to be profitable when the price of oil plummeted in the early 1980s.

Arco's executives also decided that the high-priced oil scenario had a relatively low probability compared with the other two scenarios. Try as they might, they couldn't put together a sufficiently convincing if/what sequence of events that would drive the price of oil in the future at the same rate it had increased in the early 1970s. (Of course, they considered carefully the possibility of Mideast wars that would disrupt oil supplies. But they decided that they weren't going to bet the future of their company on the possible occurrence of a war.) They then developed a strategic plan in which Arco would not have to be dependent on high-priced oil to make investments in alternative fuels profitable. To implement this strategy, they divested themselves of the major part of their Colony Shale project in Colorado (holding back a small part of the richest property as a hedge). Arco then sold these lands to Exxon at a considerable profit.

The consequences of the difference between the planning processes in the two oil giants were enormous in this instance. Importantly, this difference was *not* in technique (Exxon also uses scenario planning on occasion). The real difference was that, when push comes to shove, Exxon executives required *the* truth —a single forecast on which to base their strategic plans. In contrast, Arco executives were not obsessed by the need for certainty; they could live with the ambiguity of contingencies (an ambiguity that accurately reflects the unpredictable complexity of life). Ironically, a change of leadership at Arco in the early 1980s brought into power several top managers with limited tolerance for such uncertainty who set out to exorcise the very traits that had differentiated Arco from their competitors. Rather abruptly, Arco's entire managerial system started to display signs of bureaucratic rigidity and a lack of comfort with confounding evidence and divergent ideas. It was not coincidental, I suggest, that by 1984 Arco was having the same problems with the strategic mix of their refineries that Exxon was having. There is a curious habit of great corporations to imitate the behavior of their less-eminent competitors.

What the sophisticated planners at the Vanguard are up to completely baffles most Old Guard managers who are conditioned to seek a *single set* of assumptions that will guide them in

the future. For, in sharp contrast, the planning methods used at
the Vanguard are designed to generate and to test *alternative*
assumptions. In fact, no Vanguard planner would ever claim to
have made an accurate prediction about the future. Even when
they use computers and sophisticated planning models, they do
not engage in pseudoscientific forecasting. Arco's Finizza,
Deere's Dave Willis, and their counterparts in the other Vanguard companies know what Mark Twain knew; the pitfalls of
"scientific" prediction are almost as great as those based on a
seat-of-the-pants guess. Wrote Twain:

> In the space of one hundred and seventy-six years the lower
> Mississippi has shortened itself 242 miles. That is an average
> of a trifle over one mile and a third per year. Therefore, any
> calm person, who is not blind or idiotic, can see that in the
> Oolitic Silurian Period, just a million years ago next Novem-
> ber, the Lower Mississippi River was upward of one million
> three hundred thousand miles long. By the same token any
> person can see that seven hundred and forty-two years from
> now the Lower Mississippi will be only a mile and three
> quarters long. There is something fascinating about science.
> One gets such wholesale returns of conjecture out of such a
> trifling investment of fact.

Since it is easy to be seduced into such scientism, Vanguard
futurists work hard to stay free from the *Megatrends*, hot-shot,
"I've-got-all-the-answers" mold. Instead of forecasting "the ten
big trends that will determine the future," they explore the many
possible ways hundreds of *minitrends* and mini events might
interact and upset corporate assumptions. So don't think of Willis
and Finizzia as either scientists or seers. At most, all they claim is
to help managers think about the future in a more sophisticated
and useful way than is done at the Old Guard or by pop futurists.

Importantly, scenarios are not the standard tools that the Vanguard use for environmental scanning—in fact, each company
uses a variety of different tools. For example, Larry Schrenk of
Honeywell had an important insight a few years back. As a
midlevel staffer in the corporation's human resources department, he wasn't in a position to directly influence the direction of
the company's strategic plans (and that wasn't his concern). But
he was worried about the absence of sophisticated human resources planning in a labor-intensive company with nearly a hun-

dred thousand employees. If the company's claim that "people are our most valuable resource" was accurate, Schrenk felt they should plan to manage and develop those resources the way an energy company would plan to use their natural resources, or a capital-intensive industry would plan to make best use of their plant and machines.

Taking the initiative to do something about this oversight, Schrenk consulted with his Honeywell colleagues, tapped the ideas of outside experts, and put together a briefing book of forecasts that included: workforce demographics, economic conditions, technological developments, social trends, legal and regulatory developments, regional and metropolitan characteristics, and relevant international trends. He also offered an analysis of the potential implications of these trends for Honeywell's human resources planning. Highly sophisticated (and carefully avoiding the *Megatrends* pitfalls of prediction and singularity), Schrenk's forecasts were appreciated immediately by managers all over Honeywell. Today, Schrenk's forecasts are incorporated in divisional plans and corporate operational plans, and constitute an important resource in Honeywell's long-term strategic planning effort. Schrenk and his colleagues now continually monitor these trends, updating them annually, and revising their analysis of the consequences for Honeywell.

Motorola's Technology Roadmap is another notable Vanguard planning tool. It is designed to project, analyze, prioritize, and coordinate new product development. The Roadmap starts with a semiannual exercise in which ten-year forecasts of technological trends are generated by the people in the company who have technical backgrounds or expertise. These trends are then examined in light of: (1) the strengths of competitors, (2) experience curves, (3) sales history, and (4) Motorola's own distinctive competencies and interests. From this raw data, a long-term product plan is created, a Roadmap that indicates when and where to allocate corporate research resources, when to begin product development, when to introduce new products (and when to take existing products out of production). This entire process is tracked in the company's periodic Management Technology Review, designed to call the attention of each operating unit to where they are on the Roadmap. In effect, this system ties futures research to workaday operational planning by making sure that everybody in Motorola is constantly asking these four questions:

Where are we?

Where have we been?

Where are we going?

How do we get there?

What is most unusual about the Motorola system is that: (a) it is an institutionalized method of insuring that basic assumptions are challenged, (b) it occurs regularly and frequently, and (c) it involves most of the people in the company. Indeed, at Motorola (as at Arco, Deere, and Honeywell) the purpose of futures research is not to develop *a* plan; instead, the goal is to *involve people in the process of planning*. Out of this learning process come new patterns of thought that allow managers to uncover new opportunities (and to deal more effectively with old problems). In effect, the managers of these Vanguard companies have liberated themselves from the atavistic human desire to engage in fortune-telling, oracle-consulting, and prophecy. They have even escaped the contemporary pseudoscientific manifestation of such activities represented by econometric modeling and other quantitative tools designed to give the single *right* forecast.

And the same thoughtful balance is carried over to the strategic plans the Vanguard make—plans that are formulated in light of their sophisticated understanding of future environments.

Vanguard Strategic Planning (To Diversify Or Not to Diversify, That Is Their Question)

Significantly, the Vanguard's most important strategic decisions—those relating to diversification—have all been made with an eye toward preserving their flexibility. Not surprisingly, the Vanguard come down squarely in the middle of the two poles of thought on the virtues of diversification: On the one hand, none is a conglomerate, and on the other hand, none is a single-product-line company. To understand why the Vanguard have sought out a position of strategic balance on the issue of diversification, we must ask them to step offstage while we review the pitfalls of the polar extremes.

Conglomeration. Like adolescent lust, the desire of large industrial bodies to merge is insatiable. Examples abound. Within the last few years, Mobil bought "Monkey Wards" for a cool $1.6

billion. Exxon followed, picking up Reliance Electric at a fire sale price of $1.2 billion. Recently, U.S. Steel laid out $6 billion for Marathon Oil. But, at the time I write this, the record for a conglomerate merger belongs to Du Pont, who shelled out some $7.3 billion for Conoco—in effect, joining Park Place and Pennsylvania Avenue with one roll of the dice!

Not all M&A activity is unnecessary, indefensible, or unwise. Some such combinations are necessary for the effective functioning of capitalism. For example, our system rewards successful entrepreneurs with a big payday when they eventually sell their companies to larger enterprises. Without this possibility of selling out, fewer entrepreneurs would engage in the risk taking and deferred gratification necessary to start new businesses. Also, mergers can occasionally create a single, strong company from the marriage of two or more weaker entities in the same industry: Atlantic Richfield is the successful result of combining three marginal oil companies, and Dayton-Hudson is a happy marriage of two regional retailers (with a third added later).

But there is no economic or managerial necessity for the merger of giant, successful, publicly held corporations in different industries. The two reasons (excuses) offered by CEO's who get the urge for a conglomerate merger are: (1) synergy, and (2) increased shareholder wealth. Unfortunately, the record of conglomerate mergers over the last decade reveals little evidence of either benefit.

Synergy is that sought-after state in which two plus two magically equals five. But what synergy can be expected from the marriage of an oil company to a department store (or a food producer to a company that makes batteries)? The obvious answers to the following two simple questions put the lie to the synergy argument: What is the source of synergy? Integration. What is the source of integration? Complementary interests. Now, then, is there any wonder why so many mergers among incompatible partners fail to meet expectations?

If the synergy argument doesn't hold up, what about increasing shareholder wealth? Here we find that asset shifting is not asset increasing, or at least it hasn't proved to be for Occidental and City Services ($4 billion), Fluor and St. Joe Minerals ($2.9 billion), General Electric and Utah International ($2 billion), Standard Oil and Kennecott ($1.8 billion), or the dozens of other big ticket acquisitions of the modern merger era. In fact, most such mergers have worked to the detriment of shareholders. Du Pont's record after acquiring Conoco is illustrative: The purchase diluted shareholder equity by 50 percent and increased corporate debt fivefold (to a tidy $5.8 billion). Indeed, to service that debt, Du Pont has had to sell off some of Conoco's assets and cut back on capital spending across the entire corporation (thus decreasing their prospects of meeting their long-term obligations to shareholders). Significantly, Du Pont admits that their decision to acquire Conoco was "made over a weekend" by former CEO Irving Shapiro and current CEO Edward Jefferson (a glorious example of the consequences of the "Do it, Try it, Fix it" style of management). Clearly, just a little *formal* planning might have been useful in making a $7 billion decision!

But the real cost to shareholders of a conglomerate M&A is that it distracts executives from their real jobs. The executive who is engaged in the enthralling fun of the acquisition hunt has little time for the basics of production and marketing. The alternative to increasing shareholder wealth by *acquiring* assets is, of course, increasing shareholder wealth by *creating* assets. Thus, merger-mad managers slight such asset-creating activities as introducing new products, expanding into new markets, and increasing productivity and efficiency. Why? Partly because creating assets involves hard work and is not nearly as exciting as the seduction involved in a merger (which, in the case of an "unfriendly takeover," is closer to rape).

Even in the aftermath of an acquisition, executives find themselves preoccupied by the consequences of the act. For example, Du Pont has run into considerable resistance from Conoco employees while trying to impose their conservative habits on folks who had long enjoyed the more freewheeling life-style of the oil industry. As a result, Du Pont managers have invested valuable time on conflict resolution that could have been more profitably applied to improving the efficiency of their chemical operations. In fact, conglomerate executives often lose entire sight of the basic tasks of management: The MBAs (Masters of Business Acquisition) who once ran ITT spent so much time buying and selling companies that they were in the complete dark about the quality of the products made in their divisions and the effectiveness of their marketing. When did Harold Geneen ever say, "Hey, what's your long-term automation plan at Continental Bakery?"

Ultimately, disillusion besets the giant conglomerate. RCA, which had acquired Banquet Foods (TV dinners) and Random House (publishing), sold these companies when they found they couldn't manage them. Ditto Colgate-Palmolive, which has unloaded Helena Rubinstein (cosmetics), Hebrew National (lunch meats), Bancroft (tennis rackets), and Lum's (fast-food restaurants). Whittaker Corporation holds the record, however, having divested some ninety companies between 1967–1983! And, in the oil industry, synergy has come to mean two plus two equals three: There is not a single example of an oil company that has displayed a smidgen of talent for managing anything but another oil company. Exxon's high-tech acquisitions, Reliance, Zilog, Vydec, and Qyx, are in worse shape postmerger than they were premerger.

And then there is Arco. In the early 1960s, if one had visited Philadelphia's stodgy old Atlantic Refining Company, Los Angeles's provincial Richfield Oil Corporation, and New York's sleepy Sinclair Oil, it is highly unlikely that one would have predicted that a great corporation would soon be forged out of such unpromising raw material. But then one would not have seen these companies through the eyes of Robert O. Anderson, son of Swedish immigrants, owner of more land than any other American, classically educated cowboy, loner, and entrepreneur *par excellence*.

Some capitalists have the gift of foresight. They can see the silk purse in the sow's ear, can see potential profit where the conventionally minded manager sees only the debits on today's balance sheet. Anderson saw in those three idling organizations the makings of a single, dynamic, superbly profitable corporation. The entrepreneur, of course, is not clairvoyant, nor is he a magician. He only appears to be these things in comparison to you and me. He is, in fact, the supreme illusionist. His trick is to work so hard and so single-mindedly as to make the course of events conform to his vision of the future. That Anderson did. When he assumed the leadership of the Atlantic Oil Company in 1965, the company had $66 million in profits on $700 million in sales and was ranked sixty-eighth on the *Fortune* 500. In 1982, Atlantic Richfield was the nation's twelfth largest corporation with earnings of $1.7 billion on $26 billion sales.

Anderson's Midas touch failed him only once, but spectacularly. In 1977, he turned the black gold of oil profits into cheap copper with the $700 million purchase of Anaconda. Curiously, it was merger alchemy that had been Anderson's strong suit in the past. But previously he had always been buying oil companies. Now, he sought to diversify. Unfortunately, where oil companies are concerned, conglomerate mergers seem always to turn into grand-scale mistakes. It is possible that Arco plowed another $700 million into Anaconda in an attempt to revitalize it before finally putting what was left of Anaconda on the block in 1984.

What lesson can be drawn from Arco's Anaconda venture? At one level, it is this: Even smart guys make mistakes. While to demand perfection of any corporate leader is unrealistic, there is reason to believe that Anderson's style of leadership contributed to the unfortunate decision to buy Anaconda. More to the point, his style *discouraged* the kind of objective analysis and healthy skepticism that should have accompanied a decision of that size and weight. While open and participative on day-to-day issues, Anderson brooked no opposition on major, strategic decisions. As a member of the task force that was pulled together to "evaluate" the merits of purchasing Anaconda put it: "We knew the decision had been made; we looked around for the numbers to justify it." (William Safire calls this "post planning.") Even today, Arco advances a variety of rationales for the Anaconda acquisition: tax advantages, the need to diversify in anticipation of the depletion of their oil reserves, and so on. None is convincing. In hindsight, conglomerate mergers always look like follies.

So what is the *real* reason why corporations do it? It is hard to prove exactly why anyone acts irrationally, but Alexandra Lajoux, an editor of *Mergers and Acquisitions*, argues that it boils down to the "frontier spirit" that still lurks in the hearts of many American executives, a desire for "adventure, conquest, success, expansion, and available wealth—a new life on free lands." That . . . and money. After all, the CEO of a $1 billion company who is earning $500,000 a year can claim that he deserves a million clams to run a newly merged $2 billion company.

So executives benefit from mergers (as do lawyers, investment bankers, and other assorted parasites) and that probably is enough to explain the appeal of this form of executive recreation.

The people who *lose* from M&A's include: employees, customers, small businesses, and society (in addition to shareholders). Here's an example that illustrates how all these stakeholders can come up short simultaneously: Let us say that Exxon wants to enter the electric transformer business. Exxon's executives either can take a billion from here or there and start a new venture from scratch, or they can buy an existing company. If they do the former, for each $20,000 or so that they invest in plant and equipment they will create a new job for the economy. (Depending on the industry in question and the technology being employed, it costs from $5,000 to $500,000 to create a job, but the principle of job creation remains the same at any amount of investment.) Hence, for a billion dollars, Exxon could start a division employing as many as 50,000 workers. They also could utilize the latest available technology—perhaps even developing new, highly productive machines and processes in their new venture. If, instead, they use their billion to buy an existing company (as they did when they acquired Reliance Electric), no new jobs will be created, old technologies will be employed, and a potential competitor will be eliminated from the market.

And, when big businesses like Exxon go on a buying spree, their acquisitions are typically financed by banks. Thus, capital that could have been loaned to entrepreneurs, expanding industries (or even used for home mortgages), is put to what is probably its least-productive use. (Think of it this way: The $1.2 billion that Exxon borrowed to buy Reliance could have been used to capitalize 1,200 new entrepreneurial businesses to the tune of $1 million each.)

Control Data's William Norris argues that there are additional negative organizational impacts that result when a takeover is *hostile:*

Hostile takeovers destroy innovation because innovation is a team effort among top executives and professional employees with different skills, including engineering, manufacturing, and marketing. Experience shows that a high percentage of the most creative members of the innovation team resign soon after the takeover. Defection is highest in small- and medium-sized target companies.

An environment in which hostile takeovers are a constant threat creates an even greater deleterious effect. Small- and medium-sized companies at the leading edges of important technologies are inviting targets. Hence, chief executives are prone to avoid investments in advanced technology with a high degree of risk, because such investments might decrease earnings in the short term and, therefore, depress the market value of the company, making it more vulnerable to a takeover.

And there is the further tendency of conglomerates to "write off" the once-successful companies that they manage into the loser's column. Lest we forget, "write off" means plant closings, job losses, bankruptcy of one-employer communities, welfare costs, and the accompanying human misery that is obscured by the neutral language of the accountant (the burden of servicing the Conoco debt forced Du Pont to eliminate some 3,000 employees from its payroll).

This is not to say that corporate executives always act foolishly when they play the conglomerate acquisition game. In an era of high inflation it is often more prudent (cheaper in the short run) to buy an existing plant or company than it is to start a new one. Thus, until inflation is brought under long-term control, corporate managers will feel the natural inclination to acquire surging through their loins. But that doesn't make it in the public interest —or even in the long-range interest of large corporations—for government to encourage executives to live out their fantasies (as it did during the reign of former Assistant Attorney General William F. Baxter). Keynes once explained that there is a great cost to society when corporations start making such "rational" decisions as "it is cheaper to acquire Getty's oil fields than to explore for our own oil." Said Keynes, "If human nature felt no temptation to take a chance . . . there might not be much investment merely as a result of cold calculation."

Conglomerate mergers and acquisitions are, then, classic examples of what George Gilder calls "sumps of wealth . . . sinks of purchasing power which divert money from productive use." Of course, most of the money that exchanges hands in the purchase of a corporation will eventually find its way back into productive reinvestment. But there is still a great deal of "leakage," as suddenly enriched shareholders buy gold, antiques, and other nonjob-creating investments. Worse, interest rates will be bid up in the process. Worst of all, taxpayers underwrite the exchange: Uncle Sam allows corporations to deduct the interest they pay on their large borrowings.

Thus, the merger of giant corporations tends to lower productivity, reduce industrial innovation, raise interest rates, drain capital away from entrepreneurial ventures, and adversely affect the national employment picture. And, sadly, the government often encourages the obscene longings of giant corporations to merge, when it should be acting like a Victorian auntie, segregating the parties for their own good—and for the good of society. Under Mr. Baxter, federal antitrust policy made as much sense as providing motel room keys to wanton teenagers.

Yet, it is difficult, if not impossible, to state precise rules concerning how much diversification is too much, when a merger creates too much concentration in a market, and when a conglomerate acquisition will have disbenefits for shareholders, consumers, employees, and society. The literature on "industrial organization" overflows with unhelpful economic theories concerning "barriers to entry," "oligopoly," "kinky demand curves," and "predatory pricing." So unhelpful, in fact, that the entire antitrust field has gotten a bad name; nearly every economist from Murray Weidenbaum on the right to Lester Thurow on the left now engages joyously in trustbuster bashing. Clearly, government actions in this domain have often been illogical: Attempting to punish IBM for their success in gaining market share was merely the most blatant of a long string of ill-conceived applications of antitrust law (and the breakup of AT&T *after* their monopoly had been broken by new technologies adds further weight to the trustbuster basher's arguments).

My own feeling is that the law and the tax code might be made more neutral and more consistent: There is no reason why companies that gain market share as the result of technical or managerial brilliance should have to fear dismemberment; there is no reason why the government should encourage conglomerate mergers through tax loopholes; there is no reason to encourage mismanagement by permitting "golden parachutes"; and there is some need to protect virgin companies (who wish to remain so) from hostile takeovers. (To discourage hostile takeover, the government might require stockowners to hold their shares a year or two before they can vote on them and prohibit the payout of dividends to those who have held stock for less than a year.) But, as much as I decry the takeovers of the Old Guard, I cannot formulate a general rule (or set of rules) on conglomeration that I'd be willing to entrust to federal bureaucrats and the courts to enforce. Moreover, I do not believe that government action is the called-for response to what is basically a managerial issue. Instead, I believe the most fruitful long-term response to merger-mania is *education*.

By reference to the experience of the Vanguard, it is possible to educate managers, journalists, stock analysts, shareholders (and finance professors) that the surest route to success is *not* along Conglomerate Drive. For instance, in the 1960s Motorola engaged in a series of erratic acquisitions but, once they recovered from their brief spell of conglomerate fever and defined for themselves a clear, cohesive strategy, the company took off like a rocket. And now that Arco is free of Anaconda, they are more able to concentrate on the things they do very well. But it is not enough to show that excessive conglomeration is almost always a mistake. The difficulty encountered in educating managers on this score is that excessive conglomeration is not the only mistake a corporation can make in its strategic diversification planning. The second extreme mistake is . . .

Too Little Diversification. Consider the example of Cummins Engine (which would have been the ninth Vanguard corporation featured in this book if it weren't for the strategic bungling of their top managers). Cummins experienced slow growth in their *only* business—large, diesel engines—throughout the 1970s, yet their top managers refused to budge from their rigid, single-product strategy. Cummins executives were proud of the fact that they had captured 53 percent of their market. But the more significant fact was that they had half of what was a no-growth market—worse, they had half of a market that was chronically the first to suffer in a recession, and the last to recover. To add incompetence to injury, Cummins completely misread their future environment: They assumed that expensive gas meant cheaper diesel fuel and this trend would create demand for their engines (a premise that turned out to be wrong in two ways: not only did gas get cheaper, diesel fuel got relatively more expensive).

For years, Cummins's friends and critics alike had urged them to branch into other businesses. But their CEO, Henry B. Schacht, remained adamant: "Diversification has no appeal to us." In 1980, the industry went into a state of depression, and Cummins didn't come out of it for some four years. The shame of this is that Cummins had done everything *else* right. They had been among the nation's leaders in employee relations, customer relations, and social responsibility. But a great corporation must strive to be great at everything, and Cummins's weakness was that they never understood environmental scanning, never understood strategic planning (and were arrogantly deaf to those who would try to teach them). That did them in—in fact, it *un*did much of the good Cummins had done for decades. Along with Dayton-Hudson, Cummins had been the only large U.S. corporation to contribute a full 5 percent of taxable profits to philanthropic purposes. Cummins's commitment to do so remains firmly in place (but the sad truth is that five percent of nothing is no contribution at all). Profitability, we should recall, is a corporation's responsibility to *all* their stakeholders. For nearly four years, Cummins thus failed them all. That they are now on the road to recovery—and actively engaged in related diversification —does little to change the fact that their recent hard times were avoidable.

Another former Vanguard company, Polaroid, has suffered from a similar strategic shortcoming. At Edwin Land's insistence, the Cantabrigians directed all of their considerable and varied technical skills into a single, narrow channel. Today, Polaroid is struggling to free themselves from overconcentration on amateur instant photography by diversifying into electronics, holography, chemicals, commercial and industrial photography, and a host of products related to their areas of technical strength (for example, Palette, which makes instant slides of personal computer graphics). Unfortunately, after fifty years of being Johnny One-Note, Polaroid is having trouble learning to sing a complete operatic score.

Again, nothing in the realm of corporate excellence is ever simple once it is fully understood. It is never simply a question of too much or too little diversification. In addition, there is always the issue of the right kind of diversification. For instance, at Cummins and Polaroid their challenge is to find *related* fields where they can make a contribution (fields that might even be countercyclical to their current product lines).

Vanguard Strategic Planning

Diversification at the Vanguard is characterized by three traits. First, while the Vanguard all produce a variety of products, all these products are logically related. Honeywell makes thermostats in one division and flight simulators for pilot training in another (but both are based on computer control systems). Control Data sells insurance, job training programs, and show tickets (all are services delivered by the computer). Weyerhaeuser sells chemicals, diapers, and houses (all are wood and paper products). Motorola makes information systems, semiconductors, and telecommunications equipment (which they unite through portable terminals that talk to central computers by a radio link). Dayton-Hudson has some six or seven autonomous businesses (all are retailers). Levi Strauss makes pants, shirts, socks, and shoes (all are moderately priced wearing apparel). Deere makes farm tractors and construction equipment (both are heavy-duty rolling stock that incorporate many interchangeable parts). And then there is the black sheep of the flock—Arco. Until recently, Arco has had several highly successful energy-related businesses (gas, oil, coal, and solar), and one not-at-all successful, *un*related business (Anaconda).

"Hold it, you are going a bit too fast, buster," the skeptic might say. "It is nice that you acknowledge Arco's failings, but back up and explain the 'logic' of some of those other connections. Try Weyerhaeuser, for instance. They also are in the mortgage banking business, a little point you failed to mention." OK, I admit that some aspects of Vanguard diversification defy the logical consistency required by a rule or a law. But I never claimed anything other than a common-sense link. Look at Weyerhaeuser, "the tree-growing people." They start by expanding into plywood, hardboard, particleboard, and fiberboard. Fiber expands into pulp, paper, paperboard, shipping containers, milk cartons, and newsprint. Left over in the process of making wood and paper are chemicals, which expand into oils, chlorine, caustics, and fertilizer (which is sold back to the tree-growing part of the company to fertilize their forests). Growing trees for their own forests expands into growing trees for other people which expands into a wholesale nursery business. Now, they've got all that wood, but people aren't buying it because they don't have money to finance the construction of a home, which expands into mortgage banking (and real estate). Finally, all that is left of the original tree is a little ooze and some hot water from the paper mill. Why not feed the ooze to shrimp and grow salmon in the hot water? Well, finally, with aquaculture they *have* strayed a bit from the original business. (That could be why aquaculture is the only part of the entire Weyco product line that continually loses money.)

The second trait of diversification at the Vanguard is that (with the exception of Arco) they only acquire companies that they know how to manage (in keeping with the deathbed advice of General Robert Wood Johnson to his successor at J&J: "Never buy a business you can't run yourself"), and they usually acquire small companies that have a special skill or technology they can't develop themselves. Motorola's Weisz explains the theory behind Vanguard acquisitions:

> Our 1940 "constitution" would have kept us out of every business we are in today. That is why we have to be alert to things so different that they can't come from our existing businesses. Instead of doing basic research, we do applied R&D and look for small companies that are doing interesting things. Not things that are too far developed—like robotics— but things like plasma technology. For example, we recently bought into a small firm in that field, and we're willing to wait years for it to develop.

Third, the Vanguard only engage in friendly takeovers. Not only must they be friendly, the culture of the merging firms must be complementary. Here's Weisz on the secret to a happy marriage:

> The first question we ask when we look at a potential acquisition is, does this company have a similar philosophy? The test: Can you close your eyes at one of their meetings and feel you are at Motorola? If not, run . . .

Apparently, there are many legally wed companies that have not consummated their marriages even years after the ceremony. For instance, Stanley Davis writes that thirteen years after Rockwell International merged with North American, the marketing types in the former and the engineers in the latter still had separate bedrooms. TRW is another unmerged merger. There is little shared learning, dissemination of information (or even much communication), between the midwestern and western partners in that marriage. As the North American Rockwell case illustrates, a little premarital corporate "hanky-panky" is often necessary to discover if the potential partners are compatible, for it is not always possible to spot compatibility at arm's length.

From a distance, the marriage of Rockwell and North American seemed made in heaven, bubbling over with the promise of connubial synergy. As it turned out, the world views of the parties were so dissimilar that they found themselves locked in a blissless union: One partner squeezed toothpaste from the bottom and the other squeezed it from the top.

Conversely, who would have bet on a successful match when that solid, midwestern, low-keyed, WASP feller Dayton-Hudson caught the eye of that aggressive, young, Jewish honey out in California, Mervyn's? But, after a trial marriage, they found that each was consumer-oriented, each believed in treating employees with respect, and each was socially responsible. Says Dayton-Hudson's Kenneth Dayton, "If our cultures hadn't been compatible, there would have been no merger, regardless of how profitable Mervyn's was." Unlike the Du Pont-Conoco merger, DH *planned* the Mervyn's acquisition carefully, during a lengthy courtship—a pattern found at Motorola, Control Data, and all the Vanguard who from time to time have found it prudent to acquire a smaller firm.

The Vanguard undertake all aspects of their strategic planning with similar care with equal formality. For instance, Levi Strauss's corporate strategy, "To cover the asses of the masses," is deceptively casual. In reality, their plan to become a diversified apparel company was not a seat-of-the-pants decision—it came about during years of tough and open debate among the Haas family and their top managers. As the plan evolved, it became clear that the company had several areas of competitive advantage as well as several areas where it could never hope to compete with specialists and low-overhead firms. When they mapped out the entire apparel industry on a matrix (like the one following), they were able to identify where they should compete and where they should not:

	BUDGET WEAR	MODERATE-PRICED APPAREL	HIGH FASHION
Children	X	X	X
Youth	X	Levi Strauss	X
Men	X	Levi Strauss	X
Women	X	Levi Strauss	X
Older People	X	Levi Strauss	X

In sum, Levi decided to leave the small, budget end of the market to low-priced importers, to leave the small, high-fashion end to the pricey and trendy "rag trade" (and to leave the clothing of toddlers to specialists). Their strategic plan became "to cater to middle America." Instead of chasing after Jordache and Calvin Klein by courting Rodeo Drive and Fifth Avenue boutiques, Levi decided to place their products "where America shops," in Sears and Penney's. Some said this was a risky strategy: "Designer jeans will eat into that market." Levi worried not, confident that the people who shop at Sears were not interested in paying a premium in a vain effort to look like Brooke Shields. After all, it's what one puts *into* the jeans that counts: flabby fanny in, flabby fanny out (even in Calvin Kleins). And the critics were dumbfounded when designer jeans created increased demand for *all* jeans: During the fancy-fanny era, Levi not only sold more jeans than ever before, they actually *increased* their market share (until the bottom fell out of the entire market temporarily in 1984).

Moreover, Levi's formal strategy was intended to increase the *flexibility* of the firm. Sears and Penney's—unlike the smaller, specialty retailers they had depended on in the past—were able to market a broader range of Levi's products, not just jeans. The big chains also offer the possibility of creating a steady and more predictable market, thus allowing Levi to plan more effectively for full employment in the future after their debacle of 1983–84.

In preparing their strategic product matrix, Levi discovered that there were holes in their line that they couldn't fill using their own skills and facilities. So they selectively acquired two or three compatible companies and merged them into the Levi culture. The reaction of Wall Street was one of panic when these acquisitions didn't pay off immediately. Robert Haas replied:

Many apparel companies live for the moment, for the season. We've grown because we've kept our long-term goals intact. We're not jumping out windows because some of our selective diversification efforts didn't meet our goals. Our goals are to steadily increase our position over a five- or ten-year period. Because we're patient, we can make mistakes, take risks, and still mature a business. We were in women's wear for ten years before we got the formula right. We were in menswear for almost ten years . . . Patience pays off in the long run.

Haas could just as well be describing the Control Data strategy. Shortly after forming CDC, William Norris began acquiring a number of small electronics firms in the Minneapolis area. His main goal was to develop the critical technological mass he felt CDC needed to become successful. Unfortunately, many of the firms Norris bought were not immediately profitable. But instead of jettisoning the divisions when they did not show short-run profits, Norris held on and waited for them to become profitable. Although a few of these investments eventually had to be written off, most became integral parts of the corporation, filling gaps in the overall CDC product line.

Patience (but not acquisitions) is also the word at Deere, where strategic planning is as deceptively simple—and as eminently complex—as at Levi. Deere's long-standing plan "to serve the 20 percent of American farmers who account for 80 percent of production" boldly anticipated the farm consolidation that began in the 1950s. Once the Deere strategy was in place it became evident that there was a fundamental obstacle in the way of its realization: It turns out that making big tractors is as cyclical a business as making big diesel engines. To avoid a Cummins-like, single-product dependency, Deere decided to diversify into construction and industrial equipment; and, to lessen their vulnerability to the downswings of the American farm economy, they moved to become a multinational corporation. In this way, their strategic plan had the dual characteristics of formal clarity on the one hand and operational flexibility on the other. The same can be said of the strategic plans of all the Vanguard companies.

This is all fine and good, the critic might contend, but it begs the important question: How do the Vanguard actually *do* their strategic planning? There must be an answer to this question. After all, in a recent article in *Fortune,* "High-Speed Management for the High-Tech Age," reporter Susan Fraker described a "briefcase full of techniques" that consultants and professors of management claim work in every corporation (at least, Ms. Fraker reports no doubts on the part of the experts nor limitations to their techniques). In contrast to this remarkable certainty, I have found no universal method of strategic planning at the Vanguard. Company and industry differences dictate that they use a variety of methods and employ a variety of planning horizons.

Moreover, I suspect that such variety would also be found

among all major corporations, if one were to look carefully and objectively. Consider three examples: First, suppose you were Apple in the highly dynamic computer business. You faced compressed product life cycles in which the timing of entry and exit is the critical factor in success. How would you do your strategic planning? Well, "do it, fix it, try it," might make some sense in this technology-driven industry. But if you are Phillips Petroleum—in the oil and chemicals business where all commodities are fungible—you find that price competition is the name of the game. Consequently, your strategic planning might involve long-term investments to increase the efficiency of process technology. Or, perhaps you are 3M, in a nondescript "industry," comprising thousands of products, each with small markets. Since each of these little cottage industries has its own product life cycle, you might evolve a highly decentralized system in which each division does their own planning. You might offer this advice to them: "Since you are basically in the business of making slight modifications of existing products, try staying close to your customers." Who does it right, Apple, Phillips, or 3M?

I'm convinced that how-to is a relative consideration. That is a fact of life that business people deny and resist. Over two decades ago, Peter Drucker explained that there was no one right method or technique for strategic planning and that it was, at base, a Socratic process. Such a process would begin with a general question such as "What business are we in?" or "What are our special competencies?" and would move on to rigorously challenge the fundamental premises of the organization in an effort to root out self-deceit and to encourage real innovation (which only occurs from looking at familiar facts in a new light). What business people don't like about the Socratic process is that it is open-ended and unpredictable (indeed, even the *second* question one asks in a Socratic analysis is unpredictable because it is entirely dependent on the answer to the first question). Now, nothing could be more unpalatable to the Old Guard than a lengthy analytical process in which, beginning with the very first question, they are forced to challenge their assumptions and in which all the rest of the analysis is unpredictably contingent on what was said earlier! Hence, hundreds of consultants have learned that one will never grow broke selling techniques to American businessmen that promise to reduce uncertainty. But, in truth, all that is generalizable about those who do strategic planning well is that they tie their plans to all other aspects of management. From environmental scanning, through strategizing, to operations, all aspects of planning are coherently integrated at the Vanguard.

Systemic Integration
(Getting It All Together at the Vanguard)

The Vanguard start their planning with a tremendous advantage over the Old Guard: They have a belief structure. Their leaders have vision, ideas, and purpose—which they articulate in their corporate objectives. For example, Apple's Stephen Wozniak set out to build a better computer, not to get rich. With that idea in mind, strategic planning was a cinch. Donald Burr, founder of People Express, started with the idea of creating an airline that was responsive to the needs of customers and employees. Given that idea, in his strategy every employee would naturally have to be a manager and an owner, not a hired hand. (Earlier, Burr had quit as president of Texas International Airlines because "It was grind, grind, grind with no better purpose than to grind out some profits. It had no vision, no excitement.") Sadly, business schools teach that ideas are *un*important, that you can finance a shoddy product to success, or successfully apply a strategic planning technique in the absence of a clearly articulated objective. Such Old Guard corporate "heroes" of the late 1970s as TI's Pat Haggerty, ITT's Harold Geneen, and United's Edward Carlson offered no belief structure to their corporations. After a while, people started to ask why were they doing what they were doing, and what the purpose was of their business activity. Old Guard executives have no answers to such questions. To them, business is merely a game; and there is no purpose to a game—it is an end in itself. Without a purpose, one cannot do long-range planning. All one can do is to engage in tactical maneuverings designed to win the current round of the game. Hence, the planning activities of the Old Guard tend to be reactive, incident-driven, episodic, and short term. That is why TI, ITT, and United went into tailspins when their charismatic leaders retired.

Because Vanguard executives know where they are going, their planning tends to be anticipatory, structured, continuous, and long term. It all starts with a clear statement of purpose. At Deere, for instance, the corporate objective is

. . . to provide those who work the land, build upon it, and there spend their leisure—on farms, in forests, in parks and open places, and in towns and cities throughout the world— reliable mechanical power and equipment of superior quality to increase their productivity and satisfaction in mutually beneficial ways.

At Dayton-Hudson, the stated objective is

. . . to serve the American consumer through the retailing of dominant assortments of merchandise that represent quality, fashion and value . . . to be premier in every facet of our business.

To meet their various objectives, Vanguard executives outline clearly stated strategies. At Deere these include: (1) product leadership (measured by market share, sales value, and profitability), (2) product design (Deere products are the same the world over), (3) single-sourcing (Deere manufactures a given component at only one location to insure quality and standardization), (4) vertical integration (they attempt to make as many of their own parts as possible), and (5) capital expenditures (sustained long-term investments in plant and technology). At Dayton-Hudson, the overall strategy includes dominance (the best assortment of merchandise), quality (of products, service, and the shopping environment), fashion (timeliness of all products), convenience (hassle-free shopping), and price (competitive value for money).

There are thus obvious differences between the Deere and DH approaches (as well there should be considering the former makes tractors and the latter sells consumer goods). Indeed, if we were to examine each of the Vanguard's strategies, we would find that the key elements were likewise dissimilar. But as different as the Vanguard strategies are, they are all held together by a common glue: a continuous, integrated, and formal planning and management process that, in the words of Dayton-Hudson CEO Kenneth Macke, "ensures consistent, well-informed, and timely decision making . . . that provides the framework for strategic planning and corporate consensus."

While such an integrated planning process is found at all the Vanguard companies, let us examine only one—Dayton-Hudson's —which can serve as an illustration of the rest. The first thing to understand is that each of DH's operating divisions has considerable autonomy (each essentially operates as an independent company). A major purpose of DH's planning process is to formalize interaction between the corporation and these divisions with an eye toward ensuring that they adhere to the company's basic objectives, and that each serves the "constituencies" listed in the DH constitution. DH's five planning phases are like the spokes of a wheel:

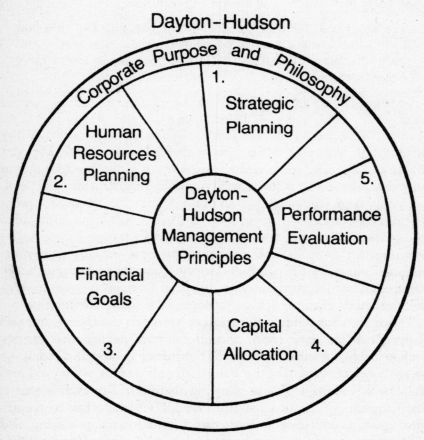

The first step in this process, strategic planning, starts with an environmental scan. Each operating company engages in futures research, examining economic, competitive, demographic, and consumer forecasts in order to identify business threats and opportunities. In light of this external analysis, attention is then turned to the internal environment, and to an identification of the operating company's strengths and weaknesses. In this way, each DH company identifies their assumptions about their environment, their assumptions about themselves, and their assumptions about the interaction of the two. Such a focus on the interaction between the environment and the organization is a key to successful strategic planning everywhere. At DH this is accomplished by an exercise in which corporate top managers review the operating company managers' missions and objectives, asking them the following kinds of questions:

- What business are you in?
- What business should you be in?
- What are your target customer groups?
- What level of service does the customer expect, and is this changing?
- What is the character of your stores?
- Is the character of the merchandise right for the stores?

After addressing such strategic issues, the focus turns to matching resources to the qualitative plan. This includes: human resources planning (does the company have the people to carry out their plan? are they being prepared for succession and appropriately rewarded?); capital allocation (DH allocates capital for the upcoming five years); and the setting of financial goals (how the company will measure the degree to which the strategic plan was achieved). The final step in the annual process is performance evaluation. Then the process starts all over again. According to Macke, the Dayton-Hudson approach is "predicated on a clear statement of the company's mission and a well-defined process that integrates strategic, financial, and human resources planning with ROI-based objectives."

What we see at DH is the antithesis of the ITT and Teledyne "holding company" mentality in which divisions are viewed as stocks in a portfolio to be bought and sold to maximize corporate wealth. In sharp contrast, in the most highly decentralized of the Vanguard companies, divisions are viewed as integral parts of the whole. At the very least, that gives division heads the confidence to act like team players.

Underlying this process is a series of fundamental assumptions that Dayton-Hudson articulates as "management principles": that superior return on investment allows high levels of investment for growth (and is, therefore, the soundest measure for financial planning); that planning is imperative and must be an ongoing process; that a participatory style of planning is the only effective kind; that divisions should have as much operating autonomy as possible; that uniform accounting practices are the *sine qua non* of autonomy; and that managers of operating divisions should be paid based on their performance. The essence of these principles (and the planning process they undergird) is that *management must be all of a piece.*

The proof of the validity of the DH approach is in the pudding. Since 1970, DH has experienced fifteen consecutive years of growth. During that time, they have climbed from fourteenth place in nonfood-retailing to fifth (in early 1984 they climbed over the nearly prone figure of Montgomery Ward). As DH grew from one hundred stores in 1970 to one thousand in 1984, earnings per share kept pace with an eightfold increase. To what does Macke attribute this phenomenal record? "Long-term planning." And they plan to keep on planning. In 1983 DH's five-year plan called for a $2.2 billion capital expenditure to add another five hundred stores.

As at Dayton-Hudson, planning at each of the Vanguard comes down to the art of integration. Motorola starts with the long-term objective of putting one of their phones and computer terminals in every car in America. In an effort to integrate that goal with corporate strategy, management development, human resources planning, organizational design, annual budgets, and the system of evaluation and rewards, they engage in a process of continuous upward and downward communications. In fact, Motorola's planning process is a near clone of Dayton-Hudson's (which is remarkable given that Motorola is a high-tech manufacturer with no retail business at all).

At Levi Strauss, integration starts with the corporate principles relating to stakeholders and with their strategic objective ("Cover the asses of the masses"). For each stage of the integrative planning process, Peter Thigpen offers a pithy categorical imperative that relates it to the overall objective: environmental scanning ("Don't be a monolithic giant; listen and learn"), operational planning ("Think long term in a short-term business"), human resources planning ("Remove obstacles to entrepreneurialism"), management systems ("Decentralization with appropriate control"), and R&D ("Make small, controlled mistakes"). This framework for meeting objectives is designed to build consistency between all parts of the system. It was put in place when the company found they were planning for the long term but rewarding people for short-term performance only. The result was that managers were too optimistic and aggressive in their objectives, which led to overcapacity, which, in turn, led to the inability to meet objectives (and, ultimately, to plant closings). From this error, Levi discovered that effective management is a complex whole that must be orchestrated with a composer's ear toward symphonic composition and coherence. To further tie rewards to structure, strategy, and objectives, Levi recently created a bonus pool for top managers that rewards them for meeting nonquantitative goals (significantly, the size of the pool is *not* a function of overall corporate profitability).

Likewise, the recipe for success at Deere has been integration, balance, consistency, and coherence. This stands in sharp contrast to the inconsistent, scattershot strategies of their prime competitors. It is useful to recall that Deere started far behind Cyrus McCormick's International Harvester, but IH squandered their lead with unwise, unrelated acquisitions (refrigerators, air conditioners), sloppy quality (they once placed a combustible gas tank on top of a red hot tractor engine), poor labor relations (they got tough with the UAW which cost them a 172-day strike), and short-term thinking (they spent too little on R&D and on new plant and equipment). In contrast, through good times and bad, Deere doggedly stuck with a plan that allowed them not only to catch their old rivals, but to leave them in the dust. Deere's fully integrated management system includes these factors (which we have considered only individually to this point):

- A Strong Dealer Organization
- Low-Cost Manufacturing
- Excellence in Engineering and Development
- A Future Orientation
- A Commitment to Quality
- Viewing the Union as a Stakeholder
- High Moral Purpose and Ethical Principles
- Strong Financial Controls
- A Three-Pronged Strategic Plan
  —Diversification into Construction Products

—International Expansion

—Focus on the Top 20 Percent of Farmers

Missing any single one of these pieces, it is unlikely that Deere could have quintupled their revenues in the 1970s (growing twice as fast as IBM and TI), unlikely that Deere could have surpassed IH and Massey Ferguson (both of which are near bankruptcy), and unlikely that they could have presented Caterpillar with a serious competitive challenge. Hence, it is not just futures research, not just strategic planning, not just any one of a dozen essential managerial activities that has allowed Deere (and the other Vanguard corporations) to succeed spectacularly in turning themselves from also-rans into leaders in their respective industries . . . In addition, it is (to use the famous words from DH's constitution) a commitment *to be premier in every aspect of our business.*

10.

HOW TO CHANGE
AN ORGANIZATION

Progress depends very largely on the encouragement of variety. Whatever tends to standardize the community, to establish fixed and rigid modes of thought, tends to fossilize society . . . It is the ferment of ideas, the clash of disagreeing judgments, the privilege of the individual to develop his own thoughts and shape his own character, that makes progress possible.

—CALVIN COOLIDGE

As the tumultuous decade of the 1960s came to a blessed end, and as Americans steeled themselves for God-knew-what in the unpromising 1970s, the eight corporations who are the subject of this book mirrored the floundering state of the nation. In the late 1960s, not one of these corporations could have been called great; not one had yet achieved Vanguard status. Atlantic Richfield—only recently formed by way of merger between two ne'er-do-well, old-line oil companies—was still a struggling corporation with, at best, an uncertain future. Out in Minneapolis, it was questionable whether Control Data—then losing in their competition with IBM in the mainframe business—would even survive the 70s. Neighboring Honeywell was in only slightly better shape, grasping for a handhold in computers and kept alive by cash generated from their old thermostat business. Our third Minneapolitan, Dayton-Hudson, was a regional retailer searching for an identity and lacking a coherent vision of what they could become. Deere, still a one-product-line company, was feeling their way toward leadership in a cyclical and somnolent industry. Motorola, going through fits and starts with ill-conceived

acquisitions, faced trouble down the line in their car-radio and
television businesses, both growing rapidly obsolete. Weyerhaeuser was the sleeping giant of the north woods, idling compla-
cently while their less-endowed but more dynamic competitors
charged ahead grabbing market share and growing at spectacular rates. Only Levi Strauss could be called an exception to this
pattern of water-treading and confusion. The then-small, privately held company was inspired by their recent success to go
public. Shortly after that event in 1971, the company experienced rapid growth which, in turn, led to the European debacle
described earlier, to domestic overexpansion, and to the loss of
the Haas family values. By the late 1970s, Levi found themselves
in the same condition of drift experienced a half dozen years
earlier by our seven other companies.

Clearly, this was an inauspicious start for the Vanguard to what
turned out to be a fairly miserable decade for U.S. corporations in
general. But, by the 1980s, six of our eight companies had turned
themselves around and were well on the way to becoming great
(and Honeywell and Levi have recently put into place excellent
plans to do so). In different industries, facing different challenges
and barriers, they each in their own way found a route to Vanguard status. If they could find such a route, there is reason to
believe that many other large, older U.S. corporations could do
the same. The question before us now is, *how?*

Each of these eight corporations changed their cultures—indeed remade themselves radically—by using *different methods*.
To repeat a central theme: Vanguard status is *not* a function of
technique; rather, it is a function of attitude and ideas. There was
no one-shot, quick fix that enabled the Vanguard to alter their old
ways. Instead, they each institutionalized a variety of change
processes—processes that, in some cases, took as long as ten years
to show clear results. While the mechanisms by which changes
were achieved at the Vanguard vary in detail, all entailed one
form or another of decentralization of decision making, monitoring of stakeholder needs, challenging of assumptions—and the
provision of appropriate rewards and incentives for all of these
activities. In this chapter we examine the how-to's of these activities, beginning with what for most companies is the *sine qua non*
of change: a clear, long-term, top management commitment to
the hard work of altering corporate culture (we also examine a
harder row to hoe: change in the *absence* of such leadership).

Planned Culture Change

It is just as absurd to talk of changing the culture of a firm to make it into something radically different from what it is, as it is to talk about manipulating one's personality to become someone you aren't. The corporate culture kick scuffed the floor when two authors of doubtful literacy (come on, fellas, *Will* Durant wrote *The Story of Philosophy*, it was *Billy* Durant who was the founding father of GM) recently defined culture in terms of the following things: symbols, slogans, heroes, rites, and rituals. While these may be *manifestations* of culture—although any graduate student in social anthropology could come up with more sophisticated examples—they are *not* culture. A culture is a system of beliefs and actions that characterize a particular group. Culture is the unique whole—comprising shared ideas, customs, assumptions, expectations, philosophy, traditions, mores, values, and understandings—that determines how a group of people will behave. When one talks of a corporation's culture, one means that complex, interrelated whole of standardized, institutionalized, habitual behavior that characterizes that firm, and that firm only. Thus, to talk about "it" is absurd: Culture is "us." To talk about top management's role in changing corporate culture is to talk about them changing *themselves,* not changing some "it" or "them" outside the door to the executive suite.

To think in terms of "it" is to fall into the trap that ensnared one Mohammed Reza Pahlavi. He tried to change Iranian culture by bringing 'em up-to-date a bit: giving women a few rights, taking away some of the power of the clergy, introducing Western education and material goods. In fact, the erstwhile Shah was a champ at manipulating symbols, slogans, heroes, rites, and rituals (remember that big party he threw out in the desert to commemorate the founding of Persepolis? That ritual set him back a few million smackers, what with the elephants and the helicopters to take folks to the party, and so on). Significantly, it is *exactly* the Shah's approach to change that is advocated by the corporate culture vultures. Indeed, the favorite story used by McKinsey consultants to illustrate "how to do a successful culture change" concerns a Silicon Valley company in which the CEO decides to "shake up his troops": He calls an offsite meeting at a nearby motel and starts into the usual, boring routine with overheads and flipcharts when, suddenly, out on the lawn land several heli-copters manned by "guards" who take the executives "captive" and whisk them off to a remote beach. There, the executives find the elements of the new "culture" the CEO has cooked up for them. There are belly dancers with the new company logo on their tummies, elephants sporting banners with the new com-pany slogan. All of this is accompanied by two days of rituals designed to demonstrate a complete break with the past. It is a great story, and I am certain that the flair with which it is told by McKinseyites (and the richness of detail that I cannot muster) more than justifies their unconscionable fees. I have only one trouble with the whole idea: I don't believe it would work. For all the Shah's fun and games, bread and circuses, rites and rituals, he failed *completely* to alter Iran's underlying fundamentalist Is-lamic values. Why should we believe that the Silicon Valley CEO would have any more success than the Shah? (That the Shah was also corrupt and authoritarian didn't help any, either; but, even if he had been honest and a nice guy, he was still going about change in the wrong way.)

Effective change builds on the existing culture. A group will reject a foreign system of values the way a healthy body rejects a virus. Dennis Stanfill, former head of Twentieth Century-Fox, is one of a long line of intelligent people who have outsmarted themselves on this score. A financial whiz kid, Stanfill violated all the norms of Hollywood when he tried to run Fox in the manner of General Electric. Stanfill didn't understand the motivations and values of creative people. He is now out of a job, and Fox is still running along in the inefficient and unprofessional way it has always functioned.

Anthropologists show that culture change occurs in one of two basic ways. The first is revolutionary. This is always the course of disaster. Whether it is a planned, Maoist-like cultural revolution, or the unplanned collapse of a primitive culture that results from contact with the powerful technology, organization, and reli-gions of the West, revolutionary culture change is always shock-ing, painful, disruptive, and undesirable. The second form is evo-lutionary. For example, over time, American culture has evolved from a rural European, Protestant, and traditionalist past to an urban, heterogeneous, secular, and modernist present. The agents of change—politicians, business leaders, inventors, union organizers, artists, writers, scholars, whoever—moved the country forward by reference to "the things that have made this country great." Name a Democratic candidate for President who didn't remind us that his is the party of Jefferson and Jackson (or a Republican candidate who didn't evoke Lincoln, much as Lincoln himself evoked the Founding Fathers)? Every one of these agents of change has known that success depends on the active support of the people, and for the people to become involved in change they must see some familiar elements of continuity. Franklin Roosevelt could succeed in changing America because he put the radical reforms he sought in the context of traditions, systems, and beliefs with which the people were familiar; in contrast, American Communist leaders of the same era failed to make converts because they tried to *impose* a system that was foreign to the traditions and values of the citizenry.

If you are starting to get the idea that altering the culture of a corporation is slow and hard work, you've got the picture. But if the leaders of a company understand that change must be based on the current culture of the company (Lee Iacocca's "new Chrysler" is still Chrysler at heart—he couldn't have turned it into a cultural clone of IBM no matter what), and if they have the patience to involve the entire organization in the process of change, it is possible to turn a company around . . . given the better part of a decade to do it. Here's how they did it at Weyerhaeuser.

Weyerhaeuser's Cultural Turnaround

Had the Shah hired Fred Fosmire to manage his "white revolution" there might still be a Pahlavi on the Peacock Throne. Instead, George Weyerhaeuser hired Fred and, thanks to Fred and a courageous team of Weyco top managers, the company is well over halfway to being one of the best-managed corporations in America. That is a remarkable accomplishment. For, in the 1970s, things were not going all that well for Weyco. Professor Fosmire of the University of Oregon was then called in to diagnose the origin of a low grade fever that was sapping Weyco's profits, productivity, and growth. After examining every corporate orifice with the thoroughness of a doc from the Mayo Clinic, Fred brought his diagnosis to G.W. (How are those for initials? Only Jimmy Carter's were more imposing!) "George, you've got a bad case of an existential paradox," Fred said (he was still a professor then and hadn't yet learned to speak English). "What I mean is that your strengths are your weaknesses. You own all this goddamn timber that makes you resource rich—and that's good. But those same easy-to-reap resources keep you from paying adequate attention to the marketplace—and that's bad."

Fred went on to explain that life had been too easy for Weyco. Great grandpapa (Frederick I) had made a fantastic deal when he purchased about half the Pacific Northwest for the price of a telegram and change. He left a patrimony that subsequent generations of Weyerhaeusers had only to harvest. Turning timber into cash was easy. So easy that the company had come to evaluate their success in terms of "return at the stump." But the real money wasn't to be made in cutting down trees—you make money from "conversion," as they say in the wood business (that's the process of turning logs into lumber, paper, cartons, and chemicals). And you need good management practices to do that productively and profitably.

But Weyco had never fully gotten the hang of business efficiency. They weren't lazy, they had just had some bad teachers. For example, they had listened to economists. Following the advice of that benighted breed, Weyco had pursued economies-of-scale with a vengeance: "Expand that mill" became the corporate motto. Not just expand it, make it fully integrated. In fact, they made *all* of their mills so fully integrated that they had huge concentrations of duplicated assets in every location.

Weyco also listened to industrial engineers who taught them about scientific management: "Go for optimal solutions, not satisfactory solutions." In pursuit of perfection, Weyco's managers broke down the jobs of workers further and further until the workers had no discretion, and until labor contracts were filled with such detail that they were thicker than the Manhattan phone book. If Weyco managers found a labor problem, they'd add another supervisor. A problem in another area, they'd add another middle manager. The attitude of throwing phalanxes of lieutenants and majors at problems spread up the organization until Weyco was engaging in what Fosmire calls "white-collar featherbedding": that is, hiring layers upon layers of managers until the hierarchy was so deep that the Weyco organization chart was interchangeable with the Chinese Army's. And, with little else to do, those in the bloated middle of the organization turned their attention to the favorite sport of bureaucrats: resisting change.

By the time Fred had finished his diagnosis, George Weyerhaeuser was feeling quite ill: "Can you operate today, Fred, before it's too late?" Fred explained that he wasn't a surgeon and, furthermore, he didn't think putting Weyco under the knife was the most effective way to treat their persistent fever: "I'm into preventive, holistic medicine, George. I think people should be responsible for their own health. You can show them that it makes sense to eat right, get exercise, give up smoking—but doing it is up to them." Anyway, Fred explained, the situation wasn't a crisis; Weyco wasn't dying. There is a difference between not being healthy and being sick, he said. Weyco just wasn't as healthy as they could be. They had good genes, a basically sound body, they were still in the prime of life, and there was reason to believe that if they got into shape that they could run the Adidas off their competitors in the great wood products marathon. But you don't get into shape for the marathon in a week or even a year, Fred counseled. "How long will it take?" George asked. "Optimistically six years, pessimistically maybe ten." "OK, you've got me convinced," George said. "Why don't you quit your job at the university and come over and whip us into shape?" "I'll quit my job and be your coach, George, but you and everyone else at Weyco will have to get *yourselves* in shape."

Let me not misrepresent fact. Importantly, the change of Weyco wasn't just a George and Fred show. It was a team effort, with support and leadership coming from vice presidents Charles Bingham, Robert Schuyler, William Ruckelshaus, and many others. Weyerhaeuser was ready for change; Fosmire was merely a catalyst. Indeed, the process started with a vigorous and sustained debate among top management about what ought to be done to change the Weyco culture. After some time, G.W. and his peers committed themselves to a decade-long effort that they swore not to back out of—come hell, high water, or a depression in the industry. The depression came shortly after the change effort was announced. Suddenly, Weyco was running in the red. All the problems that were merely problems in good times turned to crises in the depression. Now they really were sick. It was clear that if they didn't do something quick to halt the hemorrhaging, Weyco wouldn't last the ten years needed to change their culture. To have a future, and to get off the cyclical roller coaster they were on, it became clear to Weyco's top managers that they "would have to learn how to be profitable at two-thirds our present size." So the change effort was made even tougher. Management had to come up with a system for changing the culture of the company at the same time they were laying off several thousand managers. They feared that people would hear the overhead reduction message and miss the more important redesign message; they had to figure a way to keep everybody's eye on the long-term goal.

Here is the plan as finally approved by Weyco's top management: George Weyerhaeuser would issue a challenge to his managers, telling them in general what he thought the company should look like in ten years, and asking them to develop their own specific visions of what their units would look like consistent with that broader picture. The challenge, then, was *not* to reduce a specific number of employees. Instead, it was this: "How would you redesign your unit so that it would be profitable in bad times as well as good? How would you raise productivity so that you would still earn a profit even when demand was down by a third?"

Managers of units ranging from 200 to 2,000 employees met with their people to prepare qualitative descriptions of the changes they envisioned. Once they gained consensus within their group, the unit managers took their plans to the next level up for discussion. Weyco's top managers then reviewed the plans, always asking one key question: "What are the risks inherent in the changes you propose?" All of this took three months, with everyone working six days a week.

Fosmire says, "We were bleeding at the time, but we didn't want to give out head-count goals, or to rush into any cuts we would later regret. We wanted to establish a new style of thoughtful and participative management even in the midst of a crisis." Ultimately, after a year of such discussions, some 22 percent of Weyco's *salaried* work force was cut. Because conditions of severance were so generous (as we see later), there was no lasting reduction of morale. Instead, morale *improved* (especially among the hourly, unionized work force. As the middle management cuts were made, the workers saw the immediate effects on productivity and profit. Their only complaint was that the managerial cuts didn't go far enough!). White-collar morale (except among the heavily trimmed corporate staff) improved, too, for three reasons: First, Weyco employees saw that by taking the cuts now, the company could provide greater stability of employment in the future. Second, since they had been involved in the process, it wasn't something that had been imposed on them. They had, in effect, made the decisions themselves and, therefore, saw the underlying rationale. Third, and most important, they had been caught up in the long-term organizational redesign effort and were excited by the prospect of creating a great company.

With the cutbacks behind them, Weyco started the organizational change process at ever smaller, ever lower units, right down to the shop floor. Each unit was asked to develop a vision statement that explicitly described their managerial philosophy. They were asked to develop their own measures of performance. They were asked, "What kinds of capital improvements would you have to make over the next five years to achieve your goals?" At the same time, the number of levels of management required to sanction the plans of the units was reduced, thus flattening the entire Weyco hierarchy.

Once the process was set into motion, it became clear to the units that they even could act *without* permission or review. The idea was to decentralize authority, after all, and that meant giving the people on the firing line power to make the changes needed to improve their performance. To reinforce this initiative, it became clear that the Weyco reward system should be changed. In the past, compensation had been based on internal equity and on levels of outside competition. While surveys indicated that Weyco's pay was equal to or better than their competitors', many salaried people still felt the system was unfair. In the future, top management argued that each unit should develop their own reward system—one that would support their own vision and plan. Even though only a small percentage of the units immediately picked up the challenge, the people in the corporate compensation department had a fit: "*We* have to design a single system, or there will be anarchy." "No," said G.W. and the others at the top, "from now on we'll tolerate a variety of systems. In the past we had a compromise system that fit the needs of no one. Let's get some creativity in this area as well. Let us create a generous bonus pool. Let the units come up with their own measures of productivity, ones they can influence directly and ones that will allow them a fair share of the pool. We want all the productivity we can get!"

And they got a lot. Between 1977 and 1981, Weyco's return on assets had been a mediocre 15 percent. If, during that time, they had been as productive as they were in 1982–83 under the new system, their return would have been 22 percent (and they would have had led their industry instead of lagging 6 percent behind the average). Still, the central staffs complained of the possibility of chaos under the new system of decentralized self-management. Fosmire answered: "Of course there will be screw-ups. But there were *worse* screw-ups under the old system. Don't compare changes to perfection—that's the devil's proposition—compare them to the way things were before."

My long-time friend, Robert Schrank, always counsels skepticism about corporate culture stories. He knows from experience that most success stories are generated by corporate P.R. departments, by overenthusiastic but out-of-touch CEOs, or by inadequately informed journalists and consultants. "Don't believe anything about how wonderful a company is until you've seen it yourself, until you've talked to the union, to first-line supervisors, and to the people who actually do the work." I couldn't face Bob Schrank and the state of Missouri if I didn't see it for myself, so off I flew to a Weyco mill in Oregon.

The modern Weyco pulp and paper mill outside Eugene has 450 employees. Inside the mill office there is a strategy room—nothing fancy, just a big room with a beat-up table and lots of uncomfortable chairs. On the wall there is a twelve-foot "road map," a strip of "butcher paper" that bears the marks of many hands. On the top, someone has scrawled "G.W.'s corporate philosophy," and underneath has listed the corporation's stakeholders. Starting at the left-hand side of the chart is another list, this one under the heading: "Organizational Philosophy: Values and Assumptions About People and Work." Moving left to right one finds these headings: "Environmental Analysis," "Core Mission and Goals," "Desired Future Organization Outcomes: Characteristics of People, Jobs, Work," and "Key Activities." If it weren't for the obvious fact that many people had been writing on the chart, I would have suspected the hand of Professor (now Vice President) Fosmire behind this textbook change effort. But I discovered that the entire process, with the exception of G.W.'s corporate philosophy, had been managed by the folks in the mill *themselves.*

I interviewed a range of mill employees (from the manager on down) to get a feel for what was behind that impressive "road map." Lots of work, it turns out: two years of work involving all 450 employees. The process started with a visit by the mill manager to the office of the local union president to ask his cooperation in an effort to improve both productivity and working conditions. The manager was rebuffed. He tried again and again (he ended up spending two to four hours a week at the union office for nearly a year until he had established trust). The national union had said, "Don't cooperate," but the local president was won over when Weyco convinced him to visit other union leaders who had been involved in similar change efforts. Today, the union leader will drop into any Weyco office at any time. As described in Chapter Four, cooperation has replaced the traditional adversarial relationship.

But the problems in getting started weren't confined to the union. Weyco supervisors and middle managers didn't like the idea of changes that threatened *their* authority. So the mill manager started a long-term educational process that involved cross-training, information sharing, and talk, talk, talk ("redundant communications") until everyone was on board. Significantly, the trainers and "change agents" were operating managers in the mill—not shock troops imported from Fosmire's central corporate personnel staff.

Then the real change process started with meetings of small groups of shop floor workers around a flip chart. The first task was to capture the workers' perspective of what the current culture looked like, and their vision of what they wanted it to look like in the future. Everything was fair game: management style, compensation, power—all the issues that are taboo in typical quality-circle or quality-of-work-life change efforts. The visions were then consolidated in the following consensus statement:

> We will be viewed as the highest performing, best managed, most responsive, and most adaptable organization in our industry. We will have the capacity to respond to all the needs and demands of the key stakeholders in our business. We will develop a long-term relationship and a long-term commitment to our customers, suppliers, union, community, government, the Weyco corporation, and other Weyco mills.

The next step was to take these generalizations and break them down into specific goals: "Highest performing mill" was translated into "Our goal is to leapfrog our leading competitors in 1,000 days" "The commitment to the union" became: "We will have a stable, informed union coupled with a stable, informed management group, working together as a competent team to preserve the future of our business and people alike." The next step was to define specific actions for meeting the goals they had defined. Here's what the workers told the managers about dealing with the union:

"You managers aren't so smart that you can put anything over on the union."

"A weak union is a disaster. If you want action they have to be strong. Stability is necessary if union leaders are going to deal cooperatively with the company."

"To make them strong, they need information. Tell them how much money the mill is making. That'll build trust."

The managers and workers then came to an agreement that the company could not only live with the union, they would actually work to build the strength of the union by sharing information with them. A remarkable commitment. Moreover, the idea of information sharing was extended to every employee in the mill: Managers agreed to ask workers what they needed to know and to provide whatever they asked—including normally confidential cost and profit data.

The results of the change effort have been remarkable. The first area where results were spotted was increased cooperation between the operations of two major parts: a pulp mill and a paper mill. While theoretically the operation was highly interdependent (both sides of the operation jointly used the same trees), in fact, the two parts had often worked at cross-purposes, creating costs for each other. Now, as a result of the change effort, boundaries between the two groups fell and cooperation became the norm. And the bottom line was also improved as the result of better matching of raw materials to the needs of the two mills, improved maintenance and energy use, more uptime and higher machine utilization, and increased tailoring of products to meet the needs of specific customers.

I asked employees if the effort had been worthwhile and was told that, in terms of money and working conditions, the mill was now a much better place to work. They also expressed confidence that the changes would lead to greater job security. The mill manager was a bit more balanced in his appraisal: "It was one hell of a lot of work. It involved a great deal of time out of the mill. And, frankly, I was scared to death when I started, what with talking about a long-term commitment to change into the 1990s! When you start off bare-assed naked, it is hard to tell what kind of a suit you'll have at the end." In hindsight, what strikes him most is that, after two years of autonomy, the values of the mill map onto the Weyerhaeuser corporate values with near-exact consistency. That pleases him.

It pleases Weyco's top managers even more. I left the mill to attend a regional meeting in which the managers of many other mills reported on the progress of their change efforts to a group of Weyco top managers. At this informal meeting, Charlie Bingham, Weyco's executive vice president, volunteered to turn the overhead transparencies for the various presenters. He put no one on the spot. He asked helpful questions. Indeed, the only grilling was the tough questions the division managers put to *him*. For example: "What commitment do we have from you guys that you won't back out of the change effort when the economy turns around and the pressure for change is off?" His answer: "You've got G.W.'s word—and Fred and I are there to remind him he gave it."

The division managers—some with as few as 200 employees—each had a chance to report. None of the presentations had been rehearsed in front of their bosses. This was a chance for operating people to report directly to the top. One manager told about a group of his employees who formed a task force on their own to find ways to reduce energy costs. Another told how the machine operators in his division had created a training program to teach their skills to other workers. One manager told how the workers in his plant now select the machinery to buy, install it, and maintain it themselves. Other reports included one on a factory in which white-collar jobs—including sales—had been eliminated and the tasks assumed by unionized workers, and another about a worker safety council in which union workers now grill people prior to promotion to see if they understand safety measures and are technically competent for the next assignment. In one mill, workers had assumed so much responsibility that there was only one salaried person on duty in two out of three daily shifts.

Perhaps the most impressive stories concerned efforts to bring the needs of customers and the efforts of employees into harmony (as at Motorola, "quality" is key to this congruence). In some Weyco plants, employees put their names on the products they make. In one location, customers were invited into the mill to discuss their requirements and expectations with employees. In another facility, employees rented a bus to take them to a site where their products were being used. In each case, the ideas had come from the employees themselves. (Deere has introduced similar methods.)

From these presentations, it was clear to me that there had been three kinds of changes: first, in management behavior (there was delegation of authority and accountability, and managers were now more concerned with matters of "what" and less concerned with matters of "how" than they had been in the past); second, in organizational design (there was a radical decentralization and flattening of the organization); and, third, in the nature of staff work (there was less of it, and the power of staffs was greatly reduced). Yet, despite these similarities, this was no cookie-cutter approach to culture change: The diversity and variability of the actions of mill managers was as great as their commitment to overall change was complete.

I revisited Fred Fosmire to check my observations with his. I summarized for him why I thought the change effort was succeeding. "Not a bad account, not bad at all," he said, "for a *professor*. With a little real-world business experience, you'd be okay." *Vice President* Fosmire then added one key factor that he felt I had missed: "The glue." He explained that the glue that had held the whole effort together was top management's long-term commitment to planned, total organizational change—beginning with a change in their own behavior. This point was critical. Indeed, everyone with whom I spoke at Weyco saw that this was the most difficult part of the entire effort because the participative nature of the change ran counter to George Weyerhaeuser's macho style. But Fosmire explained that George Weyerhaeuser not only overcame this tendency, he actually led the effort with his steadfast commitment to the basic principles of the company, principles consistent with those of his grandfather ("We do these things not for ourselves . . .").

In November of 1981 (and, again, in November of 1982), in the midst of the recession and layoffs, and during the most challenging period of the change process, Weyerhaeuser called his top managers together and talked to them *not* about the bottom line or about "how to," but about the "basic values and responsibilities" of the corporation. Given the timing and the conditions in which these two talks were given, they stand as models of effective leadership of culture change. G.W. began the talks by saying that "the thing that has to be preserved in this period of internal and external turbulence is the basic, fundamental values of this company." In both 1981 and 1982 he reminded his top management team of the Weyerhaeuser values and responsibilities:

> In a free-enterprise society, a company's only assurance of its future is its ability to earn a profit. At Weyerhaeuser, we believe that *how* that profit is earned is critical to the Company's continued success. For this reason, we commit the Company to the following values and principles.

Integrity
- Integrity in all dealings, internal and external.

Stewardship
- Long-term, responsible stewardship of land and timber.

Fairness as an Employer
- Fair, considerate treatment of employees in a work climate that encourages the full utilization of their abilities.

Balance
- Decision making that reflects an appropriate balance between short- and long-term perspectives.
- Management decisions that balance the legitimate interests of shareholders, bondholders, employees, customers, and of the communities in which the Company is a major employer.

These fundamental values comprise criteria against which the actions of Weyerhaeuser managers will be evaluated.

To whom does Weyerhaeuser management have a special obligation?

Employees
- Employment that contributes to economic security, personal development, personal dignity and pride.

Shareholders

• A return on investment consistent with the risk and with competitive opportunities.

Bondholders

• Protection of their underlying interest through a sound, conservative capital structure.

Customers

• Conduct of our businesses in a manner that fosters long-term preferred-customer/preferred-supplier relationships.

Communities

• Management of the Company in a financially prudent manner, pursuing stability and continuity of operation, in order to be a good corporate citizen.

He concluded his remarks by saying that it was necessary in 1981 to state these values and responsibilities (and necessary to restate them in 1982), because in times of rapid change there is a "danger of expedience overcoming ethics." He also reiterated the company's commitment to total and systemic organizational redesign in which divisional autonomy was the desired end. He put no limits on the change effort, but added, "These values are what make Weyerhaeuser, Weyerhaeuser. Without them we lose our moorings, and the waters are turbulent. They *must* be preserved!"

If you find parallels between (1) the process of change at Weyerhaeuser, (2) the process of planning described in the previous chapter, and (3) the general process of management advocated in these pages—well, you are starting to understand how to run a great company! Moreover, it is significant that the successful processes of change initiated at Motorola, Levi Strauss, Honeywell, Deere, Dayton-Hudson, Arco, and Control Data have all paralleled the Weyerhaeuser experience. In each case:

• *Change built upon the unique strengths and values of the corporation.* Organizations don't start with a coherent philosophy or set of values. These evolve over time, pragmatically, and grow out of experience. Hence, new values can't be created by fiat, either.

- *The specifics of change were not imposed from the top.* Instead, there was broad and open participation of all levels of the corporation in all stages of the process.

- *Change was holistic.* Since the parts of a culture are all complexly interrelated, changing one part requires changing them all to achieve consistency between objectives, strategies, rewards, structure, training, management style and control systems.

- *Change was planned.* The long-term process was mapped out in advance, and there was a process of education in which every employee was informed about the what and the why of the effort. The process was broken down into small, doable tasks.

- *Change had top-management support.* Since the process of changing the entirety of a large organization is a slow one, there is need for commitment from the leaders of the corporation to the long, hard work involved—including the commitment to change their own behavior.

- *Changes were made in the guts of the organization.* Power relationships, information access, and reward systems all must be altered in meaningful ways.

- *There was a stakeholder orientation.* Since the goal of change must be to better meet the needs of all corporate stakeholders, the primary source of impetus and direction for change must come from the environment.

- *Change became ongoing.* Since the environment doesn't stand still and the needs of stakeholders aren't static, the idea is to institutionalize a process of continuing change.

Surfacing Basic Assumptions

Most change efforts at the Old Guard fail because they only deal with superficial levels of culture: They deal just with cultural *artifacts* (like the company logo or the style of management); or they go one level deeper and attempt to change cultural *values* (the norms and ideals of the organization). In contrast, the process of change at the Vanguard takes root because it operates not only at these two levels, but also at the deeper level of *basic assumptions.* Change at the Vanguard starts with an analysis of premises about (1) the nature of work and workers, (2) the purposes of the corporation, and (3) responsibilities to various stakeholders.

Two contrasting stories illustrate why some corporations are able to change and others are not:

The first is the sorry tale of the Cowles Media Corporation, owners of the *Minneapolis Star and Tribune.* (Control Data, Honeywell, Dayton-Hudson, Wilson Learning Corporation, and 3M notwithstanding, not *every* Minneapolis corporation is well-managed.) In fact, until recently, the Cowles empire may have been the worst-managed corporation in the entire publishing industry. Having lost *Look* in the 1960s and *Harper's* in the 1970s (the first went belly up, the second had to be literally *given* away), the down-in-the-dumps corporation saw their net income fall from $12.2 to $0.7 million between 1979 and 1982. In 1982, I was invited by several of the top managers of the company to meet with the entire executive group to discuss the Cowles "corporate culture." I started by asking the group for a few short, descriptive phrases that would best describe the culture of the company. Silence. I asked again. More silence. Finally, I was passed an unsigned note that read "Dummy, can't you see that we can't speak our minds? Ask for the input anonymously, in writing." I did, and for the next two hours I would ask them a question about their culture, they would write down answers, I would collect them and read the responses back to the group. At the end of this wearying experience I said that I worried deeply about the future prospects of any organization in which people were so afraid to speak their minds. After the session, several executives came up to tell me in private that the meeting was the best they had had since John Cowles, Jr., had assumed leadership of the corporation! Within a year of the meeting, Cowles fired several of these top managers and several others resigned in protest over one or another of his decisions. Shortly thereafter, the Cowles family fired John.

The second story is about a company that is arguably in the Vanguard league: the Federal Express Corporation. In the late 1970s, I was invited to address some thirty of the corporation's top managers on the subject of productivity. I had gotten no more than ten minutes into my talk when a young manager interrupted me and addressed a challenge to his colleagues:

"Professor O'Toole has made an interesting point about planning that runs counter to a major decision top management made a couple weeks ago. I suggest we ought to reexamine that decision now in light of what we have just learned." To my amazement, the managers picked up the suggestion and turned directly to a no-holds-barred debate. What was surprising about the discussion was that the lower-level managers present made the top managers *defend* their decision. When it was clear they couldn't defend it, the younger managers asked the bosses to change it. Which they did—then and there. This rough and tumble exchange lasted for about an hour. At the end of the time, they all got up to go to lunch without a trace of hard feelings, or a sign that anyone had won or lost face, power, or status. Apparently, this openness and willingness to raise tough questions and challenge accepted wisdom was part of the culture of the firm, for I was the only one in the room who found the exchange unusual. I had never seen such a healthy debate in *any* organization. My feeling was that if Federal Express could retain this ability to learn and to change, it was a good bet that they would continue to be a remarkable success. (The only bad news was that I never got to finish my speech . . . and they forgot to pay me!)

One can see from these two stories why the Cowles organization failed to meet the test of change, and why Federal Express has been one of the most successful corporations in anticipating and responding to technological, social, political, economic, and competitive change: Cowles was a nonlearning organization while the Federal Expressers were learners. (I understand things are better today at Cowles.) In general, the managers of the Vanguard are constantly reading and rereading, questioning, thinking, rethinking, reviewing, and revising. They are willing even to rethink their most basic assumptions; willing, in short to *un*learn the things that had led to past success but are likely to be anachronistic in the future. In fact, if I were forced to pick just one characteristic that distinguishes the Vanguard from the Old Guard it would be "openness to learning." They call every premise into question right down to its psychological foundations through a process of constructive dissent. In contrast, the Old Guard suffer from the arrogance of incompetence: a profound lack of curiosity and an overwhelming complacency. Perhaps the most damning thing that can be said about the managers of the

Old Guard is that Calvin Coolidge was more progressive than they!

At Dayton-Hudson, the word is: "Keep complacency out." They keep it out by an open management style and by "focusing on the 2 percent that isn't right." Says former DH chairman William Andres, "Some companies stress learning *among* their divisions. We stress learning from the *outside*. We feel it is more important for our people to talk with—listen to—suppliers, customers, experts, and community leaders than it is for Mervyn's managers to talk to B. Dalton managers."

At Motorola the spoils go to those who successfully challenge inappropriate managerial premises. CEO Galvin explains,

> Our challenge is to continually evidence a willingness to reach and risk, a willingness to *renew*. I saw at a young age that my father had to change to survive . . . My father was a "natural" at changing his mind. He would pound on the table telling you he was right. Then you would tell him the consequences of his decision, and he'd change his mind right there . . .

> There is no master plan that can anticipate change. That is why my father counseled, "Be in motion." He didn't believe in milking things to the end, until they became failures . . .

> We saw what happened to our former competitors Philco, Zenith, and Admiral and swore that we wouldn't let it happen to us. We looked at the companies that didn't survive, and we learned from them. As a management team we read John Gardner's *Renewal*, and we've lived by its precepts ever since.

And the attitude of renewal pervades the *entire* Motorola corporation, not just the executive suite. One Motorola manager explained to me,

> The expectation is that you will challenge any idea. The top three guys—Galvin, Weisz, and Mitchell—disagree with each other in front of their managers. The upshot is a healthy disrespect for the idea that those at the top are necessarily the wisest . . .

> Another important thing about the Motorola culture is our diversity of style and opinion. There is no such thing as the "Motorola Man." We've been a meritocracy for years. Jews,

Catholics, ethnics of all types climbed to the top faster here than in any large U.S. corporation I know of. The only question ever asked is, "Are you a good manager, engineer, or marketer?" Consequently, we've never had standardized or rigid modes of thought . . . We've never stood still.

At Arco, a similar attitude toward the virtue of speaking out pervaded the company from top to bottom throughout the 1970s (with the possible exception of Robert O. Anderson). I was once present at a meeting in which then-president Thornton Bradshaw was in the midst of answering a question about the virtues of decentralization with a glowing report on the company's recent reorganization, when he was interrupted by a young man who couldn't have been much older than thirty. "Mr. Bradshaw," he said firmly, "either you are lying to us or kidding yourself. We have not experienced any increase in autonomy as a result of the recent reorganization. It has been a change in name only. You guys at the top are still making all the decisions." I was flabbergasted that a young middle manager would have the temerity to question the veracity of a corporate president. But the real shock was yet to come. Bradshaw calmly asked the young manager for some examples of what he meant, and then went around the room asking all of those assembled if they, too, felt the decentralization was a sham. Bradshaw thanked them for their help and advice and said, in effect, that it was their obligation to tell the emperor when he was wearing no clothes. While I don't know exactly what happened after Bradshaw left the room, I do know that there were several subsequent actions to force real decision-making authority down into the operating divisions. And, I know of several other instances where low-ranked Arco managers have successfully questioned the decisions of their superiors—and lived to fight another day.

Like Motorola and Arco, most great companies see the challenging of sacred cows as a source of continuing renewal. For example, the 1981 Herman Miller Annual Report was dedicated to renewal, and CEO Max DePree explained therein what that process entails:

The part of our strategy that is renewing is our continuing to question what it is that has changed; the asking of ourselves, figuratively, what day it is. And then asking, if this is the new condition and the new day, what is the need and what is appropriate?

Max may have inherited the change "gene" from his father, D.J., a small town, religious businessman willing to listen to the wild ideas of designers from wild places like Europe, San Francisco, New York and Santa Fe—people and places foreign to the people of Zeeland, Michigan.

How can a company institutionalize what the Galvins and the DePrees do naturally? Verne Morland, an executive at NCR, suggests that the same effect can be had by hiring a corporate "fool." Like Lear's Fool, the corporate equivalent would be licensed "To challenge by jest and conundrum all that is sacred and all that the savants have proved to be true and immutable." While he or she need not be dressed in motley, spangles, and bells, the fool would be obligated to "stir up controversy, respect no authority, and resist pressures to engage in detailed analyses." In keeping with William James's observation that "genius . . . means little more than the facility of perceiving in an unhabitual way," Nancy Reeves suggests that women may be natural to this role because "they have been outside the status quo ante, and are free to marshall historic exclusion for positive ends . . . women have not learned, therefore do not have to unlearn, principles no longer pertinent . . . women might be the utterers of today's imperative blasphemies."

Another sign of renewal in a great company is the willingness to admit what is wrong about themselves. Like Cassius, they recognize "The fault, dear Brutus, is not in our stars but in ourselves." The value of this recognition is not in the act of truth telling or "confession," but in being able to admit to themselves what is wrong and thereby justify change. That is a rare trait. Visit IBM and GM and you would think that these companies had never erred in their entire existence. For example, it is unclear what IBM has learned from their personal computer experience. While it is no doubt true that IBM's new leader, John Opel, is more willing than his immediate predecessors to challenge past assumptions and to try new things, my contacts with IBM managers down the line lead me to conclude that IBM may soon experience GM-like "failure of success" as the result of their hit with the Personal Computer. Their corporate egos stroked by not one, but *two*, adoring *Time* cover stories within a year, and by a passel of other worshipful articles by journalists, business professors, and consultants, IBM managers may once again believe they have "solved the problem of management." Depending on with whom one spoke, IBM was said to have created some three to fourteen additional skunk works by early 1984. If so, this may be a sign that, like GM in the 1970s, IBM may be becoming a nonlearning organization—satisfied that they have discovered practices that are appropriate for all seasons. I was once told by one IBM manager: "When faced with another challenge like the Personal Computer, we now know how to respond. Skunk works are the wave of the future around here." Fine, if the next challenge is like the Personal Computer. But new challenges are seldom like old ones, and old responses are seldom appropriate to new challenges. Certainly, IBM has created new managerial assumptions, but it is not clear that they have created a *system in which assumptions can be continually tested* and, where proved wanting, revised. Similarly, GM has recovered from their disastrous years in the late 1970s, but have they created a learning organization that will allow them to *anticipate* problems in the future? One waits for evidence that GM has changed in that regard.

In contrast, at Levi Strauss there is a premium on admitting mistakes. Walter A. Haas, Jr., says, "One thing you can say about us: We learn from our mistakes." His son Robert has sought to further open up the Levi organization by discussing their mistakes publicly and by bringing in outsiders with diverse backgrounds to break down resistance to change (three examples of the new breed of Levi executives: Peter T. Jones, chairman of the prestigious Inter-American Foundation, Robert Dunn, former White House official, and Martin Krasney, late of the Aspen Institute).

In late 1984, Levi's Vanguard status was tried by ordeal when the company suffered the largest series of financial setbacks in their history. During the rapid growth of the 1970s, Levi had apparently acquired a lot of bad habits: insensitivity to the retailers who peddle their pants, inattention to quality, overcentralized decision making, bureaucratic "analysis paralysis," and indifference to long-range planning, all of which made it difficult for them—the world's largest apparel manufacturer—to compete with the hundreds of smaller, faster moving, mom-and-pop operations that buzzed around them like killer bees. In October

1984, Robert Haas assembled his management team and, sounding much like George Weyerhaeuser in a similar situation four years earlier, called on them to support a total organization change. He started out by accepting the blame, saying that Levi couldn't use such external events as a strong dollar and a decline in the demand for jeans as excuses. He said that the company had gotten in the habit of reacting rather than anticipating and complacency had begun to erode their capacity to innovate. His proposed solution? To commit the company to being the best, to commit the company to treating all stakeholders (particularly retailers) as partners, and to appoint as chief operating officer the only person in the firm with a sophisticated understanding of long-term planning. But, like G.W., Bob Haas put the burden of change on his people. He called for thorough and rapid decentralization of the company, creating dozens of small businesses each with the autonomy and flexibility to innovate to meet the challenge of their mom-and-pop competitors. In effect, Bob Haas said he was going to get the central staff off the back of the divisions and let them respond directly to their own constituencies.

Openness is a two-way street: While the Vanguard listen to their external stakeholders, they also share internal information with outsiders. Whereas such near-great companies as 3M, Kodak, P&G, and Cummins practice Kremlinlike secrecy, Levi, Arco, DH, and the rest of the Vanguard treat the media, scholars, and even corporate critics as stakeholders deserving of information. For example, Arco invites scholars to spend several months in residence at the company, encourages them to speak to any employee, and allows them to publish whatever they find without any conditions of censorship. As a consequence of this policy, Arco is constantly gaining the benefit of independent observation. The company recognizes this and is, in fact, probably the only company in the country that encourages scholars and experts to criticize them publicly. They even *pay* them to do so! Some seven years ago, the company issued their first "social report" to go along with their annual financial report. They reasoned that if they hired an auditor to verify their financial claims, they ought also to have a "social auditor" as well. To fill this role, they hired Milton Moskowitz, a San Francisco-based corporate critic of impeccable integrity. Moskowitz "audited" the company's record—his findings were far from uniformly glowing—

and Arco published them, as written, in the social report. Subsequently, they have commissioned Stanford professor Kirk Hanson and retired New York *Times* reporter Gladwyn Hill to do the same. What is truly remarkable is to go back a year or two later and review the published reports of these criticis: One will find that, for the most part, they will be out-of-date. This is because the company actually listens to critics and responds affirmatively to their recommendations. A secondary advantage of such openness, of course, is that it leaves no dirt for investigative reporters to "discover."

William Ruckelshaus brought such a spirit of openness to Weyerhaeuser, having learned from experience in the Nixon Administration the high cost of trying to keep the lid on information. He tells of a relevant experience when he was deputy U.S. Attorney General:

> While I was at the Justice Department, we undertook a review of FBI wiretap guidelines. I suggested that we should have a series of public hearings to get people to understand why the FBI did it, and how rare it actually was. I argued that if people knew how much documentation was needed for a tap, that a lot of the opposition based on fear and ignorance would dissipate. I suggested that the FBI might also learn something from the process. When I finished speaking, the idea was met with dead silence. Finally, one FBI agent said, "Jesus, what a stupid idea." Openness was so foreign to how they thought they should do business that they couldn't see the benefits to the organization of a little sunshine. Too many corporations are like the FBI on this score.

But not Weyerhaeuser, where all corporate files are placed in archives that are open to scholars, and where the corporate public relations department distributes articles and studies about the corporation to anyone who requests them—including articles critical of Weyco. Even when *mis*information is spread about the company's environmental record (as it was during the Senate hearings on Ruckelshaus's 1983 appointment to head the EPA), the company's response is simply to open up their records, tell the truth, and let the chips fall where they may.

Whether it is Bob Galvin being challenged by young Motorola managers in the corporate cafeteria, Bob Haas answering questions at an open forum for lower-level Levi employees, Arco bringing leaders of environmentalist groups into the corporation for discussions with top executives, or Honeywell sponsoring a company-wide seminar in which outside experts discuss both the pluses and minuses of the corporation's change efforts, *openness and learning* constitute a way of life at the Vanguard. As a consequence, continuous change is a natural, expected, and desired result.

THE TOUGHER ROW TO HOE

But what if the corporation is a closed, nonlearning entity? How can change be institutionalized when every aspect of the corporate culture militates against it? What if you are Kodak, and your policy is to play everything close to the vest—you have a "one voice" doctrine that forbids employees to discuss corporate matters with the press, scholars, or any other outsiders (you even have undercover "spies" who frequent Rochester bars looking for "leakers" of company secrets). And your policy is to promote only "homegrown" employees—your entire top management crew has worked their way up through the ranks of the company, never having lived or worked anywhere but in Rochester. And you have a history of paternalism in which there is "the company way" and no employee is free to challenge it. And, most critically, you have been fabulously successful—Kodak has historically earned at least 50 percent pretax profits on color film, while controlling some 88 percent of the domestic film market (because of this you have been saluted for decades, making every list of excellent companies).

What if you are Kodak, then, with that kind of history and, suddenly, the world changes and you are faced with (1) a decline in demand for film, (2) new technologies that undercut your basic businesses, and (3) a concerted challenge from a tough Japanese competitor who is gaining U.S. retail outlets at the clip of three thousand per year. Suddenly your profits are off by 10 percent and dropping fast. You find, in this world, that your once-vaunted employee relations (based on paternalism and *not* on participation) are a liability: You earn only $85,000 in sales per employee while your Japanese competitors bring in twice that amount. And that same employee loyalty is seriously eroded when you lay off some 3,500 workers. In response, you try the Old Guard approach (centralize, give power to corporate finance, make nonrelated acquisitions), but that doesn't work. Faced with rapid environmental, technological, and competitive change, you find that none of the old rules or techniques apply. It becomes clear that you need a completely new way to think and to act—a total organizational change.

If you were a Vanguard corporation such a change would be a natural outgrowth of the way you have been managing all along. But, in Rochester, the openness and learning needed for change are countercultural.

Fortunately, the situation is not hopeless. While overcoming Kodak's paternalism and arrogance will not be easy, there is reason to believe that the company can once again regain Vanguard status. First, they have an excellent set of traditions on which to build (great research, social responsibility, commitment to quality and service). And they see the need for holistic, planned change. Compared to Weyco, the missing ingredients at Kodak would appear to be vision and direction. That is, while they know they need to change, they don't know in which direction to go. Worse, they aren't likely to find it through their traditional top-down managerial processes. For it is highly improbable that Kodak could find a CEO who is smart enough, by himself, to outthink the technological community and the Japanese (when they got George Eastman, Kodak exceeded their quota of geniuses). But, as we saw at Weyco, George Weyerhaeuser didn't have to single-handedly "invent" the strategy that turned *his* company around. Instead, he opened up the Weyco management system and, in this way, every Weyco employee became an agent of change.

To Kodak's credit, they are pursuing similar ends (but using different means). Much as Weyco recruited Fred Fosmire to broker corporate change, Kodak has turned to Vincent P. Barabba, director of the last two U.S. Censuses. Barabba has been made Kodak's "chief of market intelligence," responsible for gathering information about consumer demographics and social trends. More important, Barabba has introduced Kodak to "Assumptions Analysis." Based on the work of my colleague, Ian Mitroff, Assumptions Analysis is a technique that formalizes what Bob Galvin, Bob Haas, Max DePree, and other great Vanguard executives do naturally and informally: that is, constructively challenge basic corporate premises to discover which are anachronistic or inappropriate. To do this at Kodak, Barabba assembles teams of up to thirty Kodak managers. The first thing Barabba gets them to do is to identify all of Kodak's stakeholders (Mitroff has developed methods for doing this that overcome the common managerial reluctance to take a broad view of the corporation's constituencies). Kodak managers will typically come up with the following kind of stakeholder list:

—customers   —federal government
—dealers   —local communities
—suppliers   —technological community
—competitors   —foreign governments
—employees   —the media
—shareowners   —ourselves

Next, Barabba will ask managers to state Kodak's prime assumptions about each of these stakeholders (again, Mitroff has techniques for surfacing such assumptions, and for developing group consensus about which are the prime assumptions). At the end of this exercise, the group will have created a list of Kodak's assumptions that is not dissimilar in form (but obviously different in substance) from the ten GM assumptions enumerated in Chapter Two. At this point, Barabba will break the group into two teams. The task of the first team is to adduce all the data, evidence, and arguments that they can think of that *support* the validity of the assumptions. The task of the second group is to advance all the evidence, data, and arguments they can think of that *belie* the validity of the assumptions. In the course of this adversarial process, it becomes clear to the entire group that some premises are more valid than others. While many premises may withstand challenge, those that are no better than witchcraft become readily apparent. The next exercise is to revise the inappropriate assumptions (or to develop new ones). The final product is a list of assumptions in which the group has considerable confidence.

Of course, what is important about Assumptions Analysis is not this final list of premises (which, at any rate, need to be regularly revised). The real value of the exercise is found in opening the group to new ideas, in getting managers in the habit of challenging sacred myths, and in preparing the organization for change. At a place like Kodak—in which there is little tradition of participation or open debate—a formal mechanism like Assumptions

Analysis can be a powerful tool for challenging the premises of the corporate Azande in a disciplined, nonthreatening way. Indeed, in late 1984, there were positive signs of change at Kodak. Most important was the decision to tackle paternalism head-on by radically decentralizing authority in the company. (My guess is that if Kodak stays at Assumptions Analysis—and builds on the momentum of the effort with further changes in corporate behavior and strategy—they can regain their Vanguard status. Says their recently retired CEO, Walter Fallon, "The real change at Kodak has been in awareness." Let's hope he's right, because that is exactly where change must begin.)

Other Places, Other Methods

The quite different processes of change used at Weyco and Kodak have the common characteristic of forcing both these organizations to take long, honest looks at themselves, to identify their strengths and weaknesses, their warts as well as their beauty marks. This kind of critical self-examination would be impossible for the Azande (or for any other closed culture). One of the *benefits* of an open society (one with a free press, opposition parties, and guaranteed rights of speech, assembly, and religion) is that there will always be someone more than willing to call attention to the emperor's embarrassing exposure. The *price* of such liberty includes: loss of some of the emperor's authority, high maintenance costs generated by the inefficiencies of individual freedom, and general dissatisfaction among those who prefer order to a raucous assembly of citizens speaking their minds. The same is true at corporations. While the Vanguard cultivate diversity of opinion in order to generate constructive dissent and change, the Old Guard much prefer conformity, loyalty, and a climate of well-modulated voices. (I once asked a PepsiCo vice president if anyone in that corporation had ever raised the issue of the morality of promoting junk food in ghetto areas where kids weren't getting enough basic foods. He answered, "If anyone would ever be so foolish as to raise the question, he'd find himself out on the street." On the occasion of a visit to the headquarters of the Phillip Morris Corporation, I noticed that *all* the executives were smoking. Was there any pressure on them to smoke to further their careers, I asked? Would a nonsmoker be considered "unclubbable?" The question was met with silence. The essence of a taboo, whether it is among the Azande or among tobacco merchants, is that it cannot be questioned.)

What is important in culture change is that there be honest self-examination; the particular technique used is incidental to this end, a mere function of the peculiarities of the organization. In fact, there are a number of quite useful mirrors into which a corporation might peer. Some companies have used "social anthropologists" to do the trick. Not *real* anthropologists in pith helmets leading native bearers laden with tape recorders and other paraphernalia, merely objective outsiders who learn about the corporation through participant observation. These individuals then write a description of the corporation, much as Evans-Pritchard prepared an ethnography of the Azande (Arco has done something similar to this from time to time).

Norwest Bank has used one of their employee task forces (see Chapter Four) to interview people at all levels of the organization about their culture. The task force identified both the characteristics of the current culture and alternative characteristics that employees felt were needed to cope with the bank's newly deregulated, highly competitive environment:

A. THE CURRENT NORWEST Culture	B. THE NEEDED NORWEST CULTURE
Self-image	**Self-image**
Proud	Confident
Demanding/self-critical	Self-critical/demanding
Insecure	Proud
Integrity	**Integrity**
Ethical	Responsible citizen
Good citizen	Honest, fair
Good place to work	Ethical
Vision	**Vision**
Not unified	Shared
Not clear	Compelling
Not used	Demonstrated
Leadership	**Leadership**
Reluctant	Visionary
Diffuse	Consistent
	Visible

Organization	Organization
Internally focused	Networking
Hierarchical	Entrepreneurial
Upward delegating	Downward delegating

Activity	Activity
Process oriented	Results oriented
Internally focused	Focused on the customer
Risk averse	Tolerant of failure

Communication	Communication
Weak across subcultures	Subcultures communicate
Conflict averse	Constructive conflict permitted
Incongruent	Words and actions congruent

Rewards	Rewards
Volume driven	Value driven
Entitlement oriented	Performance oriented
Rigid	Flexible
Not focused	Focused

After completing their analysis, the task force met several times with top management to develop the steps needed to move the bank from column A to column B. (One recommendation: Form "Stakeholder Councils" to keep top management abreast of change in the external environment.)

At Polaroid, a questionnaire has been used to elicit managerial views of their corporate culture. This instrument was used to examine the major aspects of the Polaroid culture, by eliciting responses to the following kinds of questions:

- What are the most pivotal events that have occurred since the founding of Polaroid?
- What distinctive competencies does Polaroid possess?
- What competencies does Polaroid need to develop?
- List five short, descriptive phrases or adjectives that best describe Polaroid.
- What is the best thing that has occurred at Polaroid during the past two years? (And the worst thing?)
- Is the Polaroid environment collaborative and supportive—or individualistic and unhelpful?
- Are superior-subordinate relationships at Polaroid paternalistic—or participative?
- To what extent is Polaroid open or closed to new ideas?

- When Polaroid employees are rated for raises and promotions are they judged on their performance—or on nonperformance criteria?

- Is planning at Polaroid proactive and long-range—or reactive, crisis management?

- To what extent do Polaroid employees participate in gains that come from their increased productivity?

- To what extent are Polaroid people encouraged to take risks—or to play it safe?

- To what extent is Polaroid willing to engage in critical self-analysis—or *un*willing to question basic assumptions?

- Is company performance measured by the quality or effectiveness of the product or service—or by financial ratios (management by the numbers)?

- Are new ideas carefully considered and tried whenever practical—or quickly killed off by staffs and committees?

- Is there adequate job security at Polaroid—or can you be out on your ear tomorrow?

- To what extent is [the Polaroid constitution] a realistic, action-oriented document—or unrealistic and hard to act on?

Results of the poll were then analyzed by a group of Polaroid managers to find ways to disseminate the information—and to get it acted on by top management.

The problem at Polaroid and Norwest—and at many other very good companies—is inadequate commitment to change at the top of the organization. This unfortunate situation is probably more the norm than the exception. In corporation after corporation that I visit, managers nod approvingly when I recite the details of Vanguard culture change efforts . . . then they say: "That's a top management problem. What can we, as powerless middle managers, do about it?" While the question may be legitimate, in too many cases it is an excuse, a cop-out of individual responsibility. Sure it helps to have someone great at the top—someone who'll do the tough work of leadership for us. But if such a person isn't there—and in most cases she isn't—one has the choice of despair, of resignation . . . or of taking action ourselves. While taking action is clearly the responsible choice, most people won't do it because they assume that they have to be either a hero or genius to change an organization. In fact, what it takes is a little courage and persistence. For example, in Spanish-speaking East Los Angeles, where the schools tend to be miserable and where the performance of students is equal to that of the schools, one math teacher decided to do something about it. He couldn't change the whole curriculum, or get more resources for the school, but he could teach calculus to students who previously received no math beyond algebra and geometry. At first, only a handful of kids signed up for the class. But as word of the success of the students spread—as it became known that Latino kids were actually being accepted at good colleges—more and more signed up until the entire school was infused with enthusiasm. Within a few years, almost all the teachers in the school had toughened up their courses.

Norwest Bank's Douglas Wallace is not the only individual without a power base who has successfully initiated change in a large organization. At Prudential Insurance, Morton Darrow played the role of Lear's Fool so successfully that he managed to get his Old Guard colleagues to (a) undertake the largest quality of work life program ever in an American white-collar corporation, (b) to introduce futures research long before anyone ever heard of *Megatrends,* and (c) to make Prudential a national leader in support of inner-city rehabilitation. Without a staff, without a budget, without an imposing title, Darrow courageously set himself to making Prudential the kind of place where he would be proud to work. Such actions often come at a cost. In the process of transforming their organizations, both Douglas Wallace and Morton Darrow used up all their political chips. After a while, it became clear to both that the time had come for them to voluntarily leave the companies they had dared to make great. Important, neither one regrets the choice he made. Consider the many people who have played it safe only to live to regret their timidity! Fortunately, in most organizations, courageous people don't usually face the kind of opposition that forces them to put their jobs on the line.

Robert Townsend had the right idea as far back as 1969: No support at the top? Then one must engage in "guerrilla warfare"! The best divisional, unit, middle- and upper-middle managers (and teachers, professors, lawyers, and doctors) that I've met, all assume they have authority to make the changes necessary to improve the effectiveness of their operations—unless, of course they have been specifically forbidden to do so (a rare, but not unknown occurrence). In fact, most organizations have so much slack in them that the people at the top won't find out that someone lower down is practicing sound management until it is too late for them to choke it off.

HONEYWELL'S GUERRILLAS

Honeywell is included in this book not because it is the best-managed company in America, but because it has come so far without the luxury of luck, technological breakthroughs, or dynamic leadership. Honeywell offers hope to the despairing masses of American middle-managers who are stuck in mediocre firms with lacklustre leaders. For, in the late 1960s, hardly any major U.S. corporation was less-promising material for greatness than Honeywell. The company had a traditional, hierarchical command-and-control culture built on rigid rules and roles: "It was run as if General Patton had designed the system," says one long-time Honeywell employee. Further, the company's technology was old hat. Worse yet, there wasn't even a crisis to spur action: the company was limping along earning a satisfactory profit. None of these circumstances constituted fertile soil in which to plant the seeds of change.

Change occurred at Honeywell when a small group of tenacious managers (headed by Jim Renier, then a divisional manager), decided to engage in guerrilla warfare and turn Honeywell around without initial support from the top. (They quickly gained it as their efforts bore fruit.) The change worked, in large part, because the managers engineered it in a way that was consistent with the existing culture of the firm. Believe it or not, they actually used *committees* as the prime vehicle for change! In most companies committees function to forestall change, but that had never been the case at Honeywell. Recognizing that committees were the traditional source of influence in the company, Honeywell's guerrilla fighters slowly but persistently encouraged top management to establish new committees to evaluate existing corporate practices in the areas of training, benefits, job security, entrepreneurship, productivity, middle-management development, rewards, and so on. The guerrilla fighters kept forming more and more of these cross-functional, ad-hoc committees until everyone in the company was using the language of change (the guerrilla fighters even resorted to slipping "revolutionary rhetoric" into executive speeches).

The guerrillas' real secret was that they never let up, never lost faith, never slept (that's why undermanned guerrillas often win wars against great armies). And they were particularly good at diagnosing the strengths and weaknesses of top management. For example, it was clear that Honeywell executives—like most executives—believed that the only people besides themselves who know anything about management are other top executives. This being so, the guerrillas recognized that there wasn't much they or their allies could say that would convince Honeywell's top people to change—but, if they could get executives from Vanguard corporations into the act, maybe top management would listen to them! So the guerrillas convinced their executive team to take a two-week Cook's tour of progressive companies— in the process, Honeywell's executives got the idea from their peers of what change is all about.

Working from below with quality control circles and committees, and from above with these "fly arounds" and other executive-level educational efforts, the guerrillas began to have success. Ultimately, it became natural for Honeywell executives to want to get in the act and assume the leadership of what was proving to be a successful change effort. Finally, the executives asked, "What can we do?" The guerrillas showed them two of the famous Johnson & Johnson videotapes that depicted executives debating the merits of the J & J Credo. Honeywell executives got the picture: They then went on a two-day retreat and generated their own statement of corporate values and objectives (which has since been revised in a broader, more participatory effort). Here's the good news for the despairing masses: Today, Old Guard corporations send delegations on "fly arounds" to visit *Honeywell* to learn how they changed their corporate culture! And the best news is that Honeywell's top managers now tell the visiting firemen, "We don't know how to change *your* culture . . . but we'll tell you how we changed *ours*."

Now, back to the meeting at which Polaroid managers were discussing how to bring about change in the absence of top management leadership. Before the meeting was over, all of the people present were asked to write down their final thoughts about the corporate culture questionnaire they had been reviewing, and about the problem of getting change implemented. Significantly, 25 percent of the 125 people present mentioned their *individual responsibility* for initiating change. Here are some of the phrases they wrote down: ". . . my responsibility to the culture," ". . . I can initiate change," ". . . I can make a difference," "my *own* responsibility to impact change." If they meant it, Polaroid (like Kodak) is on their way to rejoining the Vanguard!

Excuses, Excuses

I have found six common excuses for *not* attempting corporate change. In this chapter we have reviewed the Vanguard responses to each of these:

FIRST EXCUSE: "Change won't lead to perfection."
Vanguard response: "Of course it won't; compare change to the way things were, not to perfection" [Weyerhaeuser].

SECOND EXCUSE: "We're too big to change."
Vanguard response: "We did it in a company with 100,000 employees" [Honeywell].

THIRD EXCUSE: "We've got a union."
Vanguard response: "Turn them into a stakeholder and involve them in the process" [Weyerhaeuser].

FOURTH EXCUSE: "There's no top-management support."
Vanguard response: "Engage in guerrilla warfare" [Honeywell].

FIFTH EXCUSE: "We don't know where to start."
Vanguard response: "Start from the company's strengths, and start with *you*, kiddo" [Honeywell, Weyerhaeuser, Polaroid].

SIXTH EXCUSE: "We can't change now, we're in the midst of a recession" or ". . . we're in the midst of a financial crisis."
Vanguard response: "If you've got the stuff of greatness, *now* is the time to change." [See what follows directly . . .]

MANAGING CHANGE IN THE MIDST OF A CRISIS

Edwin Land once said, "The bottom line is in heaven." Actually, it is in *hell*. The true test of a company is how it acts in periods of great adversity. Any company can appear excellent in good times; the qualities of greatness become manifest only when times are bad. Thus, while it is remarkable that each of the

Vanguard succeeded in turning themselves into productive, high-performance companies during the 1970s, it is their behavior during the 1980–83 recession that cements their Vanguard status. During the recession, they not only continued the long-term process of change and continued to abide by the principles in their constitutions, they *intensified* both these commitments. As a result, each (with the exception of Levi Strauss) emerged from the recession stronger than when they entered. By 1984, each had completed the turnaround begun a decade earlier, and each is now an industry leader (or poised to become so).

Not that the Vanguard found the recession to be a piece of cake. Like most large American corporations, the Vanguard discovered their weaknesses during the long economic drought. Several of the Vanguard discovered that they were overstaffed, and they were forced to make at least some cutbacks in their white-collar ranks. (It is significant that there were no permanent blue-collar work force reductions at any of the Vanguard companies.) Noteworthy, however, is the way the Vanguard *minimized* layoffs (through the methods discussed in Chapter Four), and how they *managed* the layoffs that proved unavoidable. Look at how Weyerhaeuser eliminated 3,000 salaried positions: People up and down the line were involved in the decisions; training was provided for those who needed it; and an outplacement service was established (only 990 employees needed this service, and 75 percent of those were placed in new jobs while they were still receiving Weyco checks). Severance pay averaged $21,000 per person, and the whole effort cost $63 million. Says Fred Fosmire, "The idea was to treat those people with dignity and respect; it was money well spent." At Weyco (and at each of the Vanguard) most layoffs were achieved through early retirement and other voluntary separation programs. Wherever possible, the Vanguard used incentives rather than forced firings.

In 1984, with the market for jeans at depression levels, Levi Strauss was forced to close more than a dozen plants and lay off some 3,000 workers. Even though the company was experiencing a crisis, they didn't adopt a crisis mentality toward their workers. Instead, workers were given a minimum thirteen-week notice, a week's pay for every year they had worked for the company, continuation of medical coverage from three to six months (based on seniority), full maternity benefits for all women already pregnant at the time, counseling, outplacement, and re-

location expenses for those employees willing to transfer to other
Levi facilities where there were job openings. Moreover, the
company agreed to continue for up to three years any grants to
impacted communities that had come from a local Community
Involvement Team. Layoffs are always sad and bitter times for
employers and employees. But it is some measure of the greatness of Levi and of the spirit in which they closed their plants in
Macon, Georgia, and Denison, Texas, that, according to Milton
Moskowitz, "the assembled employees broke out in spontaneous
applause."

It is worth contrasting the Levi and Weyco layoff practices with
those of Heublein at a distillery in Kentucky where, according to
Moskowitz, "Most of the employees got the first word of their
joblessness from the newspaper or television screen," and at one
other member of the Old Guard where several hundred employees were summoned to the company auditorium one Friday afternoon and told: "You are all fired. Clean out your desks, pick up
your last checks, and be off the premises by 5:00 P.M."

Plant closings are hard to manage well, even with the best of
intentions in the best of firms—as Arco discovered when attempting to do right while closing two Anaconda facilities in
1980. Here are a few of the facts: The smelter in Anaconda,
Montana, was seventy-five years old. It was the town's *raison d'*
être, directly providing 25 percent of the town's jobs (and, indirectly, most of the rest). Anaconda's property tax bill amounted
to 40 percent of the county's total budget. If there was ever a
company town, this was it. Dependency in spades. Yet, to my
knowledge, no independent analyst has ever argued that the
company had any choice but to shut the smelter (and a nearby
refinery) down permanently.

Arco faced a projected loss of $281 million on their mining
operations in 1981 and clearly could not justify the $400-odd
million it would have cost to resuscitate the old plant or to build a
new one, for there were many materials being substituted for
copper—and there was the promise of future technological
breakthroughs that would further erode the declining demand
for the mineral. And, even where copper remained the metal of
choice, Anaconda faced increasingly keen foreign competition.
Thus, while the company had spent some $65 million over eight
years in an unsuccessful attempt to make the facilities competitive and environmentally sound, and another $15 million in re-

search to find a technology to keep production in Montana, the handwriting was on the wall. Finally, Arco's CEO Robert O. Anderson met with both of Montana's senators and a passel of local politicians and told them that Arco was forced to throw in the towel unless someone had a saving idea.

Shortly thereafter, Arco announced that, effective immediately, the facilities would be permanently shut down. In compensation, all hourly employees were to receive a $3,500 severance allowance, supplementary unemployment benefits that amounted to a year's full working pay, continuation of health benefits for a year, counseling, and early retirement for those over age 55. The communities involved would receive land for an industrial park, a Community Redevelopment Fund of $5 million, and the equivalent of what the company would have owed in taxes for a year. Arco was proud of this package, since they were required by neither law nor union contract to do much in way of compensation. Hence, by Arco's reckoning, they had made the most generous voluntary offer ever made by a company in similar circumstances.

Arco officials were subsequently stunned to find that most outside observers failed to share Arco's enthusiasm for this "alimony" package. There were four areas of criticism directed against the company:

First, Arco was accused of having *told* employees, the union, and the local community what they were going to do for them. It was argued that there had been no real negotiations, because the Anaconda parties, with no leverage and in obvious desperation, were in no position to bargain for what they really needed from the company.

Second, it was said that the closing had been precipitous. Why the rush? Things hadn't suddenly gone bad for Arco and Anaconda. The EPA was willing to grant a two-year variance on antipollution requirements, and the company was enjoying their most successful quarter ever, so why did the closure have to be immediate? A two-year phaseout, it was said, would have allowed both workers and the community to plan for the future in a more orderly fashion.

Third, it was argued that the best things a company can do for laid-off employees are to provide retraining opportunities and to underwrite their relocation expenses. But the company had little to offer on either score.

Fourth, critics asked how it was that, on the very same day the company announced record quarterly profits of $390 million, they could say that they could not afford to offer jobs at other Arco facilities to the thousand or so people being laid off? Many companies—far stodgier, far poorer, and with far worse future prospects than Arco—would have offered jobs to all those who were willing to move to other company locations.

Alas, Arco did not have good answers to these questions. Their mumbling replies indicated that they had simply moved too quickly and had considered too few options. (They also didn't seem to view Anaconda employees as their own. Some have said that the company would *not* have treated employees on the oil side of the business in this fashion. It is interesting that, long after mergers have been consummated, acquirers almost always speak of acquirees as *them* not *us.*)

Well, Arco got *close* to making a good job of a nasty business. But almost isn't good enough, especially for a company that prides itself on "managing operations with an active concern for their impact on employees [and] host communities." How can Arco be considered a Vanguard company with a performance like this on their record? The answer is that there are no companies that are free of mistakes. What separates the best from the merely good is how a company copes with their errors. Most companies respond to an old fashion foul-up by adopting a defensive attitude, or by trying to cover up the incident. At Arco, the defensive period lasted only for a few short weeks. Internally, there was a debate from the start about what had gone wrong and why. Externally, they started to admit their mistakes within months. Since the incident, the company has been wrestling with developing policies for plant closings, layoffs, and job security. On one hand, they know that they cannot go through another mass layoff; on the other, they know they cannot afford to promise more than they can deliver. In a way, the issue is a by-product of the questionable initial decision to buy Anaconda. Because all the implications of the Anaconda acquisition had not been thought through (for example, what is the responsibility to the employees of a failing company that Arco acquires?), Anderson's one bad decision has continued to haunt Arco. Importantly, this is not used as an excuse. At the company's two-week seminar for up-and-coming managers, there is now a required half-day case analysis of the shutdown in which participants debate what additional options the company had that they failed to consider. God forbid they'll have to go through such a closing again. But they are prepared to do it better and more responsibly if there is a next time. That's what learning and change are about in an organization.

After reading such a story, I realize some readers will have come this far and still not be convinced by my arguments about the Vanguard. What further evidence can I adduce to show that the way of the Vanguard is, in fact, superior to the way of the Old Guard? I admit that not even the Vanguard are able to completely insulate themselves from the impact of untoward economic conditions: As we have seen, Deere and Weyerhaeuser are particularly affected by economic downturns due to the harshly cyclical nature of the farm and home construction businesses. But what is important is how these Vanguard firms had prepared themselves for the inevitable recession, and how they coped when it finally came. Deere, which had invested their cash flow of the 1970s in research, plant, and equipment (and not in high dividends or acquisitions), had steeled themselves for the economic shock by becoming the industry leader in terms of productivity. Then, during the recession, they actually stepped up their emphasis on capital productivity. As a result of both their preparation for, and their reaction to, economic adversity they *increased* market share and earnings in the early 1980s (the worst years in the farm industry since the 1930s) while their competitors went by the boards. Weyerhaeuser, which had begun their change effort prior to the recession, continued it (as we have seen) even in the face of great adversity. And, while their competitors were cutting their operations to the bone, Weyerhaeuser spent $300 million on capital investment in 1982 (the worst year in the wood products industry since the 1930s) and was the only company in the industry that year to operate anywhere near capacity.

Motorola and Dayton-Hudson both expanded during the recession (Dayton-Hudson never lost a beat in their planned addition of stores. While Motorola did see their profits slip by 6 percent in the worst year of the recession, their archrivals TI and Intel experienced a 49 percent and 72 percent drop, respectively). Honeywell, Levi Strauss, Arco, and Control Data all increased expenditure on plant modernization and new technology while their competitors were cutting back. In fact, Arco and Control

Data had their best years relative to their competitors during the recession. And, lo and behold, the corporate and financial community even started to catch on to what the Vanguard were up to: In the 1984 *Fortune* ranking of the nation's "most respected companies," the Vanguard found themselves well placed (unlike the previous year). Sooner or later even the Azande learn that there is a better alternative than witchcraft!

11.

PHILOSOPHERS NOT ADMINISTRATORS: THE LEADERS OF THE VANGUARD

The structure of the organization can then be symbolized by a man holding a large number of balloons in his hand. Each of the balloons has its own buoyancy and lift, and the man himself does not lord it over the balloons, but stands beneath them, yet holding all the strings firmly in his hand. Every balloon is not only an administrative but also an entrepreneurial unit.

—E. F. SCHUMACHER

Here's a question I have been asking myself: What traits do Arco's (later, RCA's) Thornton Bradshaw, Dayton-Hudson's Kenneth Macke, Deere's William Hewitt, Control Data's William Norris, Honeywell's James Renier, Levi's Robert Haas, Motorola's Robert Galvin, and Weyco's George Weyerhaeuser have in common? Each is a great leader—of that I am convinced—but are they all great in the same way and for the same reasons? I search the literature on leadership for guidance. Here I find a theory based on charisma, and there one that says "The occasion makes the man." I even find a tool for identifying different "leadership styles": It is quaintly called the "Managerial Grid" (as opposed to what, the rack?). Little help from these scholarly scribblers.

But my colleague Warren Bennis has taken a more fruitful tack. He has interviewed some ninety successful men and women in an attempt to determine what qualities they bring to their jobs that inspire others to follow them. I am intrigued especially by one of these traits, which Bennis has dubbed "The Wallenda Factor." During the many decades that the great tightrope aerialist Karl Wallenda amazed the world with his daredevil feats, it seems he concentrated on one thing only—*walking* the tightrope. Then, before his last (and fatal) stunt he talked to his wife incessantly about *falling*. Later she was to say, "It was the first time he'd ever thought about that, and it seemed to me that he put all his energy into *not falling*, not into walking the tightrope." Bennis concludes from his many interviews that great leaders never think about *falling*, they think only of their ultimate goal:

> I call that peculiar combination of vision, persistence, consistency, and self-confidence necessary for successful tightrope walking—the combination I found in so many leaders—The Wallenda Factor.

That is as close to it as we are going to get. The leaders of the Vanguard indeed each have a *vision*—a clear idea of where their companies are going, what they are about, and why. They each have *persistence* and *consistency*—they stick to their principles and provide constancy to the organization in rough seas and on long voyages. And they each have *self-confidence*—they lead by example—with faith that if they do right others will follow and do right in turn.

Again, this is all so very general, so abstract, and so frustratingly unspecific. Isn't there some particular, identifiable *thing* that they all do? Isn't there a common practice among these great leaders, or some rule that they all follow?

The Deceptive Rule of Decentralization

In the midst of the relativism found in these pages, there is nonetheless one rule to which all Vanguard leaders pay heed: All practice *decentralization* of authority.

Decentralization, the oldest "rule" of management, also seems to be the only rule that is, in fact, a *rule*. It is a strange kind of rule, however—a rule by default. For all that has been learned with certainty about management since the early days when Caesar attempted to command his far-flung legions from distant Rome is this: *No one is smart enough to run a large organization.* No one, not Caesar, Alfred Sloan, or even a Vanguard executive is able to direct all aspects of a large, diversified corporation. *Size* is the problem, if we must state it in a single word. Not to say that small is beautiful—it is just that big is hard to keep track of, impossible to control. The best that can be done is to break the organization down into units that are each small enough to be managed as nearly autonomous, entrepreneurial enterprises. That's what all great leaders appear to do.

SMALL COMPANY EXAMPLES

Consider the practices of leaders of two small companies:

1. W.L. Gore & Associates, manufacturers of a range of their own wondrous inventions (including Goretex, a gossamer-thin fabric that is both waterproof and breathable), are as decentralized as they are inventive (and profitable: Between 1977 and 1982 the company's sales and earnings grew at a 40 percent annual compounded rate). Instead of the traditional, corporate pyramidal structure, Gore & Associates is a "lattice organization" (every employee may interact directly with any other employee on a one-to-one basis much like the horizontal and vertical cross-hatchings of a garden lattice). In effect, there is no hierarchy, no chain of command. No one even has a title. Says Bill Gore, "We organize ourselves around voluntary commitments . . . people manage themselves." To make this work, there obviously needs to be a tremendous amount of personal interaction. To get it, Gore opens up a new factory as soon as the population of a plant nears 200 (150 people per plant is considered ideal). Thus, while the company has only 2,000 employees, they have 27 plants. And Gore disperses these plants geographically so they won't start messing in each other's business, spoiling their creativity.

When a new "associate" is hired at W. L. Gore and Associates, he or she will be told to "look around and find something you'd like to do." This system turns every employee into an inventor or an entrepreneur. Order is maintained by an informal "sponsor" in each department—a senior associate who takes a special interest in the new associate's problems and career aspirations. Gore calls this system "un-management"—but it is really *self*-management (with critical support from more experienced associates).

Since Bill Gore doesn't give orders or get involved in making decisions, that doesn't leave much "work" for him to do. But Bill Gore actually works hard, very hard. Indeed, he moves around the organization making certain that size, bureaucracy, rules, and bad habits don't foul up the lattice. Wherever you look at

W.L. Gore and Associates you find Bill Gore talking to his associates about the philosophy that makes the company unique, and about their long-term opportunities ("You know, I'll bet we could use a membrane like Goretex to desalinate water. What do you think?").

2. Chapparal Steel is the nation's best-managed steel company. While U.S. Steel, Bethlehem, Republic, and the other giants of the industry are being forced to shut down one after another of their unproductive megamills, Chapparal's minimills are setting world records for productivity (Chapparal turns out a ton of steel in 1.6 "man-hours," compared with the Japanese record of 2.8 and U.S. Steel's snaillike 5.0). After only seven years in business, Chapparal is the fifteenth largest domestic steel producer (and is as busy as Pac-Man chewing away at the *Japanese* share of the market in the western United States).

Where an Old Guard mill may have 10,000 employees, Chapparal considers 800 too many. Why? In a small Chapparal mill managers can know every employee and involve them all directly in decision making and profit sharing. Moreover, the manager of a small mill can think of himself as the president of his own little company. In contrast, the manager of an 800-worker unit in a 10,000-employee mill will feel she has all the discretionary authority of a lieutenant in the Red Army.

To preserve a sense of ownership, expansion at Chapparal means horizontal *not* vertical growth. When they have added new mills, they have "expanded management sideways," says their president, Gordon Forward, "and if we take on any more endeavors, we're going to continue to add horizontally to retain our shallow management structure . . . We have only four levels of management, General Motors has seventeen. And some big steel companies would have trouble counting theirs."

Forward has decentralized all responsibility for personnel, safety, training, and even "keeping up-to-date on technology" to Chapparal's front-line supervisors. When these supervisors go on their mandated annual sabbaticals, they may go to Japan to learn about the latest steel technology or they may take on a special project designed to broaden their technical knowledge. The people who report to these supervisors, Chapparal's production workers, have full responsibility for the quality and quantity of work in the mill. Unlike their peers at U.S. Steel, they are paid an annual salary (that is, not by the hour), they participate in profit sharing, and they meet regularly with top management in the corporate boardroom to discuss their ideas for improving corporate performance. What work does this leave for President Forward to do? He is the firm's peripatetic philosopher. You will find him in the locker room talking technology with workers, or in a strategy meeting talking about the company's principles and objectives. But you will *never* find him telling people how to to their jobs, or what they ought to be doing that they aren't.

Gore and Forward are examples of what my colleague Larry Greiner calls "strategic actors"—managers who lead by articulating the philosophy of the corporation, by paying attention to the company's strengths, and by talking about the future (and they do this with employees at *all* levels). In contrast, Greiner describes "the trapped executive"—the administrator who attempts to solve every problem, to make minute decisions, who pays attention only to the weaknesses of the organization and to current events (and who talks only with the people who report directly to him). In essence, the function of executives like Gore and Forward is to provide the core vision and values that keep decentralized operations from succumbing to the centrifugal forces of anarchy and confusion.

Now, here's the problem: In a small company, *the power of personality* can act as the gyroscope in a decentralized operation. But in a big, mature corporation the nature of leadership must be different. The head of a firm with thousands of employees located in hundreds of locations around the globe will find that there is not enough of himself to spread around in the manner of a small company leader like Gore or Forward. Moreover, a professional manager who has worked his or her way up the corporate ranks lacks the legitimacy of leadership that comes naturally to the enterpreneurial founding father of a small company. Decentralization and leadership are thus different breeds of cat in large as opposed to small companies (but both are cats nonetheless, as we soon discover).

LARGE COMPANY EXAMPLES

Decentralization can easily degenerate into anarchy (or lethargy) in a large corporation. The clearest example of this is TRW, a company with 90 autonomous divisions and 250 separate R&D units. TRW has been on the verge of Vanguard status for years (later we consider one of their unique strengths), but their admirable freedom to experiment, to be entrepreneurial, and to be self-managing has gotten out-of-hand and bred Balkanization. Fiercely independent corporate fiefdoms refuse to share technology, learning, or resources. Moreover, there is no way for TRW's professional managers to coordinate these nationalistic mini-states to meet changing external threats and challenges. There is no way that even a charismatic Gore or Forward could *talk* these many and diverse groups into cooperation. In fact, so many opportunities are being lost that the company is now risking "war" with their divisions by attempting to negotiate a modicum of centralization. At Hewlett-Packard, another near-Vanguard corporation, decentralization has also gotten out of hand as the founding fathers fade into retirement and the company is too big to be run by one person: H-P divisions now make incompatible components for what are supposed to be "systems." Such examples should cause us to question a new "rule" of management: that excellent companies are all "hang loose." While it is true that a number of fast-growing companies are loosely organized, it would seem that is a by-product of growth, not a cause of it. Indeed, once fast-growing companies get into trouble, their looseness is often seen as a sign of sloppy management.

Even at the Vanguard, decentralization has its costs and its complications. Three instances: In the 1970s, Atlantic Richfield's corporate staff was far and away the most progressive in the oil industry, but management practices in Arco's far-flung divisions were often no better than the Neanderthal practices of Union Oil. At Honeywell, divisional independence is a fetish—and a costly one. Not only is there duplication of some activities (two separate divisions make their own computer circuit boards; there are three separate training centers offering overlapping courses), cooperation has suffered from provincial pride: When one division decided to conduct a series of seminars on quality circles they assembled their own faculty—even though three or four extremely knowledgeable people on the subject were available only twenty minutes away in corporate headquarters. At Levi, decentralization led to the formation of subcultures whose values ran counter to cherished corporate principles. In all three of these instances, there was little that the folks in central headquarters could do about checking the independence of their divisions. As corporation after corporation (and central government after central government) has discovered, divisional managers (and colonial administrators) can be *ordered* to fall into line —but the chances are they will successfully resist orders that are *imposed* from the top. What to do?

The Nature of Leadership in a Decentralized Organization

Since the early part of this century, the primary problem of big-company management has been to find ways to simultaneously obtain the benefits of centralization *and* decentralization. GM's Alfred Sloan thought he had solved the problem by decentralizing operations while centralizing financial controls. But TRW, HP, Honeywell, Arco, and every other company (whether Old Guard or Vanguard) that has tried the Sloan approach has found that it is not enough. While centralized financial controls are *necessary* in any large, decentralized corporation, they are *insufficient*. (Worse, as we have seen in our discussions of the Old Guard, financial controls by themselves ultimately distort the purpose of the organization.)

Dayton-Hudson—the most decentralized of the Vanguard Corporations—has come the closest to resolving the big company centralization/decentralization dilemma. The resolution wasn't easy, and it required the complete rethinking of the nature of leadership in a large corporation. Start with some remarkable facts: In 1973, when DH's annual revenues were $1.4 billion, there were 250 people in their Minneapolis headquarters; a decade later, when revenues had reached over $6 billion, there were still 250 people overseeing their 100,000-employee empire. DH's staff can remain so thin because their executives would no sooner become involved in store management than the White House would call the captain of an aircraft carrier to advise on catapult maintenance (while Jimmy Carter might have been tempted to proffer such advice, we should remember that management wasn't exactly his *forte*).

Says DH's CEO Kenneth Macke, "We start with the proposition that responsibility must be fixed at the store level. If you push profit responsibilities down there, then you must push all other responsibilities down, too." I once challenged Macke on this, asking him what he would do if he visited a B. Dalton store and found an instance of clear *mis*management. Wouldn't he then call B. Dalton's president and raise hell? "Let me tell you a story," Macke replied. "Last winter I was cutting through our flagship Dayton's department store [across the street from head-quarters] on the way back to my office after lunch when I passed the tearoom. In the old days, the tearoom was very popular. Ladies would come into town to make a day of shopping, and they would socialize in this grand old room. On this particular day, I noticed there were only two old ladies (in white gloves and snoods, no less) sitting in the tearoom while being attended to by four waiters and waitresses. As I made my way out of the store, I walked by our new yogurt stand, and there was a bloody mob scene, with about three dozen young people trying to catch the attention of one completely shell-shocked yogurt jerk. Now, professor, what would you have done if you were in my shoes?"

"Simple," I replied, "I would have walked back to the tearoom, grabbed three of the idle employees, and shoved them behind the yogurt bar where they could be productive." Macke sat back, amused, silently shaking his head. "O.K., what did you do?" I asked. "Nothing." "Nothing?" "If I had jerked the Dayton company president's wire, he would have jerked the store manager's wire, and he would have jerked the floor manager's wire, and he would have jerked the yogurt jerk! Pretty soon, everybody in the whole corporation would be depending on me to play puppeteer. If you really want people to take initiative, you can't be commanding them at the same time. The only way you can lead in a large corporation is by example. Now, if the Dayton stores started losing money chronically, I'd ask the president why. If he couldn't figure it out, I might then say, 'Try walking by the tearoom some afternoon.' But, if I'm doing my job, we should never come to that level of detail."

There is no doubt that DH's decentralization provides them with a host of good things: flexibility, entrepreneurship, market sensitivity, managerial specialization, and an institutionalized change mechanism. Unfortunately, there is another side to the story. As at Levi and Arco, many of the good things about the DH culture get diluted by the time they reach their far-flung stores. Indeed, the benefits of centralization—integration, control, synergy, quick action, learning, the avoidance of duplication, and the core values of the central company—have been devilishly hard to maintain in DH's decentralized operations.

Significantly, decentralization wasn't a problem at DH as long as the company was small and the charismatic Dayton family dominated management. But as company stores multiplied faster than rabbits in a hutch, and as the last of the Daytons retired from active involvement in the corporation, the centralization/decentralization problem emerged. Even though profits were pouring in, the distinctive cultural features that had differentiated DH from their Old Guard competitors were being lost. By the end of the 1970s, DH's then-chairman William Andres recognized that, if something wasn't done, they would soon become just a rich Montgomery Ward. And the next step after that would be to become exactly like Monkey Wards—that is, poor. Says Andres, "Lately, we've come to realize that with our rapid growth—and with many new executives coming in—we need to do a better job of passing along the gospel."

In 1983, after a year of consultation, the "gospel" according to Dayton-Hudson was published. DH's constitution, "Management Perspectives," is a 118-page document that spells out the company's entire, unique management system, starting with stakeholder obligations, running through corporate planning, and down to financial controls. Significantly, the seven presidents of DH's operating companies were *not* asked to reproduce the book and pass it down the line. Instead, when the presidents asked what they might do with the book, Andres and Macke obliquely suggested that the seven might each consider meeting with the people in their respective divisions and, with them, writing their *own* documents. "Of course, we hope they do so, and of course we hope what they come up with is consistent with our corporate principles," says Macke, "but I'm not going to *tell* them what to write, or even *tell* them that they have to write something. If they don't see the benefits of doing what we have done, then we have not done our jobs as leaders, and they shouldn't copy us."

Macke is in many ways the antithesis of the ascendant model of the "great" corporate leader. Unlike the now-storied Forrest Mars, founder of the Mars Candy Company, Macke doesn't run around DH facilities picking up scraps of paper from the floor. Unlike Baltimore's famous mayor, William Schaeffer, who drives around town twelve hours a day, seven days a week, personally directing the filling of potholes and the removal of trash, most lower level DH employees have never set eyes on Macke, and most probably wouldn't recognize his name if they heard it. No doubt, both the Mars Corporation and the city of Baltimore became success stories because they were blessed with obsessive

personalities at their helm who were willing to sacrifice friend-
ship, family, and private interests in the single-minded pursuit of
corporate eminence. But who has the energy or the dynamism to
run a Dayton-Hudson (let alone an IBM or a GM) by herself? And,
even if one did have such energy, is manic "management by
walking around" the most effective way to run a big (as opposed
to a small) company? Significantly, "Martians" became so dependent on old Forrest that they didn't get in the habit of "picking
up after themselves." After Forrest retired, strife, political infighting, and gross mismanagement became the rule at Mars.
Baltimoreans, too, grew accustomed to standing around waiting
for Schaeffer to tell them what to do next. Leaders of great
institutions, in sharp contrast, leave a legacy of greatness. As we
shall see, not only do they leave worthy successors (unlike Mars
and Schaeffer), they leave structures, systems, and habits of behavior that live on after they have gone.

The DH approach of leadership by example is thus quite different from the Chapparal and Gore approach of leadership by
personality (although both systems are based on ultimate principles and on a clear philosophy). By necessity, the large company
approach to leadership must be more formalized and institutionalized. (If Gordon Forward dies, retires, or quits to become a full-
time break dancer, the Chapparal culture could be lost overnight
—a risk that a large company cannot afford to take.) As we saw in
Chapter Six, in many respects entrepreneurial leaders are one
breed of cat and professional managers are another. And, while
there is no doubt that the tasks of executives in new and small
companies differ in many ways from those of executives in old
and large companies, Ken Macke shows that it is possible to be
both a great leader *and* a great manager.

Leadership Role of the Board

Kenneth Dayton, the last of his family to manage Dayton-
Hudson, realized that his retirement might mean the loss of all
that his family had hoped to create with the corporation. Hence,
he devoted the last few years of his tenure to institutionalizing
the unique DH culture. His chosen mechanism was one never
before employed in a large U.S. corporation: He utilized the
board of directors.

There is no greater waste of human resources to be found in

American corporations than the way boards of directors are typically used. In most cases, corporate boards serve only to rubber-stamp the decisions made by top management. Even those who are the worst offenders in this criminal misuse of talent accept this indictment: Harold Geneen writes that 95 percent of boards "are not fully doing what they are legally, morally, and ethically supposed to do. And they couldn't, even if they wanted to." No doubt boards do act in times of crisis (when a corporation faces bankruptcy and it is obvious that the CEO must go, or when there is the threat of a hostile takeover), but under normal circumstances they do exactly what management expects of them: nothing. The only exceptions I know to this generalization are found at Dayton-Hudson and at the smaller Lord Corporation. In both cases, corporate boards are utilized to institutionalize leadership.

The DH constitution says that it is the board's function

> . . . as representatives of the shareholders to be the primary force pressing the corporation to the realization of its opportunities and the fulfillment of its obligations to its shareholders, customers, employees, and the communities in which it operates.

In effect, the DH board has the same job description as the CEO of a small company! The board functions as "strategic actors," keeping management focused on the company's principles and on the future. Again, like a small company CEO, the DH board does *not* get involved in administration or in day-to-day management decisions—instead, they monitor the major decisions of management to insure that these are consistent with the vision found in the DH constitution. Why is this necessary? Says Kenneth Dayton,

> All managers become dictators eventually, even if they start out benign. Once a corporation goes public, managers start to act as if it were their private preserve. That is why you need the board. Their role is to be the force pressing the corporation to fulfill its broader and long-term responsibilities.

Kenneth Dayton's last act as chairman of the DH board was to restructure it in a way that would perpetuate its leadership function of instilling and protecting corporate values. To do this, he amended the DH constitution to specify the functions, structure, and makeup of the board. Specifically, these changes were designed to insure the independence of the board and to insure that it remain representative of all the corporation's major constituencies.

To insure board independence, the constitution calls for all but two of its members to be outsiders. These outside members constitute the "executive committee" of the board. They, and only they, deal with matters of executive review, compensation, and appointments. They, and only they, nominate new members for the board and determine the board's functions and agenda.

To insure diversity, the constitution specifies a mix of board members, including people with backgrounds in the consumer goods industry, the marketing industry, consumer affairs, government, and several from the broader Minneapolis community. Interestingly, the DH constitution is also specific about who is *in*eligible: "We want no investment bankers, lawyers, retirees, or professional directors."

In addition, the constitution specifies the criteria to be applied in choosing board members. Not only must they be young (no one over fifty-three is eligible for an initial appointment), they must have the following character traits:

- Integrity.

- Wisdom.

- Independence.

- Valid business or professional knowledge and experience that can bear on DH's problems and deliberations.

- Proven record of accomplishment with excellent organizations.

- Understanding and general acceptance of DH's corporate philosophy.

- An inquiring mind.

- Willingness to speak one's mind.

- Ability to challenge and stimulate management.

- Orientation to the future.

- Willingness to commit time and energy.

While the list is a tad idealistic—try naming one person (other than yourself) who would qualify—it is most remarkable in that the traits DH seeks are exactly the *opposite* of those the Old Guard seek in their directors.

In essence, then, the qualities of leadership found in great small companies have been institutionalized at DH through three mechanisms: a strong and independent board; top managers who lead decentralized operations by example; and a constitution that clearly spells out the values, objectives, and managerial philosophy of the firm.

The Lord Corporation (a medium-size, privately held, high-technology company located in Erie, Pennsylvania) uses similar mechanisms . . . but with a twist. "I want the board in the ball game, not selling peanuts," says Lord's CEO, Don Alstadt:

> To use the language of engineers, the board can reduce the "impedance" between the inside and the outside of the corporation. That means they can break down managerial allegiance to the status quo by constantly informing us of change in the external environment. But they will only be able to do so if we make full use of their talents . . . only if we listen to them.

Alstadt is rare among corporate CEOs in that he is a listener (even some Vanguard CEOs tend to be chronic lecturers). Alstadt spends over 20 percent of his time visiting universities listening to leading scholars and gathering intelligence in the areas of technology and management. And some of the professors he meets in his travels find their way onto the Lord board of directors. "We use the board *not* to tell us how we are doing, but how to do it better," says Alstadt. To this end, he has created a "strategic committee of the board" responsible for advising him on long-term planning (in a high-technology company, it makes sense for scholars who are on the cutting edge of technological change to be in such a role). Lord's board members (including Carnegie-Mellon president Richard Cyert, Polytechnic Institute of New York president George Bugliarello, and director of MIT's Center for Advanced Engineering Myron Tribus) have even made films about emerging technological and management trends for distribution to the entire Lord work force. Says Alstadt,

Because we in top management are obviously listening to (and learning from) our board, the entire company comes to view us as *learners* rather than *knowers*. You see, we aren't afraid to let our people in on the secret that we don't know everything. In fact, we believe that people are more likely to follow those who they see as learners. Paradoxically, then, leadership comes from learning and listening, *not* from knowing and bossing.

I can hear the excuses: "What a great idea . . . too bad board matters are a top management issue and thus out of my bailiwick." Come on, listen to what some of Honeywell's guerilla fighters are doing: One Honeywell division has appointed an internal board of directors, consisting of external stakeholders and managers from other Honeywell divisions who function to focus the strategic direction of their division.

Internal boards are also used at all sixteen of the Kollmorgen Corporation's divisions. In fact, Kollmorgen goes a step further and makes all corporate policy by consensus of a "partners' group" composed of the sixteen divisional presidents and corporate officers. Kollmorgen was compelled to adopt a radical structure when rapid growth in their printed circuit board business made them too big for the industry they were in. Small mom-and-pop competitors (who were able to customize their products) had been chewing into the larger and less flexible Kollmorgen's market share when Kollmorgen responded by breaking their circuit board division into five separate businesses. Within a year, the division went from a *sales* volume of $280,000 per month to a $280,000 monthly *profit*. Today, all the Kollmorgen CEO does is stand under his expanding balloons making sure they don't get so big that they burst.

Weak Egos and Strong

Why don't other CEOs follow Alstadt's lead and make fuller use of corporate boards? Simply because macho "do it, fix it" types don't like to admit that there is anything they don't know. In most organizations the executive ego thus gets in the way of effective leadership.

The executive ego also gets in the way of effective decentralization of authority. While most executives believe that it is their duty to solve everyone else's problems, in contrast, Levi's Peter Thigpen describes his role as empowering others: "All I do is remove blocks." At Levi, DH, Motorola, and Deere, one finds leaders dedicated to the principles that the higher level should never absorb the functions of the lower; that the burden of proof should lie with those who want to deprive the lower of its freedom; that the center will gain in authority and effectiveness *if* the freedom and responsibility of divisions are carefully preserved; and that rewards should go to those who independently find imaginative ways to support the goals and philosophy of the corporation. Adherence to these principles allows Peter Thigpen, Ken Macke, and other Vanguard leaders to enable their subordinates to do their work, inspire them to do it well, and allow the necessary authority to gravitate to the point in the organization where it belongs.

Recently, management consultant Robert Half reported that the typical corporate CEO works 56.9 hours per week. And they spend their time literally *running* their shows. Says Half: "In business, unlike politics, a dictatorship works best. When one person makes the major decisions, it is efficient." Half (and others who believe that great leaders must be obsessive, decisive, macho manipulators) should meet the quiet-spoken, reserved, careful and thoughtful William Hewitt, Thornton Bradshaw, and Robert Galvin. They don't ever seem to be working—except when they are enabling and empowering others.

Great leaders are seldom the smartest people in their organizations, but they *are* willing to surround themselves by people who clearly outclass them intellectually. Both Paul and Robert Galvin had that rare leadership trait of enough self-confidence to surround themselves with brighter men (there are precious few women engineers). Paul surrounded himself with the likes of Daniel Noble (who designed the first FM mobile communication system and the first walkie-talkie, among other accomplishments) and made no bones about the fact that Noble was the technical genius of the operation. In turn, Robert has brought in the best minds from Texas Instruments and IBM and given them the freedom to shine that they lacked in their former corporations. And Robert's number two, COO William Weisz, is pound-for-pound the brightest mind I've ever met in an executive suite —but Galvin isn't jealous of him and isn't intimidated. And Weisz can speak for the corporation without Galvin's prior approval.

Similarly, most executives in Edson Spencer's shoes would be threatened by having someone like Jim Renier, a more charismatic leader than himself, in the number two spot (ditto Arco's Robert O. Anderson and the more brilliant Thornton Bradshaw). And George Weyerhaeuser didn't fret that the popular and charismatic William Ruckelshaus would erode his glamour and authority with the company's external audiences. Spencer, Anderson, and Weyerhaeuser have the self-confidence that allows them to be more effective leaders than if they were uncertain of their abilities and surrounded themselves with mediocre managers.

While this trait of executive self-confidence may appear neither important nor rare, I suggest that it is both. For example, Senator Edward Kennedy, a man of at best average intelligence, has forged a successful career on the abilities of his staff—everyone of whom could have taken his college exams for him and gotten A's. In contrast, Elliot Richardson, arguably the smartest man to serve in a cabinet post in the second half of this century, would enter each new federal department he headed and systematically eliminate every star likely to shine brighter than he (I feel free to criticize him on this score: He never even bothered to try to get rid of *me* when I worked for him at HEW).

The leader who is too uncertain of himself to employ more talented others ends up undercutting his own legitimacy in the long run for, as Warren Bennis notes, self-confidence is a key to "walking the tightrope." People won't follow an executive out on the rope if they can tell he is afraid of falling himself. In contrast, a Robert Galvin will step out on the wire with such enthusiasm that an entire corporation will follow him across—never considering that he or they might fall.

Managers who fear the abilities of their subordinates also encounter another problem: They cannot adequately fulfill the essential function of choosing a competent successor.

Passing the Baton

One often-overlooked test of executive greatness is whether he or she leaves the organization with a qualified *next* generation of leadership. This is a difficult test that few executives pass because succession planning is a hated task (like writing a will, it reminds one of one's mutability). Not only is the function of developing a successor unpleasant for many executives, the failure to fulfill it often goes unnoticed until after the baton is passed. Then, when the next runner's torpor becomes apparent to all, it is too late for the organization. That, at least, was the story of Polaroid and Edwin Land.

Edwin Land is living proof of the complexity of effective management. He was a hero in the classical Greek sense: He was a giant among men; but he was fatally flawed. His flaw was an overweening pride that prevented him from appointing a worthy successor. Land was, for many years, the Karl Wallenda of American technology. In the days when Polaroid was small, Land would fire up his troops and inspire them to undreamed-of heights of creativity. They would achieve the impossible because Land believed that he and they could do it. He was like Bill Gore or Gordon Forward—only on a grander scale. Not only was he a technical genius, he was the philosopher king of big business. Land was a man of *ideas*. Indeed, there is not an idea found in these pages that Land didn't have, write about, and put into practice by the late 1960s. Just one example, lest we forget his accomplishments in examining his flaw:

In 1958, Polaroid's picture-in-a-minute process was a decade old. But it was quickly becoming old hat. Tiresome, in fact. Consumers no longer were willing to wait a minute. Worse, they had had it with the messy film they had to peel off (and then figure out where to dispose of the "disposable" backing). Faced with a potential consumer rebellion, Land boldly decided to break with Polaroid's long-time film purveyor, Kodak, and to make his own film—clean, dry, fast, film with beautiful colors. To make such film, it was clear that Polaroid would need to build their own plant and machines. When Land proposed to do just that, Wall Street said he was bonkers. But he did it and did so in a way that the plant would still be state-of-the-art technologically twenty-five years later. For example, Land got his technical people so hyped up that they walked out on the tightrope and built a *single* machine that combined sixteen separate parts into a film pack (at the rate of seventy-five packs per minute).

But don't forget that Land believed in *balance*. Polaroid had two equal goals: *technical* quality and efficiency and *human* satisfaction. Land's idea—original at the time—was that the separate systems in the new plant—the machinery, the product, and the organization—had to mesh. The designers of Land's new plant said that the people who made the film would "be established as a group that will experiment in the art of managing their own conduct. It will be their responsibility to establish rules for themselves with regard to work schedules and pay." Here is what Polaroid's "plant of the future" offered workers in the early 1960s:

- Changing tasks as a regular feature of employment.
- The opportunity for workers to identify with the end product.
- Freedom to act and to decide.
- Freedom of physical movement (workers weren't tied to a machine).
- Balance between the mental and physical aspects of all tasks.
- An attractive physical environment.
- The opportunity to learn.

Here's how Polaroid delivered on just the last of these promises: Workers at all levels were taught about technology, taught how to accept responsibility, and taught how to work closely with their peers. To do this effectively, Polaroid established job rotation and career ladders based on learning. Blue-collar workers could actually *learn* their way into white-collar jobs! For example, Polaroid constructed a fifteen-step career ladder in which all employees would alternate between operational jobs (injection molding, for example) and staff jobs (quality control lab work, for example) rotating back and forth as they learned their way up the ladder to higher responsibilities. Along the way, workers were offered courses in physics, math, photography, writing, and grammar. The idea was to train everyone to do everything in the plant and, thus, eliminate all supervisors. For the first eighteen months of operation, all employees spent four hours on the job and four hours in training. Not until twenty years later would a plant come anywhere near to being as revolutionary in concept as this. In the early 1960s, Polaroid was not only a Vanguard corporation, they were *the* Vanguard corporation.

Alas, it was not to last. The company got big and autonomy gave way to centralization, self-management to bureaucratization, generalism to specialization, and cooperation to competition. Land was too busy in the lab to take notice. And, if truth be told, he was an indifferent manager who had little idea of how to preserve the cherished advantages of his old small company in his new big one. Fortunately, there was a young manager at

Polaroid who knew how—and everyone at Polaroid knew he knew it. His name was Tom Wyman and he was the element of hope at Polaroid between 1965 and 1975. As senior vice president, general manager of the company, and chairman of the management committee, he demonstrated that he knew how to keep Edwin Land's brilliant ideas operational after Land had lost interest in them and had gone back to the lab. "Appoint Tom Wyman as your successor, Dr. Land," everyone pleaded. "Pass on the mantle." "Give him the power to run the day-to-day operations." "We need competent management."

Herein lay the great man's tragic flaw. Land would have none of this business of sharing power in *his* company. Polaroid was Edwin Land, Edwin Land was Polaroid. Egocentric, threatened, hurt, Land passed the mantle to his safe, colorless, long-time crony, William McCune, leaving the dynamic, popular, and competent Wyman out in the cold. It was as if Land had followed Confucius's bad advice to "Have no friends equal to yourself." Polaroid has not yet fully recovered from Wyman's departure, and the managerial system that once made Polaroid great is now all but lost.

What could have saved Polaroid? For one, the board of directors. But Land had always wanted a weak board, uninformed and dependent upon him. He got what he wanted and, as a result, during some five years of chaos, the board stood by passively as Polaroid's prospects further deteriorated in the late 70s and early 80s. Indeed, nearly everyone at Polaroid had grown dependent on Land (much as Mars employees had grown dependent on Forrest Mars). A paradox of greatness is that charismatic leaders relieve their followers of the necessity of developing their own leadership skills. After the great one retires, they find that no one has had sufficient practice in the arts of leadership and, like Polaroid today, they drift.

It needn't have been so. Had Edwin Land been aware of another model of leadership practiced out in California during the same era, he might have chosen a different course, and Polaroid might still be a Vanguard company. Had Edwin Land studied the top management structure of TRW, he would have discovered an alternative to the disastrous course he had set for himself. Land's closest living parallel is, without doubt, Simon Ramo. Both are brilliant technicians, first-rate entrepreneurs, arrogant, egotistical . . . and *miserable* managers. Ramo is the R in TRW. While clearly the most powerful personality in that organization for twenty-five years, the highest title he ever held was vice chairman of the board. Instead of holding the post of chief executive officer, president, or any other operating position (any one of which he was entitled to by virtue of his ownership position and stature as a scientist), Ramo *chose* to function as TRW's director of research. In effect, he allocated research dollars among various claimants. In so doing, he determined the long-range future of that high-tech corporation. In this job, he could be Wallenda without having to be an administrator (which, God knows, he could never have been. For Ramo is a nonstop lecturer. If he has ever listened to *anyone* in his life, the event went unrecorded). As we have seen, TRW's system of management is far from perfect—but things would have been *worse* had Ramo been at the helm. For all his faults, Ramo thus saw where he could make his optimal contribution to TRW. In contrast, Land insisted on being Polaroid's CEO, chairman of the board, and director of research. He should never have been the first, it is arguable whether he should have been the second, and it is clear as the light he analyzed that no one was more qualified than he to be the latter.

IMPORTANT: The situation I describe is not unique to Polaroid. CDC's William Norris could easily have been another Edwin Land. In fact, he has much the same virtues and weaknesses as Land (lacking only Land's technical brilliance). But, at a key point in Norris's career, he turned over operating authority in the company to two younger men: Norbert Berg and Robert Price. Norris then withdrew from day-to-day management activities and focused on two things: developing the firm's philosophy and allocating a pool of long-term risk capital (à la Ramo). Furthermore, Norris, to whom no act is without meaning, sent a strong message to his company when he made Berg his heir apparent: Berg will one day become the only CEO of a large American corporation who has risen to the top with a background in human resources (significantly, such a background is quite common among Japanese CEOs). Norris's legacy to Control Data was thus made complete when he provided for succession and insured that his successor represented the unique values of the corporation. "We've set the course for the next fifty years," says Norris with characteristic overstatement.

What we find at Control Data, TRW (and at the Lord Corporation as well) is that the creative leader manages the R&D function but not the operations of the company. These three examples put the lie to the notion that "when a company becomes large, the founding father must be put out to pasture before he screws things up with his crazy, nonprofessional ideas." In fact, the task is to find an appropriate role for the founding father.

The Legacy of Founding Fathers

The moment Edwin Land was eased out of Polaroid, the iconoclasts set to work debunking all he stood for, blaming him for all that was bad in the company, giving credit to others for all that was good. Treated like the Gang of Four, Land became a nonperson in the company whose name was once synonymous with his own. While such corporate patricide is understandable, it carries an extremely high cost. In the case of Polaroid, the cost may be the very values that could undergird a much needed change effort. Destroying Land has meant destroying what was perhaps the clearest and most progressive business philosophy ever articulated. Everything Land stood for is consistent with what is now known about how to run a great company. That he was an incompetent *administrator* is undeniable—but Polaroid may be throwing the baby out with the bath water in dismissing his *philosophy* on those grounds. As a result, Polaroid's guiding culture is at risk.

Polaroid's struggle with Land's legacy is not *sui generis*. Since the cultures of all corporations are rooted in the values of some "founding father," the passing of this individual will have an enormous impact on any organization. As we have seen, Sloan's legacy to General Motors was paralysis. He didn't leave the company with a role model of leadership by example, with a clear philosophy, or with an independent board; instead, he left them with an inflexible system of rules. Walt Disney's legacy to his company was even more paltry: He didn't even leave a system. He left only the memory of his charismatic personality. While he was alive, Disney made all corporate decisions, he was always "right," and no one else ever had the experience of leadership. Consequently, for years after his death, Disney executives sat around doing all they had been prepared to do: nothing. Until 1985, when dealing with an important issue, there was only one argument that carried weight in the company: "Walt would have wanted it this way." (Peter Drucker tells the story of Nick Kelly, who served as Walter Chrysler's lawyer and, after Chrysler's death, as the Chrysler Corporation's legal counsel. For years after Chrysler's passing, Kelly would "get in touch with the ghost of Walter P." whenever the company faced a tough decision. At such moments, Kelly would excuse himself, go into his office, pull the drapes, switch off the lights, and conjure up Chrysler's spirit. Kelly would then walk back into the boardroom and report, "This is what Walter P. would have done." According to Drucker, the Chrysler executives would then make a decision.) Harold Geneen's legacy at ITT is similar. For decades Geneen was ITT— he made all the decisions. Without him, the company now suffers from both an identity crisis and the paralysis of dependent children who have suddenly lost their paternalistic papa. (Part of the problem at ITT, of course, was that the Great One wouldn't let go. Geneen "fired" his hand-picked successor, Lyman Hamilton, when he began to reverse some of Geneen's policies.)

What this says is that no leader can be considered great if he does not instill the traits of leadership in his successors. My argument is quite radical: I'm suggesting that such charismatic giants of industry as Sloan, Geneen, Disney, Land, Chrysler (and I'll throw in Henry Ford and George Eastman while I'm at it) failed the final test of leadership in that none left a successor who was in turn a great leader. In contrast, I suggest that the relatively unknown Kenneth Dayton was a great leader in that his successor is as good as himself and, in turn, Kenneth Macke is preparing the next generation of leaders at Dayton-Hudson by giving them the independence needed to develop their own leadership skills. (Indeed, a common trait of the Vanguard seems to be that they each have a stageful of fine young leaders waiting in the wings.)

Ken Macke devotes about half of his time to the career development of the top hundred or so DH employees. To make sure that this group does the same for their subordinates (and so on down the line) the company presents an annual "CEO Development Award" and a parallel "Staff Development Award." Macke says that developing "bench strength" is every DH manager's duty. And a manager's first responsibility is to have a "backup" ready in the wings. Says Macke:

> I can remember being asked this question just a few weeks after I had started my first management job at Dayton's: "Who's going to take your place?" A year ago, right after I

was named CEO, one of our directors approached me and asked, "Who's going to succeed you?"

This is not to relieve the current generation of their leadership responsibilities if they have been *in*adequately prepared by their predecessors. Indeed, the Vanguard can be distinguished from the Old Guard by the way they manage the transitions from entrepreneurial leadership to managerial leadership, and the subsequent transitions from one generation of professional managers to the next. The immediate problem faced by the first-generation, professional managers is, of course, *legitimacy.* Where the founding father could, by virtue of his ownership and entrepreneurial success, *command* the loyalty of his followers, the professional manager is often seen as an *il*legitimate heir to executive power. ("Just who does that bastard think he is?") When faced with such initial resistance and skepticism, most newly appointed professional executives retreat into a cocoon of bureaucratic systems and rules in an attempt to establish some authority.

The reaction of Vanguard leaders is exactly the opposite. On taking charge, they immediately make reference to the values of the founding fathers (no Polaroid-like expunging of the Old Man's achievements), and they articulate how they will build on the strengths of the existing culture to achieve even greater things. For example, when William Hewitt took over at Deere, to all the world he seemed to have had everything going against him: He was a young, inexperienced San Franciscan suddenly in control of an old line, conservative, midwestern firm. *He overcame this handicap with ideas.* He renewed the company's historical commitment to excellence, quoting John Deere. ("I won't put my name on a plow that doesn't have in it the best that is in me.") Hewitt knew he couldn't order the company to rekindle the fire of excellence that burned in the breast of founder Deere, but Hewitt believed he could lead them by his own examples of integrity, honesty, competence, responsibility, receptivity, supportiveness, vision, and imagination. When they were tempted to play it safe, he showed them that they were really made of more entrepreneurial stuff. When they were tempted to be satisfied with second best, he showed them the greatness that was hidden in them. When they wanted to build a conventional headquarters, he spent years patiently getting them used to the idea that they *deserved* the highest-quality building their money could buy. In the end, by encouraging them and not by commanding them, he brought out all the potential of the enterprise. "He showed us how good we were" was the way a Deere manager put it when Hewitt retired.

As William Hewitt, Robert Haas, Robert Galvin, Jim Renier, and other young executives who have assumed the reins of troubled companies have found, transitions in leadership are only successful when the heir acts with vision, confidence, consistency, and resolve. In short, the second and third generation of leaders, like the first, must be willing to get out on the tightrope. And, without ideas, no one will follow. No rules, controls, commands, or orders will induce people to take the risks needed for greatness. In matters of leadership, there is thus no substitute for ideas.

(Because of the unavoidably masculine nouns and pronouns that dominate this section, I feel it necessary to add a point concerning the only founding mother of whom I am aware, Mary Kay Ash. Founder of Mary Kay Cosmetics, Ash is one of the most thoughtful corporate leaders in America—a fact usually overlooked because of the hoopla that surrounds her business. But if one listens closely, it is clear that she uses ideas to inspire tens of thousands of salespeople to walk the tightrope with her. While I wish there were additional examples, Mary Kay Ash stands as evidence that the true qualities of leadership are not determined by the sex of the executive.)

The Overlooked Quality

Does that do it? Have I adequately answered the question with which I began this chapter? Is the ability to encourage employees to dizzying heights of performance the common characteristic of Vanguard leaders? Is great leadership the preparing and empowering of the next generation of leaders? Or is great leadership, as my colleague Steven Kerr writes, not a technique at all but a social value that strikes a responsive chord in followers because it mimics the participatory processes of our democracy? Certainly, it is all of these things, but I fear I have still fallen short of capturing the essence of greatness. For there are many executives who are masters at creating productive institutions who do not begin to approach the ineffable qualities of Messrs. Bradshaw,

Macke, Hewitt, Norris, Renier, Haas, Galvin, and Weyerhaeuser. In fact, I have only described *one half* of the task of a leader of a great corporation. In addition to internal leadership, the top manager of a great company exerts leadership in the broader society. The leaders of the Vanguard, unlike the leaders of many very good companies, use the resources of their institutions to improve the quality of life. They bring the prestige of their offices to bear on issues of social justice, much as they use their positions to create moral symmetry within the confines of their respective companies. A point to which we now turn . . .

12.

MORAL COURAGE: THE *SINE QUA NON* OF GREATNESS

> . . . Three outstanding attitudes—obliviousness to the grow-
> ing disaffection of constituents, primacy of self-aggrandize-
> ment, [and the] illusion of invulnerable status—are persistent
> aspects of folly.
>
> —BARBARA TUCHMAN

Let an executive practice "management by walking round,"
let him be employee-oriented, let her be committed to total
consumer satisfaction, let him lead by articulating the values of
the firm, let her cut through bureaucracy with entrepreneurial
behavior, let him be obsessive about productivity and product
quality, and he or she will have created a very good company,
indeed. But this executive will *not* be a great leader, for he will
have done only half his job: He will still not have made an adequate contribution to society; she will still not have created an
institution worthy of the great society of which it is a part. This
otherwise excellent executive lacks what conservative thinkers
call "virtue." In the words of John Adams, virtue is "a positive
passion for the public good."

It is that passion that distinguishes the leaders of the Vanguard
from those who head the Old Guard. Irving Kristol asks the
question that haunts Vanguard leaders, "Can men live in a free
society if they have no reason to believe it is also a just society?"
Like Kristol, the Vanguard leaders respond with a resounding *no*.
Says Levi's Walter A. Haas, Jr.:

Business legitimacy is being questioned on two broad fronts
—its conduct, structure, and attitude as an institution, and its

performance as a supplier of goods and services to the public. In both areas . . . what the public hears and sees has created an atmosphere among them that can be described only as one of substantial and growing mistrust . . . Any American corporation—or American corporations collectively—can reach the end of the trail by failing to respond to the pressures of the sociopolitical world just as surely and just as fatally as by failing to respond to the pressures of the marketplace.

That American corporations "can reach the end of the trail" is attested to by public perceptions—and misperceptions—of big business. In a summary of public attitudes toward corporations, Seymour Martin Lipset reports (in the conservative journal *Public Opinion)* that, while Americans overwhelmingly support the free-enterprise system, "The overall evaluation of business is far from positive." In general, polls show that Americans feel corporations operate almost exclusively for the benefit of managers and stockholders. When asked who these corporations *should* serve, the vast majority of Americans say business should *also* operate for the benefit of customers, employees, and society as a whole. And a 1982 Harris Poll found that some 70 percent of Americans give business a negative rating on meeting basic responsibilities to employees, consumers, and society. That Americans believe there is an imbalance of corporate concerns is underscored by a 1983 Opinion Research Corporation survey. This poll revealed that Americans believe the average business earns thirty-seven cents profit on each dollar of sales (the actual rate is less than four cents). Mobil Oil raises the alarums over this misperception in an "editorial advertisement" headlined "The Profits of Doom":

One thing *is* certain: Until more Americans understand economics, there will continue to be public outcries against business profits—and misguided laws and regulations promulgated as a result.

Mobil then suggests the Old Guard approach to dealing with a public that questions corporate legitimacy:

Given all the readily accessible facts proving corporate profits *aren't* excessive, you've got to wonder who or what is to blame for the ignorance about the economic realities of the marketplace. We think it reflects a basic lack of knowledge about economics itself . . . or more precisely, a *lack of economics education.*

Levi's Walter Haas looks at the same data and comes to a different conclusion:

> Over the years, we've spent millions of dollars on economic education. But these millions of dollars have not stemmed the tide of business criticism. The thesis behind this spending has been, "If only those people understood, they would be more sympathetic." It is my judgment that economic education—while it can be useful and informative—has not and will not attack the mistrust problem.

And how does Haas propose to solve the "mistrust problem"? *By altering the behavior that causes the mistrust.* He proposes that business "make alliances with many sectors of the public," and "deal ethically and openly" with "employees, shareholders, customers, and not the least, the general public." He concludes,

> The social responsibility of business requires establishing standards of excellence in all phases of operation—such as truth in advertising, quality of products, accuracy of labeling, appropriate disclosure, job content, working conditions, and upward mobility for women and minorities.

Haas thus implicitly argues that Americans mistrust Mobil and other large corporations with some reason. It is possible that the public concludes that Mobil's profits are excessive because they read Mobil's *own* pronouncements: It is Mobil, after all, who buys space in newspapers to proclaim that the only legitimate function of a corporation is to maximize shareholder wealth; it is Mobil who buys newspaper space to oppose the excess profits tax; and it is Mobil who misguides the public when they announce their profits as "up 50 percent over last quarter" instead of accurately saying "up from 3 percent to 4.5 percent."

Moreover, the polls suggest that most public perceptions are accurately based on corporate *performance,* not on economic ignorance. For example, the great majority of Americans are convinced that private corporations are far more efficient than government at providing quality goods and services, and at developing, introducing, and marketing new products. Indeed,

Americans oppose governmental interference in those aspects of business where the market is self-regulating (they oppose wage and price controls, central planning, and the like) and favor governmental actions only in areas where the market is *not* self-regulating (environmental protection, worker- and product-safety, employment discrimination, and the like). That the public is able to thus distinguish the market failures that economists call "externalities" and "neighborhood effects" from effective market mechanisms is hardly a sign of economic ignorance!

The label of ignorance is more accurately placed on the leaders of the Old Guard who, when they argue "we have no social responsibilities beyond remaining profitable" are their own worst enemies. As Barbara Tuchman so clearly illustrates in *The March of Folly*, it is a distressing and dangerous habit of nations to pursue policies contrary to their own interests. And so it is with corporations. Where it is Tuchman's intent to encourage government leaders to have the courage to embrace feasible alternatives to those policies that will lead to their own destruction, I wish to warn the Old Guard that their shortsighted behavior will lead to "the end of the trail" more surely than the actions of any enemies of free enterprise.

Mr. B's Moral Leadership

I can think of no corporate executive who was more willing to challenge the self-destructive policies of his industry than Thornton Bradshaw. One of the most daring moves ever made by the freewheeling entrepreneur Robert O. Anderson was making Bradshaw his number two at Arco. This was not an easy or an obvious choice. Oil industry executives tend to be monosyllabic types who call wearing silver belt buckles "dressin' up." In contrast, Bradshaw was a sophisticated, Eastern, university professor who was about as uncomfortable on an oil rig as an Oklahoma roughneck would have been teaching in Harvard's Hallowed Halls (whence Bradshaw migrated). As careful, articulate, and as skilled in dealing with people as Anderson was weak in each of those respects, Bradshaw provided a fine complementarity and counterbalance to Anderson's cowboy capitalism. Together, Anderson and Bradshaw forged a unique mixture of entrepreneurialism and social consciousness that came to characterize Arco's corporate culture.

In the early 1970s, while Anderson and Bradshaw were waiting for Arco's oil to start to flow through the great Alaskan pipeline from Prudhoe Bay to the waiting tankers at Valdez, they spent a great amount of time seminaring-it-up at Colorado's fabled talk tank, the Aspen Institute for Humanistic Studies. (In fact, Anderson personally underwrote that organization through a debt-ridden decade, putting up as much as a half million dollars of his own money in a given year.) At Aspen, the Arco duo often came into contact with people who despised everything they stood for. There, they met environmentalists, consumerists, government regulators, unionists, counterculture gurus, civil rights activists and leaders of the nascent women's movement. It was a heady time to be in Aspen (literally as well as figuratively: One had the impression, at times, that the whole town might float away on a cloud of cannabis smoke!). This environment could not always have been hospitable for the eminently conservative Mr. A and Mr. B. But, significantly, they didn't recoil from the attacks on big business and big oil that they were frequently subjected to at Aspen. They didn't retreat to the defensive carapaces that became home for so many others in their industry. Instead, they *listened* to their critics.

Not only did they listen themselves but, during the 1970s, they sent about a hundred of Arco's top managers to Aspen for two weeks each of the same treatment. Much of what the Arco people heard they didn't like; much they couldn't begin to agree with. But they stayed and listened (and continued to pay the bills of those who abused them and their industry). There is not, I hasten to add, the slightest trace of masochism in the character of any Arco manager I've ever met. While I don't have a clue as to why they sat through the kinds of attacks popular at the time—talk of "profiteering," "capitalist repression," "naked abuse of corporate power," and the like—it is my impression that the reason had little to do with a fondness for self-flagellation. It is my guess that they were simply so shocked and scared that they thought it prudent to stay and try to understand their enemies.

Anderson, Bradshaw, and the other Arco executives got the message. They went home to corporate headquarters in Los Angeles and introduced policies that were brilliantly suited to the times and, as it would soon turn out, particularly appropriate as responses to the crisis of public confidence in the U.S. oil industry that came in the wake of the 1973 Arab oil embargo. These policies included a combination of splashy philanthropy, careful corporate conduct, and courageous public policy stances—all made thrice as effective through clever public relations and advertising.

Arco's philanthropic record was marked as much by imagination as by generosity. Like almost every other corporation with a fat coffer, Arco gave to hospitals, universities, symphony orchestras, museums, and to such special and, no doubt, worthy causes as bike teams and the New Orleans Preservation Hall Jazz Band. What made Arco unique was that they also gave—and gave generously—to environmentalists and other groups not known to be fellow-travelers of big oil. For example, they gave The Nature Conservancy a $1 million grant to purchase the 55,000-acre Santa Cruz Island off the Southern California coast in order to preserve it as a wilderness area. Arco's support of environmentalists like the Sierra Club and Jacques Cousteau, and of such cultural activities as highbrow public television programs, the arty movie festival "Filmex," and modern art museums in Los Angeles bought the company credibility with the upper-middle-class elite who wield disproportionate political power. Arco's activities at home and at Aspen gave the company entrée to the media, to special interest groups, and to other liberal power bases from which the likes of Phillips Oil and Mobil Oil were barred.

Mobil, of course, tried some of the same with their support for high-quality public television programs. But the effect of this left-handed gesture was more than vitiated by the pummeling liberals were taking from the corporation's mailed right hand, one Herbert Schmertz. In the aforementioned weekly newspaper ads that ran on editorial pages across the country, Schmertz—Mobil's vice president for public affairs—castigated and berated the very same liberal elite that Arco sought to woo with concern and money. A trip to the city halls and legislatures in the cities and states where Mobil and Arco each do business, or a visit to the offices of the members of Congress who deal with energy matters, will confirm whose approach worked best.

But saying Arco's Anderson and Bradshaw were more effective with oil industry critics and with government leaders than their Mobil counterparts Rawleigh Warner and William Tavoularas is only to argue for honey over vinegar as the best way to catch bears. In the final analysis, can we say something more of Messrs. A and B than that they were cleverly manipulative? This question is made doubly difficult to answer by the mixed signals that the corporation itself sent out from time to time. It is clear that, within the walls of Arco, there were highly placed executives who argued that giving money to the likes of the Sierra Club was tantamount to a condemned man helping his executioner to tie a surer knot in the fatal noose. Anderson and Bradshaw were always careful not to offend these internal critics. On several occasions, after they had responded imaginatively to the needs of some organization not noted for its affection for corporate capitalism, A and B would reassure their top management that they had acted "only to advance the self-interest of Arco." They thus presented some of the few instances in history where men have done good, only to then offer as an alibi that "in our hearts we remain impure!"

Throughout the 1970s, Anderson and Bradshaw did good, there can be little doubt of that. There can also be no question of their being do-gooders. Rather, they merely did what they felt society required of an oil company with deep pockets. Thus, they did the right thing because they felt they *had* to do it. Nonetheless, they did what was right. In sharp contrast, their competitors responded to societal challenges either by going on the defensive or going on the attack. Clearly, Anderson and Bradshaw had mixed motives—at times, they almost seemed schizophrenic. But since we can never be sure of the motives of others—often, we cannot even sort out our own motives—it seems prudent to judge the company solely on the basis of their *actions*. Moreover, it seems ungenerous and unwise to question the motives of those who do good, for there are so few of them!

Hence, we probably should accept on face Bradshaw's complex response to the question of why Arco became so deeply involved in environmental and social issues:

Because they go with the territory. As every shareholder and, indeed, every American understands, we are not living in conventional times. And so, if this company chose to act as corporations once did, its actions would be rejected because they did not look beyond the dollar signs to see the people . . . We are doing what we feel is prudent and effective and honestly acknowledges some of our obligations to a social and economic system that has made it possible for us to prosper and grow.

It is important to understand that Bradshaw was talking here about something more than philanthropy. If nothing else, he was a stickler for consistency. When he talked about "corporate obligations to a social and economic system" he meant, as he said in 1976, *everything* the company stood for:

> All I can say is that the social dimension of business today is as broad as the corporation itself; it is neither first nor last among our objectives, but an ongoing part of everything we do. No decision is made in the boardroom of Atlantic Richfield without first considering its social and political implications. Our lives are thus made far more difficult, more troubled, frequently more concerned—and yet infinitely richer in a very human sense. I would make that bargain any time.

Bradshaw's moral leadership came at a high price. His call for national energy planning and for general reform of the oil industry led him to alienation from his peers. Speaking up in L.A.'s famed California Club—where the city's most powerful old men bump stomachs—against the club's policy of admitting only white, male Christians alienated him not only from the club's membership, but from the city's power elite. (Accidentally, I picked this up firsthand. I was a guest at a meeting at the California Club at which a group of members were planning a large conference. Naively, I nominated Bradshaw as a speaker. The backlash came with a thunderous crack: "I'd rather have Jane Fonda than that, that . . . traitor!") Bradshaw paid a heavy price for this courageous leadership when a group of trustees of the University of Southern California vetoed his appointment to the presidency of that institution, apparently finding Mr. B's liberal Republicanism a bit too much to stomach. (Bradshaw's consolation prize was the executive suite of RCA where one of his first moves was to end cronyism by appointing an independent board of directors dominated by outsiders.)

The words that come to mind in describing Bradshaw are harmony, tension, fairness, and courage. Hence, Bradshaw's social leadership—even his call for national energy planning—did not make him the darling of the left anymore than his tough-mindedness on profit made him the beloved of the right. For example, Arco has an unusually active and nonpartisan Civic Action Program in which, in 1981 alone, some three hundred government officials and political candidates spoke to Arco employees. One such speaker was the novelist Gore Vidal, then a candidate for the U.S. Senate from California. Vidal is a left-wing Democrat who makes no bones about wishing to see Big Oil neutralized, if not nationalized. He addressed a standing-room-only crowd at the Arco headquarters in Los Angeles in what doubtless was his first invitation to speak in the den of his *bête noire.* Not being one to miss an opportunity to be ungrateful, ungenerous, and outrageous, he proceeded to attack his host. In particular, Vidal singled out the man who he said symbolized the oil industry's profiteering, greed, tax avoidance, exploitation of the poor and minorities, abuse of political poor, despoilation of the environment, and general capitalistic lack of human decency. And who was this traitor to the public interest? None other than Thornton Bradshaw. Ironically, the room in which Vidal spoke looks out on the California Club. Now, a man who can be attacked by the right wing and by the left wing from both sides of the same street clearly understands how to balance conflicting interests!

Bradshaw succeeded in turning the tide of public opinion—while not in favor of Arco, at least to a position where it was more neutral and objective. This illustrates how the job of a Vanguard leader differs from that of an Old Guard executive. As Walter A. Haas, Jr., says, the Vanguard leaders "make alliances with many sectors of the public." And ethical behavior is the prerequisite for these alliances. For only ethical behavior will gain public trust.

Vanguard Ethics

Each of the Vanguard corporations has the equivalent of an ethical code that states their position on conflicts of interest, foreign practices, and similar matters. Such codes *guarantee* nothing—they merely *inform* all employees of corporate standards. While this information is necessary, not even in the best of circumstances will it be sufficient. As in any organization with tens of thousands of workers, there are some individuals in each of the Vanguard who from time to time are tempted to skirt the law. What is important is the fashion by which leaders of the Vanguard have dealt with wrongdoings and wrongdoers. For instance, when Levi settled a $12 million antitrust suit, they responded by hiring a lawyer to instruct all managers and salespeople about the requirements of the law. Later, the first person caught playing fast and loose was fired. In another instance, ethical considerations relating to bribery were among the factors considered in withdrawing from business in an Asian country. (While there is nothing wrong with the Azande believing in witchcraft—it is plain madness for *you* to believe in it!)

When one talks of ethics, the immediate objections raised are: "There is no way to anticipate all problems in a single code"; "It all depends on the situation"; and "Ethics is an individual, not a corporate matter." Such relativistic justifications for unprincipled inaction are belied by the Vanguard, where ethical behavior simply means adherence to a few common-sense principles, such as:

- Obey the law.
- Tell the truth.
- Show respect for people.
- Stick to the Golden Rule.
- *Primum non nocere* (above all, do not harm)—the first rule of medical ethics.
- Practice participation not paternalism.
- Always act when you have responsibility (that is, when you have the capacity or resources to act, or when those nearby are in need and you are the only one who can help).

In essence, knowing the right thing to do is not difficult (the foregoing list is merely a codification of the principles by which moral people in all Western societies try to raise their children). *The bind comes in applying personal standards of behavior to organizational behavior. That requires real leadership.* Ultimately, then, it is the behavior of the leader that establishes the ethical tone of a corporation. If he is beyond reproach, if she rewards right behavior in others, and if he is totally intolerant of wrongdoing, the chances are that nearly everyone in an organization will also behave ethically.

For example, during the Nixon-era wage and price controls, it became obvious to Weyerhaeuser's financial people that there was plenty of room to get around the intent of those infamous "anti-inflation" measures. In fact, the Weyco people discovered that their major competitors were already "cheating." When the Weyco officers then took the news to George Weyerhaeuser that competitors were gaining an advantage as a result of unethical behavior (and that Weyco would lose millions of dollars if they didn't follow suit), Weyerhaeuser replied, "I don't agree with this law, but we must obey it no matter the consequences. And we must obey the *spirit*, not merely the letter of the law." The word at Weyerhaeuser is that their leader (who is an inveterate table thumper) was only once seen in a *total* rage: That was when he discovered that several of his troops had engaged in price fixing. "There is only one rule around Weyco on which George is adamant: You don't sully the Weyerhaeuser name," says one long-time employee, "and I think everyone has gotten that message."

The same is true at Motorola. One manager told me, "We could make a potful of dough selling technology to the Russians that isn't *quite* restricted by our government. But no one would dare broach the subject with Bob Galvin. He adamantly puts principles before profit." When an internal audit revealed bookkeeping "discrepancies" in a Motorola sales department, Galvin directed twenty managers to make retribution by contributing some $8,500 to charity.

Recently PepsiCo has won praise because their president is "obsessive" about work details. He is said to drive employees seven days a week in a single-minded effort to make PepsiCo the industry leader by any means (including heavy promotion of caffeine and sugar among ghetto children). In contrast, the only thing that the Haases, Bob Galvin, and George Weyerhaeuser are "obsessive" about is ethical behavior. That contrast illustrates the clearest single difference between great and merely good companies. Let's see how a strong ethical base undergirds all Vanguard efforts to build alliances with their external publics.

CONSUMER SAFETY

Adherence to the Golden Rule once caused Levi Strauss to reject the opportunity to purchase twenty-five thousand yards of denim made of a blend of cotton and the "miracle" material, lycra spandex, when it first came on the market. Even though obtaining it on an exclusive basis would have provided Levi with a significant jump on their competitors, Levi decided to pass up the opportunity because they didn't want their customers to bear the risk of a product for which there were no established quality standards. As a result, a leading competitor enjoyed a significant increase in sales for over six months while Levi undertook tests to provide quality benchmarks with which to protect their customers.

And adherence to *primum non nocere* caused Levi to spend a fortune to reduce formaldehyde levels in the finish of Sta-Prest pants below government standards, even though there was no evidence of harm to consumers or to employees. Why act then? Because Levi has a principle of monitoring all chemicals used by suppliers to discover any *potential* for harm.

John Deere's record of leadership in product safety includes the development of the first rollover protective structure for tractors (which led to industry standards for both farm and construction equipment), color- and shape-coded controls that can be located by tractor operators quickly and surely by sight or touch, and industry-leading noise abatement in all their products. At both Deere and Levi, serving customers thus means more than mere market subservience to immediate wants. It means accepting a moral responsibility for *anticipating* problems that could affect consumer welfare in the long term . . . that is, caring about their *needs* as well as their *wants*.

Environmental Protection

For over a decade, Arco has been committed "To manage operations with an active concern for their impact on employees, host communities, and the physical environment." Here are some of the credits they've earned in this regard: (1) The Council on Economic Priorities has ranked Arco number one in the nation in controlling air and water emissions from their refineries. (2) The company's internal, self-imposed health and safety standards make OSHA's fiats appear lax in comparison. (3) The company has health/safety and environmental "audit teams"— groups of middle-managers who spend from one to two weeks at an Arco facility (other than their own) evaluating the performance of the facility and making recommendations for improvement to the facility manager and the company president. (4) In 1977, the company committed $1 million to support a private nonprofit organization dedicated to settling environmental disputes through mediation instead of litigation. (5) Ever on the alert to avoid oil spills, the company has outfitted each of the tankers in their fleet with double antiexplosion systems, and the most sophisticated accident-avoidance apparatus . . . well beyond the requirements of the law. (6) In such company towns as Valdez, Alaska, Tonopah, Nevada, and Gillette, Wyoming—all "garden spots" where no sane person would live if there weren't a compelling economic reason—Arco makes even the federal government look chintzy when it comes to ameliorating the impact of their activities on the host community. Schools, roads, housing, sewers—you name it—an Arco company town beats Anytown, USA, for all the amenities. (7) In big cities where Arco has facilities, they have been a leader in carpooling, supporting mass transportation, and other environmental and energy-saving activities. (8) In "headquarters" cities like Dallas, Denver, Philadelphia, and L.A., Arco's architectural standards give other companies fits of jealousy. And so on. If it weren't for their Anaconda problems, one could list enough credits to make Arco look like the eco-freaks of industry. Why did Arco do these things? Because they felt they *had* to do it, certainly. But, in addition, they did the right thing because of Anderson and Bradshaw's commitment to the principle of respect for people. Humanist ethics were at the heart of all the philosophical statements made by Messrs. A & B during their reigns.

Weyerhaeuser has long been the leader of the forest products industry in terms of environmental protection. As the standard-setter in toxic- and solid-waste disposal, the relatively clean air over, and clear water running through, Weyco lands earned them the Audubon Society's highest "praise" of a private corporation: In a 1974 issue of *Audubon*, Weyco was called "Best of the S.O.B.'s." How did the company earn this ringing endorsement? By adhering to the ethical "principle of participation." Before Weyco allows any of their plans for land or facility development to be set in concrete, they consult with all relevant stakeholders. In the mid-1970s, Weyco eyed an old Du Pont operation on Puget Sound that had one of the few ports in the area with water deep enough to accommodate the big ships the company was preparing to use to ship logs to Japan. Fully two years before the company would even take title to the property, they held open hearings in which they patiently listened to the concerns of the Sierra Club, the Audubon Society, the Steelhead Trout Club (and some three hundred individuals who represented only their own interests). The company sought to learn from these publics, so that they could then find ways to win their consent. This process of participation is long, frustrating, and often painful (environmentalists are not noted for their politic characterizations of lumber company executives). Why do it, then? Says G.W., "We try to get some breadth of viewpoint, and then get ahead of it. We've got the time, and are prepared to take the trouble."

Weyerhaeuser executives recognize that the sensitivities of environmentalists are as legitimate in their own way as the world's needs for lumber and paper, and they believe that by working cooperatively with their publics a valid and workable compromise can be achieved. To satisfy both economic and environmental ends requires adherence to the ethical principles of "truth telling," "respect for people," and "responsibility." For example, when the Sierra Club was lobbying to set aside an area in the Cascade Mountains larger than Rhode Island as a "wilderness area" (read: no cars allowed), Weyco became involved because some of their timberlands abutted the designated area and, if the Sierra Club's proposal were adopted, almost every conceivable economic activity on the Weyco lands would have been halted. Weyco's response was to meet with the Sierra Club, disclose all Weyco interests in the matter, and to make available Weyco maps and data (the Forest Service maps and data that the Sierra Club was using turned out to be grossly inaccurate). After many shirt-sleeve sessions, Weyco and the Sierra Club jointly arrived at a plan in which nine thousand additional acres would be included in the wilderness set-aside, in exchange for a "multiple-use" designation for adjoining lands.

Weyco's approach is self-interested but not adversarial. Says George Weyerhaeuser, "We want to surface issues [before they become contentious] to be ahead of criticism—to be our own advance critics." When the environmentalists are right, Weyco graciously concedes (for example, to protect bald eagles, the company agrees not to cut timber an eighth of a mile around nesting birds). And when environmentalists are wrong, Weyco merely presents the data that makes their case. (For example, environmentalists believed that deer wouldn't cross an open area more than a quarter mile wide and, hence, demanded a restrictive limit to clear cutting. Weyco responded not by Mobil-like name-calling, but by dispatching a team of scientists who collected meticulously detailed data showing that there were as many deer droppings in the middle of open areas as at the fringes. Q.E.D.)

Big deal, the cynic might say, what's so special about that? A lot, it turns out. Urban-based environmentalists often fail to understand the culture of lumbermen and, hence, fail to appreciate Weyco's unusual behavior. I learned the difference through a shocking experience in 1969 at a Northwest operation of one of Weyco's major competitors. Because trout need shade to survive, this company had been asked by the Sierra Club to leave a single line of trees standing along the bank of a river running through an area being clear-cut. The company invited the environmentalists and television crews in to show them that the trees had indeed been left standing alongside the stream. The next day, the head logger chopped down all the remaining trees. When I asked him why he did it, he replied, "Who the hell do they think they are telling me how to run my business on private land?"

Loggers clearly lack the sensitivities of a John Muir—a problem even Weyerhaeuser faces in their field operations. For example, a William Ruckelshaus announcement of new federal toxic wastes regulations was greeted with something less than enthusiastic acceptance by Weyco field managers. Explains Ruckelshaus,

> At first, some of the old-timers saw the regulations as "unreasonable governmental interference in their jobs." We tried turning the situation around by starting from a different assumption. We said "We are doing this because we don't want to hurt any of our *own* people." Remarkably, it was difficult for some field operators to even see workers as their own people. We finally convinced them, but it was a lesson for me in how different the world is out here from what I thought it was sitting in a D.C. office.

In fact, at Deere and Arco, as well as at Weyco, environmental leadership has had to start with changing the attitudes of employees before it was possible to change the attitudes of environmentalists. Clearly, the art of leadership is not in knowing the right thing to do (could it ever be right to dump poison where it might harm others?), but in having the *courage* to get others to accept an unpopular course. Paradoxically, moral men and women will behave immorally in organizations because it takes tremendous courage for an individual, even one at the top, to challenge the collective representations of a group. It is this courage that is absent in Old Guard organizations.

INDUSTRY LEADERSHIP

Thornton Bradshaw, Walter Haas, Jr., Kenneth Dayton, George Weyerhaeuser, and, above all, William Norris, have accepted the ultimate responsibility of leadership: They attempt to educate their less-perceptive peers in other corporations. This is a particularly courageous act, for the eleventh commandment of American business is "Never disparage the efforts or ideas of your fellow executives." In fact, as Barbara Tuchman illustrates, saving people from their narrowminded, "wooden-headed" errors is never appreciated. The barrier is pride. Great corporations, like great nations, fall prey to snow blindness because of the stiff-necked refusal of leaders to admit that conditions have changed since they set their original course. Tuchman writes how George III repeatedly and unwittingly rubbed salt in the wounds of the American colonists, making rebels where none had existed before. She shows that the British Government's suicidal error was *not* in their original mistake of taxing the American colonies, but rather in later refusing to retreat from taxation when it was clearly producing contrary results. Edmund Burke was the lone voice of sanity in Parliament when he courageously argued against the continuation of the hated taxes, "They tell you that your dignity is tied to it. This dignity is a terrible encumbrance to you for it has of late ever been at war with your interest, your equity, and every idea of your policy."

To call attention to shortsightedness—especially if the change being proposed requires the humiliating cessation of self-defeating acts—places the visionary in conflict with the comfort and the pride of his audience. Thus, when Thornton Bradshaw called for the elimination of the oil depletion allowance because it generated public hostility against the oil industry, when Walter Haas, Jr., called for large corporations to make alliances with the public to reduce mistrust of business, when Kenneth Dayton called for corporations to increase philanthropy as an alternative to further governmental control of the nonprofit sector, and when William Norris called for American corporations to establish cooperative research projects to counter the Japanese threat to the computer industry, each was met with the same lack of sympathy with which George III's ministers received Burke's clear-sighted and rational warnings.

On these matters, it took a decade for events to prove these Vanguard leaders right (much as it took a decade for events in America to validate Burke's warnings). It takes great courage (and moral obstinacy) to repeat an unpopular warning for ten years, and that is perhaps why there are so few courageous leaders in American industry. But while the acceptance of their ideas by their peers is the *desideratum,* Vanguard leaders believe in doing right even when they know that neither such acceptance (nor the validation of history within their lifetime) will be forthcoming. For example, Honeywell's approach to public affairs runs so counter to the practices of American business that CEO Edson Spencer can neither hope to win the hearts and minds of his counterparts, nor can he hope to live to see history prove him right. Unlike any of their competitors, Honeywell has only one corporate representative working in Washington—and he is forbidden to lobby on any legislation in which Honeywell has a direct stake. Even though Honeywell is one of the nation's prime defense contractors, they remain silent on political issues relating to defense appropriations and authorizations. Spencer says, "Those decisions must be resolved on what is in the national interest, not on what is in the interest of a defense contractor." Arco's approach to political lobbying was similar. Throughout the 1970s, the company had several hundred employees in their government affairs division under vice president Donald Henriksen. Henriksen, a deep-voiced, 6'6", former Stanford basketballer, could clearly have won by intimidation if that were his style. Instead, he used finesse rather than corporate muscle to score points for Arco in state legislatures and in Washington. Henriksen believed that good laws come about *not* from armtwisting, but from an informed decision-making process. What Arco lobbyists mainly do is to provide legislators with the kind of high quality staff work they can't afford themselves. Arco provides them with full, accurate, and objective information—even when the data seem to contradict Arco's position on a particular bill. Henriksen argues that the most important thing for the company to have in the long run is credibility with lawmakers.

When Dayton-Hudson "went public" in 1967 they disclosed to the very investors whose capital they sought that DH dividends could be constrained by the fact that the corporation was committed to donating 5 percent of taxable profits to social causes. When Levi published their stock prospectus in 1971 they, too,

gave potential shareholders fair warning that the company's social philosophy might not always result in short-term profit maximization. Could Spencer, Henriksen, the Daytons, or the Haases
have ever hoped that others would follow their lead, or that the
world would hail them for their vision? Surely, such hope must
have been far from the minds of the Haases when Levi became
the first corporation to integrate plants in the South in the 1950s,
among the first to hire and train ghetto residents and to support
minority businesses in the 1960s, and among the first to publish
their affirmative action statistics in the early 1970s. They did so
for only one reason: because these were the right things to do. By
definition, moral courage is incompatible with a guarantee of
success. If principled actions were undertaken only when the
actor had some assurance of eventual popular acceptance, there
would be no moral leadership in this world.

URBAN DEVELOPMENT

When many American corporations were beating a retreat to
the suburbs in the early 1970s, Arco, Levi Strauss, Dayton-Hudson, Weyerhaeuser, Deere, Honeywell, and Control Data were
each making separate and unique commitments to inner-city
redevelopment. In 1970, Arco was the first large corporation to
build in downtown Los Angeles in decades and, in the early
1980s, was the first to support developer James Rouse's efforts to
create public/private partnerships to renovate ghetto housing.
Levi Strauss kept their original inner-city facility open long after
the neighborhood had been abandoned by all other industry (and
Levi built a park for the community, to boot). While moving their
own headquarters to the woods, Weyerhaeuser rehabilitated historic buildings and built new ones in a seedy area of Seattle and is
currently revitalizing the historic area of central Tacoma. In
addition, Weyerhaeuser is supporting the revitalization of neighborhood housing in Tacoma—and Deere is doing the same in
Waterloo, Iowa.

"Minneapolis slum" is an oxymoron, but in the late 1960s,
Honeywell found their headquarters located in what was, at best,
a run-down area. The company was tempted to fly to the suburbs
but, instead, they stayed and turned their old brick factories into
attractively remodeled brick offices (while creating an enormous
park for the community on land once used as the corporate

parking lot). In 1971, Honeywell launched a Neighborhood Improvement Program, in which they built or renovated eighty old houses near their corporate headquarters and gave financial assistance to two hundred other residents to make property improvements. One neighborhood building was renovated and leased for a dollar a year to a community job training center. In addition, the company formed a nonprofit light manufacturing business which employs 9 full-time and 27 part-time workers, all of whom were local residents who had been chronically unemployed for years.

Dayton-Hudson demonstrated their commitment to inner-city Minneapolis by keeping their flagship store downtown and by facilitating the redevelopment of the area by putting their headquarters in an urban development project. In addition, the company donated $1 million in 1977 to the revitalization of an eighty-eight-block neighborhood five minutes from downtown Minneapolis. This neighborhood had deteriorated into an eyesore of neglected homes, abandoned buildings, and littered streets. By 1981, some 332 homes had been rehabilitated, 89 new homes built, hundreds of trees planted, and a community-betterment campaign launched that involved some three thousand community residents.

In the late 1960s, as we have seen, Control Data started placing factories in depressed areas and providing training and jobs therein for minority residents. This experience grew into the City Venture Corporation, a cooperative enterprise involving business, professional, governmental, and religious organizations who seek holistic solutions to urban problems. City Venture stresses the formation and growth of new, small businesses in run-down urban areas (and offers residents a share of ownership in those businesses to involve them directly in determining their own economic futures). In Toledo, Philadelphia, Baltimore, Miami, as well as in Minneapolis, Control Data's City Ventures have sought—not always with perfect success—to provide training, health care, transportation, and affordable housing to the communities being revitalized.

Civic Virtues: The Minneapolis Story

In Minnesota's Twin Cities, Control Data, Honeywell, Dayton-Hudson, 3M, General Mills, and dozens of smaller businesses like the Wilson Learning Corporation have created institutions in which business, labor, civic groups, and government work together for the betterment of the community. In Minneapolis-St. Paul, voluntary organizations bring citizens together to discuss common problems and to *act* to solve them—actions such as community redevelopment projects, low-cost housing, and job creation. This public/private cooperation is, in no small part, responsible for the fact that Minneapolis is the only major city in the frost belt *not* losing population, and one of a handful with low rates of unemployment. These achievements cost money, let there be no mistake about that. For example, forty-five firms are members of the "Minnesota 5 Percent Club" in which each company donates at least 5 percent of taxable profits to their communities. And another twenty-five to thirty companies give 2 percent. (In contrast, in greater Los Angeles, where the population is nearly ten times larger than the Twin Cities, there is only *one* large corporation—Arco—that donates even 2 percent.)

In addition to giving money, Twin City managers give their time. The Metropolitan Council is an innovative urban planning body composed primarily of private sector members. Over sixty companies are members of the Minnesota Project on Corporate Responsibility, an active forum in which executives heighten their understanding of their social obligations.

And it isn't just executives who get into the act. Over thirty corporations are members of the Minnesota Corporate Volunteerism Council which coordinates the activities of thousands of Twin City employee-volunteers. In 1983, the federal government gave Honeywell a President's Volunteer Action Award, given each year to the two corporations that lead the nation in employee volunteerism. In one unusual Honeywell program, six hundred retirees engage in voluntary activities in welfare agencies, hospitals, schools, and recreational and civic organizations. In addition, Honeywell gives grants to community organizations in which employees volunteer time (ditto DH, Arco, Weyco, and Levi). Currently, Honeywell is evolving a four-step process of social responsibility: First, they give money to support a worthy activity; second, they provide volunteers; third, they build partnerships with other organizations to add further support; and, finally, they internalize the activity and make it a part of the company's operating system. They have progressed to step four with child care, Vietnam veterans assistance, and their retiree program.

But why Minneapolis (and not, say, Providence, Philadelphia, or Pensacola)? Some argue that the Minneapolis experience is due to "a unique ethnic homogeneity" (that is, almost everybody is white). But, hell, the folks in Burlingame, Bismarck, and Beverly Hills are even *whiter*, and they do next to nothing, so that can't explain it. Others argue that it is so cold in Minneapolis that people cooperate just to get warm. Actually, the *worst* season in Minneapolis is *summer* when it is too darn hot and sticky to cooperate with anybody on anything, so that can't explain it, either.

I believe that the attitudes of the Minneapolis business community are not based on Scandinavian values, cold (or hot) extremities, the northern lights, or anything other than the old ethical "principle of responsibility." Simply put, Minneapolitans believe they have an obligation to put something back into the community from which they take so much. As the folks at Dayton-Hudson and Honeywell will tell you, corporations have obligations to society because they benefit from things they either don't pay for, or don't pay enough for. Private corporations benefit from hospitals, schools, libraries, museums, university research, and a host of other components of the social and economic infrastructure. While corporate taxes may underwrite some of these activities, most are obtained at a discount, or for free (for example, Arco did not pay the private University of Southern California for educating the 800 USC graduates on their payroll. So when Arco makes a grant to USC, it should not be considered a gift. Arco *should* pay—otherwise they are getting a free ride).

A heightened sense of obligation to one's community is called the public virtue of *civitas*. The Committee for Economic Development has recently studied seven large U.S. cities (including Minneapolis) where private corporations have worked with local governments to revitalize rotting central areas. The CED argues that the first requirement for such collaboration is a *civic bond,* or "a civic culture that fosters a sense of community." As one who lives in Los Angeles, where there is little discernible sense of community, I am struck by this powerful insight: The CED business leaders recognize that a sense of community is the *sine qua non* of revitalizing not only our cities, but our nation. In Minneapolis, *civitas* means that corporations accept the following obligations to the community:

- Providing the goods and services the community needs.
- Providing steady employment.
- Improving the standard of living and quality of life.
- Paying a fair share of the community's tax burden.
- Behaving ethically (doing no harm, obeying the law, telling the truth, respecting people, living by the Golden Rule, and practicing participation).
- Encouraging employee citizenship and volunteerism.
- Philanthropy.

How do Minneapolis corporations justify these activities to their shareholders? Says a Dayton-Hudson vice president, Peter Hutchinson: "We can't conceive of a situation where there would be a conflict between meeting our obligations to shareholders and meeting our obligations to society." That is, Minneapolitans believe that the high quality of life created by the spirit of cooperation makes Minneapolis a wonderful place to live and do business. And, by putting something back into the community from corporate coffers, managers and workers become as loyal and committed to their companies as they are to their community. Now, if they could only do something about their beastly weather!

PHILANTHROPY

Of all the items on the preceding list of community obligations, only the last is problematical. Philanthropy is not, *prima facie*, a moral responsibility. In fact, the case is often made that corporate philanthropy is *im*moral. Milton Friedman says that it is no better than stealing from shareholders when an executive gives corporate profits to charity, spends money to reduce pollution beyond what is required by law, or "hires hard-core unemployed instead of better-qualified available workmen." Friedman says:

In each of these cases, the corporate executive would be spending someone else's money for a general social interest. Insofar as his actions in accord with his "social responsibility" reduce returns to stockholders, he is spending their money.

Insofar as his actions lower the wages of some employees, he is spending their money.

Friedman's indictment of philanthropy does not stop here at the accusation of theft. Far worse, he accuses the corporate philanthropist of unconstitutional, antidemocratic behavior. For when an executive decides, first, to give away some percent of a corporation's profit and, second, to do so in a way that is different from how the stockholders would have spent it, "he is, in effect, imposing taxes on the one hand, and deciding how the tax proceeds should be spent, on the other." Friedman asks who elected the executive to fulfill these governmental functions:

This process raises political questions on two levels: principle and consequences. On the level of political principle, the imposition of taxes and the expenditure of tax proceeds are governmental functions. We have established elaborate constitutional, parliamentary, and judicial provisions to control these functions, to assure that taxes are imposed so far as possible in accordance with the preferences and desires of the public—after all, "taxation without representation" was one of the battle cries of the American Revolution. We have a system of checks and balances to separate the legislative function of imposing taxes and enacting expenditures from the executive function of collecting taxes and administering expenditure programs and from the judicial function of mediating disputes and interpreting the law. Here the businessman—self-selected or appointed directly or indirectly by stockholders—is to be simultaneously legislator, executive, and jurist. He is to decide whom to tax by how much and for what purpose, and he is to spend the proceeds . . .

This is not a crank argument. Indeed, Friedman's concern is shared by many on the left. The left-wing argument builds on Friedman's, adding that corporate donations give executives illegitimate and excessive *power* to influence society. Better to tax the money away, say the leftists, and let democratically elected bodies decide on how it should be allocated. These arguments—and an admixture of greed—have apparently had some influence on corporate thinking. According to the Conference Board, less than 30 percent of all corporations make any contributions at all. (Among large corporations—which are the businesses most likely to give—the average amount given has hovered around 1 percent for decades.) Ben M. Heineman, president of Northwest Industries, probably speaks for the majority of corporate executives when he says,

> We should never forget we are giving away other people's money, that vicarious generosity can be corrupting and become an ego trip for some company official . . . In the absence of genuine, direct benefit to our stockholders, we think we should restrict the level of giving.

(That Mr. Heineman doesn't apply the same standards to his energetic allocation of the profits of Northwest shareholders to his favorite politicians doesn't, by itself, discredit his argument. He no doubt would argue that these political contributions are an insurance policy against overregulation, even nationalization, of "his" railroad—and that, of course, is in the interest of Northwest shareholders.)

Given these strong objections to philanthropy, what justification is offered by Arco, Levi, Weyco, DH, and Honeywell—who stand among the nation's most active and generous practitioners of the art? Of all the many arguments they offer ("self-interest," "business can't prosper in an unprosperous environment," "corporations have social obligations as well as economic"), the most convincing is based on the ethical principles of "capacity," "proximity," and "unique qualifications." Here's an illustration of these principles: If a person is being mugged and you are a 6'5", 240-pound tight end standing nearby, you have a moral responsibility to directly and physically intervene (the principle of capacity). If you are a 95-pound, sixty-year-old woman, you have *no* moral responsibility to intervene in the mugging, because you lack the physical capacity—but you still have a moral responsibility to call for help (the principle of proximity). If you are a healthy fifteen-year-old boy on your way home from baseball practice, you probably have a responsibility to clonk the mugger one with your Louisville Slugger (the principle of unique qualifications).

The Vanguard argue that their moral obligation to engage in philanthropy is based on their capacity, proximity, and unique qualifications. That is, they have the resources to deal with issues and problems that they understand better than government, and on which government can't, won't, or shouldn't act. Hence, the first rule of philanthropy at the Vanguard is "no safe investments." Whereas the government will not risk taxpayer money on individuals or organizations with nontraditional backgrounds, the Vanguard will "bet on the come" on people and projects who show promise rather than proof. Indeed, the Vanguard concede the point to Friedman that, if they were to do exactly what government does, then there would indeed be no moral justification for them to continue their "undemocratic" philanthropic practices.

The Vanguard answer the objections of the left by democratizing their giving. Clearly, it is not in the public interest for the likes of Mr. Heineman to feed his ego by directing corporate funds to *his* favorite causes. This problem of "executive legislation" is solved by involving employees in the process of grant allocations. This is accomplished in several ways—establishing grant-review committees composed of employees, providing matching grants for employee contributions, distributing funds to decentralized operations, and involving employees directly in philanthropic decisions (for example, Levi's Community Involvement Teams). With the exception of Control Data, each of the Vanguard uses at least three of these four devices. (Motorola uses two.)

Still, there are some large allocations that must be centralized in order to be effective (Dayton-Hudson's million dollar rehabilitation of the Minneapolis neighborhood, for example). Who should make these decisions? *Not* corporate executives. At the Vanguard, eleemosynary activities are conducted by independent corporate foundations, which are headed by professional administrators. That doesn't mean that corporate officers have no say in the operations of Vanguard foundations. In fact, they establish foundation *policy* (typically, the board of a corporate foundation will be composed of corporate officers or have a majority of corporate officers), leaving *operations* to a professional director.

However, to completely separate corporate policy from foundation policy might satisfy the radical left, but it would do violence to the principle of "unique qualifications." Each of the Vanguard foundations has chosen to limit their activities to a very few areas of special competence related to the mission of the company. (Where Levi Strauss specializes in community, family, Hispanic, and women's issues, Weyerhaeuser specializes in improving the quality of life in communities where the company has a significant number of employees, and in issues related to forest management.) Indeed, Weyco's philanthropy is based on what William Ruckelshaus calls "the intersection concept." As president of Weyco's $4 million-plus foundation between 1979–83, Ruckelshaus articulated this concept, arguing that

> . . . corporate philanthropy differs from other forms of private giving: *Charitable activities by corporations should be focused on those issues that are of mutual benefit to the general public and enlightened corporate self-interest.* Only in this way can corporations justify the increasingly large amount of money being distributed for charitable purposes.

This philosophy is remarkably similar to Dayton-Hudson's, where a studious effort is made to integrate the giving program with overall business strategy. For example, DH's B. Dalton division is deeply involved in reducing the level of illiteracy (an obvious concern for a bookstore chain). Through programs designed to *teach* adults to read, and others to *encourage* young people to read, B. Dalton employees are trying not only to solve the problem but to prevent it as well. I use the word "employees" advisedly. It is not just money, but volunteers that B. Dalton is devoting to their literacy effort. In addition to donating $3 million dollars over four years, B. Dalton employees, from salesclerks to regional vice presidents, volunteer their time as tutors—and, in many cases, get paid release time from work to do so.

The principles of capacity, proximity, and unique qualifications come together when corporations play to their strengths and experience, as when Deere supports research into the world food problem and underwrites an artist-in-residence for culture-starved Moline, when Weyerhaeuser assists communities in southwest Washington that were devastated by the floods that followed the eruption of Mt. St. Helens, and when SmithKline sends thirty-five MDs to underdeveloped countries for a year of postdoctoral public service (you don't have to be a member of the Vanguard to do good).

How could it be honestly claimed that any of these activities gives corporate executives undue influence and power, that they are undemocratic, or that they constitute theft from shareholders (or even a betrayal of their long-term interests)? Why not ask the shareholders? It turns out that they don't see eye to eye with Messrs. Friedman and Heineman on this issue. In 1983, Dayton-Hudson polled their shareholders to identify the extent of investor support of the DH philanthropic policy. The stockholders were told that, in 1982, the corporation donated $11.2 million (fully 5 percent of pretax profits); then they were asked what they, as owners, would recommend to management about corporate giving in the future. Nearly three quarters of those polled supported either increasing or maintaining the 5 percent policy (31 percent favored "increasing contributions even if it costs a few cents per share"; 42 percent favored continuing at the current level; 5 percent favored reductions "so DH can increase dividends"; and 22 percent had no opinion). In a separate poll, DH employees offered equally high levels of support for the company's philanthropic policies.

Now, are you convinced of the merits of corporate giving? William Norris isn't.

CDC'S DEMURRAL

Before I met William Norris, I was convinced that it was impossible for a corporation to exert moral leadership without generously engaging in social giving. I'm no longer so certain. Norris is the sort of person who makes one rethink one's every assumption. There is simply no one like him in American business. Although he is the chief executive of the nation's seventy-sixth largest corporation, he does not associate himself with the managerial philosophy of his peers, nor does he behave any more like them than an astronomer mimics an astrologer. Step into his office and you are immediately struck by how different his aerie is from that of other top executives: Norris' office looks *used*, like a journalist's or a lawyer's, and not like the neat and sterile drawing rooms that shelter typical CEO's. His desk is strewn with papers. (When I visited him, he was busy writing his eighteenth lengthy pamphlet on the subject of the relationships of business, technology, and society.) His walls are lined with shelves, all chock-full of books and disheveled in the way a library is when its contents are used regularly. Papers, studies, reports, scientific and technical monographs, and other documents overflow the shelves and litter the floor. There is every imaginable kind of document, even law books. (When Norris entered an antitrust suit against IBM, he taught himself the law and successfully brought the Armonk behemoth to its knees, winning a several-hundred-million-dollar out-of-court settlement that he personally negotiated. "It was too important to trust to the lawyers," he explains.)

The crotchety and cantankerous Norris once said, "Whenever I see everybody going South, I have a great compulsion to go North." And so it is in the area of corporate philanthropy. If Norris had his way, CDC wouldn't give a nickel to charity (as it is, they do their United Way duty, but not much more). Norris explained to me why he doesn't believe in corporate philanthropy. First, he believes that philanthropy never solved a social problem, nor could it:

> Foundation after foundation, you look at their reports, and hell, there are hundreds of little projects, $10,000 here and $5,000 there, and what have they got to show for it? You can see, Christ, they're not really accomplishing very much.

Norris believes that the traditional corporate philanthropic approach of giving 1 or 2 percent of profits is "commendable," but "far from adequate." He points out that such corporate giving doesn't even keep up with inflation and, "In order to bridge the gap created by the Reagan administration budget cuts, corporate giving would have to increase by something like 150 percent." In effect, he sees corporate philanthropy as being about as useful as "spitting in the ocean" (he didn't exactly say *spitting)* when it comes to addressing such major social issues as urban blight, poverty, unemployment, and job training.

Second, Norris argues that philanthropy is unlikely to ever become ingrained in the culture of a corporation:

> After a while you get tired of doing good. It makes the boss feel like a white knight for a little while. But the employees say of the boss, "Well, if the old man gets a kick out of doing that, fine, let him do it." The employees are willing to participate up to a point. But they don't see how it's really helping them. And when push comes to shove in a recession, employees pressure executives to cut contributions rather than their salaries.

I immediately think of Levi, Arco, Dayton-Hudson, and Honeywell whose very special programs *do* involve employees, and these companies are obviously exceptions to Norris's criticism. But they *are* exceptions, and Norris's point is no doubt valid in general. So what do you do? Ben Heineman gets to this point and he concludes: *do nothing.* But Norris won't associate himself with the Old Guard merely because he has a disagreement with the Vanguard. Norris is a thinker, an analyst, not a seeker of excuses for inaction. After winning the IBM suit—and seeing that the corporation could not survive in *mano a mano* competition with Big Blue—Norris set himself to challenging every assumption on which CDC had been based, including their then-conventional notion of corporate responsibility. He concluded that even the Vanguard approach of his fellow Minnesotans was too narrow and "peripheral to real problems, like job creating, urban and rural poverty, and overhauling an educational system that has gone to hell." Sure, philanthropy is fine for helping museums and theatre companies, but Norris had bigger fish to fry:

> So we abandoned the traditional, do-gooder concept because it was too narrow, in favor of one that says we should address society's unmet needs as profitable business opportunities. In that way, you're not worrying about doing good or doing well. You're really doing what needs to be done. And solving social problems is no longer a peripheral (and thus expendable) add-on to your real business—it *is* your business. Now it's true that addressing major unmet needs is longer term than the traditional strategy. But the traditional strategy is not working well these days.

So Norris created the unique CDC strategy, forming not only the City Venture Corporation described earlier, but Rural Venture, Inc. (to address rural poverty by bringing the efficiencies of large-scale farming to small, "family" farms); MEDLAB (a mobile pathology lab that serves isolated areas such as Indian reservations); Fair Break (a job-training and career-counseling program for high school dropouts); and several other businesses (like PLATO) designed to make money while addressing major social problems.

So, what does one conclude from CDC's demurral to the Vanguard position on philanthropy? No doubt, Norris has demonstrated that giving is not a necessary element in greatness, provided that (a) the corporation makes explicit why they are not giving, and (b) the corporation exerts moral leadership in meeting social problems through other, more effective, means. Since this latter requirement entails rare qualities of courage and imagination, it is my conclusion that philanthropy will remain the more common approach of the Vanguard.

The Real Bottom Line

Perhaps the greatest obstacle to achieving Vanguard status is the inability of corporate leaders to see the difference between their traditional practices and the practices of the New Management. For example, George Weissman, the CEO of Philip Morris, recently gave a talk in which he challenged Milton Friedman's notion that corporations should not engage in philanthropy. Weissman argued that a corporation "must consider its expenditures for corporate social responsibility as seriously as it considers expenditures for marketing, administration, and the other costs of doing business." He then asked rhetorically, "Does all that responsibility pay off?" His answer:

> What I do know is what's happened to Philip Morris in the thirty-five years I have been with the company. We have gone from sixth place to become the largest cigarette manufacturer in the United States . . . In thirteen years, we have taken Miller from eighth to second place in the beer industries of the United States and the world. In five years we have made 7-Up a strong contender in the world soft drink industry. So while I can't tell you that being actively responsible has helped us, I sure can tell you that it hasn't hurt.

This is near self-parody by a myopic executive who cannot see that making and selling cigarettes, alcohol, and junk food may be legal, profitable, and, in some ways, even necessary, but could never be called "socially responsible." A company—like his—in which some employees have signs on their desks that read "Thank You for Smoking," could not be considered great regardless of the amount of money they make, the efficiency with which they meet customer needs, or the level of charity in which they engage.

Similarly—but nowhere near as blatantly—the likes of GM, IBM, and Kodak cannot be considered great no matter how well they do in other aspects of their business if they fail to practice stakeholder symmetry, fail to be committed to high purpose, fail to become learning organizations, and fail to try to become the best at everything they do. Ultimately, the key trait of moral leadership described in this chapter is what separates the eminent from merely very good corporations. What the leaders of such fine companies as GM, IBM, and Kodak fail to see is the profound difference between their behavior and the behavior of the Vanguard. The leaders of the Vanguard display moral courage not only when they risk their good standing in their industries by calling for reform, but also when they invest heavily in new products and technology (instead of skimping on R&D in order to pad their dividends), when they provide high-quality goods that exceed industry and government standards, when they take actions that will bear fruit only for future generations, when they eschew paternalism and share power and profits with employees, when they use their vast resources creatively to improve the state of the managerial art, and when they look at themselves in the mirror and challenge their most comfortable assumptions.

In exerting moral courage, Vanguard leaders not only lay the groundwork for the long-term success of their companies, they lay the foundation for the continued survival of corporate capitalism. According to a 1983 Gallup poll, only 18 percent of Americans placed great confidence in U.S. business leaders. And it was not just the negative press generated by unfriendly takeovers, golden parachutes, inflated salaries, insider trading, and bankruptcies that have brought scorn on a system that deserves better of its leaders. In addition, polls show that the public is reacting to the lack of affirmative, moral leadership on the part of business executives. Because large corporations are increasingly seen as national resources—engines of development creating capital, jobs, markets, products, and technology for the nation—the long-term trend is to hold them accountable for their social, political, technological as well as their economic performance. Hence, traditionally run corporations that have persisted in viewing themselves as purely economic institutions have failed to meet the expectations of the public. As a consequence, society has sought to bring corporations under greater social control—regulatory, judicial, and legislative. Ironically, then, the net effect of the Old Guard's insistence on exercising managerial prerogatives has been to lessen the domain of their managerial discretion.

In response, Robert V. Krikorian (head of Rexnord, arguably a Vanguard company) has taken the lead in calling for business "self-regulation." He suggests that business leaders have violated the public trust by "falling down in honesty, integrity, and responsibility to society. In other words, ethical considerations." He calls upon the heads of American corporations to join him in regaining the public trust by behaving with the kind of moral courage described in this chapter.

Krikorian warns that if corporate leaders do not come to behave with John Adams's "positive passion for the public good," they will live to see their freedom to operate severely curtailed by government. In short, Krikorian sees American business on a "march of folly" by pursuing policies contrary to their own self-interest. That was, by the way, Bill Holden's point in *Executive Suite.*

13.

In Search of Justice: The Theory Behind It All

> If humans are not perfect, what nonsense it is to think we can invent a perfect society. The best possible society, which can never be anywhere near ideal, has to be the one best able to correct its mistakes, to develop new ideas, adjust to new circumstances. The writers of our Constitution understood that even the best minds and hearts make mistakes.
>
> —Flora Lewis

IMPORTANT: Corporate managers are *not* required to read this chapter. My task of illustrating that it is in the self-interest of executives to adopt the principles of the New Management was completed with the last chapter. They may now get to work implementing what they have learned from the Vanguard! Nonetheless, there is still one burden yet to complete. I still must attempt to convince others in society that business executives should be given the opportunity to practice the New Management. It must be shown that all citizens and all groups—consumers, employees, environmentalists, trade unionists, men and women of all colors, ages, classes, and interests—would benefit were the principles that guide the Vanguard come to be embraced as standard business practices in America. I now turn to this difficult task. It is difficult because I cannot *prove* that something never tried would indeed work (I can only offer a theoretical justification for my conviction that it would work if tried). And my task is also difficult because of the wide variety of goals and values found among Americans. While we all desire a more just society, we each would define a condition of societal justice in slightly different ways. To some Americans, justice is a state of perfect freedom. To others, justice is equality. To still others,

justice equates with a high standard of living and full employment. Finally, some believe that a high quality of life is the *sine
qua non* of justice. In a pluralistic democracy like America, people have different goals, values, objectives, and desires, and
therein lies the source of ideological and political conflict.

But there is a constant running through these various views of
justice. To most Americans, justice is seen to hinge on the nature
of the relationship between society, on the one hand, and the
enterprises that produce its goods and services on the other. Put
another way, the behavior and performance of productive enterprises is seen by people of all ideological colorations as having a
powerful influence on whether the public experiences justice (or
injustice). Consequently, a central domestic political question in
this nation is always how to control, direct, or tweak the behavior
of corporations in order to produce greater social justice.

It is that unstated question which has underlaid all that has
gone before in these pages. In short, this book is not simply about
corporate excellence. It is about more than that: The underlying
concern is with new ways to manage that would enhance social
justice. Clearly, this is a controversial issue (and that, perhaps, is
why it is ignored in many recent managerial treatises). But to
ignore it is to miss the primary reason why *all* citizens should be
concerned with the management of large enterprises: Corporations affect the degrees of freedom and equality we all experience, and they determine our standard of living and the quality
of our lives. Mobil's decision to explore for oil internationally
rather than domestically, General Motors' joint ventures with
their Japanese competitors, RCA's retreat from the video disk
business, Levi's affirmative action program, Kodak's efforts to
spur innovation and productivity, Motorola's work-sharing policies, Dayton-Hudson's philanthropy—none of these actions (nor
thousands of others taken daily by the nation's largest corporations) is purely a *private* matter, for each has *public consequences.* Indeed, the sum total of these private managerial actions does much to determine whether or not Americans
experience a sense of social justice.

All well and good, but if justice means different things to different people—if we each have our own unique values—how in the
devil's name can such diffuse objectives be addressed? If he
wants liberty, she wants equality, some want efficiency, and oth-

ers a high quality of life . . . well, you can't please them all, can you?

No, you can't please them all, for there is no way in a free society to force or to entice all citizens to share the same vision of justice. But, in another sense, yes, you can please them all. For the trick of democratic governance is to create policies that are responsive to many competing values *without* creating a wishy-washy compromise that satisfies no one. That this can be done—and that the Vanguard point a way to doing so in the American political economy—is the major point of this book.

There's a rather simple theory behind this assertion, a theory that undergirds all that has been presented so far and lends coherence to the many disparate points that have been advanced. Since this theory is based on common sense and everyday experience, it is neither obscure nor academic—at least no more so than the principles of pluralistic democracy on which it is based. Here it is . . .

Four Views of Justice

To understand how the Vanguard offer the hope of greater social justice, one must begin with the four "great themes of political argument" (George Will's phrase). These themes are: liberty, equality, efficiency, and the quality of life. As political economists have long recognized, agendas for change in public policy emanate from core beliefs or values. For example, those who hold personal freedom as the highest good naturally come to advocate policies that reduce the role of government. Because these so-called *libertarians* believe that the concentration of power in the hands of the state is the greatest threat to individual freedom, they seek to ensure justice by deregulation, decentralization of authority, and by putting resources in the hands of individuals and private organizations. To those who believe equality is the highest good, free markets are seen as the cause of unjust disparities in income and power. *Egalitarians* thus seek to limit the power of private corporations and to use government as the means for a more equal distribution of income and wealth. Then, again, if one's highest goal is economic efficiency and growth, one will be attracted to the policies of the Japanese and northern European economies. These *corporatists* thus wish to build cooperative arrangements between business, government, and labor in order to maximize economic production and improve the national standard of living. Finally, there are those to whom a clean environment and a high quality of life are the ends to which all effort should be directed. These *humanist/environmentalists* advocate policies to conserve natural resources, halt conspicuous consumption, reduce pollution, and put workers in control of small-scale, decentralized enterprises. In grossly oversimplified form, these four themes represent the polar forces tugging at our political economy.

Two things about these four alternatives are of particular significance to those who are interested in the possibilities and consequences of the New Management: First, few Americans are extremists who would hold completely with any one of these ideologies. Second, these polar positions are in constant conflict with each other. In fact, they are typically portrayed as trade-offs, zero-sum positions in which an increment of one value leads to a consequent, equivalent loss of its opposite. For example, the political and economic history of the West since the Enlightenment is often depicted as a state of conflict between those who desire liberty and those who desire equality. It is said that, for any increment of equality gained in society, there is a concomitant loss of liberty (and vice versa). For example, Mao's China was probably the most egalitarian of all modern societies (the ratio of incomes of the highest to the lowest paid individuals was as low as 5:1), but this equality was achieved at a considerable loss of political liberty (censorship, book banning, banishment—even death to dissenters). On the other hand, pre-Depression America probably had as much economic and political freedom as has ever existed, but there were enormous gulfs between the rich and the poor (the ratio of the incomes of the highest to the lowest paid individual may have been as high as 1,000,000:1). We can see why liberty versus equality has been called the great trade-off of Western society.

But, in our increasingly complex world, there are clearly more than two sets of values in conflict. For example, since the beginning of the industrial era, there have been those for whom economic efficiency has been the highest goal. For the sake of growth and technological progress, these individuals have been willing to sacrifice other ends. In opposition are those people primarily, even exclusively, concerned with what they call the quality of life. It can be said that for any given increment of environmental quality a society gains, a measure of efficiency is lost (as when, for example, a "scrubber" is placed on an industrial smokestack). At times, then, efficiency versus the quality of life is the great trade-off of the modern era.

With these four competing values in mind, it is possible to represent "the great themes of political argument" graphically:

Liberty

Quality of Life   vs.   Efficiency

Equality

On this quadrant, there are not only trade-offs between liberty and equality on one axis, and between the quality of life and efficiency on the other, but also between equality and efficiency (as when progressive rates of taxation reduce the incentive of the poor to work), between the quality of life and equality (as when environmental regulations force the closing of a plant, causing unemployment among blue-collar workers), between the quality of life and liberty (as when one is forbidden to smoke in public), and between liberty and efficiency (as when one pays taxes to support national defense). All of the great political and economic issues that are debated in Washington can, thus, be depicted on this quadrant as conflicts between those with differing values and goals.

And whose are the "right" values? Objectively, none can be shown to be better than the others. Values, after all, are matters of individual preference and choice. As such, it is incumbent on a democracy to treat all four value sets (and their dozens of permutations and combinations) as legitimate. The genius of democracy is that it respects individuals with different values and seeks constantly to find ways of getting as much liberty, equality, efficiency, and the quality of life for society as possible. In short, a pluralistic democracy attempts to satisfy all competing interests.

Moreover, since few people are ideologues, most of us want as much of all four values as we can get. But in each decision made, each law passed, each regulation formulated, the imperfectability of human institutions causes one value to be favored over another. But not the same value every time. Therefore, the various constituents in a democratic system will never be fully and finally satisfied. Conservationists, corporate executives, church leaders, and consumers—each with different values and different objectives—will alternately find themselves pleased or displeased by the policies that emanate from the capital. But, even when *dis*pleased, they will never grow so irrevocably disenchanted as to challenge the legitimacy of the system. Democracy is thus a condition of continuing tension and dissatisfaction. It is also the only condition that modern men and women accept as just.

Why Extreme Solutions Are Unjust

That Americans reject radical or extremist programs of change is nearly a truism. A few years back, I sought to demonstrate the point by asking thirty-nine influential men and women from government, business, labor, journalism, and special interest groups to evaluate scenarios that described what the relationship of large enterprises would be to the society at large if the various agendas of libertarians, egalitarians, corporatists, and environmentalists/humanists were each enacted. The four alternative scenarios were not wild, science fiction accounts of utopian (or dystopian) states. Instead, they were composed of proposals that had recently been put in the hopper in the Congress. Significantly (if not surprisingly), all four scenarios were rejected as unacceptable by the vast majority of the panelists. Instead, they greatly preferred a fifth, more moderate alternative in which the relationship of corporations to society "continued to develop along patterns established in previous decades, with no major discontinuities or radical surprises." It is important to note that this panel comprised the most outspoken leaders of special interest groups that I could identify, individuals whose stated beliefs were far more extreme than those of typical Americans. Indeed, when I have given these scenarios to more typical Americans, their evaluations are far more negative *about all four* than are the evaluations of the panel of opinion-leaders and -molders. Indeed, I suggest that one could not find an extreme, ideologically based proposal for change in the relationship of corporations to society that could win the support of more than a tiny minority of the citizenry.

The lesson here is that there is not, nor can there ever be, a final "solution" to the problem of democracy—no optimal mix of programs, no final resting place on the values quadrant that will produce a utopia acceptable to the entire citizenry. Utopia is simply impossible to achieve in a society in which there are differing values. Democracy is thus for now and forever a dynamic process. The resources of the nation must be continually managed, husbanded: gathered then shared, gathered then redistributed . . . each person or group sometimes gaining, sometimes losing, but always expecting to be treated fairly and with respect. When the system is working in this fashion, it can be said to be just. Even the most alienated of citizens recognizes this fact. As Jesse Jackson said during the 1984 presidential race, "Democracy doesn't guarantee success, it only guarantees opportunity." Hence, the process of democracy is, at its core, the creation of "moral symmetry" between those with competing values. Again, to use a phrase of George Will's, the process tends toward "an equilibrium based on justice."

It is this equilibrium which would be radically upset if the nation were to pursue one or the other of the various extreme courses now being advocated for altering the relationship of corporations to society. For example, the adoption of laissez-faire for large corporations would be anathema to those who seek greater social equality and security, to those who seek consumer protection and clean air and water, and to those who seek to stabilize unemployment levels (and accomplish other ends that require collective action). Similarly, egalitarian solutions, if adopted, would create unacceptable consequences in the eyes of libertarians, corporatists, and humanists (in terms of decreased incentives for performance, greater bureaucracy, less entrepreneurial innovation, a decline in freedom and in the overall material standard of living as the nation became less competitive in world markets). Corporatist solutions, too, would fail to generate the support of significant minorities (who, taken together, would constitute a majority), because the only thing Americans fear more than the power of big business or big labor or big government is the possibility of the three forces combining their power in unholy consort. And humanist policies are rejected by their opponents on the ground that they would lead to a decline in material progress and in the standard of living (unacceptable consequences to libertarians, egalitarians, and corporatists alike).

The opposing policies put forward by members of extreme ideological camps thus fail for many reasons, the primary one being that each is inherently an either/or proposition. Indeed,

the last two U.S presidential elections have been contested between those, on the one hand, who believe greater justice will
result from freeing the forces of the market and those, on the
other hand, who believe greater justice will result from increasing the degree of government industrial planning. But what reason do we have to believe that either of these policies could ever
hope to succeed given the animosity of its opponents—individuals whose cooperation (or, at least, compliance) is needed for
success?

And those who advocate foreign-made ideologies forget that a
society will always reject policies that do not build on existing
cultural ideas or social institutions. Japan's Ministry of International Trade succeeds because it is consistent with that country's
tradition of cooperation. France's voluntary national planning
worked in the 1970s because it built on the ties of the leaders of
government and business that had been formed when both attended the *grandes écoles*. Such traditions are simply absent in
the United States. Instead, nearly opposite traditions—pluralist,
adversarial institutions, and competing interest groups—lead the
body politic to reject such foreign transplants. (This is not to
mention the obvious: Such European policies as national planning and training programs have done little to correct the economic problems on that continent. And, while similar corporatist
practices may have had some success in Japan, there is no reason
to believe they could succeed here, because they are based on
institutional arrangements that are countercultural in the American context.)

Whatever America chooses to do to create greater social justice
must build on the nation's traditional values, including individu-
alism, voluntary association, limited government, civil rights, private property, adversarial checks and balances, and, above all,
social, political, and economic pluralism.

Thus, each of the extreme alternatives—traditional laissez-
faire, egalitarian redistribution of wealth, national industrial
planning, and small is beautiful—is not only unjust (in that each
would do violence to the legitimate values of the majority of the
citizenry), each can be shown to be ineffective, impractical, un-
workable, and impossible to implement given the traditions and
institutions of American society. In addition, each is so burdened
with unattractive side effects as to make it unacceptable.

The Middle Course

Given the impossibility of success of any of the major ideological alternatives for changing the nature of the relationship of corporations to society, I conclude that the best course for America would be to encourage enlightened corporate behavior. If the majority of large corporations were to embrace New Management principles, I believe there would be a heightened sense of social justice in America. Moreover, this course is practical, consistent with national traditions and institutions, free from significant side effects, and responsive to the pluralistic objectives of the citizenry. Certainly, enlightened corporate management would not be easy to engender, nor would it lead to a utopia, but it would nonetheless be easier to achieve and have fewer negative consequences than any of the alternatives based on an extreme ideology. And, to reject it on the ground that it would not be perfect, but merely better than the feasible alternatives, is to again accept the devil's proposition.

Here are some ways in which the policies of the Vanguard address some of the legitimate concerns of the four great American political themes:

- Libertarian concerns are addressed by the self-regulation of the Vanguard. Through voluntarily meeting the needs of all stakeholders, the Vanguard reduce the necessity of appeals to government for intervention in the market and in the private affairs of corporations and citizens. By engaging in voluntary philanthropic activities, and by addressing society's major problems as business opportunities, the Vanguard reduce the scope, range, and, thus, the coercive power of the government.

- Egalitarian concerns are met through employee stock ownership and profit sharing. Worker capitalism more effectively meets the problems of income disparity than does state ownership and state redistribution—and does so without the drawbacks of bureaucratic inefficiency. Vanguard full-employment strategies reduce the effects of booms and busts on workers. And increasing the authority and scope of *external* boards of directors builds an institutional check on the abuse of corporate power.

- Corporatist concerns for growth, efficiency, and international competitiveness are met by the Vanguard's commitment to: research and development, the fullest utilization of human resources, the latest technology, the most effective planning, and the use of domestic production facilities.

- Humanist concerns are met by the Vanguard policies of decentralization into small work units, worker participation, and quality of work life programs. Environmentalist concerns are met by the Vanguard's voluntary efforts to provide worker health and safety, consumer safety, and environmental protection at levels that exceed what is demanded by government regulation.

Significantly, Vanguard practices address the legitimate concerns of each ideological group without transgressing the concerns of the others: Libertarian needs are achieved without the sacrifice of equality; equality is achieved without the sacrifice of liberty; and a high quality of life and a high standard of living are achieved simultaneously. Importantly, in this condition of moral symmetry, America would not simply be in the center of the values quadrant—that is, having a little of each desired social objective. Instead, the nation would have as much as possible of each value (imagine that the compass is three dimensional, and you are looking down on it from above). By definition, this middle ground is the only place on the values quadrant where all citizens would experience a sense of justice.

Justice in the Nation and in the Corporation

If this description of balanced values sounds vaguely familiar, the *déjà vu* comes from a parallel discussion in Chapter Three. Recall the four basic alternative approaches to internal corporate organization and management: The first school argues that corporations must be structured to reflect the real differences between individual abilities, talent, and willingness to work. These "meritocrats" believe in extremely high pay differentials between jobs at the top and those at the bottom of the organization. They believe that mobility up the hierarchical ladder should be rapid for those who can successfully perform their jobs. The second school believes that employees should be protected against virtually every form of risk by numerous "entitlements" and limits on managerial discretion. They believe workers should have guaranteed job security and that workers should be paid equally (or as close to equally as possible). The third school believes that jobs should be narrow in scope and engineered for maximum efficiency. Performance should be monitored closely, and there should be an elaborate incentive system providing frequent rewards to employees who do their jobs efficiently. The fourth school believes that organizational policies and practices should be designed to enhance personal growth and development. The goals of these approaches were diagramed earlier as follows:

A. MERITOCRACY
(Merit and Freedom)

D. HUMANISM	vs.	C. BEHAVIORISM
(Quality of Life)		(Efficiency and Order)

B. EGALITARIANISM
(Security and Equality)

Significantly, these schools of managerial thought map almost directly onto the four schools of political thought described in this chapter. Again, whose goal is right? Which school offers the best approach to organization effectiveness? Recall that the Vanguard corporations answer the question in this way: "We want as much merit, as much efficiency, as much security, and as much work quality as we can get in our organization." In effect, a Vanguard corporation is a social institution that believes rewards for merit *and* incentives for efficiency *and* a base of security *and* opportunities for human growth are all needed to create a sense of justice among employees. The task of internal management is to find ways to simultaneously satisfy these four competing but nonetheless legitimate objectives. As we looked at the Vanguard corporations, we saw that there is no single route to this goal. Every corporation must respond in a way that reflects its particular size, history, industry, locale, and mix of workers and managers. Moreover, every corporation must constantly be responding, reorganizing, altering its incentives, rearranging its rewards, and redesigning its work tasks as environmental circumstances change and as employee values, needs, and desires change. We saw that there is no one best way to organize a corporation. In effect, there is no one best place to be on the managerial quadrant, as there is no one best place to be on the democratic values quadrant.

We have before us an interesting instance of institutional parallelism: A great democratic nation appears to have much in common with a great corporation. Consider the characteristics of great *nations*. In the most advanced democracies, the role of government is to balance the conflicting demands of individuals and groups, each with differing values, and each possessing different objectives. A modern democratic government is responsive to *all* of the nation's interest groups, constituencies, and citizens. When a government does this well, it is viewed as fair, just, and legitimate by the vast majority of its people. In just societies, governance is dynamic, complex, and multidimensional. In contrast, less democratic governments tend to favor one ideology, one interest, or one class. Consequently, they are viewed as unjust, unfair, and illegitimate by those whose views and positions are unheard, unrespected, or ignored. In these unjust societies, the process of governance is static, simple, and unidimensional. The latter are brittle and ultimately break under the torque and tension of historical forces; the former change, grow, and survive.

Now consider the characteristics of great *corporations*: Like the great nations, they change, grow, and survive. Unlike organizations that fail to pass the test of history, a great corporation is governed by a paramount philosophy of responsiveness to all its constituencies, both internal and external. Moreover, the great corporation is a microcosm of the great nation of which it is an integral part, reflecting both the pluralistic values of the society and its process of democratic governance. Du Pont's former CEO Irving Shapiro explains why this latter characteristic is essential:

> The dual test of an organization is how well it performs its chosen functions and how well it matches the values of the society that charters it. If it is competent but hostile to the mores of society, or acceptable in that regard but incompetent in its delivery of goods and services, then it forfeits its legitimacy.

And that is the heart of the matter. I do not pretend to make the case that the parallels between my two quadrants represent an empirical finding about institutions or constitute some law about society. The parallels are, I suspect, a little too neat. Indeed, if one has problems with them, may I suggest substituting eight, twelve, or any number of points on the compass and calling them what you will. The real purpose of the quadrants is twofold: First, to illustrate that the process of governance within the Vanguard closely replicates the process of governance in the greater society (and this congruence is likely to lead to corporate policies more in keeping with the desires of a pluralistic society than would an authoritarian process that is insensitive to competing claims). Second, the quadrants illustrate by way of familiar themes that balance is at the heart of all institutions and societies that manage the trick of being at once stable and dynamic.

The Hard Work of Pluralistic Governance

While everything may appear smooth-running in a totalitarian state, the course of events in a democracy is perpetually bumpy. And, like democratic states, the Vanguard corporations are marked by continuing tension, stress, conflict, disagreement, competing interests, divergent goals, painful changes, contradictions, ups and downs, self-doubt, and a modicum of healthy self-criticism. There are, I must add again, significant groups within the Vanguard who are opposed to New Management practices, much as there are groups in our Republic who are at any time opposed to the policies of the incumbent administration.

The perpetual lot of institutions in a modern, democratic society is flux and spirited disagreement among those with competing values. The leaders of the Vanguard corporations are not simply resigned to this fact—they cherish it, nurture it, and recognize that in it is the source of continued renewal. The leaders of these corporations, like the framers of the American democracy, realize that their organizations are not potentially perfectible. America's founding fathers knew that they were constructing no utopia. They saw that conflict, tension, and turmoil were the order of their day and foresaw that that would be the order of the future as well. Hence, they did not set out to design a system so perfect that it would run on smoothly forever, without struggle or change. Instead, they created a system of checks and balances—of separation of powers—and other institutional means for managing the conflict they knew was inevitable. Indeed, they didn't see conflict as evil (Jefferson relished it; in fact, he saw it as the source of progress, of continual change).

What worried the Nation's founders was that one party would emerge from the struggle as a permanent winner, and other parties would be perpetual losers. That, they feared, would destroy the legitimacy of the system by eroding the moral basis of its popular support. Hence, the founders saw leadership as managing or balancing the constant and never-abating demands of those with different values or objectives, and *not* as defining the one path to truth. Importantly, the founders believed that truth —what is right for society—was not eternal, static, or written. What is right is dynamic and continually emerges from the free interplay of competing ideas. As Lewis Lapham puts it, "The premise of American democracy assumes a raucous assembly of citizens unafraid to speak their minds."

In many key respects—but not all—the philosophy of our democracy and the philosophy of the Vanguard corporations run parallel. As we have seen, none of these companies is a placid utopia. Life inside them is full of competing claims and neverending tensions. But their leaders have created systems of internal governance that correspond roughly to the system of balances found in the broader society. For example, each is highly decentralized, with specific powers granted to their autonomous divisions, and with limitations on the authority of their central staffs. Still, the central authority maintains control—like Schumacher's man with a handful of helium-filled balloons—in what Motorola's Bob Galvin calls "a check-and-balance" culture. In addition, we have seen that each of the corporations has a simple, eloquent statement of philosophy that serves (much like the U.S. Constitution) not as a detailed guide on how to manage daily operations, but as a moral touchstone to refer to at times of difficult choice. The documents contain ultimate values to which all members of the organization can subscribe . . . points of transcendent consensus in a dominion of competing claims. The CEO of a Vanguard corporation is not an authoritarian: His position, like the position of the President of this Republic, is a bully pulpit. He leads not by direction but by example, persuasion, Socratic questioning, and by creating structures and opportunities in which the genius of his people may flourish. The chief executives of Vanguard corporations pay great heed to the wisdom of a "raucous assembly" of constituents unafraid to speak their minds. Out of this tumult arises the raw material for effective action. The Vanguard executives listen to all sides, but are dictated to by no side. In short, they are unlike some conservative politicians who are insensitive to the legitimate demands of certain groups in society; but also they are unlike many liberal politicians who are prisoners to the demands of every special interest.

Because it is not morally possible to either ignore or always to satisfy the demands of all constituencies, Vanguard executives live in a state of perpetual tension. I suspect that it is this uncomfortable tension, more than any other factor, that discourages many Old Guard executives from joining the ranks of the Vanguard. As E. F. Schumacher writes:

> [Some] people find it most difficult to keep two seemingly opposite necessities of truth in their minds at the same time. They always tend to clamor for a final solution, as if in life there could ever be a final solution other than death. For constructive work, the principal task is always the restoration of some kind of balance.

Apparently, what attracts some people to management is the opportunity to be decisive and adamant, to take a clear and consistent stand, and to "do it, fix it, try it." In short, they want to be a "boss." To these people, such activities as balancing short-term and long-term goals, balancing the needs of employees and shareowners, and balancing economic and environmental needs is simply evidence of weak, indecisive leadership.

But the Vanguard executives see things in a different light. They do not see the balancing of equal but competing values in terms of either/or. To learn more about this belief, I made it a point to ask every Vanguard executive I interviewed the same question: "How do you decide when forced to make a tough trade-off between the conflicting needs of two stakeholders?" It came as a continual surprise to me that one after the other of these leaders refused to answer my question. Apparently, they do not believe in zero-sum games. They argued that, with a little imagination and commitment, one could always arrive at a solution that would serve—if not fully please—the interests of all parties involved. In one way or another, the Vanguard managers all echo Arco's William Kieschnick:

> [I] disagree with anyone, including social critics, who see responsible social behavior and effective entrepreneurial

performance as conflicting corporate goals. The conflict is a myth.

As one who was schooled in the harsh realities of textbook economics where everything is cast in terms of trade-offs, in which there are always winners and losers, and in which the first rule is that you can't have your cake and eat it, too, I initially found this contradiction to my academic training hard to reconcile. But the more I talked to the managers of the Vanguard corporations, and the more I learned about their companies, the less relevant what I had *read* about how to run a company seemed. Like our nation, these companies are full of paradoxes: They pursue entrepreneurial ends by cooperating with the government, they ignore opportunities to make easy money while making a lot of money pursuing higher ends, and they reconcile opposites which, it turns out, are not irreconcilable.

Corporations and countries? Is this analogy farfetched? I don't believe so. Indeed, the characteristic of moral symmetry in the nation that is mimicked in great corporations can be found in all institutions large and small. I could just as well have chosen the family. For as the French root *(ménage)* of the word suggests, management is similar to the care of a household. The image is that of husbandry: Through the judicious use of resources, the good parent cares for *all* the members of the family, *all* of whom are seen as having legitimate claims on the group's collective resources. Sometimes junior must be favored; other times, all must come to the support of sister. But the family bond will erode if it is perceived that one member always commands an unfair share of household resources—financial or emotional.

There are no rules for managing households. There is no one best way to constitute, coordinate, or cohere the various members of the family. Instead, household management is an ongoing process, the success of which depends on a perception of justice or fairness by all family members. Sue may not get her way this time; but her time will come. And, at all times, her claims are considered; at all times she is shown respect.

Even when this tiny organization is running smoothly, family members are likely to experience some dissatisfaction, because he doesn't always get his way, and she doesn't always get hers. Dissatisfaction and conflict are, after all, inescapable aspects of the human predicament. But if there is symmetry in their treatment, neither he nor she will be so displeased as to challenge the legitimacy of the family—or to quit it.

In truth, Tolstoy was right in a way. All happy families are the same: They all practice moral symmetry.

Limitations of the Theory

But the problem with the Vanguard approach is that it still founders on the devil's proposition: If every corporation were managed in this way, the world would still not be perfect. Indeed, because the world is by nature imperfect, not even the Vanguard companies practice all the things at all times that would be necessary to satisfy the objectives of all their many constituencies. As we have seen, each of the Vanguard has major blindspots or shortcomings. Moreover, even if all corporations behaved as progressively as the Vanguard (an unlikely state of affairs given the amount of effort that would entail), there would still be injustice in America, there would still be unsolved social problems. For example, unemployment could not be solved by corporations acting alone. Instead, this would require the cooperation of business, unions, educational institutions, and government at all levels to create a range of pragmatic and dynamic solutions to what, in effect, are many unemployment problems (the problem of teenage unemployment, the problem of technological unemployment, the problem of regional unemployment, the problem of black, urban unemployment, and so on). While corporations would have a role to play in addressing each of these various problems, no one of these forms of unemployment would be susceptible to solutions emanating from the private sector acting alone. The same would be true with regard to health, education, welfare, and countless other governmental responsibilities.

Hence, there would still be an important role for government even in an America in which the majority of large corporations behaved as the Vanguard do today. But the size of government would probably not grow (and might even be somewhat reduced). Almost certainly, there would be a reassessment and a reassignment of the relative functions of government and business: Government would do what it does best; business would do what it does best; and both would work together on the few remaining problems that required cooperation (problems that would be few in number and would *not* require formal alliances that concentrated power in ways that threaten the rights of the citizenry).

Could it ever come to pass that the majority of corporations would follow the lead of the Vanguard? Only if shareowners, unionists, consultants, the media, politicians, educators, employees, and all those who have influence in society continually bring home the point to the leaders of the Old Guard (and to the leaders of the financial community) that such a course would not only be better for society, it would also be better for competitive, corporate capitalism in the long run. Indeed, the way of the Vanguard is probably the only alternative available to corporations that would allow them any real freedom to operate in the future. The leaders of the Old Guard must learn that they will not be permitted to turn the clock back to the days when an undemanding public would accept single-stakeholder laissez-faire behavior among large corporations. And, while corporations have experienced a much needed respite from further governmental control during the Reagan administration, social pressures against big business are again building as the result of the failure to correct long-standing social injustices. Hence, while corporations have been taken off the firing line in the short term, the long-term trend continues to run against them. It is our duty—those of us who are not corporate managers—to educate business leaders about the ultimate folly of pursuing a course that runs against their self-interest, and ours as well.

In conclusion, I would not trust corporate executives anymore than I would trust Marxist commissars to provide society with justice. Powerful groups will always betray the public interest if that is in conflict with their perceived private interests. But if corporate leaders can be taught that, by paying heed to their constituencies, they will achieve their self-interest in the long term, they might behave more like sensitive, democratically elected officials (and parents of happy families), and less like the self-important Russian apparatchik that the Old Guard occasionally resemble. *If,* of course, is the operative word. All I know for certain is that the various alternatives to educating executives about the principles of the New Management are fraught with greater difficulties and higher social costs. And, as the examples of the Vanguard show, we have at least some evidence that America's managers are educable.

EPILOGUE:

WHAT'S PAST IS PROLOGUE

The only thing new in the world is the history you don't know.
The only thing that changes is the names we give things.
—HARRY TRUMAN

Bill Holden did *not* invent the New Management. Even as early as 1954, the ideas his character espoused in the film *Executive Suite* had been around for a long time. Ecclesiastes and Harry Truman were right: There is not much new under the sun except the names we give to things.

In fact, at the end of *Executive Suite,* while the houselights were being raised, the names of some of the creative forerunners of the Vanguard philosophy should have appeared as credits scrolling rapidly down the screen:

Adam Smith who, in 1776, saw that profits were the means and not the end of business activity: "For to what purpose is all the toil and bustle in this world? What is the end of avarice and ambition, of the pursuit of wealth, power, and avarice?" His answer: the welfare of society.

Charles Fourier who, in 1808, advocated profit sharing. He suggested that 30 percent of profits should go to capital, 45 percent to labor, and 25 percent used as incentive pay. Fourier also believed that workers would be most productive in jobs that met their particular interests and psychological needs. And, as these change over time, Fourier believed in a kind of free internal labor market in which workers would self-select tasks that suited them best at any given stage in their careers. (Fourier also believed that the extension of women's rights is the basic measure of all social progress.)

Robert Owen who, between 1813 and 1825, showed in his highly profitable spinning mill in New Lanark, Scotland, that managerial reform and economic efficiency go hand in hand. Instead of pursuing profit maximization, Owen spent money on improving the working conditions in his mill. His business partners contended this was a waste of money, but Owen countered that the very success of the mill stemmed from the money spent on employees. Among Owen's many ideas were worker education, employee stock ownership, the decentralization of factories into small units, and the rearrangement of technology to meet both human needs and the economic need for efficiency.

Jeremy Bentham who, in the early 1800s, advanced the notion that it was possible to tie justice to efficiency in the political economy, and his younger friend, *J.S. Mill*, who, in the 1840s, saw that the true realm of economics was not abstract mathematical laws but rather ethics and morality.

Count Henri de Saint-Simon who, in the early 1820s, proposed the radical notion of pay for performance. He believed in joining science and industry to create a new industrial order based on advanced technology and meritocracy. He argued that business reform was in the long-term self-interest of the owners of capital.

William G. Warden who, as president of the Atlantic Refinery in 1887, wrote to his boss John D. Rockefeller that the Standard Oil trust should drop its adversarial posture and work cooperatively with suppliers, employees, and shareholders, or face dire consequences at the hand of society. Warden warned Rockefeller that there was "a bitter cry in the oil regions, and the cause is laid at our door . . . and if we listen to it and are wise enough to try to mitigate it, we may turn the tide in our favor." If not, Warden warned, the trust might be broken up.

James Cash Penney who, in 1913, was the first businessman to prepare a corporate constitution in which his company's obligations to stakeholders were enumerated:

1. To serve the public, as nearly as we can, to its complete satisfaction.
2. To expect for the service we render a fair remuneration, and not all the profit the traffic will bear.
3. To do all in our power to pack the customer's dollar full of value, quality, and satisfaction.
4. To continue to train ourselves and our associates so that the services we give will be more and more intelligently performed.

5. To improve constantly the human factor in our business.

6. To reward men and women in our organization through participation in what the business produces.

7. To test our every policy, method, and act in this wise: "Does it square with what is right and just?"

Mary Parker Follett who, in the 1920s, argued that business must be seen as a service to society. She argued against the traditional managerial notion that business was a purely selfish occupation and that executives should only serve their communities by "sitting on the school board or some civic committee at night," or engage in philanthropy upon retirement. "The much more wholesome idea . . . is that our work itself is to be our greatest service to the community." She wrote that the larger purposes of business "include more of those fundamental values for which most of us agree we are really living." To Mary Follett, management was not a narrow administrative function, it was central to the formation of a new and more just social order.

Chester I. Barnard who, in 1938, wrote that the function of an executive is to strike a balance between competing claims in an organization. Barnard, who had served as the president of New Jersey Bell, wrote that the executive's responsibility was to formulate the purpose of the organization, to create a process in which the needs of individuals could be satisfied along with the needs of the organization, and to relate the entire internal system to the needs of the external environment.

Joseph Scanlon who, in the 1940s, created a system in which the conflicts between capital and labor could be managed in a way that workers would become more productive and the organization would become more humane. Through participation in decision making and in the fruits of their increased productivity, workers would become more responsible and more competent.

Herbert A. Simon who, in 1946, suggested that many of the "principles" of management were rationalizations of behavior rather than laws, and *Douglas McGregor* who, in 1960, wrote, "Every managerial act rests on assumptions . . . which are by definition not subject to question." Both Simon and McGregor argued for the need to challenge the premises of the managerial voodoo that passed as "scientific knowledge."

W. Edwards Deming who, in the late 1940s, argued that American managers should abandon the behavior that led to their past success and adopt a new philosophy of management dedicated to productivity and quality. He argued that the way to motivate employees to seek these two goals was not through slogans, pledges, or asking them to be nice to customers. The secret, Deming argued (and, ironically, it was only the Japanese who listened) was to involve workers as problem solvers.

And, finally, *Peter Drucker* who, in the late 1940s, wrote that corporations are human, social, political, indeed, moral phenomena in addition to being economic entities. Drucker also was one of the first scholars to stress the many *responsibilities* of management to corporate stakeholders.

There is little that the corporations described in these pages have added to these seminal insights. Nonetheless, there is a certain genius in taking the best ideas from those who have gone before and applying these in new combinations to contemporary situations. And that is what the Vanguard executives have done with particular insight, skill, and care. Wisdom may mean many things, but it is certainly the ability to apply prudently what one knows from the past to what one expects of the future. The past is prologue. The older the newer: The Vanguard are the avant-garde.

NOTES AND
REFERENCES

Observant readers will note that I almost always refer to a corporation in the third person plural. That is because I do not believe that a corporation is an *it* with a will or a life of *its* own. Indeed, Americans are wrong to say, "General Motors *is* committed to such and such a policy; the company stood by *its* earlier decision." In Britain, they have it right. There, one says, "General Motors *are* committed to such and such a policy; *they* stood by their earlier decision." The distinction is not idiosyncratic. It is crucial, because "corporation" is merely a name given to a group of people who voluntarily join together to achieve some common end that they could not realize acting alone as individuals. That these people can make of their collective enterprise what they will is an important point of this book.

Most of what I report in these pages was learned at the source. Unless otherwise indicated, all facts, numerical data, and quotes are derived from corporate publications, unpublished corporate documents, or from interviews with corporate personnel. *Important:* Nothing I have written about any company is confidential or privileged. Readers seeking further information or documentation may obtain it at a good business library or directly from the corporations in question. The references that follow deal only with information I have culled from external sources.

Prologue
P. 9   The phrase "moral symmetry" is George Will's. The phrase "clean hands" management is James Fallows's.

Chapter One
P. 15   The philosophical roots of this book are to be found in Mary Parker Follett's Collected Papers, *Dynamic Administration* (edited by H. C. Metcalf and L. Urwick), Harper & Bros., 1941; Chester Bernard's *The Functions of the Executive*, Harvard University Press, 1938; and Peter Drucker's *Management: Tasks, Responsibilities, Practices*, Harper & Row, 1973.
P. 23   The exception is George Weyerhaeuser, the CEO of Weyerhaeuser.
P. 26   Northrup quote in *New Management*, Vol. 1, No. 1, 1983.
P. 27   The AM international story is told in *Business Week*, January 25, 1982, and in Susie Gharib Nazem, "How Roy Ash Got Burned," *Fortune*, April 6, 1981.
P. 28   Exxon published their forecasts in a series of pamphlets in the late 1970s and early 1980s called "Exxon Company U.S.A.'s Energy Outlook 1980–2000." The consequences of pursuing these forecasts are documented in *Business-Week*, June 7, 1982, pp. 88–93.
P. 31   The argument I am making about Mobil was illustrated clearly in a *Wall Street Journal* editorial during the Ford Administration entitled "La Donna e Mobil," August 27, 1975. The neoliberal flap is reported in Charles Peters's

"Tilting at Windmills" column in *The Washington Monthly*, January 1984. The bottom line was reported in *Business Week*, Oct. 17, 1983, pp. 76–87.

P. 32   Warren Bennis, "The Wallenda Factor," *New Management*, Vol. 1, No. 3, 1984.

P. 36   I review this research on worker productivity and motivation in *Work in America*, M.I.T. Press, 1973, and *Making America Work*, Continuum, 1979.

P. 36   The Harvard professors' article was: Robert H. Hayes and William J. Abernathy, "Managing Our Way to Economic Decline," *Harvard Business Review*, July-August 1980.

Chapter Two

P. 49   "Raucous assembly" is a phrase of Lewis Lapham's.

P. 49   The company is the Frito-Lay division of PepsiCo.

P. 51   Herewith is the famous Johnson & Johnson's Credo:

We believe our first responsibility is to the doctors, nurses and patients, to mothers and all others who use our products and services. In meeting their needs everything we do must be of high quality. We must constantly strive to reduce our costs in order to maintain reasonable prices. Customers' orders must be serviced promptly and accurately. Our suppliers and distributors must have an opportunity to make a fair profit.

We are responsible to our employees, the men and women who work with us throughout the world. Everyone must be considered as an individual. We must respect their dignity and recognize their merit. They must have a sense of security in their jobs. Compensation must be fair and adequate, and working conditions clean, orderly and safe. Employees must feel free to make suggestions and complaints. There must be equal opportunity for employment, development and advancement for those qualified. We must provide competent management, and their actions must be just and ethical.

We are responsible to the communities in which we live and work and to the world community as well. We must be good citizens—support good works and charities and bear our fair share of taxes. We must encourage civic improvements and better health and education. We must maintain in good order the property we are privileged to use, protecting the environment and natural resources.

Our final responsibility is to our stockholders. Business must make a sound profit. We must experiment with new ideas. Research must be carried on, innovative programs developed and mistakes paid for. New equipment must be purchased, new facilities provided and new products launched. Reserves must be created to provide for adverse times. When we operate according to these principles, the stockholders should realize a fair return.

P. 51   Albert P. Blaustein, "Constitutions, the Good and the Bad," New York *Times*, September 9, 1983. If all of the Vanguard constitutions are similar, are they not, then, all fungible (and, hence, meaningless)? Here is what Blaustein says:

All constitutions have to be autochthonous. That's a key word meaning "arise from the self." It must spring from the soil. It must be *the* constitution

to represent the needs of these people. We cannot put constitutions together like prefabricated henhouses.

Like J & J's credo, all of the Vanguard constitutions are sketchy. Does their
lack of detail indicate that they are less-than-useful guides for behavior? Here's
Blaustein, again:

> You might say that some of the British colonial constitutions are bad be-
> cause they try to take care of everything. A constitution can't work if it tries
> to spell everything out. Here's a beauty: The Yugoslav constitution guaran-
> tees the human right of family planning. As soon as you go into too much
> detail, you open up a hornet's nest. On the other hand, some of the French-
> style constitutions in Africa fail because they don't say enough. They say,
> "We ascribe to the principles of the UN." Well, what does that mean?

P. 55   Alfred E. Sloan, *My Years with General Motors*, Doubleday Anchor,
1972.

P. 58   DeLorean's inside account is J. Patrick Wright's *On a Clear Day You Can
See General Motors*, Wright Enterprises, 1979.

P. 60   E.E. Evans-Pritchard, *Witchcraft, Oracles and Magic Among the
Azande*, Clarendon Press, 1937.

P. 75   Robert Levering, Milton Moskowitz, and Michael Katz, *The 100 Best
Companies to Work For in America*, Addison-Wesley, 1984.

Chapter Three
Below are sketches of four ideal workplaces, each committed to a single-
minded application of one of the broad philosophical schools of work organization and employee motivation.

A.   *The Meritocratic Workplace*
The A Corporation is a hierarchical organization with dozens of rungs up
the ladder. Mobility is rapid for those who can successfully perform their
jobs. Elaborate tests ensure that all promotions are based on merit and not
on favoritism, seniority, or any other discriminatory factor. There are extremely great differences in pay for jobs at the top of the ladder as opposed
to those at the bottom. The rewards for hard work, intelligence, and entrepreneurial behavior are extremely high. This is made possible, in part,
because the company offers no fringe benefits and passes the savings on to
its employees who are then free to buy their own insurance policies, pension plans, and so forth.

There is no union at A. Length of employment is on an individually
negotiated, contract basis. In fact, turnover is encouraged: People who
don't make it up the ladder are quickly washed out of the corporation.
There is an internal job market with active bidding for all jobs. Entry-level
jobs are filled by advertising in local papers with a full description of job
tasks and conditions of employment. On occasions when no one is willing to
do the work at the advertised rate of pay, A will alter the conditions until an
adequate supply of workers is produced.

Although one can earn a very good living working thirty-five hours per
week, there are considerable rewards for those who work longer hours.
There are no set hours, vacations, or holidays: Each employee takes as
much time off whenever he wishes on the understanding that he is never

paid for time when he isn't working. The key philosophical words used in the firm's organizational manual are: Negotiation, Competition, Mobility, Merit, and Wealth.

B. The Egalitarian Workplace

At the B Corporation all employees except corporate officers are union members. The workers are represented by the workers' rights committee (WRC) comprised of members elected from the union ranks. The chairperson of the WRC sits on the board of directors. A closed shop is maintained, and the WRC has the right to refuse employment of a new hire as well as has approval over all decisions which affect worker health, safety, compensation, and employment. All work is supervised by employees who are union members. Each corporate officer implements policy through a designated union member.

Compensation and employee benefits are determined by collective bargaining. Seniority is the basis for pay differentials. Workers and their dependents receive full dental, hospital, medical, and mental health services from a health maintenance organization (HMO) which is supported completely by contributions from the corporation. During a disability, an employee's income is continued at the predisability level. Disability of dependents is also covered. The disability plan is paid for by the corporation, and the benefits are paid as long as the disability continues.

The union has won Japanese-like lifetime job security for all workers. By terms of the union contract, each worker is guaranteed employment at a forty-hour-per-week rate until the worker elects retirement. Workers are entitled to full retirement benefits at age sixty. The monthly pension is equal to the worker's average monthly pay during his year of highest earnings. Once retired, the monthly pension is inflation-indexed and full benefits are provided to dependent survivors. The worker does not contribute to the pension plan.

A group life insurance plan provides a death benefit of five times the worker's annual salary. Also, the workers have auto, homeowners, legal expense, and liability insurance coverage under group plans. Their group insurance premiums are paid by the corporation.

C. The Behaviorist Workplace

At the C Corporation, planning, coordination, and control functions are highly centralized, but the hierarchy is relatively flat with few levels. In large part, this is due to the use of sophisticated data processing control devices and information systems which have eliminated many middle management positions. Below top management, jobs are engineered for maximum efficiency. They are narrow in scope and are performed according to prescribed sets of work rules. Job performance is monitored closely, and performance data are routinely entered into a centralized computer. An elaborate incentive system provides frequent rewards to employees who perform their jobs effectively. The central feature of the incentive system is the "credit unit" which employees can exchange for extra cash or for privileges such as time off from work, access to company recreational facilities, low-cost, company-guaranteed loans, and tuition remission at local educational institutions. Employees receive credit units at randomly selected times if their performance is observed to meet or exceed their assigned standards. To promote punctual attendance, the company gives extra credits to employees for arriving at work on time. Employees who accumulate good attendance and safety records are also awarded extra credits.

Because most jobs (other than top management positions) at C are easily learned, the company does not require any special skills of job applicants. Unpopular jobs are filled by providing special incentives including higher wages, extra credits, and company-sponsored annual vacations. Frequently, the company has surprise beer parties for the employees when productivity has been particularly high. The plant is designed to look like a garden, with almost all machine noise covered by music and the sound of waterfalls. The company-subsidized cafeteria offers gourmet meals at a discount to all employees.

D. *The Humanistic Workplace*

At the D Corporation 75 percent of the stock is owned by employees. Employee representatives constitute a clear majority on the board of directors. They are elected for three-year terms in balloting by all employees on a one-worker-one-vote basis. Few individuals hold clearly "management" positions. The scope of duties of these individuals is spelled out in the company's constitution, a document which was written by the workers themselves. The managers are appointed by the board, with the consent of the entire workforce, in a secret ballot.

The firm's constitution also includes a "bill of rights." The preamble to the constitution commits the firm to pursue a policy of "individual development." After meeting a minimal profit objective necessary to retain full employment, the company's primary goal is to provide each employee with maximum choice in pursuing his or her own career interests and personal goals. While all tasks and production goals are set by shop-floor level committees, individual workers are free to choose among jobs that offer varying degrees of participation, challenge, complexity, stress, teamwork, and work schedules. The company has developed a measuring tool for matching individual desires with the job needs of the organization. While some limits to choice are imposed by the number and variety of jobs available in the company, rotation among jobs is encouraged, and training is provided to prepare people to undertake increasingly difficult tasks.

The cornerstone of the philosophy of individual development is the company's system of continuing education. To help individuals to meet their needs and desires for growth, all jobs are designed to be learning experiences, as far as this is technically possible and to the extent it is wanted by each worker. Employees are rewarded for teaching each other. The local university offers degree-granting courses on the plant grounds, and these are paid for by the company whether they are job-related or not. Sabbaticals are also available to workers.

New employees are recruited into the firm by the workers themselves and become full voting members of the community after a one-year probationary period. Employees can be fired only by unanimous vote of the board (or by two-thirds majority of the board and two thirds of the entire work force.

P. 83   In 1979, my colleague Kenneth Brousseau and I asked a sample of 98 business students and an expert panel of 39 corporate executives, scholars, trade unionists, and government officials to rank order the desirability of the four organizations just described. As the following summary chart illustrates, there was some dissensus among the various subgroups of our panel.

RANK ORDERING OF DESIRABILITY
OF ALTERNATIVE 1990 CORPORATIONS

	Scenario	Business Students	Corporate Executives	Business Professors	Government & Unionists
A.	Meritocracy	1	1	2	3
B.	Egalitarianism	4	4	4	2
C.	Behaviorism	3	3	3	4
D.	Humanism	2	2	1	1

To gain some understanding of the reasons behind the panelists' stated preferences, we administered a complementary questionnaire that elicited the panelists' assessments of the potential social, economic, managerial, and psychological outcomes or consequences that they would expect to find in each of the four types of corporations. The brief analysis that follows is based on our statistical correlation of some several dozen items on that questionnaire with the rank ordering of the panelists' preferences among the four types of companies. For purposes of clarity, I've simplified greatly what are, in fact, many complex and subtle statistical differences between the groups.

It is interesting that the evaluation of the corporate executives and the business students exhibit the same rank order of preferences. The only difference in evaluation is that the attraction to the humanist scenario was considerably stronger among the younger people (that is, it is ranked closer to meritocracy in terms of desirability). Moreover, there was a significant difference in the imputed reasons for the preferences of the two groups: The corporate experts were attracted to meritocracy for *economic* reasons, while the students were attracted for *social* reasons. In this respect, the values of the students were closer to those of their teachers than to those of their future employers.

In addition, there were a few other differences between the university and corporate experts' rating of consequences. For example, although egalitarianism was viewed by the professors as the least productive and least effective of the four, it received higher ratings than from the executives in terms of its effects on social consequences (except individual liberty, responsibility, and sense of efficacy). Moreover, while the professors viewed humanism as unlikely to enhance efficiency, it was rated as slightly more likely than meritocracy to increase the quality of goods and services. Similarly, professors felt more strongly than executives that humanism was more likely than meritocracy to boost the standard of living and equality of opportunity.

In contrast to the corporate experts, the university experts—like their students—appear to have given more weight to social and humanistic considerations. However, they do not appear willing to totally ignore productivity and economic efficiency in favor of optimizing social outcomes. This is indicated by their rating egalitarianism (which was seen as the second most beneficial scenario in terms of social consequences, but the least productive and efficient) as their *last* choice.

From this exercise, we concluded the following:

- Managers feel they can live with a humanistic workplace, even if it isn't their first choice.
- The values of older managers square with those of younger managers. This is in keeping with several recent studies that indicate that some of the values of youth are contagious and are, in fact, being caught by corporate executives.
- Meritocracy and humanism are a compatible set of values. That is, individuals who are basically meritocratic in their values are quite open to humanist values while they are closed to egalitarian or behavioralist alternatives.

Source: James O'Toole, Kenneth Brousseau, and August Ralston, "Employee Entitlements in the Eighties," Center for Futures Research, Graduate School of Business, University of Southern California. Monograph. December 1979.

Pp. 85–87   Jan Erteszek describes the Olga philosophy in "The Common Venture Enterprise," *New Management*, Vol. 1, No. 2, 1983.

Pp. 87–90   DePree describes the Herman Miller philosophy in "Theory Fastball," *New Management*, Vol. 1, No. 4, 1984.

Chapter Four

P. 106   For a detailed discussion of employee stock ownership see my article "The Uneven Record of Employee Ownership," *Harvard Business Review*, November-December 1979.

P. 111   Hewlett-Packard also plans for full employment in this way. William Hewlett tells how HP's system responded when put to the test in 1973:

During that time, orders were coming in at a rate less than our production capability. We were faced with the prospect of a 10 percent layoff—something we had never done. Rather than a layoff, we tried a different tack. We went to a schedule of working nine days out of every two weeks—a 10 percent cut in work schedule with a corresponding 10 percent cut in pay for all employees involved in this schedule. At the end of a six-month period, orders and employment were once again in balance and the company returned to a full work week. The net result of this program was that all shared the burden of the recession, good people were not turned out on a very tough job market, and, I might observe, the company benefited by having in place a highly qualified work force when business improved.

And it is exactly this kind of planning that Levi Strauss has failed to do. Here's what Peter Thigpen, president of Levi Strauss says:

Looking at typical corporate growth patterns over the last few years, one would find something like this: +12 percent, +35 percent, +5 percent, +15 percent, −5 percent, +20 percent. During the recession we started to think about how to plan so that our own pattern in the future will be +10 percent, +10 percent, +10 percent, +10 percent. *If* we can achieve that pattern, *then* we will be able to provide true job security for all our people.

P. 113   I am indebted to my friend, John Van Doren, for his explication of the devil's proposition, "which is that because nothing can be known perfectly, nothing can really be known at all, that there is no knowledge, no truth, no reason to argue about anything." I've taken some liberties in expanding the proposition; but what the hell.

P. 113   Fred Foulkes and Anne Whitman, "Full Employment, Product/Market Strategies and Other Considerations," Human Resource Policy Institute, Boston University, 1984.

P. 116   Edgar H. Schein, "Does Japanese Management Style Have a Message for American Managers?" *Sloan Management Review*, Fall 1981, and "Organizational Socialization and the Profession of Management," *Sloan Management Review*, Winter 1968.

P. 124   Robert Townsend, *Further Up the Organization*, Knopf, 1984.

PP. 126–128   Douglas Wallace and Janet Dudrow, "How Information Flows Upstream at a Minneapolis Bank," *New Management*, Vol. 1, No. 1, 1983.

P. 136   Some observers have taken the notion of the need for a "community" and turned it into a prescription for how to run a company, to wit: "A strong and consistent culture is the key to corporate success." The best companies, then, have the strongest cultures. This is fine as far as it goes—which is not very far. After all, many institutions have strong and consistent cultures—the American Communist Party, the Benedictine monks, the U.S. Marines, the Dallas Cowboys, and the American Association of University Professors—to select an illustrative cross-sample!

How can one say, then, that excellent organizations have strong cultures, when many organizations with strong cultures would be rejected as models of excellence by large shares of the U.S. population? Moreover, how can strong cultures be offered as a characteristic of excellence when there are many significant exceptions to the rule (while it is true that most successful corporations have strong cultures, it is *also* true that many *un*successful companies have strong cultures).

P. 139   To the outsider, Arco appears genuinely schizophrenic about issues of equality. On the one hand, Arco probably does more for the minority communities in the cities they serve than does any other large U.S. corporation (for example, they trained dozens of black ex-offenders to manage gas stations; they build sports facilities and sponsor sporting events for kids in central cities). On the other hand, the company sponsors the memberships of executives in clubs with discriminatory practices. Even when Arco does bad, it tries to do good. Of course, they do not sponsor memberships in these clubs to do bad or to perpetuate discrimination; rather, they do so because they feel that it is necessary for executives to belong to these organizations in order to have access to the people with whom they must do business. Inside these clubs, Arco executives have reputations for fighting to remove discriminatory policies (see Chapter Twelve for support of this assertion). To Arco, the trade-off is between equality and efficiency, and they come down reluctantly but not completely on the side of efficiency.

Chapter Five

PP. 142–144   For more on China, see my article "The Good Managers of Sichuan," *Harvard Business Review*, May-June 1981.

P. 143   I may be guilty here of putting Peter Drucker's notion that profit is a "cost" of doing business in the mouth of a Chinese manager. While I admit the translation isn't literal, Drucker's general point was understood by the Chinese, of that I am convinced.

P. 144   Friedman's quote is from a New York *Times Magazine* article cited in Chapter Twelve. But he makes the case more cogently in his book, *Capitalism and Freedom*, University of Chicago, 1962.

P. 146   Alstadt quote, in personal conversation.

P. 150   "You've Come a Long Way Baby . . . ," *Forbes*, July 23, 1979.

P. 151   "The Outsider's Touch That's Shaking Up Mennen," *Business Week*, February 1, 1982.

P. 152   "Far-Out Firm: Seeking to Aid Society Control Data Takes on Many Novel Ventures," *Wall Street Journal*, December 22, 1982.

P. 156   "Motorola Moves Further into Technology with Its Risky Decision to Buy Four-Phase" *Wall Street Journal*, Dec. 11, 1981.

P. 158   "Will Money Managers Wreck the Economy?" *Business Week*, August 13, 1984, quoted was Leon G. Cooperman.

PP. 158–159   "A Tale of Two Companies," *Forbes*, March 6, 1978. Here is an excerpt from the article:

> While Weyerhaeuser often conducted itself with an air of *noblesse oblige,* G-P was a scrapper. Weyerhaeuser talked about trees as if only God (and a good Weyerhaeuser forester) could make one, but to Cheatham trees were —well, a business like any other. To get the land he wanted he borrowed heavily, cut the trees to pay back his lenders and planted new ones. Weyerhaeuser, by contrast, saw its forests as wood banks. The trees were there to be cut today or tomorrow. G-P went heavily into debt at a time when Weyerhaeuser had virtually no long-term debt. But Cheatham got his trees, paying with borrowed money and assuming that inflation would eventually bail him out.
>
> Unlike Weyerhaeuser, which has strong ties to the Northwest, G-P has never shown much regional loyalty. Cheatham expanded into the Northwest in the 1950s, so that by 1962 G-P was the largest private employer in the state of Oregon. But as the price of standing timber soared, he shifted operations back to the South, where purchased timber was cheaper. Last year 70 percent of G-P's earnings came from Southern operations. Weyerhaeuser, too, has been moving more of its operations to the South, where it owns 3 million acres of trees, but 2.8 million acres—much of it premium old growth—still remain in the Northwest, where increasingly strict environmental laws are beginning to affect harvesting practices even on private lands. "If Weyerhaeuser has a fault, it's that they're loyal to their towns," says one Northwest admirer. "They hardly ever close out a location."
>
> Some Weyerhaeuser critics claim that the company spends more lavishly than it needs to on maintenance and on research and development. "There's no question that, if there is a Cadillac job being done, we are doing

it," Weyerhaeuser replies. "Does that affect the bottom line?" he asks rhetorically, and answers: "Yes."

Penn Siegel, forest products analyst for Drexel Burnham Lambert, estimates that Weyerhaeuser's maintenance and repair spending is half again as high proportionally as that of its major competitors. That works out to a bottom line difference of 40 cents or so a share on earnings of $2.30. The critics say much the same thing about Weyerhaeuser's research, on which it will spend around $60 million this year. G-P, which spends only a fraction of that, does its research at the plant level—while Weyerhaeuser is just completing an elaborate, centralized laboratory.

In a very real sense, Weyerhaeuser seems to be more captive of its own history than a master of its fate. G-P is embarked on another five-year program in which it hopes to double earnings; it is already ahead of schedule. Weyerhaeuser, by contrast, recently reorganized in an apparent effort to decentralize decision making and give clear profit responsibility to local managers. If successful, the reorganization would merely put Weyerhaeuser where G-P already is: G-P plant managers are famous for being as familiar with financial facts as they are with timber technology.

Chapter Six
A fuller report of this study can be found in my article, "Declining Innovation: The Failure of Success," *Human Resources Planning*, Vol. 6, No. 3, 1983. I am indebted to Dr. Nirmal Sethia for his invaluable assistance on the study.

Chapter Seven
P. 182   Edward E. Lawler, "Whatever Happened to Incentive Pay?" *New Management*, Vol. 1, No. 4, 1984.
P. 183   For more information on these polls, see Lawler, ibid., and my book, *Making America Work*, Continuum, 1981. The Chamber of Commerce poll is reported in *Nation's Business*, December 1981, p. 55.
P. 197   For an excellent comparison of Deere and International Harvester, see Tom Redburn, "Lesson in Strategy," Business Section, Los Angeles *Times*, August 8, 1982.
PP. 201–203   Trotter and Koestler quotes from Arthur Koestler, *The Act of Creation*, Macmillan, 1964.

Chapter Eight
P. 213   George Gilder, *Wealth and Poverty*, Bantam Books, 1982.
P. 214   Iacocca quote in "The Breakdown of U.S. Innovation," *Business Week*, February 16, 1976. Du Pont executive quoted in same article.
P. 215   Pat Haggerty quoted in Robert Kirk Mueller's *The Innovation Ethic*, American Management Associations, 1971.
PP. 217–218   Bro Uttal, "Eastman Kodak's Orderly Two-Front War," *Fortune*, September 1976.
PP. 235–236   Judge Lord made these remarks in his courtroom in approving a $4.6 million suit against the A. H. Robins Company on February 29, 1984. The judge addressed himself to E. Claiborne Robins, Jr., the firm's president; Carl D. Lunsford, senior vice president for research and development; and William A.

Forrest, Jr., vice president and general counsel. Source: "A Plea for Corporate Conscience," *Harper's*, June 1984. Here is more of what the judge had to say:

. . . If one poor young man were, without authority or consent, to inflict such damage upon one woman, he would be jailed for a good portion of the rest of his life. Yet your company, without warning to women, invaded their bodies by the millions and caused them injuries by the thousands. And when the time came for these women to make their claims against your company, you attacked their characters. You inquired into their sexual practices and into the identity of their sex partners. You ruined families and reputations and careers in order to intimidate those who would raise their voices against you. You introduced issues that had no relationship to the fact that you had planted in the bodies of these women instruments of death, of mutilation, of disease.

. . . Your company, in the face of overwhelming evidence, denies its guilt and continues its monstrous mischief.

Mr. Forrest, you have told me that you are working with members of the Congress of the United States to find a way of forgiving you from punitive damages that might otherwise be imposed. Yet the profits of your company continue to mount. Your last financial report boasts of new records for sales and earnings, with a profit of more than $58 million in 1983. And, insofar as this court has been able to determine, you three men and your company are still engaged in a course of wrongdoing. Until your company indicates that it is willing to cease and desist this deception and to seek out and advise the victims, your remonstrances to Congress and to the courts are indeed hollow and cynical. The company has not suffered, nor have you men personally. You are collectively being enriched by millions of dollars each year. There is no evidence that your company has suffered any penalty from these litigations. In fact, the evidence is to the contrary.

. . . Mr. Robins, Mr. Forrest, Dr. Lunsford: You have not been rehabilitated. Under your direction, your company has continued to allow women, tens of thousands of them, to wear this device—a deadly depth charge in their wombs, ready to explode at any time. Your attorney denies that tens of thousands of these devices are still in women's bodies. But I submit to you that he has no more basis for denying the accusation than the plaintiffs have for stating it as truth. We simply do not know how many women are still wearing these devices because your company is not willing to find out. The only conceivable reasons that you have not recalled this product are that it would hurt your balance sheet and alert women who have already been harmed that you may be liable for their injuries. You have taken the bottom line as your guiding beacon and the low road as your route. That is corporate irresponsibility at its meanest.

Chapter Nine
PP. 240–241 For a cogent discussion of the key players in the strategic planning game, see Walter Kiechel III, "Corporate Strategists Under Fire," *Fortune*, December 27, 1982.
P. 243 John Naisbitt, *Megatrends*, Warner Books, 1982.
PP. 245–246 The model used at Deere is called Interax and was developed by

Selwyn Enzer. See his paper, "Interax, An Interactive Model for Studying Future Business Environments," Center for Futures Research, Graduate School of Business Administration, University of Southern California, Los Angeles, December 1979.

P. 252   The Du Pont Conoco fallout is discussed in "Du Pont: Straining to Pay the Price of Its Conoco Victory," *Business Week*, May 10, 1982, and "After the Merger Du Pont Still Likes Conoco," *Business Week*, May 30, 1983.

P. 254   Alexandra Reed Lajoux, "Mergers: The 'Last Frontier' of American Business?" *New Management*, Vol. 1, No. 2, 1983, pp. 22–29.

P. 256   "Do Mega-Mergers Drive Up Interest Rates?," *Business Week*, pp. 176–180.

P. 261   Howard Schwartz and Stanley Davis, "Matching Corporate Culture and Business Strategy," Management Analysis Center, Cambridge, MA (undated).

P. 264   Susan Fraker, "High-Speed Management for the High-Tech Age," *Fortune*, March 5, 1984.

Chapter Ten

P. 275   The book in question is Terence E. Deal and Allan A. Kennedy, *Corporate Cultures*, Addison-Wesley, 1982.

P. 290   I am not speaking "out of school" here; the sad story is recounted in Thomas Moore, "Trouble and Strife in the Cowles Empire," *Fortune*, April 4, 1983.

P. 294   D. Verne Morland, "Lear's Fool: Coping with Change Beyond Future Shock," *New Management*, Vol. 2, No. 2, 1984.

P. 294   Nancy Reeves, "The Frozen Asset," *New Management*, Vol. 1, No. 3, 1984.

PP. 299–301   Richard Mason and Ian Mitroff, *Challenging Strategic Assumptions*, Wiley Interscience, 1981.

P. 310   Milton Moskowitz, "Good and Bad Ways to Handle Layoffs," San Francisco *Chronicle*, July 13, 1984.

Chapter Eleven

PP. 315–316   Warren Bennis, "The Wallenda Factor," *New Management*, Vol. 1, No. 3, 1984.

PP. 317–318   Lucien Rhodes, "The Un-Manager," *INC.*, August 1982.

PP. 318–319   "A Maverick and His Minimill," *Industry Week*, December 12, 1983.

P. 319   Larry E. Greiner, "Senior Executives as Strategic Actors," *New Management*, Vol. 1, No. 2, 1983.

P. 325   Harold Geneen, *Managing*, Doubleday, 1984.

P. 327   Donald M. Alstadt, "Institutionalizing Leadership," *New Management*, Vol. 2, No. 2, 1984.

P. 328   Arnold F. Kanarick and David Dotlich, "Honeywell's Agenda for Organizational Change," *New Management*, Vol. 2, No. 1, 1984.

P. 329   The principles are a paraphrase of those advocated by E. F. Schumacher in *Small is Beautiful*, Harper & Row, 1973.

P. 338   Steven Kerr, "Leadership and Participation," in Arthur Brief (ed) *Research on Productivity*, Praeger, 1984.

Chapter Twelve

P. 343 Seymour Martin Lipset, "Note to Readers," *Public Opinion*, April/May 1980 and "Opinion Roundup," *Public Opinion*, October/November 1982. Also see "The recession sours voters on business," *Business Week*, May 31, 1982, and New York *Times*, "Gallop Poll Results," Section 3, August 19, 1984.

PP. 343, 355 Barbara W. Tuchman, *The March of Folly*, Knopf, 1984.

P. 356 Honeywell's position on military contracts is controversial. While I was visiting Honeywell, Spencer held an open meeting with his employees and answered a number of questions from the floor. He re-emphasized Honeywell's position that the company and its employees deplore war of any kind, but that Honeywell will continue as a military supplier as long as the government of the United States asks, but added that Honeywell does not take any stand on U.S. defense policy. He suggested that the way to change the government's policy is through elected officials and not through corporations such as Honeywell.

PP. 361–362 Milton Friedman, "The Social Responsibility of Business Is to Increase Its Profits," New York *Times Magazine*, September 13, 1970.

P. 369 "Notable and Quotable," *Wall Street Journal*, February 9, 1984.

PP. 370–371 Robert V. Krikorian, "The Time for Self-Regulation Is Now," Ethics Resource Center, Washington, D.C., November 16, 1982.

Chapter Thirteen

PP. 374–381 For a fuller description of these ideological positions, of the agendas that flow from them, and of the responses of American leaders to them, see my article, "What's Ahead for the Business-Government Relationship," *Harvard Business Review*, March-April 1979.

P. 383 Irving S. Shapiro, "The Process," *Harvard Business Review*, November/December 1979.

P. 387 Corporations and families. Am I attempting to create an analogy that doesn't exist? I don't think so. Consider the words of James Bere, the chief executive of Borg Warner, a corporation that is striving valiantly to achieve Vanguard status. Speaking to his top managers about how to change the culture of Borg Warner, Morris advised them to always "seek the middle ground":

Now, if you are the chief breadwinner, you look at your responsibilities and say that you believe in being a good provider *and* a loving parent to your children at the same time. Sometimes those two goals come into conflict. But when the demands of those two roles overlap, you don't stop trying. You look for ways to respond creatively, to give and take. To find the middle ground and still hold true to the basics of both beliefs.

INDEX